LEGAL RESEARCH SKILLS FOR SCOTS LAWYERS

AUSTRALIA
LBC Information Services Ltd
Sydney

CANADA and **USA**
Carswell
Toronto

NEW ZEALAND
Brooker's
Auckland

LEGAL RESEARCH SKILLS FOR SCOTS LAWYERS

**By Karen Fullerton, MA (Hons), LL.B., Dip.L.P., Solicitor
and Megan Macgregor, LL.B. (Hons), Dip.L.P., Solicitor**

Lecturer in Law, Napier University
and
Solicitor, Anderson Strathern

LONDON
W. GREEN/SWEET & MAXWELL
1999

Published in 1999 by
W. Green Limited of
21 Alva Street, Edinburgh, EH2 4PS
(http://www.wgreen.co.uk)
Typeset by Wyvern 21, Bristol
Printed in England by
Redwood Books Ltd, Trowbridge, Wiltshire

No natural forests were destroyed to make this product;
only farmed timber was used and replanted

A C.I.P. catalogue record for this book is available from the British Library

ISBN 0 414 012 992

The moral rights of the authors have been asserted

ACKNOWLEDGEMENTS

I would like to express thanks to Ian Crossland, Nicholas Grier, Paul Arnell and Janet Paterson for reading chapters in draft form and making helpful comments and corrections. I would also like to thank Harris Cooper for displaying infinite patience with his wife — situation normal! I must also acknowledge three lads who were not so patient. I would also like to thank my mother, Lanya Scott and my father, David Fullerton for their support and encouragement.

Karen Fullerton

I would like to thank the Commercial Department at Anderson Strathern and especially Simon Brown and John Kerr. My mother and father, Alex and Mitzi, deserve a big hug for all their encouragement which was much appreciated. A very special thank you to John Calderwood for being so supportive — cooking, cleaning and keeping the cat occupied — without you this book would not have been possible.

Megan Macgregor

FOREWORD

Information has become one of the key issues as we end the 20th century. We have moved from the "Information Revolution" to the "Information Age" Governments produce papers of varying hues on it. It is increasingly seen as a major business asset: "the right information at the right place at the right time is essential for effective conduct of business." (The Hawley Committee Agenda)

It has become clear to the legal profession that it does not differ from other businesses in this respect. For it too, it is essential to provide "the quality and quantity of information for effective operation, ensuring that, at every level, the information provided is necessary and sufficient, timely, reliable and consistent." (Hawley)

For the legal profession there is also forecast a paradigm change, with many aspects of legal services being delivered through powerful and accessible information technology based systems made available via the Internet. In this scenario, lawyers become, as Professor Richard Susskind says in *The Future of Law*, "the legal information engineers whose knowledge forms the basis of the legal information services."

In all of this, the legal research skills of the practitioner will become increasingly important. Consequently, this work will be of immense value to those already practising — particularly with regard to the sections on electronic sources. Despite the authors' claims that "it is not intended to be a reference work for law librarians", it is inconceivable that any law librarian would wish to be without a work that provides so much information on current Scottish sources.

But primarily this is a work for students. The authors are to be congratulated on producing a text which will ensure an opportunity for those embarking on a career in the legal profession in Scotland to acquire the research skills essential for their future success. The book also presents an implied challenge to the law schools to match its structured approach with appropriate courses. Neither teacher nor pupil can afford to be without this user-friendly work.

John A. Sibbald
Society for Computers and the Law
September 1999

CONTENTS

TABLE OF ABBREVIATIONS

A.C.	Appeal Cases (Law Reports)
A.J.I.L.	American Journal of International Law
A.P.S.	Acts of the Parliament of Scotland 1124–1707 (Record edition)
All E.R.	All England Law Reports
B.C.C.	British Company Cases
B.Y.I.L.	British Yearbook of International Law
C.F.I.	Court of First Instance
C.L.	Current Law
C.L.J.	Cambridge Law Journal
C.M.L.R.	Common Market Law Reports
C.M.L.Rev.	Common Market Law Review
Ch.	Chancery Division (Law Reports)
E.A.T.	Employment Appeal Tribunal
E.B.L.R.	European Business Law Review
E.C.	European Community
ECHR	European Court of Human Rights
ECJ	European Court of Justice
E.C.L.R.	European Competition Law Review
E.C.R.	European Court Reports
ECSC	European Coal & Steel Community
EEC	European Economic Community
E.E.L.R.	European Environmental Law Review
EFTA	European Free Trade Association
E.H.R.L.R.	European Human Rights Law Review
E.H.R.R.	European Human Rights Reports
E.I.P.R.	European Intellectual Property Review
E.J.I.L.	European Journal of International Law
E.L.J.	European Law Journal
E.L.R.	The Edinburgh Law Review
E.L.Rev.	European Law Review
E.P.L.	European Public Law
E.T.S.	European Treaty Series
EU	European Union
Env.L.R.	Environmental Law Reports
Euratom	European Atomic Energy Community
Fam.	Family Division (Law Reports)
Fam. L.R.	Greens Family Law Reports
G.W.D.	Greens Weekly Digest

Hous. L.R.   Greens Housing Law Reports
I.C.J.   International Court of Justice
I.C.J. Reports   International Court Reports
I.C.J. Yearbook   Yearbook of the International Court of Justice
I.C.L.Q.   International and Comparative Law Quarterly
I.C.R.   Industrial Cases Reports
I.L.M.   International Legal Materials
I.L.R.   International Law Reports
I.R.L.R.   Industrial Relations Law Reports
J.C.   Justiciary Cases
J.C.M.S.   Journal of Common Market Studies
J.I.L.T.   Journal of Information Law & Technology
J.L.S.S.   Journal of the Law Society of Scotland
J.R.   Juridical Review
L.Q.R.   Law Quarterly Review
M. or Mor.   Morison's Dictionary of Decisions
M.L.R.   Modern Law Review
Med.L.R.   Medical Law Reports
O.J.   Official Journal of the European Communities
O.J.L.S.   Oxford Journal of Legal Studies
P.C.I.J.   Permanent Court of International Justice
Q.B.   Queen's Bench Division (Law Reports)
Rep.L.R.   Greens Reparation Law Reports
S.C.   Session Cases
S.C.(H.L.)   Session Cases, appeals to House of Lords
S.C.C.R.   Scottish Criminal Case Reports
S.C.L.R.   Scottish Civil Law Reports
S.I.   Statutory instrument
S.J. or Sc. Jur.   Scottish Jurist
S.L.C.R.   Scottish Land Court Reports
S.L.G.   Scottish Law Gazette
S.L.P.Q.   Scottish Law & Practice Quarterly
S.L.R.   Student Law Review
S.L.R. or Sc. L.R.   The Scottish Law Reporter
S.L.R. or S.L. Rev. or   Scottish Law Review and Sheriff Court Reporter
Sc.L.R.
S.L.T.   Scots Law Times
S.L.T. (Land Ct.)   Scots Law Times (Land Court Reports)
S.L.T. (Lands Tr.)   Scots Law Times (Lands Tribunal reports)
S.L.T. (Lyon Ct.)   Scots Law Times (Lyon Court Reports)
S.L.T. (Notes)   Scot Law Times, Notes of Recent Decisions
S.L.T. (Sh. Ct.)   Scots Law Times, Sheriff Court Reports
S.N.   Session Notes
Sh. Ct. Rep.   Sheriff Court Reports
S.P.E.L.   Scottish Planning and Environmental Law
T.C.   Reports of Tax Cases
U.N.T.S.   United Nations Treaty Series
W.L.R.   Weekly Law Reports
Y.E.L.   The Yearbook of European Law

TABLE OF REGNAL YEARS*

Sovereigns	Commencement of Reign	Length of Reign
		Years
William I	October 14, 1066	21
William II	September 26, 1087	13
Henry I	August 5, 1100	36
Stephen	December 26, 1135	19
Henry II	December 19, 1154	35
Richard I	September 23, 1189	10
John	May 27, 1199	18
Henry III	October 28, 1216	57
Edward I	November 20, 1272	35
Edward II	July 8, 1307	20
Edward III	January 25, 1326	51
Richard II	June 22, 1377	23
Henry IV	September 30, 1399	14
Henry V	March 21, 1413	10
Henry VI	September 1, 1422	39
Edward IV	March 4, 1461	23
Edward V	April 9, 1483	—
Richard III	June 26, 1483	3
Henry VII	August 22, 1485	24
Henry VIII	April 22, 1509	38
Edward VI	January 28, 1547	7
Mary	July 6, 1553	6
Elizabeth I	November 17, 1558	45
James I	March 24, 1603	23
Charles I	March 27, 1625	24
Commonwealth	January 30, 1649	11
Charles II†	May 29, 1660	37
James II	February 6, 1685	4
William and Mary	February 13, 1689	14
Anne	March 8, 1702	13
George I	August 1, 1714	13
George II	June 11, 1727	34
George III	October 25, 1760	60
George IV	January 29, 1820	11
William IV	June 26, 1830	7
Victoria	June 20, 1837	64
Edward VII	January 22, 1901	9
George V	May 6, 1910	26
Edward VIII	January 20, 1936	1
George VI	December 11, 1936	15
Elizabeth II	February 6, 1952	—

*The Scottish Kings are not given, inasmuch as the Scots Acts are cited by year and chapter not by regal name, year and chapter.

†Charles II did not ascend the throne until May 29, 1660, but his regnal years were computed from the death of Charles I, January 30, 1649, so that the year of his restoration is styled the twelfth of his reign.

Chapter 1

INTRODUCTION

PURPOSE OF THIS BOOK

This is a book primarily intended for the Scottish law student but it will also be of interest to trainees and practitioners who want to update their knowledge about legal research. The literature contains several books on legal research skills but they tend to devote only a short section to Scots law. There is a lack of information on current Scottish information sources. This book is intended to fill this gap.

The book is designed to be a user-friendly guide to researching Scots law. It includes many diagrams to aid explanation. It also includes worked examples and exercises. The key information sources are covered, with electronic sources being referred to throughout. In recent years electronic sources of information have become so important that they cannot be regarded as an optional extra. Therefore four chapters are dedicated to the mastery of electronic sources of information and on-line searching techniques. The book will be complemented by on-line updates accessible via Green's website. It is worth pointing out that effective legal research should use an appropriate mixture of paper and electronic sources. They should be used to complement each other. The exclusive use of either paper or electronic sources is not to be recommended.

Scottish lawyers cannot focus solely on Scottish law. United Kingdom and E.C. law (and indeed some aspects of public international law) are all integral to our system of law. There are therefore chapters dealing with these areas of law. Details of English law are not covered. The book is intended for the Scottish lawyer and there are already many texts covering the situation south of the border.

1.1 STRUCTURE OF THE BOOK

The book is in three parts: Part I deals with the different types of legal information and retrieval strategies; Part II concentrates on electronic sources; Part III covers research skills.

1.1.1 Part I

The two leading sources of Scots law, legislation and cases, have each been covered in two chapters. The intention is not only to describe and explain the main information sources but to include information on how to understand cases and legislation and to make effective use of them in your research. Different search strategies are provided for accessing information from different standpoints. This includes searching by name, searching with incomplete details and searching by subject. To provide you with an appreciation of all the different sources, various alternative ways of finding the information are described. You may not always have access to the most comprehensive or most current sources. It is therefore important to understand the properties of a range of sources so that you are in a position to evaluate their accuracy and currency and therefore their usefulness to you.

Case law is discussed in chapters 2 and 3. Chapter 2 is intended as an introduction to case law and covers law reporting, the principal series of law reports (both modern and older series) and the skills of reading and analysing cases. It also includes a section on taking efficient notes from a case report. Chapter 3 concentrates on aids to tracing cases and different search strategies that can be adopted.

Legislation is discussed in chapters 4 and 5. Chapter 4 provides an introduction to the various types of legislation and the legislative process. It starts by discussing legislation from the pre-1707 Scottish Parliaments and then looks at the Westminster Parliament and the new Scottish Parliament. There is discussion of the legislative process in order to help explain the various documents that are produced. The layout of a statute and a statutory instrument is discussed and advice given on reading, understanding and interpreting legislation. Chapter 5 concentrates on aids to tracing legislation and the different search strategies that can be adopted.

Chapter 6 contains short sections on a range of information sources of relevance to the Scots lawyer. They range from the Institutional Writers of the seventeenth to nineteenth centuries to current awareness websites. The main intention is to provide details of information sources for students but some practitioner-orientated materials are also included.

Chapter 7 looks at some legal information sources which are relevant for U.K.-wide legal information but which exclude Scots law (either wholly or partially). The sources covered have been limited to those which are widely available in Scotland.

Chapter 8 concerns the increasingly important European dimension to our legal system. It is intended to highlight features of the European system which are of relevance to the Scottish legal researcher, to introduce the principal sources and the key documents of European law and to suggest search strategies for finding information about European law. Chapter 9 discusses public international law and search strategies for locating key materials. Given the importance of electronic information sources in European and international law, separate appendices of useful websites are included for each of these chapters.

Chapter 10 deals with an information-retrieval system called Current Law. The reason for an entire chapter being devoted to Current Law is that it has the most comprehensive range of information available in one data-retrieval system and it is widely available throughout Scotland. It can be a very quick way of finding information but it requires the user to become acquainted with its various idiosyncrasies. Many students find Current Law difficult to master and so detailed discussion of the various component parts of the system, worked examples and an exercise have been included.

1.1.2   Part II

Electronic resources in general and the Internet in particular have significantly changed the way we access legal materials. Many organisations have decided to make legal information publicly available on the Web. The legal profession in Scotland is making increased use of the Web to find case reports, statutes and regulations. There are however many other useful resources available, including journal articles, news reports and current awareness materials.

In order to take advantage of the resources available to lawyers on the Web you must have a basic understanding of the way the Internet works. Chapter 11 is designed as a basic introduction to the Internet and its jargon. Many students will already be familiar with email and will probably have used the Web for recreational purposes. Using the Web for legal research presents new challenges and can be both exciting and intimidating.

One of the biggest challenges for lawyers is simply managing the vast amount of on-line information available. Chapters 12 and 13 show you how to find the information you need quickly and effectively. Chapter 12 introduces the reader to Web search tools and explains how to use them properly. Chapter 13 describes the principal electronic legal resources currently available as a starting point for your research.

Chapter 14 will help you to make effective use of the materials you will find during your exploration of the Internet and is divided into two sections: the first part of the chapter sets out the criteria by which you should evaluate information found on the Internet; the second part shows you how to incorporate your Web research into bibliographies and sets out citation and referencing styles for electronic information sources.

1.1.3   Part III

This section of the book deals with research skills in the broader sense, as opposed to information-retrieval skills. The chapters follow the stages of the research process. Chapter 15 concentrates on the investigation process. Chapter 16 looks at how to read, evaluate and reference the material you research. Chapter 17 discusses how to make use of your findings to produce high quality pieces of work.

Chapter 15 examines the legal investigation process. It looks at how to get the most out of lectures and tutorials. It covers various search strategies for the efficient gathering of relevant information. Legal research can involve focusing on the substantive rules — such as examining the legal rules for controlling pollution or analysing how the courts have interpreted the wording of the principal pollution offence. However, legal research is not restricted to looking at legal rules in isolation. Socio-legal research examines how law operates in a variety of social spheres, *e.g.* whether the pollution legislation has changed attitudes and behaviour towards polluting activity. In recognition of this fact chapter 15 includes a brief discussion of the methods of data collection which are common to all the social sciences — questionnaires, interviews and observation studies.

Chapter 16 discusses what to do with the information once you have found it. It includes reading techniques, the evaluation of documentary material and record keeping. It also discusses referencing conventions and the construction of a bibliography.

Chapter 17 deals with how to use your research to produce work of a high standard. This includes essay writing, problem solving techniques and guidance on how to prepare an oral presentation. The presentation of research and the evaluation of your own work are also covered. Finally, revision strategies and exam technique are discussed.

1.2   STYLE OF THE BOOK

This book is not intended to be read from cover to cover. It is envisaged that it will be referred to when appropriate. It is intended to be used as a manual not read as a novel. It has been designed so that it is easy to find information. It does not hide information in paragraphs of prose and instead adopts a checklist approach. Most, but not all, of the chapters contain flow diagrams in order to aid understanding. They have been included to help explain the use of some of the more confusing sources. Extensive cross-referencing has been used to enable the reader to move easily around the text. However, there is, by necessity, a small amount of repetition. This has been included in an attempt to make the book as user-friendly as possible and to prevent the constant turning of pages.

It is envisaged that the reader will check the contents list to identify the section of the text on a particular area. When in the library, or in front of a PC, trying to use the various sources, the reader may find it helpful to read through the worked examples. Use the information source to locate the material in the worked example. You should then find it easier to use the source to find your own material. Bear in mind that the worked examples are correct at the time of printing but that the nature of law is such that the position could have changed by the time you are working through the example.

Part III (Chapters 15,16,17) covers general research skills. It is suggested that these should be read at the start of your university career and then referred to later as the need arises, i.e. when an essay is set or as the exams loom.

We have concentrated on sources which are widely available to students in Scotland, official sources of information and information sources which allow free access. This book does not claim to cover all information sources. It is not intended as a reference work for law librarians.

This book is not intended to provide an introduction to the Scottish legal system. There are many excellent works which already do this. References are provided to point the reader to texts which deal with specific aspects of Scots law in greater depth.

1.3   ELECTRONIC SOURCES

An increasing amount of legal information is becoming available electronically. A legal researcher cannot now ignore electronic information sources. They should be regarded as a tool — one of the many tools in legal research. They are not the solution to all problems (and in reality they can create their own problems). However, they do have an important role to play. Electronic sources need to be used properly otherwise they can end up retrieving large amounts of irrelevant information and wasting a considerable amount of time (and money). You need to think about why you are using a particular source. Do not use an electronic source just because it is something new or because it is fun. You should assess which is the most appropriate source and which will locate material most efficiently. The answer will not automatically be electronic sources. It can still be quicker to find information using some of the paper sources.

Electronic information sources are evolving all the time. As technology improves this development will continue at a rapid pace. Information on the Web is also subject to change. All websites mentioned are correct at the time of publication but they will quickly become out of date. It is, therefore, recommended that you visit the on-line updates for this book at Green's website. These will contain up-to-date information. Please note that the authors are not responsible for the content of any website referred to in the text.

1.4   WHAT IS LEGAL RESEARCH?

" 'Legal research' is not merely a search for information; it is primarily a struggle for understanding." (M.J. Lynch, "An Impossible Task but Everybody has to do it — Teaching legal Research in Law Schools'' *L. Libr. J.* 1997, Vol. 89, Pt 3, p. 415). Legal research skills do not just consist of learning how to use a law library. It is not enough just to locate information — you have to be able to understand and use the information once it has been located.

Legal research starts even before you get to the law library. It involves deciding what is relevant to your research. This may require the use of problem solving techniques to identify the relevant legal issue. After you have located the information, you have to be able to read, understand and evaluate it. You will then be in a position to make effective use of that material by using it to construct your arguments and to provide authority. Finding the information is a very important, but small, part in the research process.

Finding the leading case on the definition of causation in pollution law is not the same thing as finding the law which will help you advise whether X has "caused" pollution. It is only the first step. Other steps might include:

> reading and analysing the case;
>
> reading the authorities it refers to;
>
> reading cases which have referred to it;
>
> reading articles which have commented on the case;
>
> thinking about the arguments in the case;
>
> and finally, applying the rules laid down to X's set of circumstances.

1.4.1   Legal research skills

In the past legal research skills were barely taught. However, they are now seen as increasingly important. It is obviously important that a law student leaves university with an awareness of the basic principles in the important substantive areas of law. The authors firmly believe that the next most important piece of knowledge that a graduate should have developed is the ability to carry out legal research. When you leave university and gain employment the substantive law that you have learnt will soon be out of date. You will be expected to be able to find out what the law is **now** — not to dig out your old notes and find out what it was in the past.

Lawyers need to be able to carry out research in a way that is: precise, accurate, current, and comprehensive. All university level students need to make good use of their research, be it in essays, presentations, assessments or exams. This book hopes to help students develop these skills.

1.5   The Nature of Law

The very nature of law poses problems for the law student. When you go to university to study law, do not expect the lecturers to tell you what the law is. There is often no single, definitive answer. Instead there are shades of opinion of differing weight. "Psychiatrists have suggested that a student who enters upon the study of law is in search of the security provided by certainty. He expects to find a fixed unchanging body of unambiguous rules which, once absorbed, will furnish a clear solution to any legal problem which arises in a professional lifetime. It is not like that at all." (W.A. Wilson, *Introductory Essays on Scots Law* (2nd ed., 1984), p. 1).

Legal literature can be divided into primary and secondary materials. Primary materials represent the law and include statutes and cases. They are not someone's view about the law. Secondary materials are those which have been collected and interpreted by someone else. Secondary sources do contain commentaries on the law. Examples of secondary sources are encyclopaedias, books, journals and indexes. As a student you cannot avoid having to become familiar with primary materials. It is important not to rely solely on secondary sources. They are dependent on the author and may be out of date. You may find that nothing has been written on a topic.

Some legal materials are regarded as more authoritative than others. You should be aware of the level of authority attached to the sources which you are using. Cases can be reported in several different series of law reports. There will usually be one series which is regarded as more authoritative. In Scotland the Session Cases series is regarded as the most authoritative. If a case is reported there and in other law reports, you should refer to the report in Session Cases.

Some sources of legal information are official and some are unofficial. There is a very important distinction. You can rely on the accuracy of official information. It is authoritative. For example, the official publication of E.C. legislation is in the *Official Journal of the European Communities*. There are many other versions of E.C. legislation which have been produced commercially. They may be easier to access but the content is not authoritative because it has not come from an official source. You should not be discouraged from using unofficial sources (they do after all reprint the official text) but it is important to be aware of their status.

One feature of the law that causes the law student problems is that it changes all the time. However, not all of it changes at the same pace. Some law may remain unchanged for decades or even centuries, while other areas of law change on an annual basis. This means that awareness of the most up-to-date sources of information is necessary, but equally you need to be able to find older works. It cannot automatically be assumed that, just because something is old, it can be ignored.

The importance of finding up-to-date information is stressed repeatedly throughout this book. Basing advice to a client on outdated authorities could make your advice completely wrong. In doing so, you would have acted negligently.

Law students have to come to terms with the fact that the study of law is a precise discipline. Language is used in a precise way. Lawyers use words such as "aforesaid", not to be particularly obscure, but in order to make the meaning beyond doubt. Documents drafted by lawyers (such as contracts and wills) may give rise to significant consequences and may be read some time after they are written. It is therefore vital that the document accurately reflects the original intention.

Precision is also required in the way documents are read. The study of law involves paying attention to detail. The difference between "may" and "shall" can be crucial to advising a client on a course of action. Researching the law also has to be carried out in a precise way. It is not sufficient to have a vague or hazy knowledge of the law. You need to be able to find the relevant rule and to ensure the currency of your research. A reflection of the need for precision can be found in the nature of law books. Law books differ from other books. You will find that law books contain more precise indexing systems than other books. They contain extra information such as tables of cases and statutes. New editions of law books are frequently produced. This is to take account of the fact that the law is constantly changing. You must always take care to consult the most recent edition.

Not only are law books different for other books but law libraries are different from other libraries. They will tend to contain many more periodicals and reference materials. The law library is a vital component in your studies at university. If you learn how to use it effectively you will enhance your studies and you will find that it will bring benefits to you long into your professional career. It is presumed that you will be given information about your own university library and so subjects such as searching library catalogues have not been covered. A library exercise has been included in the appendices. This should enable you to test your knowledge and ensure that you know your way around the primary materials in a law library.

Within a law library the sources of law are not always easy to access.

> "there is an enormous and constantly changing mass of decisions, legislative enactments, and administrative rules from which the lawyer must speedily and accurately extract the law applicable to a specific problem... The task is immeasurably increased because these decisions, as made, and these rules, as enacted, are not published in a subject or classified arrangement but, instead, by jurisdiction and date of decision or enactment." M.O. Price, H. Bitner, S.R. Bysiewicz, *Effective Legal Research* (4th ed., 1979), p. 2.

Collections of statutes and cases are published in chronological order due to (a) the vast number being produced, (b) the need for prompt publication and (c) tradition. In order to facilitate searching these materials various aids have been developed. They attempt to help access legal information in more meaningful ways. These aids include citators, tables, digests and indexes. However, some of the facilitating aids can themselves prove difficult for the inexperienced user.

The law student has to face the unpalatable fact that there is no single source that will answer a legal problem. There is no one place where you can find all of the law. There is no right way of finding information; instead there are lots of different methods, with different coverage, different searching facilities, different formats, etc. In order to evaluate the material he retrieves, the researcher must be aware of the strengths and limitations of the various information sources. This book offers comments about different information sources and highlights particular strengths and weaknesses.

The Scottish law student faces particular problems in researching the law. Legislation emanating from the Westminster Parliament applying exclusively to Scotland can be difficult to find. Lack of parliamentary time or interest in the intricacies of our legal system has resulted in a piecemeal approach to Scottish legislation. The increased use of Miscellaneous Provisions Acts to amend the law on a range of subjects has contributed to the difficulty in finding Scots law.

United Kingdom texts tend to concentrate on the larger jurisdiction of England and Wales. There may be a short chapter or perhaps just a paragraph pointing out that Scottish law is different. Worse still, some texts exclude mention of Scotland altogether. Scots law has been poorly served by providers of legal information. Even the electronic sources have, in the main, failed to include exclusively Scottish material. Only one of the electronic databases contains Scottish legislation. A final, but not unimportant point, is that dedicated Scottish law books are more expensive than their U.K. counterparts. The reason claimed is the small size of the potential market.

Despite these difficulties, it is an exciting time to be studying Scots law. When one of the authors was at university in the eighties, doubt was expressed as to whether Scots law would exist as a distinct system by the end of the century. Now, with the advent of the Scottish Parliament, its future is assured and we can look forward to researching Scots law well into the next millennium.

The law in this book is correct as at March 31, 1999.

Chapter 2

AN INTRODUCTION TO CASES

2.1 THE IMPORTANCE OF CASES AND THE DOCTRINE OF JUDICIAL PRECEDENT

You will come across cases throughout your study of law at university and beyond. It is essential that you become familiar with the different series of law reports, the various ways of locating cases and the layout and content of a reported case. This chapter will cover law reporting, the principal series of law reports and the skills of reading and analysing cases. Chapter 3 will concentrate on aids to tracing cases and different search strategies that can be adopted. European Community cases are discussed in chapter 8 and cases concerning international law are covered in chapter 9.

Case law is important as it is one of the primary sources of Scots law, second only to legislation. The doctrine of judicial precedent allows judgments in previous cases to influence decisions in later cases. The strict version of this doctrine, *stare decisis*, means that "A single decision from a qualifying court will bind all future courts dealing with the same point of law." (M.C. Meston *et al*, *The Scottish Legal Tradition* (new enl. ed., 1991), p. 11). Greater discussion of the doctrine of judicial precedent will be found in: *The Laws of Scotland: Stair Memorial Encyclopaedia*, Vol. 22 and D.M. Walker, *The Scottish Legal System* (7th ed., 1997), pp. 414–456.

This definition encompasses two important concepts surrounding the earlier decision: (a) it has to be binding, that is from a qualifying court, and (b) it has to be "in point". This means that it concerns the same point of law. If both of these elements are in place the later court must follow the earlier decision. This is the theory but, in practice, there are techniques which the judiciary can employ to avoid following a binding precedent — see A.A. Paterson and T.St.J.N. Bates, *The Legal System of Scotland* (3rd ed., 1993), Chap. 14.

2.1.1 The status of the court

Previous cases can be binding or persuasive on a current case. The status of the previous case will depend on the position in the court hierarchy of the court which heard it. In general, decisions from a court higher in the hierarchy will bind a lower court. Courts can be bound in the following circumstances:

Civil Courts

Sheriff Court	**bound** by decisions of	Inner House; House of Lords and European Court of Justice/Court of First Instance*
	usually follows	decisions of own Sheriff Principal
	not bound by decisions of	other sheriffs, Sheriffs Principal or Lords Ordinary
Sheriff Principal	**bound** by decisions of	Inner House; House of Lords and European Court of Justice/Court of First Instance*
	not bound by decisions of	sheriffs, other Sheriffs Principal or Lords Ordinary
Lord Ordinary	**bound** by decisions of	Inner House; House of Lords and European Court of Justice/Court of First Instance*
	not bound by decisions of	sheriffs, Sheriffs Principal or other Lords Ordinary
Inner House	**bound** by decisions of	either of its Divisions; House of Lords and European Court of Justice/ Court of First Instance*
	has power to overrule a previous Inner House decision by convening a larger court	
	not bound by decisions of	sheriffs, Sheriffs Principal or Lords Ordinary
House of Lords	**bound by** decisions of	European Court of Justice/Court of First Instance*
	has power to overrule its own previous decision (Practice Statement [1966] 3 All E.R. 77, [1966] 1 W.L.R. 1234, HL)	

* Decisions concerning meaning or effect of any E.C. law/treaty (European Communities Act 1972, s.3).

The effect of the House of Lords decisions on Scots law

> Decisions in Scottish appeals are binding;
>
> Decisions in non-Scottish cases on statutory provisions which are applicable in both jurisdictions are probably binding;
>
> Decisions in non-Scottish cases on areas of law which are different are not binding but can be persuasive if they concern matters of general jurisprudence.

This is discussed in greater depth in *The Laws of Scotland: Stair Memorial Encyclopaedia*, Vol. 22, paras 270–285.

Criminal Courts

District Court	**bound** by decisions of	"A magistrate sitting in the district court is probably bound by rulings of any superior criminal court or of a single judge or sheriff" Walker, D.M., *The Scottish Legal System* (7th ed., 1997) at p. 428.
Sheriff Court	**bound** by decisions of	A single judge in the High Court of Justiciary (Trial) and High Court of Justiciary (Appeal)
	not bound by decisions of sheriffs	
High Court of Justiciary (Trial)	**bound by** decisions of	High Court of Justiciary (Appeal)
	not bound by decisions of	Single judges in the High Court of Justiciary (Trial)
High Court of Justiciary (Appeal)	**has power to overrule**	A previous High Court decision by convening a larger court
	not bound by decisions of	House of Lords

2.1.2 Which parts of the previous decision are binding?

Not all of the previous case (precedent) is binding, only the part which deals with the reasoning on the same point of law. This is referred to as the *ratio decidendi*. This is discussed in more detail in *The Laws of Scotland: Stair Memorial Encyclopaedia*, Vol. 22, paras 334–345. The *ratio decidendi* will be explored later in the chapter para. 2.4.2.

2.1.3 Importance of current status of a case

It is not only important to know the details of a case, it is also essential to be aware of the current status of that case. The law changes all the time. The status of a case does not remain static. A decision may be appealed to a higher court, which may overturn the original decision. Even when a final decision is reached in a case it may be overruled by a later case and thereafter play no part as a precedent.

There are various things that can happen to a case during its lifetime. These are referred to in the following terms:

Affirmed

The present court agrees with the decision of a lower court concerning the same case.

Applied

The present court accepts that is bound by the *ratio decidendi* of a previous case and applies the same reasoning in the present case.

Approved

The present court agrees that a decision made by a previous lower court was correctly decided.

Considered/Discussed/Commented on

These all mean that the present court has discussed the earlier case.

Distinguished

The present court decides that an apparently binding precedent is not in point. It has found material differences between the two cases. It, therefore, does not have to follow the previous case. However, the previous case still remains as authority for future cases which are in point.

Overruled

The present court rejects a previous decision of a lower court. The earlier decision is struck out and can no longer be used as authority.

Reversed

The present court disagrees with the decision of a lower court concerning the same case.

2.2   THE REPORTING OF CASES

2.2.1   Reported Cases

A huge number of cases are heard by the courts every year but only a small number of cases are reported in law reports. Reporting in the law reports is very different to being reported in a newspaper. Cases are reported by newspapers to entertain/inform the newspaper's readership. Cases which are reported in the law reports are cases which carry some legal significance, *i.e.* cases which introduce a new principle into the law or which interpret a piece of legislation for the first time. Cases which are reported tend to be appellate decisions which in reality represent a tiny minority of cases litigated in court.

The editors of the various law reports decide which cases are reported and this can mean that the same case appears in several different series of law reports.

How do the editors decide which cases to report? They would all tend to answer that they report cases which are legally significant but what exactly does this mean? The criteria used by the editor of the SLT (Supplied courtesy of Greens) are as follows:

1. Cases which make new law, either because they deal with novel situations or extend the application of existing rules.

2. Cases where the judges restate old principles of law in modern terms or which are examples of modern applications of old principles.

3. Cases where the law is clarified by an appellate court when inferior courts have reached conflicting decisions; also non-appellate decisions discussing issues regularly litigated, *e.g.* subsistence of missives.

4. Cases which interpret legislation, unless the matter is peculiar to the parties involved.

5. Cases which interpret clauses in, for example, contracts and wills, which are likely to be of wider application.

6. Cases where the courts clarify points of practice or procedure.

7. Cases which, while turning on their facts, may be of guidance in comparable cases, *e.g.* decisions of quantum and certain instances of interim interdict.

Cases which turn purely on questions of fact, trite law, bad pleading or which generally contain nothing which has not already been laid down in reported cases are not reported.

2.2.2 Unreported cases

Unreported cases can be cited in court and the fact that a case has not been reported has no effect whatsoever on its weight as a precedent.

In the past it was very difficult to obtain transcripts of unreported cases. This has become easier with the advent of electronic databases which include selected unreported cases, *e.g.* Lexis and Lawtel. Transcripts of unreported cases can also be obtained for research purposes by contacting the Operations and Policy Unit at Scottish Courts Service, Hayweight House, 23 Lauriston Street, Edinburgh EH3 9DQ.

A permanent record of proceedings is not automatically kept for all cases heard in court. In criminal cases no transcript is kept of summary trials. The same is true for small claims and summary cause cases in the sheriff court.

2.2.3 What is a Law Report?

A law report is not a verbatim account of the whole court proceedings. It is the judicial decision on a point of law. A law report is concerned with the legal issues and not the factual evidence. A law report will not contain an account of the evidence, examination-in-chief, cross-examination, etc. The only facts to be included in a law report are those relevant to the legal reasoning in the case.

2.3 HOW CASES ARE PUBLISHED

2.3.1 The development of law reporting in Scotland

Early Scottish law reports were known as "Practicks". These date from the fifteenth century to the early seventeenth century. They are hardly recognisable as a law report as we understand them today. They have been described as "embryo law reports" (Stair Society, *An Introductory Survey of the Sources and Literature of Scots Law* (1936), p. 27). They tended to be notes compiled by judges for their own use. Publication was not envisaged. They were brief and consisted of details of legal principle and the parties' names.

Examples of published collections of Practicks are:
Balfour's Practicks (1469–1579), Spotiswoode's Practicks (1541–1637), Hope's Minor Practicks (1608–1633) and Hope's Major Practicks (1608–1633). More details about the Practicks can be found in the Stair Society publication, *An Introductory Survey of the Sources and Literature of Scots Law* (1936), chap. 3.

In the seventeenth century many different individuals published private collections of case reports. Lists can be found in paras 2.3.7.1 and 2.3.7.2 below. Gradually law reporting became more formalised. A large step forward occurred at the beginning of the nineteenth century with the restructuring of the Court of Session. From 1821 cases from the Court of Session were reported in the Session Cases and the modern system of law reporting was born.

2.3.2 Modern law reporting

Some introductory points:

- Some cases appear in many different series of law reports. If this is the case, the most authoritative law report for that jurisdiction should be cited. In Scotland, the most authoritative series of law reports is the Session Cases, followed by the Scots Law Times.

- Some series of law reports are full text and others are digests/summaries, *e.g.* Session Cases is a full text series; Green's Weekly Digest contains short summaries of cases.

- Some series are general and others are specific to one area of law. The main series of law reports are general (they cover cases on every different subject) and law reports are published in chronological order. Specialist series publish according to subject matter, *e.g.* Environmental Law Reports. They will only include cases concerning environmental issues.

- Most series of law reports are bound in annual volumes. The current year's issues appear as slim paper booklets prior to being bound into annual volumes. They will usually be located beside the annual volumes in a law library.

2.3.3 The Principal Modern Series of Law Reports

Title **Session Cases**
Abbreviation S.C.
Citation Since 1907 the citation has been as follows:
Each annual volume consists of three parts which are paginated separately:
(a) Scottish cases decided by the House of Lords, referred to as S.C.(H.L.), *e.g. Slater v. Finning Ltd* 1997 S.C. (H.L.) 8;
(b) cases decided by the High Court of Justiciary, referred to as J.C., *e.g. Gellatly v. Heywood* 1997 J.C. 171;
(c) cases decided by the Court of Session, referred to as S.C., *e.g. Kennedy v. Smith* 1997 S.C. 51.

The series of Session Cases which appeared between 1821 and 1906 are referred to by the names of the five respective editors:

First Series	Shaw S.	16 vols.	1821–1838
Second Series	Dunlop D.	24 vols.	1838–1862
Third Series	MacPherson M.	11 vols.	1862–1873
Fourth Series	Rettie R.	25 vols.	1873–1898
Fifth Series	Fraser F.	8 vols.	1898–1906

These are cited by the volume number, the initial of the editor and the page number, *e.g. M'Calman v. M'Arthur* (1864) 2 M. 678. This indicates that you will find the report in Session Cases, third series, Vol. 2, edited by MacPherson, at page 678.
The series began by covering decisions in the Court of Session. The House of Lords (Scottish appeals) was covered from 1850 and was separately paginated, *e.g.* (year) 3 M. (H.L.) page no. The High Court of Justiciary was included from 1874 and was paginated separately, *e.g.* (year) 2 F. (J.) page no.

Period covered 1821 to present

Publisher and Editor	W. Green for The Scottish Council of Law Reporting, R.F. Hunter
Comments	In Scotland the Session Cases series of law reports is the most authoritative. The judgments are revised by the judge prior to publication. Be wary of separate pagination.
Available in	Paper only at present
Courts covered	House of Lords, Court of Session, High Court of Justiciary, Lands Valuation Appeal Court
Format	These reports are arranged as follows:

- list of judges in the courts covered;
- index of case names — accessible by either party's name. These are arranged in three sections under the relevant court: Court of Session (includes Lands Valuation Appeal Court), Court of Justiciary and House of Lords;
- case reports are arranged in separate sections and paginated separately. They appear as follows:

House of Lords
Court of Justiciary
Lands Valuation Appeal Court
Court of Session

At the back of each volume is the following information:
- Index of Matters — a subject index. It includes "Words and Phrases" as a heading.
- Cases referred to judicially in that volume in alphabetical order of the first party.
- Cases affirmed, reversed, commented on, etc., in that volume, in alphabetical order of first party's names.

Updated	six times a year.
Consolidated indexes	No consolidated index but information from Session Cases is included in the Faculty Digest. See para. 3.1.3.3.

Title	**Scots Law Times**
Abbreviation	S.L.T.
Citation	
Full report from superior court	*Aitken v. Reith* 1997 S.L.T. 2
Notes of a report	*F. MacGregor v. MacNeill* 1975 S.L.T. (Notes) 54
Sheriff Court report	*Cavanagh v. Godfreys of Dundee Ltd* 1997 S.L.T. (Sh. Ct.) 2
Land Court report	*Crofters Commission v. Mackay* 1997 S.L.T. (Land Ct.) 2
Lands Tribunal of Scotland report	*Tennant v. East Kilbride District Council* 1997 S.L.T. (Lands Tr.) 14
Lyon Court report	*Douglas-Hamilton, Petitioner* 1996 S.L.T. (Lyon Ct.) 8
Previous citation convention between 1893–1908	Citation was by volume, *e.g. Thomson v. Landale* (1897) 5 S.L.T. 204
Period covered	1893 to present
Publisher and Editor	W. Green, P.A. Nicholson
Comments	Be wary of the separate pagination.

Not just law reports but also contains articles and professional information. Historically published with less time delay than Session Cases. Recently the difference has been greatly reduced.

Available in	Paper and CD ROM. The CD-ROM allows access to cases between 1893–1997. You can search by keyword, names or citation.
Courts covered	House of Lords, Court of Session, High Court of Justiciary, Sheriff courts, Scottish Land Court, Lands Valuation Appeal Court, Lands Tribunal for Scotland and Court of the Lord Lyon.
Format	The annual volumes consist of the following information:

- List of judges in the Court of Session.
- The law reports are arranged in sections relating to the court which heard the case. The sections are separately paginated and contain separate indexes of cases, case reports and indexes of cases according to subject matter. The sections are:

Superior courts
Sheriff courts
Scottish Land Court
Lands Tribunal for Scotland
Lyon Court

- News section. This includes:

Subject index

Articles

Acts of Adjournal/Sederunt

Appointments

Obituaries

Parliamentary news

Book reviews

General information

Coming events

Court

Business changes

Taxation

Since 1989 two annual volumes have been produced.

Volume one contains:

List of judges in Court of Session

Superior court cases and indexes

Volume two contains:

Index of all cases in the two volumes in one index, but organised in separate sections

News section

Cases and indexes for cases in Sheriff Court, Scottish Land Court, the Lands Tribunal of Scotland and the Lyon Court

Publication Published weekly. Cumulative indexes are published after every ten issues.

Consolidated indexes 1961–90 covers cases reported in the S.L.T. during these years and includes: alphabetical index of cases

subject index

index of cases considered

1991–date. Index is updated annually.

CD-ROM version allows access to cases between 1893–1997.

Title	**Scottish Civil Law Reports**
Abbreviation	S.C.L.R.
Citation	*e.g. Watson v. Renfrew District Council*, 1995 S.C.L.R. 82
Period covered	1987 to present
Publisher and Editor	The Law Society of Scotland/Butterworths, Sheriff D. Kelbie
Comments	Commentaries are included for selected cases
Available in	Paper only
Courts covered	House of Lords, Court of Session, Sheriff Court
Format	Annual volumes contain the following information:

- Index of cases reported by name — accessible by both parties' name.
- Digest of cases — arranged by subject matter. ''Words and phrases'' is included as a heading.
- Statutes, Statutory Instruments and Court Rules judicially considered.
- Cases judicially considered.
- Case reports. The cases are arranged in three sections: full reports, notes and quantum. All three are paginated as one. Some of the cases are accompanied by commentaries by experts in the area of law concerned.

Updated	six times a year.
Consolidated indexes	Index 1987–1996. This consolidates the information contained in the first four tables above for the period.

Title	**Scottish Criminal Case Reports**
Abbreviation	S.C.C.R.
Citation	*e.g. H.M.Advocate v. Penders*, 1996 S.C.C.R. 404
Period covered	1981 to present
Publisher and Editor	The Law Society of Scotland/Butterworths, Sheriff G.H. Gordon
Comments	Commentaries are by the editor
Available in	Paper only
Courts covered	High Court of Justiciary, Sheriff Court
Format	The annual volumes contain the following information:

- List of judges in the High Court of Justiciary
- Index of reported cases — accessible by both parties' names

- Digest of cases according to the subject matter which includes ''words and phrases'' as a heading
- Statutes and Statutory Instruments judicially considered
- Cases judicially considered

Case reports. Selected cases are followed by commentaries.

Updated	six times a year.
Consolidated indexes	Index 1981–1990 contains the following tables relating to the period covered:

Cases reported

Digest of cases

Statutes and Statutory Instruments judicially considered

Cases judicially considered

The Index includes cases reported in Justiciary Cases, S.L.T. and S.C.C.R. Supplement 1950–80.

The 1995 annual volume contains an update of this index with consolidated tables for 1991–95.

The Scottish Criminal Case Reports Supplement (1950–1980). This addition to the series contains a selection of cases decided by the High Court between 1950–80 which had not been previously reported.

It contains the following information:

- Index of cases reported — accessible by both parties' names
- Digest of cases according to subject matter
- Statutes and Statutory Instruments judicially considered between 1950–80
- Cases judicially considered between 1950–80
- Case reports

Title	**Green's Weekly Digest**
Abbreviation	G.W.D.
Citation	Within G.W.D. the cases are referred to by issue number and paragraph number, e.g. *Fry's Metals v. Durastic*, G.W.D. 1990 5–272
	This case will be found in the 1990 folder in issue 5 at paragraph 272.
Period covered	1986 to present
Publisher and Editor	W. Green, P. Nicholson
Comments	It reports all decisions of the Scottish courts received by W. Green. Reports of significance are subsequently reported more fully elsewhere.
	Arranged by subject
Available in	Paper only
Courts covered	House of Lords, Court of Session, High Court of Justiciary, Sheriff Court, Scottish Land Court.
Format	Annual Service Files contain:

- Index of cases digested (alphabetical by first party's name)
- Index of subject matter
- Table of statutes considered
- Table of quantum of damages
- Case digests

Updated	40 times a year. Cumulative indexes are published three times a year.
Consolidated indexes	Index 1986–1991 — consolidates all four indexes for that period.

2.3.4   Specialist series of Scottish law reports

Title	**Greens Reparation Law Reports**
Abbreviation	Rep.L.R.
Citation	*Forbes v. City of Dundee District Council* 1997 Rep.L.R. 48
Period covered	1996 to present
Publisher and Editor	W. Green, D. Kinloch
Comments	Includes commentaries
Available in	Paper
Courts covered	House of Lords, Court of Session, Sheriff Court
Format	Editorial and case reports. Some cases are in note form.
Updated	six times a year.
Consolidated indexes	Annual consolidated index containing an alphabetical list of first named parties and an index of subject matter.

Title	**Greens Housing Law Reports**
Abbreviation	Hous.L.R.
Citation	*Cook v. Renfrew District Council*, 1998 Hous.L.R. 14
Period covered	1996 to present
Publisher and Editor	W. Green, R. Sutherland
Comments	Includes commentaries on the cases.
Available in	Paper
Courts covered	House of Lords, Court of Session, Sheriff Court, Lands Tribunal for Scotland, Decisions of Local Government Ombudsmen, Housing Association Ombudsmen.
Format	Editorial
	Case reports
Update	six issues a year.
Consolidated indexes	Annual consolidated index containing an alphabetical list of first named parties and an index of subject matter
Title	**Greens Family Law Reports**
Abbreviation	Fam.L.R.
Citation	*Donnelly v. Green*, 1998 Fam.L.R. 12
Period covered	1997 to present
Publisher and Editor	W. Green, R.P. Macfarlane
Comments	Commentaries are provided
Available in	Paper
Courts covered	European Court of Human Rights, House of Lords, Court of Session, Sheriff Court
Format	Editorial
	Subject index
	Case reports
Update	six issues a year.
Consolidated indexes	Annual consolidated index with an alphabetical list of first named parties and an index of subject matter.
Title	**Scottish Land Court Reports**
Abbreviation	S.L.C.R.
Citation	*e.g. Broadland Properties Estates Ltd v. Grant*, 1997 S.L.C.R. 1
Period covered	1913–present
Courts covered	Scottish Land Court
Format	Contents
	Index of cases (Alphabetical order of first party)
	Case reports
	Digest of cases via subject headings
Title	**Scottish Planning Appeal Decisions**
Abbreviation	SPADs
Publisher	The Planning Exchange in association with the Scottish Office Enquiry Reporters Unit
Coverage	Planning appeal decisions by the Secretary of State
Updates	Monthly

2.3.5 Reporting of Scottish cases in England

Some Scottish cases will appear in the following English series of law reports:

>   Appeal Cases
>
>   Weekly Law Reports
>
>   All England Law Reports

The English law reports are covered in chapter 7.

2.3.6 Specialist series of law reports covering the U.K.

There is an increasing range and number of specialist series of law reports. Examples include:

British Company Cases (B.C.C.)

Environmental Law Reports (Env.L.R.)

Industrial Cases Reports (I.C.R.)

Industrial Relations Law Reports (I.R.L.R.)

Medical Law Reports (Med.L.R.)

Reports of Tax Cases (T.C.)

2.3.7 Older Series of Scottish Law Reports

Title	**The Scottish Law Reporter**
Abbreviation	S.L.R. or Sc. L.R.
Period covered	1865–1924 (vols 1–61)
Courts covered	House of Lords, Court of Session, Court of Justiciary, Court of Teinds
Format	Contents
	Index of cases (either party's surname)
	Index of Statutes
	Index of Subjects
	Case Reports
	(all paginated together)

Title	**Sheriff Court Reports (Sh. Ct. Rep.)** (usually to be found bound as **Scottish Law Review And Sheriff Court Reporter**)
Abbreviation	S.L.R. or S.L.Rev. or Sc.L.R.
Period covered	1885–1963 (vols 1–79)
Courts covered	Sheriff Court
Format	First part contains collections of the Scottish Law Review. These contain articles and professional news/information.
	Second part (all in the one volume) is Sheriff court reports:
	Contents
	Index of cases (either party)
	Digest of cases accessible via subject headings
	Scottish Land Court Reports
	Index of cases
	Case reports
	Digest of cases accessible via subject headings

Title	**Scottish Jurist**
Abbreviation	S.J. or Sc. Jur.
Period covered	1829–1873
Courts covered	House of Lords, Court of Session, Court of Justiciary, Court of Teinds
Format	Contents
	Index of Matters (subject index)
	Index of case names
	Court of Session (pursuer and defender)
	Court of Session (defender and pursuer)
	House of Lords
	High Court of Justiciary
	English decisions generally applicable to Scots law
	Scottish cases

Title	**Morison's Dictionary of Decisions**
Abbreviation	M. or Mor.
Period covered	1540–1808
Format	This collection of cases consists of 22 volumes. There are 19 volumes of cases. Volumes 20 and 21 contain a digest of cases from the main volumes. Volume 22 contains supplementary material. There is an Appendix which includes cases which were reported while the Dictionary was being published.
	The work is paginated continuously throughout all the volumes. It is not referred to by volume number but by year and page number, *e.g. Johnston v. Napier* (1708) M. 16511.

Other works are frequently kept with Morison's Dictionary:

Morison's Synopsis (1808–1816)

Tait's Index. This contains an index of the cases in Morison's Dictionary in alphabetical order of pursuer.

Brown's Supplement (1628–1794) (B.S.). This covers cases which were not included in Morison's Dictionary.

2.3.7.1   *Old reports which covered House of Lords decisions in Scottish appeals*

Brown's Synopsis of Decisions (1540–1827)

Robertson (1707–27)

Craigie, Stewart and Paton (1726–1821)

Dow (1813–1818)

Bligh (1819–1821)

Shaw (1821–1824)

Wilson & Shaw (1825–1835)

Shaw & Maclean (1835–1838)

Maclean & Robinson (1839)

Robinson (1840–41)

Bell (1842–1850)

MacQueen (1851–1865)

Paterson (1851–73)

From 1850 Scottish appeals to the House of Lords were reported in Session Cases, see para. 2.3.3 above.

2.3.7.2   *Old reports which covered Court of Session decisions*

Morison's Dictionary of Decisions (1540–1808)

Brown's Synopsis of Decisions (1540–1827)

Durie (1621–1642)

Brown's Supplement (1622–1794)

English Judges (1655–1661)

Stair (1661–1681)

Gilmour and Falconer (1665–1677)

Dirleton (1665–1677)

Fountainhall (1678–1712)

Harcarse (1681–1691)

Dalrymple (1698–1718)

Forbes (1705–1713)

Bruce (1714–1715)

Kames (Remarkable Decisions) (1716–1752)

Edgar (1724–1725)

Elchies (1733–1754)

Clerk Home (1735–1744)

Kilkerran (1738–1752)

Falconer (1744–1751)

Kames (Select Decisions) (1752–1768)

Hailes (1766–1791)

Bell (1790–1792)

Bell (1794–1795)

Hume (1781–1822)

Deas and Anderson (1829–1833)

Scottish Jurist (1829–1873) see para. 2.3.7 above

Scottish Law Reporter (1865–1924) see para. 2.3.7 above

Faculty Collection/Faculty Decisions (Old Series) (1752–1808)

Faculty Collection/Faculty Decisions (New Series) (1808–1825)

Faculty Collection/Faculty Decisions (Octavo Series) (1825–1841)

Bell's Dictionary of Decisions (1808–1832)

From 1821 Court of Session cases were reported in Session Cases, see para. 2.3.3 above.

2.3.7.3   *Old reports which covered High Court of Justiciary decisions*

Shaw (1819–1831)

Syme (1826–1830)

Swinton (1835–1841)

Broun (1842–1845)

Arkley (1846–1848)

Shaw (1848–1851)

Irvine (1851–1868)

Couper (1868–1885)

White (1885–1893)

Adam (1893–1916)

From 1874 decisions of the High Court of Justiciary were reported in Session Cases, see para. 2.3.3 above.

2.3.7.4   *Old reports covering decisions of other courts*

Fergusson (1811–1817) — Consistorial Court

Murray (1815–1830) — Jury Court

McFarlane (1838–1839) — Jury Court

Shaw (1821–1831) — Teind Court

2.3.7.5   *Old reports of Sheriff Court decisions*

Guthrie's Select Sheriff Court Decisions (1854–1892)

Scottish Law Review (1885–1963), see para. 2.3.7 above

Sheriff Court decisions have been reported in Scots Law Times since 1893. More detailed information on old Sheriff Court records can be found in the Stair Society publication, *An Introductory Survey of the Sources and Literature of Scots Law* (1936) chap. 10.

Many of the old collections of reports were reprinted at the beginning of this century in a series called *Scots Revised Reports*, which contains:

Selected cases from Morison's Dictionary, part of the Faculty Collection/Faculty Decisions, House of Lords Appeals, Shaw, Dunlop, Macpherson and cases reported only in the Scottish Jurist between 1829–65.

More detailed information on the old series of law reports can be found in Stair Society, *An Introductory Survey of the Sources and Literature of Scots Law* (1936) chap. 4.

2.3.8   Citation conventions

In order to find cases in the various law reports it is necessary to become familiar with the referencing system for cases. The reference for a case is called its "citation". The citation of a case is made up of five elements:

- name of the case — this will usually be the names of the parties involved;

- year in which the decision was reported;

- volume number of the relevant report, if applicable;

- abbreviation for the name of the law report — a table of abbreviations appears at the start of the book;

- page number of the volume at which the case report begins.

In order to trace a case, follow the citation, *e.g.*

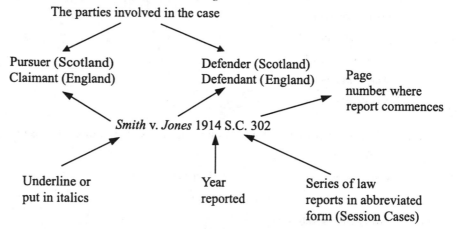

The parties involved in the case

Pursuer (Scotland) / Claimant (England)   Defender (Scotland) / Defendant (England)   Page number where report commences

Smith v. *Jones* 1914 S.C. 302

Underline or put in italics   Year reported   Series of law reports in abbreviated form (Session Cases)

The parties are usually referred to by the pursuer's name followed by defender's name. If the case is appealed the order is reversed.

2.3.8.1   *Criminal cases*

In cases where solemn procedure is used, the Crown is referred to as Her Majesty's Advocate (H.M.A.). If the case is prosecuted under summary procedure, the surname of the Procurator Fiscal is used to represent the Crown.

In certain cases where anonymity is to be preserved the parties are referred to by initials, *e.g. A v. B.*

In England, criminal cases are cited, *e.g. R v. Smith.* The R stands for Rex or Regina depending on whether there is a king or queen on the throne at the time.

2.3.8.2   *Others*

In shipping cases the name of the ship involved is often used.

Unreported cases are cited as follows: name, the date of judgment, abbreviated form of the court and the word "unreported" in round brackets.

2.3.8.3   *Use of brackets in Scottish case reports*

The convention is that where the date is an essential part of the reference to the volume, the year is **not** put in brackets. If the date is not essential, it is put in round brackets or it may not be given at all.

The five series of Session Cases between 1821 and 1906 are referred to by citing the first letter of the surname of the editor or chief reporter, *e.g. Goldston v. Young* (1868) 7 M.188. This indicates that it was the 7th year of Macpherson's editorship.

After 1906 the year was essential in citations and brackets are not used, *e.g. Errol v. Walker*, 1966 S.C. 93.

The earliest volumes of Scots Law Times (1893–1908) are cited by volume number using brackets, *e.g. Peden v. Graham* (1907) 15 S.L.T. 143.

After 1908, the year alone is used and is therefore essential. No brackets are used, *e.g. Dunfermline D.C. v. Blyth & Blyth Associates*, 1985 S.L.T. 345.

In summary, no brackets are used by the modern Scottish law reports. Square brackets are **never** used in Scottish case citations. In contrast square brackets are used by most modern English law reports, *e.g.* The Law Reports, the All England Law Reports and the Weekly Law Reports.

2.3.8.4   *Summary—Using the citation details to locate the report of the case.*

name and citation

↓

identify the series of law reports
from the abbreviated form in the citation,
if necessary check one of information sources
on abbreviations listed in para 2.3.9

↓

locate appropriate volume
of series of law reports

↓

turn to the page number
and the case should commence on that page

N.B.: Take extra care when consulting law reports which have separate paginations.

2.3.9   **Abbreviations — how to find their meaning**

The list of law reports in para. 2.3.3 has included the appropriate abbreviated forms. If you come across an unfamiliar abbreviation, the following sources can help:

- D. Raistrick, *Index to Legal Citations and Abbreviations* (2nd ed., 1993).
- *The Laws of Scotland: Stair Memorial Encyclopaedia.* There is a table of abbreviations at the beginning of each volume in the series.
- Current Law — Monthly Digest, Year Book and Case Citators all have lists of abbreviations.
- Lawtel provides a list of abbreviations in its case law section.
- Legal Journals Index. Each issue has a list of abbreviations for all the journals indexed.
- P. Osborn, *Concise Law Dictionary* (8th ed., 1993).

2.4   READING CASES

2.4.1   **Anatomy of a case**

Reading cases is a skill that you will develop through practice. The anatomy of a case has been included to introduce you to the layout of cases. Do not expect to fully understand the first case that you read. It will take time to get used to the format and language used by the judiciary.

The case below appeared in the Session Cases. Case reports in other series of law reports will be similar but not identical. Different features of the law report are marked with numbers which correspond to the following list:

[1] The names of the parties

[2] The date when the case was heard in court. The opinion of the court is usually delivered some time after the actual hearing. There is then a further lapse of time before the case will appear in the law reports. In this instance, the case was heard in July 1997 and appeared in the first issue of Session Cases for 1998.

[3] The judges who heard the case

[4] In criminal cases the first named party is usually the Crown and the accused (the pannel) would be the second party. However, here the pannel has appealed the original decision and he has become the first named party; he is referred to as the "appellant". The Crown is referred to as the "respondent".

This case has been initiated under summary procedure and the Crown is therefore referred to as the surname of the Procurator Fiscal in whose area the case is being taken. Here the Crown appears as Robert T. Hamilton who is the Procurator Fiscal in Dunfermline. In cases taken under solemn procedure the Crown is referred to as H.M.Advocate.

The names in italics opposite the parties' names are those of their representatives in court. The representative for the Crown is referred to as "QC, A-D". The Q.C. stands for Queens Counsel and means that he is a senior advocate. The A-D stands for Advocate Depute.

[5] The section in italics is written by the editor of the law report. It gives an indication of the subject matter of the case and the legal issue involved. The first words indicate the heading under which this case is classed in the subject index for the law reports. This case will appear twice — once under Crime — Malicious Mischief and again under Words & Phrases — "Detriment".

JC   1

[1]   BETT v HAMILTON   A

No 1   Lord Sutherland, Lord Johnston
[2]   23 July 1997   and Lord Dawson   [3]

[4]   ROBERT JOHN BETT, Appellant — *M E Scott*
              ROBERT T HAMILTON (Procurator fiscal, Dunfermline), Respondent — *Campbell,*
                                           QC, A-D

[5]   *Crime — Malicious mischief — Whether material patrimonial loss required — Pannel charged*   B
        with maliciously moving video surveillance camera resulting in detriment to the benefit which a
        bank had attempted to secure by having camera — Whether loss of benefit to be obtained from
        use of camera constituted malicious mischief — Whether "detriment" meant simply "implied
        disadvantage" — Whether crime constituted

        Words and phrases — "Detriment"   C

[6]   A pannel was charged on a libel, the terms of which narrated that he had maliciously
        moved a video surveillance camera with a pole or similar instrument so as to point the
        camera in such a direction that it did not show or record activity in an area which it had
        been set to cover, whereby the running costs associated with the camera were wasted and
        the building was exposed to increased risk of housebreaking, theft and vandalism. The
        pannel tabled a plea to the relevancy of the charge in that it did not set forth a competent   D
        charge of malicious mischief. The sheriff held that the acts of the pannel had resulted in
        detriment to the benefit which the bank had attempted to secure by having a surveillance
        camera. He considered that the bank suffered a financial loss in that the running costs of
        the camera were incurred without any benefit and also the bank was exposed to the unneces-   E
        sary risk of vandalism or housebreaking being committed at its premises. The pannel
        appealed.
            Held (1) that what was required for a charge of malicious mischief was that there should
        be a wilful intent to cause injury to the owner or possessor of the property, which injury
        might be either in the form of physical damage or in the form of patrimonial loss; (2) that
        the running costs of the camera would have been incurred in any event even if it had been   F
        pointing in the right direction, so that what had been lost to the bank was such benefit as
        they might have obtained from the fact that the camera was pointing in the correct direction
        and possibly deterring vandals or thieves; and (3) that to describe such loss of benefit as
        patrimonial loss extended the latter concept too far and was altogether too speculative; and
        appeal *allowed.*

[7]   ROBERT JOHN BETT was charged in the sheriffdom of Tayside Central and Fife at Dunfermline
        at the instance of Robert T Hamilton, procurator fiscal there, with a contravention of the Criminal
        Law (Consolidation) (Scotland) Act 1995, sec 52(1) and a charge of malicious mischief. The   G
        pannel tabled a plea to the relevancy in respect of the charge of malicious mischief. After hearing
        parties, the sheriff made certain deletions to the charge and held that the charge set forth a
        relevant charge of malicious mischief. The terms of the charge are as set forth in the opinion of
        the court.
            The pannel appealed to the High Court of Justiciary.

[8]   *Cases referred to:*
        Advocate (HM) v Wilson 1983 SCCR 420
        Monro (George), July 17, 1831 (unreported)   H

        Textbook referred to:
        Alison, *Criminal Law*, ii, 451

[9]   The cause called before the High Court of Justiciary, comprising Lord Sutherland, Lord John-
        ston and Lord Dawson for a hearing on 23 July 1997. *Eo die* the opinion of the court was   I
        delivered by Lord Sutherland.

[10]

A   OPINION OF THE COURT — The appellant was charged on summary complaint with a contravention of the Criminal Law (Consolidation) (Scotland) Act 1995, sec 52(1), the relevancy of which is not challenged, and a further charge purporting to set out an offence of malicious mischief. The appellant tabled a plea to the relevancy of the second charge. The sheriff made certain deletions to the charge (which the Crown did not argue before this court should be restored) and thereafter held that the remainder constituted a relevant offence of malicious mischief. The terms

B of the charge, as they now remain, are as follows: "The Royal Bank of Scotland, having at their own expense, placed and operated a surveillance camera so as to show and record activity at the front of the building occupied by them in East Port, Dunfermline, for the purpose of enhancing the security of said building by deterring persons from acts of housebreaking, theft and vandalism at said building and making it possible to identify those who carry out such acts, you did on 7 December 1996 in said East Port, Dunfermline, maliciously move said camera with a pole or similar instrument so as to point said camera in such a direction that it did not show or

C record activity in the area which it had been set to cover whereby the running costs associated with said camera were wasted and said building was exposed to increased risk of housebreaking, theft and vandalism." The view taken by the sheriff was that the acts of the appellant resulted in detriment to the benefit which the bank had attempted to secure by having a surveillance camera. He considered that the bank suffered a financial loss in that the running costs of the camera were incurred without any benefit and also the bank was exposed to the unnecessary risk of vandalism or housebreaking being committed at its premises.

D   Counsel for the appellant before this court submitted that actual injury or harm, damage or patrimonial loss had to occur before mischief could be established. Neither wasted running costs nor the increased risk of housebreaking or theft or vandalism could constitute mischief. In *HM Advocate v Wilson* it was held that physical injury or damage was not necessary provided that there was an element of patrimonial loss. The accused in that case had activated an emergency stop button wilfully, recklessly and maliciously and brought a power station generator to a halt, causing a loss of production of electricity which had to be replaced at a cost of £147,000. Lord

E Justice-Clerk Wheatley, having set out Hume's definition of malicious mischief, said that the basic constituents involved in the crime of malicious mischief were that it had to be a deliberate and malicious act to damage another's property or to interfere with it to the detriment of the owner or lawful possessor. He went on to say: "It is clear from the words used in the libel that the Crown seek to establish that the act of the respondent founded upon was deliberate and malicious. The Crown further seek to prove that this act resulted in a generating turbine being brought to a halt for an extended period of time with a consequential loss of generated electricity.

F In terms of Hume's second ground *supra* this would be an interference with the employer's property and the wording of the libel is such as to be habile to carry the inference that the initial positive wilful, reckless and malicious act was intended to harm the employer by causing patrimonial injury ... To interfere deliberately with the plant so as to sterilise its functioning with resultant financial loss such as is libelled here is in my view a clear case of interference with another's property which falls within Hume's classification of malicious mischief, and consists with the words in the phrase." Counsel therefore accepted that it is not necessary to

G prove physical damage but argued that there must at least be some material patrimonial loss before the crime of malicious mischief can be established. In the present case, as far as the running costs of the camera were concerned, these costs would have been expended anyway and there was no additional cost. What was lost, if anything, was the benefit to be obtained from the use of the camera. The same argument applied to the other part of the complaint which narrated that the bank lost the benefit of the security of the surveillance camera. That was not something which constituted patrimonial loss. It is clear from what the Lord Justice-Clerk said in *Wilson*

H that when he used the word detriment he was referring to patrimonial loss. The only other case involving detriment to an owner which was held to constitute malicious mischief, apart from *Wilson*, was an unreported case referred to in Alison, *Criminal Law*, ii, 451 (*George Monro*, July 17, 1831) where an accused was convicted of opening a barrel, thus allowing the contents to escape, causing loss to the owner of the contents. Accordingly it was submitted that loss of benefit was not the same as patrimonial loss and was insufficient to warrant the charge of

I malicious mischief.

JC   BETT v HAMILTON   3

> In reply the Advocate-depute founded on the words of Lord Justice-Clerk Wheatley that to   A
> interfere with the property of another to the detriment of the owner would be sufficient. The
> word "detriment" in his submission simply implied disadvantage. The bank in the present case
> had installed this camera for a particular purpose and incurred costs in the running of that security   B
> device. If the purpose was destroyed or interfered with then the running costs were wasted and
> thus became a patrimonial loss. He submitted that where outlay is incurred to maintain a benefit,
> if the benefit is destroyed then the continuing costs constitute patrimonial loss. Furthermore loss   C
> of protection from vandalism or theft is a serious matter. The camera was installed to protect
> the bank against the risk of serious crime and this risk could be quantified in financial terms.
> For these reasons he submitted that there was an ascertainable patrimonial loss in this case and   D
> that accordingly the charge was relevant.
>   In our opinion the Crown have not averred sufficient in this case to constitute a relevant
> charge of malicious mischief. What is required in such a charge is that there should be a wilful   E
> intent to cause injury to the owner or possessor of the property. This injury may be either in the
> form of physical damage or in the form of patrimonial loss. We do not consider that the matters
> referred to by the Advocate-depute properly constitute patrimonial loss. The running costs of
> the camera would have been incurred in any event, even if it had been pointing in the right   F
> direction, and accordingly what has been lost to the bank is such benefit as they might have
> obtained from the fact that the camera was pointing in the correct direction and possibly deterring
> vandals or thieves. The same can be said of the loss of security which they might have sustained
> through the absence of this camera performing its proper function. In our opinion to describe   G
> such loss of benefit as patrimonial loss extends the latter concept too far and is altogether too
> speculative. The bank on these averments suffered no financial loss whatsoever and therefore
> there is no patrimonial loss. We shall therefore allow the appeal and sustain the appellant's plea   H
> to the relevancy of the second charge on the complaint.

[11]   THE COURT allowed the appeal.

[12]   *More & Co — The Crown Agent*   I

[6] This is the headnote or rubric. It is a summary of the case and is not part of the law report proper. The temptation to read only the headnote of a case should be resisted. It should not be relied upon as accurate. It is written by the editor of the law reports and not the judge. Another reason not to rely solely on the headnote is that the significance and interpretation of a case can change over a period of time. The headnote remains frozen at one point in time and is not altered.

   The headnote will give a summary of:

   (a) Material facts
   (b) Legal issues involved
   (c) Decision of the court

[7] This section outlines the judicial history of the case.

[8] The entries in italics are the authorities referred to in the case. Here, there is a list of cases and a book. You will see that the cases include an unreported case. The fact that a case is not reported has no effect on its status as a precedent. Alison is one of the Institutional Writers (see chapter 6, para. 6.2). In the past only books by authors who were dead would be referred to in court. This convention has been relaxed in recent years and modern authorities do now appear.

[9] This section gives details of the court, the judges and the date of the hearing. In Scotland presenting the judgment of the court is referred to as delivering the opinion of the court.

[10] The opinion of the court is the most important part of the case. In this case there is only one opinion/judgment. Cases can have just one judgment or can have multiple judgments. This makes it more difficult to understand the reasoning as they may reach the same decision but adopt

different reasoning. A case can have no *ratio decidendi* as a result. In recent years the courts have tended to provide one judgment, with the other judges stating that they have read it and agree with it. However, if they wish, judges can still present their own reasoning. If they dissent with the majority view, their full judgment will appear.

There is no one style that judges use to write a judgment. Judgments tend to be individualistic. They are sometimes clear and easy to understand but sometimes they are the complete opposite. Gradually judgments are becoming more reader-friendly with headings being used for ease of reference.

The capital letters which appear down the side of the page allow a precise reference to be given to part of the opinion, *e.g.* Lord Sutherland starts to discuss the case presented for the appellant at 1998 J.C. 2 D.

[11] The outcome of the case.

[12] The agents acting in the case. Here More & Co. is the firm of solicitors representing the pannel. The Crown Agent is the term used for those acting on behalf of the Crown.

2.4.2   Analysis of cases

In the real world, of course, the outcome is the most important part of a case, but to those studying law it is almost irrelevant. The major point of interest is the reasoning which the court adopted in order to reach its conclusion. This is referred to as the *ratio decidendi*.

There is no agreed definition of the *ratio decidendi* and little clear guidance exists on how to identify it. Lawyers will often disagree about the content of a particular *ratio decidendi*. The situation is further complicated by the fact that some cases may have no *ratio decidendi* at all, while others may have more than one. The *ratio decidendi* of a case does not always remain the same. Later cases can re-interpret it and it is possible for a rule which emerged from the original case to be expanded or contracted over a period of time.

Traditional texts tend to be unhelpful with comments such as ''recognising the *ratio* will come with practice''. Reading such statements can be frustrating but there is no easy way of learning how to identify the *ratio decidendi*. It requires skills of analysis and interpretation. One way of developing these skills is to read as many cases as possible. You will gradually become familiar with the general format of judgments. If you read cases from law reports which contain commentaries you can check whether your understanding of the case is the same as that of the commentator. More detailed discussion of the *ratio decidendi* can be found in W. Twining and D. Miers, *How to Do Things with Rules* (3rd ed., 1991), chap. 8, G. Williams, *Learning the Law* (11th ed., 1982), chap. 6 and J. A. Holland and J. S. Webb, *Learning Legal Rules* (4th ed., 1999), chap. 6.

2.4.2.1   *Tips for reading cases*

- You do not need to pay the same amount of attention to all the cases. Pay more attention to leading House of Lords judgments.

- Concentrate on cases which are the first to define a principle or interpret a statute. Cases which are illustrative of a rule are not as important as those which expounded the rule in the first place.

- Do not waste time on cases that have subsequently been overruled unless you are specifically interested in an historical perspective of an area of law.

- Do not spend time reading dissenting judgments unless you are particularly interested in the conflicting arguments.

- Concentrate on the leading judgment. It tends to be the most important.

2.4.3   **Preparation Of A Student Case Note**

A student case note is essentially a summary of all the important information in a case. It should only be about one or two pages of A4. The length will depend on the importance of the case. You should not copy out great chunks of the case. The information should allow you to:

- find the case again

- understand the case

- appreciate why the case is important

- use the case effectively in an essay or an exam

A case note should contain the following:

1. Details about the case

    (a) names of the parties

    (b) citation (and any alternative citations, if known). This is so that you can find the report if one law report is missing from the library or if you have to use a library with fewer facilities.

    (c) court which heard the case (the names of the judges may be relevant). The court is important because of the doctrine of judicial precedent. If you know which court heard the case, you have an idea of how much weight is likely to be attached to the decision.

    (d) the result. This means whether the appeal was allowed or whether the defender was liable, etc. You should note whether the decision was unanimous or whether a judge or judges dissented.

2. Précis of the *material* facts. Material facts means facts that are legally relevant to the judge's decision. This is to help you appreciate the application of the law in the specific circumstances of the case and to help you understand the operation of the law in practice. It will also help you identify the case.

3. Issue(s) of law raised in the case.

4. Decision made by the court. The decision reached on the legal issues raised.

5. Reasons for the decision made by the court. This is the most important part of the case report and should take up the most space.

6. Additional comments

    (a) A quotation. Judges sometimes say things in a clear succinct way. You may want to put such a quotation in an essay or it may help to clarify something for you. Perhaps a case contains some famous dicta and you may want to take this down word for word. Any quotation should be short.

    (b) Your own opinion of the case. Perhaps you doubt the reasoning. Your lecturer or an article has criticised the case.

    (c) You would want to note if the court has done something significant, such as overrule another case or interpret a piece of legislation for the first time.

You could make up a file of individual case notes or alternatively you could put your notes on small index cards. Whichever method you use, make sure that you store them alphabetically. This should enable you to find the relevant case note easily. Adopting a card index system has the added benefit of forcing you to make your notes concise as they have to fit onto the card. This could also be done in electronic form.

Example of a student case note

Bett v Hamilton, 1998 J.C. 1
High Court of Justiciary sitting as an appellate court
Appeal was allowed

A bank installed a surveillance camera situated to record movement at the front of its premises. Bett was accused of moving the camera so that it no longer covered the area at the front of the bank. The bank continued to pay the running costs of operating the camera while it was out of position and thus not protecting their premises.

What constitutes the offence of malicious mischief? Hume had defined it as requiring a deliberate and malicious act to damage another's property or to interfere with it to the detriment of the owner or lawful possessor. Particular issue was whether "detriment" required patrimonial loss or whether some disadvantage would be sufficient.

Decision — Patrimonial loss was required

Reasons for the decision

The offence was defined as requiring "a wilful intent to cause injury to the owner or possessor of the property. This injury may be either in the form of physical damage or in the form of patrimonial loss". The running costs would have been incurred even if the camera had been pointing in the correct direction. There had been no loss merely a loss of benefit. Loss of benefit did not constitute patrimonial loss.

Chapter 3

SEARCH STRATEGIES FOR FINDING CASES

3.1 AIDS TO TRACING CASES

There are five different types of aids to tracing cases:

- The series of law reports themselves and their various indexes
- Full text electronic databases
- Digests of cases contained in collections which are indexed in various ways
- Citators
- Commentaries on case law and indexes of such commentaries

These will now be discussed in turn.

3.1.1 The series of law reports themselves and the various indexes which they contain

3.1.1.1

Source	**The series of law reports themselves and the various indexes which they contain**
Case coverage	Varies according to the series of law reports. For details of the English series see chapter 7. The important Law Reports Index is dealt with below.
Scottish material	For details of the Scottish law reports, see chapter 2. A very useful new tool is the CD-ROM version of the Scots Law Times reports from 1893 to 1997. This allows searching by case name, citation and keywords.
Comments	Not all series contain the same indexes, *e.g.* some series have separate tables of words and phrases judicially considered. Other series include the information in a subject index under "W" for word. The subject categories adopted are also variable.
Updates	Varies according to the series of law reports.
Hints on use	Make sure you look for cumulative versions of the indexes. This will save you having to check the annual volumes, The consolidated indexes are usually published separately but should be located next to the appropriate series of law reports in the library.

3.1.1.2

Source	**The Law Reports Index**
Case coverage	This index provides a continuous indexing system to the principal English law reports from 1951 to date. It contains: All cases reported in The Law Reports, The Weekly Law Reports, The Industrial Case Reports.

	References to cases reported in:
	All England Law Reports, Criminal Appeal Reports, Lloyd's Law Reports, Local Government Reports, Road Traffic Reports, Tax Cases and Tax Case Leaflets.
Scottish material	Only important Scottish cases are covered.
Updates	The Index is contained in four volumes referred to as the "Red Indexes": 1951–60, 1961–70, 1971–80, 1981–90. There is an additional volume from 1991–98. This is updated by Pink Indexes which are published several times a year. More recent updates of the Index can be found at the beginning of each issue of the Weekly Law Reports.
Hints on use	The index contains nine different tables.
	Check table of cases reported and table of cases judicially considered. To ensure that you are up to date, check through: (1) Red Index; (2) Pink Index; (3) Weekly Law Reports. For more details see chap. 7, para. 7.3.1.2.

3.1.2   Full-text electronic data bases

3.1.2.1

Source	**Lexis**
	This is a full text on-line legal database.
Case coverage	The Scottish cases available in full-text are:
	Reported cases:
	Session Cases: November 1944 onwards
	Scots Law Times: May 1945 onwards
	Scottish Criminal Case Reports: January 1981 onwards
	Scottish Civil Law Reports: February 1986 onwards
	Unreported Cases:
	Scottish House of Lords decisions: July 1986 onwards
	All Inner House decisions: January 1982 onwards
	All Outer House decisions: January 1985 onwards
	Lexis contains the full text of nearly all reported English decisions since 1945 and many unreported cases since 1980.
Scottish material	Headnotes (case summaries) are not included for Scottish cases.
Comments	Use of this database is not cheap and charges apply per minute of use.
	Lexis is a LITERAL search system. It contains no law — only words. All Lexis can do is to compare the words which are given to it and offer you any which correspond.
	It is essential to plan a search strategy in advance.
Updates	The system is updated regularly but there tends to be a time delay of at least several weeks.
Hints on use	Scottish material — Access is via the SCOT library.
	U.K. material — Access is via the ENGGEN library.
	See chapter 13, para. 13.4.3 for more detail.

3.1.2.2

Source	**The internet**
Case coverage	From 1996, all House of Lords cases. Some Court of Appeal and High Court cases are also available.
Scottish material	From September 1998, opinions from the Court of Session and High Court of Justiciary are available. Web address: http://www.scotcourts.gov.uk
Comments	House of Lords cases — the cases are listed in alphabetical order and not chronological order.
	Scottish case website — ability to search by keyword or by structured search. This facility allows you to search by: type of opinion, date, judge, pursuer, defender, type of action.
Updates	House of Lords decisions appear within two hours of the judgment being issued. Scottish cases are updated on 2 p.m. on the day the opinion is issued.
Hints on use	See chapters 11–14.

3.1.3   Digests of cases contained in collections which are indexed in various ways

3.1.3.1

Source	**Current Law Year Books and Monthly Digests**
Case coverage	Digests of all reported cases since 1947 and references to cases (no matter when

	they were reported) which have been considered, applied, overruled, etc., by the courts since 1947.
Scottish material	Full coverage of Scottish material in Current Law since 1991. Prior to that only in the Scottish Current Law Series. The Year Books have a separate section for Scottish material. The index at the end of each Year Book does not have a separate Scottish section. Scottish material is indexed under the appropriate subject heading. You are alerted to the fact that it is a Scottish reference if the reference given ends with a capital "S".
Comments	The headings only appear if there is material included under that heading so the headings can vary from Year Book to Year Book. The choice of subject category is sometimes not ideal and you may have to check under several different terms, *e.g.* if you want to check if there have been any cases concerning water pollution, you might have to check under environment, pollution and water.
Updates	Monthly
Hints on use	Check the relevant subject headings in the Year Books and the latest Monthly Digest. These will lead you to a digest of the case and to citations in the law reports. See chapter 10, paras 10.2 and 10.3 for more details.

3.1.3.2

Source	**Current Legal Information**
Case coverage	Digests of all reported cases since 1986.
Scottish material	Full coverage of Scottish material
Comments	It allows you to cross-reference to digests of other cited cases, details of the legislation considered and any journal articles or case notes that have been listed in Legal Journals Index.
Updates	Monthly for CD-ROM version, daily for on-line.
Hints on use	See chapter 13, para. 13.4.5 for more details.

3.1.3.3

Title	**The Faculty Digest**
Case coverage	1868–1922, Vols. 1–5. Vol. 6 — Indexes covering 1868–1922 Faculty Digest Supplements 1922–30, 1930–40, 1940–50, 1951–60, 1961–70, 1971–80, 1981–90. Information is organised in the Supplements as follows: ● Cases digested by subject matter ● Cases judicially referred to (including English cases referred to in the Scottish courts but not Scottish cases referred to in English courts). ● Statutes, Acts of Sederunt, Statutory Orders, etc., judicially commented on — arranged by year ● Words judicially defined ● Index of cases in the digest — alphabetical order (both parties)
Scottish material	Courts covered: House of Lords, Court of Session, High Court of Justiciary, Lands Tribunal, Land Court. From 1981–90 Supplement it also covers sheriff court cases, Scottish Criminal Case Reports and Scottish Civil Law Reports.
Comments	Useful for tracing older Scottish cases.
Updates	New Supplement published every ten years.
Hints on use	It allows searches to be made by subject, names of both parties, legislation, cases judicially referred to and words judicially defined.

3.1.3.4

Source	**Lawtel** This is an on-line legal database accessible via the World Wide Web or direct dial.
Case coverage	It contains summaries of reports from newspapers and a range of cases from the major English series of law reports. The coverage starts from January 1, 1980. From 1995 it also includes all handed down judgments from the English High Court, Courts of Appeal and the House of Lords. If a case is subsequently reported in the law reports Lawtel inserts the citation into its material.
Scottish material	*N.B.* the coverage of Scottish material is patchy. It only covers Scottish cases which are followed in England.

	Comments	For U.K. material it is the most up to date source for very recent cases in newspapers, the principal law reports and unreported cases.
		Subscription service.
	Updates	It is updated daily.
	Hints on use	Choose the case law option from the initial menu. This will take you into a search facility where you type in key words to locate the material which you require. More detailed information is contained in chapter 13.

3.1.3.5	Source	**The Daily Law Reports Index**
	Case coverage	Started in 1988 and covers law reports contained in daily newspapers.
	Scottish material	It included law reports from *The Scotsman* before publication ceased.
	Updates	Fortnightly.
	Hints on use	Searches can be made by names of both parties, subject and by legislation.

3.1.3.6	Source	**The Digest (formerly the English & Empire Digest)**
	Case coverage	It covers case law of England and Wales and has a selection of cases from Scotland, Ireland, Canada, Australia, New Zealand and other Commonwealth countries. 90 volumes.
	Scottish material	Predominantly English, but contains selected Scottish cases in footnotes.
	Comments	The Digest tends to be the most widely available source of information about Scottish cases in England. The current edition is the green band re-issue edition which dates from 1971.
	Updates	Annual Cumulative Supplement and a Quarterly Survey of recent developments.
	Hints on use	More details can be found in chapter 7, para. 7.3.4.

3.1.3.7	Source	**Shaw's Digest**
	Case coverage	House of Lords decisions 1726–1868 and Scottish superior courts 1800–1868.
	Comments	The Faculty Digest was a continuation of Shaw's Digest.
	Hints on use	This digest does not always appear in the same format and different editions are bound differently. Cases are arranged by subject. There are indexes of pursuers' and defenders' names at the end of a volume or, if produced in several volumes, in the final volume.

3.1.3.8	Source	**Scots Digest**
	Case coverage	House of Lords cases 1707–1947 and cases from Scottish superior courts 1800–1947.
	Comments	This was superseded by Scottish Current Law.
	Hints on use	This digest also appears in different formats. Cases are arranged by subject. The volumes contain a table of cases and table of cases judicially considered.

There is a Digest of Sheriff Court Cases reported in the Scots Law Times between 1893–1943. Digests of old Scottish cases have been covered in chapter 2, para. 2.3.7.

3.1.4   Citators

	Source	**Current Law Case Citators**
		The citators are published in several parts and contain an alphabetical listing of case names.
	Case coverage	All reported cases since 1947 and references to cases (no matter when they were reported) which have been considered, applied, overruled, etc., by the courts since 1947.
		If the case has been reported more than once, each alternative citation is given.
	Scottish material	Full coverage of Scottish material in Current Law since 1991. Prior to that only in the Scottish Current Law Series.
		Scottish cases are listed separately and follow the listing of English cases.
	Comments	This is the best starting point *unless* the case is very recent (within the last month) or old (pre-1947 and not commented on by the courts since 1947).

A version of the Case Citator is available in Current Legal Information. It covers the period from 1977 to date. It excludes Scottish cases.

Updates   Monthly — published in the Monthly Digests which appear in cumulative form each month.

Hints on use   Remember to check the Scottish section, it follows the English cases.
                                    See chapter 10 for more details.

3.1.5   Commentaries on case law and indexes of such commentaries

3.1.5.1   **Source**   **Legal Journals Index**
          Case coverage   Started in 1986.
                                    References to case notes and articles which discuss cases.
                                    This index covers all journals published in the U.K. which are devoted to law or frequently contain articles on legal topics.
          Scottish material   Scottish journals currently covered: Edinburgh Law Review, Journal of the Law Society of Scotland, Juridical Review, SCOLAG, Scots Law Times, Scottish Law Gazette, Scottish Licensing Law & Practice, Scottish Law & Practice Quarterly, Scottish Planning & Environmental Law
          Comments   This is also available as part of Current Legal Information on CR-ROM and on-line.
          Updates   Paper version and CD-ROM versions monthly; on-line daily.
          Hints on use   Paper version: access is via the case index. Cases are cited by either party or by subject headings. See chapter 6, para. 6.8.1.1.
                                    Current Legal Information version allows you to search by field (case name is one of the fields) and by free text.

3.1.5.2   **Source**   **Tables of cases in textbooks**
          Case coverage   Depends on the text. Usually the citation and page reference to where it is discussed in the text.
          Scottish material   Make sure that you use a Scottish text.
          Comments   Make sure that you use the most current text that you can find.
          Updates   Depends on the text.
          Hints on use   Tables of cases in textbooks are usually found at the beginning of the book after the contents page. The cases are listed in alphabetical order of the first named party.

3.1.5.3   **Source**   **The Laws of Scotland: Stair Memorial Encyclopaedia**
          Case coverage   This encyclopaedia gives a commentary on Scots law. It is arranged alphabetically in broad areas of the law and contains articles on each area. The encyclopaedia consists of 25 volumes which began to appear from 1986 onwards. The first re-issue has recently been published.
          Scottish material   A Scottish encyclopaedia.
          Updates   Annual Cumulative Supplements and Service binder is updated three times a year.
          Hints on use   You can search by subject or by the first party's name.
                                    To search by subject: ⇒ Consolidated Index ⇒ Relevant volume which contains a table of cases ⇒ Annual Cumulative Supplement ⇒ Service Binder
                                    To search by case name: ⇒ Consolidated Table of Cases ⇒ Table of Cases in latest Annual Cumulative Supplement ⇒ Service Binder
                                    Full details in chapter 6, para. 6.3.1.1.

3.2   SEARCH STRATEGIES FOR FINDING CASES

This section deals with the different ways of finding cases. This will allow you to find cases from different starting points; for instance you may want to explore a new area of law or your knowledge of a case may be incomplete.

There are usually many ways of finding legal information. This section contains lists of various alternative sources along with comments as to their strengths and weaknesses. The most comprehensive sources are listed first, followed by the more limited sources. It is not a simple matter of listing the best and worst sources. A lot may depend on the facilities that you have available to you. You may be fortunate enough to have access to a well-resourced law library. However, you may be faced with finding information with much more limited facilities available to you. Resources are also important. The cost of some of the electronic sources is not inconsiderable and access may be restricted on cost grounds.

The following search strategies are considered:

- Finding cases by name only. This should allow you to find cases when you have lost the citation or where you have an incorrect citation. See para. 3.2.1.

- Finding cases by subject. This should allow you to search where you may be interested in a specific subject area and have little or no knowledge of the case law. See para. 3.2.2.

- Finding cases on words or phrases. This allows you to ascertain if a certain word or phrase has been interpreted by the courts. See para. 3.2.3.

- Finding cases interpreting legislation. This covers the situation where you know of a specific legislative provision and you want to find out if any cases have considered it. See para. 3.2.4.

- Current status of a case. You may want to know whether a case is still binding law, whether it has been commented on or overruled. See para. 3.2.5.

- Finding out about a very recent case. It is very important to be aware of current developments in the law. New cases are reported daily and the sources for very recent cases tend to be different from those for older cases. See para. 3.2.6.

- Finding cases from other courts/tribunals, *e.g.* Lyon Court, Lands Tribunal, EAT, social security, tax, customs. See para. 3.2.7.

- Putting cases into context — recent cases and older cases. See para. 3.2.8.

At the end of each section there is a diagram summarising the alternative sources.

3.2.1   Finding Cases By Name Only — Citation Unknown

3.2.1.1   *Current Law Case Citator*

This is the best starting point *unless* the case is very recent (within the last month) or old (pre-1947 and not commented on by the courts since 1947). Current Law includes all reported cases since 1947 and references to cases (no matter when they were reported) which have been considered, applied, overruled, etc., by the courts since 1947. The latter appear in the citator along with their own citation and the Current Law reference for the case which has commented upon it.

The citators are arranged alphabetically by the name of the first party. The citator will provide you with the citation for the case. This enables you to locate it in the relevant series of law reports.

See worked example in para. 3.2.1.15 below and for more details on how to use the Case Citators, see chapter 10.

3.2.1.2   *The Laws of Scotland: Stair Memorial Encyclopaedia*

To search by case name, check the following:

- Consolidated Table of Cases
- Table of Cases in latest Annual Cumulative Supplement
- Service Binder

More details are contained in chapter 6, para. 6.3.1.1.

3.2.1.3   *Lexis*

On-line by subscription. See para. 3.1.2.1 above for details of case coverage and chapter 13 for general information.

3.2.1.4   *Tables of cases in relevant textbooks*

Tables of cases in textbooks are usually found at the beginning of the book after the contents page. The cases are listed in alphabetical order of the first named party.
    This depends on you knowing the area of law involved.
    Make sure that you find the most current edition of the textbook.

3.2.1.5   *Indexes in the law reports*

The most useful law reports index now available in Scotland is the Scots Law Times CD-ROM. This allows you to search by case name or keywords. It covers cases from 1893–1997.
    In order to use the paper volumes of the various series of law reports you need to know both the likely series of law reports and the approximate date.
    Most series of law reports include indexes of cases for a specific volume and may have cumulative updates covering many years. The indexes are usually accessible from either party's name. See chapter 2 for details of the Scottish series and chapter 7 for the English series.

3.2.1.6   *The Law Reports Index*

This index provides a continuous indexing system to the principal English law reports from 1951 to date. Remember that only selected Scottish cases are covered. See para. 3.1.1.2 above.

3.2.1.7   *Lawtel*

On-line by subscription. It is updated every 24 hours and contains summaries (not full text) of reports from newspapers and a range of cases from the major series of law reports. It also covers unreported cases from the Court of Appeal and the House of Lords.
    It is the most up-to-date source for very recent cases reported in newspapers and the principal law reports. The coverage starts from January 1, 1980.
    N.B. the coverage of Scottish material is patchy. It only covers Scottish cases which are followed in England. See chapter 13.

3.2.1.8   *Legal Journals Index*

This source started in 1986 and contains a case index which goes back to 1986. This allows cases to be traced by reference to either party. It contains references to case notes and articles which have discussed cases.

3.2.1.9   *Daily Law Reports Index*

Published from 1988. The service covers *The Times, Financial Times, Independent, Guardian* and *Lloyds List*. Check parties' name index.

Indexes helpful for locating older cases

3.2.1.10   *The Index to Morison's Dictionary*

This covers cases from 1540–1820. Se chapter 2, para. 2.3.7.

3.2.1.11   *Scots Digest*

House of Lords cases from 1707–1947 and cases from Scottish superior courts from 1800–1947. See para. 3.1.3.8.

3.2.1.12   *The Faculty Digest*

This covers cases from 1868–1990. See para 3.1.3.3 and worked example in para. 3.2.1.19 below.

3.2.1.13   *The Digest*

This is predominantly an English reference work. Scottish cases are referred to after English counterparts.

Check the consolidated table of cases to find the correct volume number. The case table in the appropriate volume refers to the paragraph number. See chapter 7, para. 7.3.4.

3.2.1.14   **How to find a citation for a case where you only know the parties' names:** See diagram A on facing page

3.2.1.15   **Using Current Law to find a citation for a case by name only:**
⇒ Step 1: Check through the Case Citators in chronological order. Remember that if it is a Scottish case you should check in the Scottish section. If you are not sure if it is Scottish, you should check *both* the English and Scottish sections of the citators. Cases are listed in alphabetical order of the first named party. If the case appears its full citation(s) will be next to it.
⇒ Step 2: You should then check the Table of Cases in the most recent Monthly Digest.

> Example

Find the citation for *Galt v Goodsir*. You know that the case is Scottish but nothing else.
⇒ Step 1: Check the Case Citator volume 1948–1976. Make sure that you check the Scottish section. There is no entry.
⇒ Step 2: Check the Case Citator volume 1977–1997. Again make sure that you check the Scottish section. Here there is an entry for the case and two citations are given: 1982 S.L.T. 94; 1981 S.C.C.R. 225.

3.2.1.16   **How to find a case if you remember the name AND the year but *not* the citation:**
Check the appropriate Year Book and look in the Table of Cases at the beginning of the Year Book. All cases included in the Year Book are listed alphabetically.

3.2.1.17   **How to find a case if you remember the year and the subject matter only:**
Check the appropriate Year Book and look under the subject heading.

3.2.1.18   **How to find details of a case:**
Full text:
Locate the case by checking in the Case Citators (see above). Following the name of the case you will find all the citations for the case. For the full text of the case go to the appropriate law report.
A summary of the case:
Locate the case by checking in the Case Citators. Opposite the case the first entry will be for a paragraph number where the case is digested in a Current Law Year Book. The reference is made up of the year/paragraph number. The paragraph number of the digest is always shown in bold. Turn to the appropriate Year Book and you will find that the entry for the paragraph number will contain a digest of the case.

A. Finding Cases by Name only

Best sources	Current Law Case Citator + latest Monthly Digest or	Stair Memorial Encyclopaedia Consolidated Table of Cases, Annual Cumulative Supplement, Service Binders or	Lexis - SCOT library	
if unavailable	Table of Cases in relevant texts *find most recent edition* or	Indexes in law reports *helpful if you know approximate date* or	Legal Journals Index *only cases which have been commented on* or	The Law Reports Index *only selected Scottish cases*
if not found in Current Law Case Citator the case could either be:				
very old	Index to Morison's Dictionary 1540-1820 or	The Scots Digest 1800-1947 or	Indexes in law reports *SLT CD-ROM* or	The Faculty Digest 1868-1900 or · The Digest *selected Scottish cases*
very recent	Internet Scottish from 1998; House of Lords from 1996 or	Newspapers *accessed by* The Daily Law Reports Index or	A weekly-series report, *e.g.* G.W.D. or S.L.T. or	Lawtel *limited Scottish coverage*

Example

In the previous example we established that *Galt v Goodsir* appeared in the Case Citator volume 1977–1997. How can you find out details about it in the Current Law system?

⇒ Step 1: Locate the case in the relevant Case Citator. Here we have already established that it is Case Citator volume 1977–1997. Opposite the entry for the case is a reference that says "Digested 82/**4292**".
⇒ Step 2: Turn to the Year Book for 1982 and specifically to paragraph number 4292. The entry contains the following information:

> "Identification of driver
> [Road Traffic Act 1972 (c. 20) ss. 6(1) and 168(2)]
> *Held*, that an admission by the owner of a car made under s. 168(2) of the Road Traffic Act 1972 that he had been the driver two days before was admissible evidence against him on a charge under s. 6(1), although the result of the laboratory test was not known to the police when the request under s. 168(2) was made: *Galt v. Goodsir* 1982 S.L.T. 94."

3.2.1.19 **If the case does not appear in Current Law, it could mean that it is either very old or very recent.**

Example

Find the case *Branford's Trustees v. Powell*.

This case does not appear in Current Law.
   Check the Faculty Digest.
   Volume 6 is an indices volume covering 1868–1922. Check in the Cases in Digest Table. There is no entry for this case.
   The Supplement volumes need to be checked on a volume by volume basis.
   Volume 1922–1930 does contain a reference to this case and refers you to page 29. The entry there gives a summary of the case and alternative citations: 1924, S.C. 439; 61 S.L.R. 306 and 1924, S.L.T. 334.

Reference to this case could also be found by checking the Consolidated Table of Cases in the *Stair Memorial Encyclopaedia*. See chapter 6, para. 6.3.1.1.

3.2.2 **Finding Cases By Subject**

3.2.2.1 *General reference works*

Major reference works

The Laws of Scotland: Stair Memorial Encyclopaedia
You can search by subject by checking:

- Consolidated Index
- Relevant volume which contains a table of cases
- Update by checking Annual Cumulative Supplement
- Update by checking Service Binder

See example in para. 3.2.2.11 below and chapter 6, para. 6.3.1.1 for more details.

Halsbury's Laws of England

See chapter 7 para. 7.4.

General reference texts

These tend to have been updated over the years and run to several editions. Make sure that you use the most up-to-date edition.

Gloag & Henderson, *An Introduction to the Laws of Scotland* (10th edn., W. Green, Edinburgh 1995.)

D.M. Walker, *Principles of Scottish Private Law* (4th edn., Clarendon, Oxford 1989).

General reference works tend not to provide much detail about the case but should provide you with its citation. If you want a fuller discussion of the case go to a dedicated textbook.

3.2.2.2 *Dedicated textbook*

This will probably be referred to by your lecturer or in a general reference work. If not, check the keyword/subject index in the library catalogue.

3.2.2.3 *Current Legal Information*

Check the Current Law Cases section. This covers cases from 1986. You can search by field (this includes subject or keywords) or free text. This will lead to a digest of the case and citations in the law reports. See chapter 13.

3.2.2.4 *Current Law*

Check the relevant subject headings in the Year Books and the latest Monthly Digest. These will lead you to a digest of the case and to citations in the law reports.

The Year Books have a separate section for Scottish material. The index at the end of each Year Book does not have a separate Scottish section. Scottish material is indexed under the appropriate subject heading. You are alerted to the fact that it is a Scottish reference if the reference given ends with a capital "S".

Check the appropriate subject heading in the index at the back of the Year Book. The headings only appear if there is material included under that heading so the headings can vary from Year Book to Year Book. The subject categorisation can sometimes leave a lot to be desired. Be prepared to search under related terms. For more details see chapter 10, paras 10.2 and 10.3.

3.2.2.5 *Lexis*

On-line by subscription.

See para. 3.1.2.1 above for coverage of cases and chapter 13, para. 13.4.3 for general information.

3.2.2.6 *Subject indexes in various series of law reports*

The CD-ROM version of the Scots Law Times reports 1893–1997 allows you to search by keyword.

Session Cases, paper version of the Scots Law Times, Scottish Criminal Case Reports, Scottish Civil Law Reports and Green's Weekly Digest all have subject indexes. The ease of use will depend on whether you know the approximate dates and/or the frequency of consolidation volumes of the subject indexes. If the date is unknown and there are no consolidated indexes, you would be left searching annually volume by volume. For details of the Scottish series see chapter 2. The English series of law reports are covered in chapter 7.

3.2.2.7 *Lawtel*

On-line by subscription. This is the most useful source for very recent cases in the newspapers but remember that only limited Scottish data is available. See chapter 13, para. 13.4.2.

3.2.2.8   *Daily Law Reports Index*

Useful for very recent cases. See para. 3.1.3.5.

3.2.2.9   *Legal Journals Index*

Search under subject heading. Remember this will only reference cases discussed in journals. See para 3.1.5.1.

3.2.2.10

B. Finding Cases by Subject only

Best starting points:

> Stair Memorial Encyclopaedia
> *regularly updated but may still need to update further*
>
> or
>
> dedicated textbook
> *use most up to date edition*
> *and then Current Law to bring you up to date*
>
> or
>
> reference work such as
> Gloag & Henderson or
> Walker
> *use most up to date edition*
> *and then Current Law to bring you up to date*

If unavailable:

⇒   Current Law Year Books and Monthly Digest
       But subject index categories can be problematic

⇒   Lexis
       Uses a literal word search

⇒   Current Legal Information
       Good search facilities but coverage limited

⇒   Subject indexes in law reports
       Means that you need to know which jurisdiction and approximate date.

⇒   Lawtel
       But remember patchy Scottish coverage

⇒   Daily Law reports Index
       Mainly English newspapers

⇒   Legal Journals Index
       But only includes cases discussed in articles

N.B. If do not find anything try changing your search term, e.g. pollution, environment, waste.

Example

Using the *Stair Memorial Encyclopaedia* to find a case by subject:

Find out if there any cases on the meaning of "causation" in the principal water pollution offence.

The heading to search under would be water pollution.
⇒ Step 1: Either check the Consolidated Index. Under "water pollution" is a sub-heading called "control" and beneath it "offences"; or
Check the spines of the bound volumes. Volume 25 includes the heading "Water and Water Rights".
⇒ Step 2: Check the Contents page of the relevant volume, look under "Water and Water Rights" and find within that heading a section on pollution — paragraphs 394–428, page 111.
Before checking any further, it is important to be aware of the date of the volume. On the page opposite the list of contents there is a statement that the law stated in the volume is in force as at a certain date. The date given for volume 25 is November 30, 1988. It is obvious that steps will have to be taken to update the information contained in the volume.

Turning to the relevant section you find that paragraph 401 discusses control over water pollution. It mentions the principal offence and in a footnote contains details of cases on causation. It mentions the key Scottish authority of *Lockhart v. NCB*, 1981, S.C.C.R. 9; 1981 S.L.T. 161 and the leading English House of Lords case of *Alphacell v. Woodward* [1972] A.C. 824; [1972] 2 All E.R. 475 (H.L.).

This is not the end of the search. This has only covered the law up to 1988.
⇒ Step 3: Now check the Annual Cumulative Supplement. It will also contain a statement as to the date the law stated in it is in force. Currently it is up to December 31, 1998. The Cumulative Supplement is arranged in the same way as the bound volumes. Turn to volume 25, paragraph 401. Here you will find that other cases are mentioned — *Wychavon D.C. v. NRA* [1993] 2 All E.R. 440 QB and *Empress Car Co. (Abertillery) Ltd v. NRA* [1998] 1 All E.R. 481, H.L.
⇒ Step 4: As a final step you should check the Service Binder. In this instance there is no new entry.

3.2.3   Finding Cases On Words Or Phrases

3.2.3.1   *Current Law*

Check the Words and Phrases Judicially Considered Tables in the appropriate Year Books and the latest Monthly Digest. The table lists words and phrases alphabetically. Beside a particular word or phrase will be the paragraph number for where the case is digested. If you want to look at the actual case report, the digest entry will include a full citation reference.

Example

Find a recent Scottish case which considered the word "introduced".

⇒ Step 1: Check the Words & Phrases Judicially Considered Table in the latest Monthly Digest and look for an entry followed by "(S)". This denotes that it is Scottish. The December 1998 Monthly Digest refers to:
"introduced, 5 C.L. 569 (S)".
⇒ Step 2: The 5 refers to the fifth volume of the year. Check the May volume of the Monthly Digest at paragraph number 569. That paragraph contains a digest entry for the case which considered the word "introduced" — *Christie Owen & Davis PLC v. King* 1998 S.C.L.R. 149.

3.2.3.2   *Subject indexes of law reports*

The subject indexes of many law reports include "Words and phrases" as a subject heading. Law reports which do this include: Session Cases, Scottish Civil Law reports, Scottish Criminal Case Reports, the Faculty Digest and The Law Reports Index. The SLT CD-ROM version of the reports from 1893–1997 allows searching by keyword or phrases.

The Consolidated Indexes to the All England Law Reports contain a "Words and phrases judicially considered" table.

3.2.3.3   *Books*

Publications specifically dealing with the interpretation of Words and phrases.
Scottish publications include:
W.J. Stewart, *Scottish Contemporary Judicial Dictionary* (W. Green, Edinburgh 1995)
and
A.W. Dalrymple and Gibb, *Dictionary of Words and Phrases* (W.Green, Edinburgh 1946).
United Kingdom publications include Stroud's *Judicial Dictionary* and *Words and Phrases Legally Defined*. See chapter 6, para. 6.4.1 for more details.

3.2.3.4   *Halsbury's Laws of England*

The Consolidated Index (volume 56) to *Halsbury's Laws of England* has a Words and Phrases Table. This includes words which are defined or explained in Halsbury's Laws. A worked example is contained in chapter 7, para. 7.4.7.

3.2.3.5

> ### C. Finding Words and Phrases interpreted by the Courts
>
> Most comprehensive source:
>
> > Current Law — words and phrases index (Year Books and Monthly Digests)
>
> Alternative sources:
>
> ⇒ Subject indexes of most law reports either include "Words and Phrases" as a subject heading or have a Table of Words and Phrases Judicially considered
>
> ⇒ Specialist publications/ dictionaries
> *but may still need to update*
>
> ⇒ *Halsbury's Laws of England.* Words and Phrases Table in Volume 56
> *useful for UK-wide material*

3.2.4   Finding Cases Interpreting Legislation

Most of the sources listed below started by referencing statutes alone but now include various forms of delegated legislation.

3.2.4.1   *Current Law*

The Legislation Citator lists cases opposite the entry for the legislation. See worked example in para. 3.2.4.12 below and chapter 10, for more details.

3.2.4.2   *Current Legal Information*

Check the Current Law Cases section. This covers cases from 1986. You can search by field (this includes legislation) or free text. This will lead you to a digest of the case and citations in the law reports. See chapter 13, para. 13.4.5.

3.2.4.3   *Lexis*

On-line by subscription. Details of case coverage are given in para. 3.1.2.1 above. General information is in chapter 13, para. 13.4.3.

3.2.4.4   *Law reports indexes*

Scots Law Times has an alphabetical subject index and under the words ''statutes and orders'' legislation judicially considered is listed in alphabetical order.

    Scottish Civil Law Reports has a table in each volume of ''Statutes, Statutory Instruments and Court Rules Judicially Considered''. This information is consolidated in the 1987–1996 index.

    Each volume of Scottish Criminal Case Reports has a ''Statutes and Statutory Instruments Judicially Considered'' table. These are consolidated in the 1950–80 supplement and the 1981–1990 index. The 1950–80 index contains reference to High Court of Justiciary cases heard before the S.C.C.R. came into existence and previously unreported.

    The Faculty Digest contains indexes of ''Statutes, Acts of Sederunt, Statutory Orders etc. judicially commented on''. Volume 6 contains an index for volumes 1–5; thereafter each volume of the Supplement has its own index.

    The Consolidated Indexes to the All England Law Reports contain a table of ''Statutes Judicially Considered''.

3.2.4.5   *The Law Reports Index*

This contains various tables:

> Table of statutes judicially considered
>
> Table of statutory instruments judicially considered
>
> Table of overseas legislation judicially considered
>
> Table of E.C. legislation judicially considered
>
> Table of international conventions judicially considered

See chapter 7, para. 7.3.1.2.

3.2.4.6   *Tables of statutes in relevant textbooks*

Tables of statutes in textbooks are usually found at the beginning of the book, after the contents page and next to the table of cases. The entries will refer to passages in the text that discuss the legislation. Relevant cases may also be discussed at the same point in the text.

    This depends on you knowing the area of law involved.

    Make sure that you find the most up-to-date edition of the textbook.

3.2.4.7   *Legal Journals Index*

This has been published since 1986. Check the legislation section. Statutes are listed alphabetically. Reference is made first to the whole Act and then section by section. This should identify articles which have discussed the legislative provisions and the articles themselves may refer to relevant cases. See para. 3.1.5.1.

3.2.4.8   *Halsbury's Statutes of England*

A comprehensive and regularly-updated source but which excludes exclusively Scottish material. See chapter 7, para. 7.2.1.

3.2.4.9   *Lawtel*

On-line by subscription. Useful only for very recent cases and mainstream cases from 1980. Remember the limited Scottish data available. See chapter 13.

3.2.4.10   *Daily Law Reports Index — Legislation Index*

This is useful for very recent cases. See para. 3.1.3.5.

3.2.4.11

D. Finding Cases interpreting Legislation:

Most comprehensive source:

    Current Law Legislation Citators

Alternative sources:

⇒ Lexis

⇒ Current Legal Information
limited period currently available

⇒ Law reports indexes of legislation judicially considered
Usefulness depends on the availability of consolidated versions of annual indexes

⇒ The Law Reports Index
Limited coverage of Scottish cases but useful for English material

⇒ Textbooks accessed by tables of statutes
Make sure you find the most current edition

⇒ Legal Journals Index — Legislation Index
Only useful where an article has been written about the legislation (or part thereof)

⇒ Halsbury's Statutes
Limited Scottish coverage

⇒ Lawtel
Only covers cases since 1980 and contains patchy Scottish coverage

⇒ Daily Law Reports Index — Legislation index
Useful for very recent cases

3.2.4.12 **How to find out if any cases have taken place concerning a particular statutory provision:**
⇒ Step 1: Check through the Legislation Citators in chronological order. Look under the piece of legislation. If a case has taken place, it will appear opposite the statute or section thereof.
⇒ Step 2: You should then check the most recent update for the citator in the Statutes Service File.

Example

Find out if any cases have concerned Sched. 1 of the Scottish Land Court Act 1993.

⇒ Step 1: Check the Statute Citator in the Legislation Citators volume 1989–95. In order to locate the chapter number, check the alphabetical list of acts at the beginning of the volume. The chapter number is 45. Once armed with the chapter number you can turn to the citator itself. Look under 1993 and within that year at the entry for chapter 45. When you have located the entry for the Act look for the section number. After Sched. 1 is a case: *Maciver v. Broadland Properties Estates*, 1995 S.L.T. (Land Ct.) 9.

We have so far identified one case which has concerned the relevant section.

⇒ Step 2: Check the Statute Citator in the Legislation Citators volume 1996–98. There are no entries.
⇒ Step 3: Check the latest edition of the Statute Citator in the Statutes Service File. Again there are no entries for cases under Sched. 1 of the Act.

We can now be certain that (up to the last month) only the one case mentioned above has concerned Sched. 1 of the Scottish Land Court Act 1993.

3.2.5   Current status of a case

3.2.5.1   *Current Law*

Check through the Case Citators and the latest Monthly Digest. See example in para. 3.2.5.7 and chapter 10, para. 10.4.

3.2.5.2   *Lexis*

On-line by subscription. See para. 3.1.2.1 for case coverage and chapter 13 for general information.

3.2.5.3   *The Law Reports Index*

Check section on cases judicially considered. See para. 7.3.1.2.

Checking the status of old Scottish cases

3.2.5.4   Faculty Digest

This covers cases from 1868–1990. Check Tables of "Cases Judicially Referred to". See para. 3.1.3.3 and example in para. 3.2.5.8.

3.2.5.5   Scots Digest

Check tables of "Cases judicially commented on" in relation to the Scottish superior courts from 1800–1947. See para. 3.1.3.8.

3.2.5.6

> **E. Finding the Current Status of a Case**
>
> Best source:
>   Current Law Case Citators updated by latest Monthly Digest
>
> Alternative sources:
>
> ⇒ Lexis
>
> ⇒ The Law Reports Index — section on cases judicially considered
>   *but limited coverage of Scots cases*

> **Checking the status of old Scottish cases (pre-1947 and not in the Current Law case Citators):**
>
> ⇒ The Faculty Digest — Tables of Cases Judicially Referred to *covers 1868–1990*
>
> ⇒ The Scots Digest — Tables of Cases Judicially commented on *covers 1800–1947*

3.2.5.7   **How to find out if a case has been commented on by the courts, distinguished or overruled:**

⇒ Step 1: Check through the Current Law Case Citators in chronological order. Remember that if it is a Scottish case you should check in the Scottish section. Cases are listed in alphabetical order of the first named party. Opposite the entry for the case will be details of whether the case has been judicially considered. It will state whether the case was applied, distinguished, followed, referred to, etc.
⇒ Step 2: You should then check the Table of Cases in the most recent Monthly Digest.

Example

Has *Galt v. Goodsir* been judicially considered?

⇒ Step 1: In the previous example we established that *Galt v. Goodsir* appeared in the Case Citator volume 1977–1997. Opposite the entry for the case we also find two references to judicial consideration:

"applied 89/4924
followed 90/5753."

These references are to digests of cases which respectively applied and followed *Galt v. Goodsir*.

The digests may be sufficient for your purposes. If not, they will contain the citations for the cases and you can then read the decisions in the relevant law reports.

⇒ Step 2: Check the Case Citator 1998. There is no entry.

⇒ Step 3: Check the Table of Cases in the latest Monthly Digest. Again, there is no entry.

We can conclude that (unless there has been a development in the last month) *Galt v. Goodsir* has been judicially considered on two occasions.

3.2.5.8   **How to find out if an older case has been commented on by the courts, distinguished or overruled:**

Example

Has *Crombie v. M'Ewan* 1871 23 D. 333 been judicially considered?

⇒ Step 1: Check Faculty Digest. Volume 6 Indices volume contains a Table of Cases Judicially Referred to. This contains an entry for the above case. It was applied in *Gray v. Smart* 1892 19 R. 692, 29 S.L.R. 589.

⇒ Step 2: The Supplement volumes need to be checked one by one:

1922–1930	no entry
1930–1940	no entry
1940–1950	entry — it was followed in *Brady v. Napier & Son* 1944 S.C. 18, 1943 S.N. 71, 1944 S.L.T. 187.
1951–1960	no entry
1961–1970	no entry
1971–1980	no entry

⇒ Step 3: The search has to be completed by checking Current Law Case Citators:

1977–1997	no entry
1998	no entry
December 1998	no entry
latest Monthly Digest	no entry

3.2.6   Finding out about very recent cases

3.2.6.1   *The internet*

Court of Session and High Court of Justiciary

From September 1998 opinions from the Court of Session and High Court of Justiciary are available via the internet. The site is updated at 2 p.m. on the day an opinion is issued. Web address (free):
http://www.scotcourts.gov.uk
You can search by keyword or by structured search. This facility allows you to search by: type of opinion, date, judge, pursuer, defender, type of action.

House of Lords

House of Lords decisions are currently published within two hours of publication of the judgment. Cases are listed alphabetically in one table covering the period from 1996 to the present. House of Lords website (free):
http://www.parliament.the-stationery-office.co.uk/pa/ld199697/ldjudgmt/ldjudgmt.htm

The Court Service website

http://www.courtservice.gov.uk/cs_home.htm
This service is free at the moment. It allows access to judgments of the Courts of Appeal (Civil and Criminal Divisions) and Queens Bench Division (Crown Office) since April 1996. Full texts of the judgments are provided. The search facilities allow you to search for judgments from 1998 onwards by keywords. You need to know details of the case in order to search for cases prior to 1998.

The Incorporated Council of Law Reporting for England and Wales website

http://www.lawreports.co.uk
This site gives free access to the details of cases that have been or will be reported in the Law Reports, Weekly Law Reports and Industrial Case Reports. Click on Recent and Forthcoming Law Reports.

3.2.6.2   *Newspapers*

English daily newspapers which publish law reports are: *The Times*, *The Financial Times*, *The Daily Telegraph*, *The Independent* and *The Guardian*. *The Scotsman* used to publish law reports but has recently ceased to do so.

3.2.6.3   *Lawtel*

On-line by subscription. This source is updated every 24 hours but has limited coverage of Scottish cases. See chapter 13, para. 13.4.2.

3.2.6.4   *Current Legal Information*

The on-line version is updated on a daily basis. The CD-ROM is updated every month and has a "What's new this month" section in its Current Law Cases. This arranges new cases by subject heading. Click on the subject heading and it will take you to a list of recent cases. Click on the entry for the case and you will be taken straight to a digest of the case. See chapter 13.

3.2.6.5   *Justis — Daily Judgments*

This is an on-line subscription service for the English courts.

3.2.6.6   *Law reports which are published weekly*

In Scotland the Scots Law Times and Green's Weekly Digest are both published weekly.

In England the All England Law Reports and the Weekly Law Reports are published weekly. The Pink Index to the Law Reports is also updated frequently.

Note that there is usually a time delay between a judgment being given and the case being reported in the law reports (even the weekly series of law reports). The delay will tend to be a couple of months.

If the judgment was delivered in the past few days or weeks try the websites above, daily newspapers or Lawtel. The first law report series in Scotland to carry a case will be Green's Weekly Digest. This will contain a brief summary of the case.

3.2.6.7   *The Daily Law Reports Index*

This is an indexing system of newspaper reports and is updated on a fortnightly basis. See para. 3.1.3.5.

3.2.6.8   *Current Law Monthly Digest*

See chapter 10.

3.2.6.9   *Lexis*

On-line by subscription. There is usually a time delay of several weeks before information appears in Lexis. See chapter 13.

3.2.6.10   *Legal Journals Index*

This will locate any journal articles or notes abut the case which have been published. See para. 3.1.5.1.

3.2.6.11

F. Finding a very recent Case

Sources updated on a *daily* basis:

⇒ Internet sites are updated on day a decision is given

Scottish Courts website: http://www.scotcourts.gov.uk

House of Lords website: http://www.parliament.the-stationery-office.co.uk/pa/ld199697/ldjudgmt/ldjudgmt.htm

⇒ Newspapers
⇒ Lawtel
⇒ Current Legal Information
⇒ Justis Daily Judgments

Sources updated *weekly*:

⇒ Weekly law reports, such as Green's Weekly Digest and the Scots Law Times
⇒ Weekly journals

Sources updated *monthly*:

Current Law Monthly Digest

3.2.7   Finding cases from other courts/tribunals

Court of the Lord Lyon

Since 1950 selected cases from the Lyon Court have been reported in the Scots Law Times.

Scottish Land Court

Decisions are published as the Scottish Land Court Reports. See Chapter 2, para. 2.3.4. From 1964 onwards selected cases have been published in the Scots Law Times. You will also find decisions published as an appendix to annual reports by the Scottish Land Court.

Lands Valuation Appeal Court

Decisions are published in Session Cases (since 1907) and the Scots Law Times (since 1893).

Lands Tribunal for Scotland

Selected cases have been reported in the Scots Law Times since 1971.

Tribunals

Administrative tribunals are not bound by the doctrine of judicial precedent and are generally less formal than a court. Some of the cases appear in the law reports but only a small number. They tend to be reports of cases which have been appealed from a tribunal to a court. Many tribunals do, however, publish their decisions.

    Immigration Appeals and Value Added Tax Tribunals Reports are both published by the Stationery Office. Selected decisions of the Social Security Commissioner are also published by the Stationery Office. Commissioners' decisions are cited by a prefix "R", followed in brackets by the abbreviated form of the series to which it belongs *e.g.* R(SSP) related to statutory sick pay. Unpublished reports are prefaced by the letter "C". Unpublished reports may be accessible at the Commissioner's offices.

    Decisions of the Employment Appeal Tribunal (E.A.T.) are published in the Industrial Cases Reports and the Industrial Relations Law Reports.

3.2.8   Putting cases into context

In order to put any case into context you need to appreciate where it lies in the development of the law in whichever subject area. There are many different ways of locating material to facilitate your understanding of the relevance of a case:

1. Examine your lecture notes.

2. Text books.

3. Some series of law reports contain commentaries on selected or all cases. Examples include Scottish Criminal Case Reports, Scottish Civil Law Reports, Green's Family Law Reports, Green's Housing Law Reports and the Environmental Law Reports.

4. Journal commentaries or case notes. Journal commentaries or case notes can be located by searching:

⇒ The Legal Journals Index since 1986. Check in the Case Index (see para. 3.1.5.1).

⇒ Current Law. Check under the appropriate subject headings in the Year Books and the latest Monthly Digest. See chapter 10, paras 10.2 and 10.3.

⇒ The Scots Law Times often contains articles on recent cases.

⇒ Specialist journals may contain commentaries on recent relevant case law, *e.g.* Green's Criminal Law Bulletin, Green's Civil Practice Bulletin, Green's Employment Law Bulletin, Green's Family Law Bulletin, Green's Reparation Law Bulletin, Green's Property Law Bulletin, Green's Business Law Bulletin. They are published bi-monthly and contain commentaries about recent cases.

⇒ Index to Legal Periodicals (a limited amount of Scottish material is included see chapter 6, para. 6.8.1.4).

⇒ The Daily Law Reports. See para. 3.1.3.5.

5. Current Law Case Citator. This gives you references to any subsequent cases which have considered the case. The relevant case reports can then be examined. See chapter 10, para. 10.4.

3.2.8.1   *Understanding the relevance of a very recent case (within the last month)*

1. Check through daily newspapers and weekly published journals. You should also check journals published on the internet.

2. If nothing has been written about it, you will have to make your own analysis of the case.

3.2.8.2

G. Putting Cases into context

- Lecture notes.

- Text books.

- Some series of law reports which contain commentaries on selected or all cases.

- Commentaries in journal articles or case notes.

- Current Law Case Citator. This gives you access to later cases which may have considered the case.

3.2.8.3

H. Understanding the relevance of a very recent case (within the last month)

- Daily newspapers.

- Comment published on the internet.

- Weekly published journals.

- Make your own analysis of the case.

Further Reading:

A. Bradney *et al.*, *How to Study Law* (3rd ed., Sweet & Maxwell, 1995).

P. Clinch, *Using a Law Library* (Blackstone, 1992).

J. Dane and P.A. Thomas, *How to Use a Law Library* (3rd ed., Sweet & Maxwell, 1996) chap. 8.

D.D. Mackey, *How to Use a Scottish law library* (W. Green, 1992).

D.R. Hart, "Scotland" in J. Winterton and E.M. Moys, *Information Sources in Law* (2nd ed., Bowker Saur, 1997).

V. Stevenson, *Legal Research in Scotland* (2nd ed., Legal Information Resources Ltd, 1997).

D.M. Walker, *The Scottish Legal System* (7th ed., W. Green, 1997).

Chapter 4

LEGISLATION

INTRODUCTION TO LEGISLATION

Legislation is the major source of Scots law today. You will encounter numerous pieces of legislation in your career at university and beyond. Familiarity with the concept of legislation and the various formats in which it appears is essential to the study of law. Chapter 4 will introduce you to the various types of legislation and the legislation process. It will also cover the skills of reading and understanding statutes and statutory instruments. Chapter 5 will concentrate on aids to tracing legislation and different search strategies which can be adopted.

The principal form of legislation in the U.K. is Acts of Parliament, which are sometimes referred to as statutes. Legislation affecting Scotland can emerge from the Scottish Parliament, the Westminster Parliament and the European Community institutions. European legislation is dealt with in chapter 8. The Westminster Parliament is the supreme legislator in the U.K. The Scotland Act 1998 has devolved some legislative powers to the Scottish Parliament but it has retained what are referred to as "reserved powers" to the Westminster Parliament.

U.K. legislation can be divided into primary legislation, such as an Act of Parliament, and delegated (sometimes referred to as secondary or subordinate) legislation. Primary legislation is made by the Westminster Parliament and involves a process of parliamentary scrutiny. Delegated legislation can be made by an individual or a body who has been given the power to legislate by the Westminster Parliament. A key difference between the two types of legislation concerns challenges to their validity. The validity of Acts of the Westminster Parliament cannot be challenged in court. The validity of delegated legislation can be so challenged. The validity of legislation emerging from the Scottish Parliament is also open to challenge.

An Act of Parliament can alter the general law of the land, in which case it is called a Public General Act. However, it is also possible (although much less common) to affect only private interests by Act of Parliament. This type of Act is called a Local and Personal Act — see para. 4.3.3 below.

Once an Act has become law it can be altered. The term used is "amended". An Act may be amended many times. The amendments may in turn be amended. An Act cannot be amended by something said by a judge in a case or by the comments of a member of the Government in the House of Commons. It can only be amended by later Acts of Parliament or statutory instrument.

Acts of Parliament do not cease to have the force of law just because they are old or have not been applied for a long period of time. An Act remains part of the law until it is repealed. This means that it ceases to be part of the law. Whole Acts or parts of Acts can be repealed. An Act can be repealed in one part of the U.K. but remain law in another area. Acts can be repealed by later Acts or by delegated legislation (providing it is within its powers). You may encounter the term "desuetude". This doctrine held that there was implied repeal of an Act that was not used for a long period of time. If it applies at all now, it applies only to pre-1707 Scots Acts.

4.2   PRE-1707 SCOTTISH LEGISLATION

Regiam Majestatem is the name of a work commonly regarded as containing the earliest collection of Scottish legislation. It dates from either the late thirteenth or fourteenth century. The *Stair Memorial Encyclopaedia* (vol. 22, para. 512) refers to it being "essentially a commentary on the procedures of the royal courts". It is not a completely Scottish document in that it is based on an English work (*Tractatus De Legibus et Consuetudinibus Regni Anglie* by Glanvill). However, it is not just a copy of the earlier work — it has adapted it to describe the legal system that was developing in Scotland. Another work of the period is the *Quoniam Attachiamenta*. It is a Scottish work and concerns procedure in the feudal courts. The two works are usually printed together. The modern edition of *Regiam Majestatem* is edited by Lord Cooper, Stair Society, Vol. 11, 1947. There is a recent edition of *Quoniam Attachiamenta* edited by T.D. Fergus, The Stair Society, Edinburgh 1996.

There is a lack of information about early Scottish legislation due to "the loss of our public records, the most valuable of which were carried off into England, first by Edward I, and afterwards by an order of Oliver Cromwell, about the middle of the seventeenth century. Apart from six isolated rolls of 1292–3, 1368–9 and 1388–9, there are no original parliamentary records existing prior to 1466." — *An Introductory Survey of the Sources and Literature of Scots Law*, The Stair Society, Edinburgh 1936, p. 4.

4.2.1   Sources of legislation from the pre-1707 Scottish Parliaments

Legislation from the pre-1707 Scottish Parliaments is usually referred to as Scots Acts. There are two main sources of Scots Acts. *Acts of the Parliaments of Scotland 1124–1707*, edited by T. Thomson and C. Innes was published during the nineteenth century. This is known as the *Record edition*. It has been called the "authoritative edition" (P.G.B. McN[eill] "Citation of Scots Statutes" 1959 S.L.T. (News) 112). The other collection is *Laws and Acts of Parliament 1424–1707* by Murray of Glendook. The author of the above article goes on to refer to this as "a collection of statutes which is neither official nor authoritative, and which is full of inaccuracies". The content of the two works does not always agree and the numbering of Acts is different. The Registration Act 1579 referred to below could be referred to as A.P.S. III 142 in the *Record edition* or 1579, c.75 in Glendook's work. It is given the chapter number 13 in the *Record edition* but Glendook's work refers to it as chapter 75.

Details of other early editions of Scots statutes are given in *An Introductory Survey of the Sources & Literature of Scots Law*, The Stair Society, Edinburgh 1936, chapter 1.

Scots Acts which were still in force in 1908 were reproduced in a single volume called *Scots Statutes Revised 1424–1707*. The Statute Law Revisions (Scotland) Act 1964 repealed many Acts of the old Scottish Parliament. Acts which were still in force following this Act were reprinted in *The Acts of the Parliaments of Scotland 1424–1707*, published in 1966.

4.2.2   Citation of Scots Acts

The correct citation of Scots Acts is by the short title or by the calendar year and chapter number or by the volume, page and chapter number of the *Record edition*. The Acts did not originally have short titles but all surviving Scots Acts were given short titles by Sched. 2 of The Statute

Law Revision (Scotland) Act 1964. An example from Sched. 2 is the Act formerly known by "For pwnishment of personis that contempnandlie remanis rebellis and at the horne". It acquired the short title The Registration Act 1579.

Prior to 1964 Scots Acts were cited by calendar year and chapter number in the Glendook edition or by the volume and page number of the *Record edition*. This is still the case for Scots Acts which have been repealed.

4.2.3   Tracing Scots Acts that are still in force

There are a small number of Scots Acts which are still in force today. It is possible to trace these Acts by checking the Chronological Table of Statutes and updating your search by using the volumes of the Current Law Legislation Citators and the latest edition of the Citator in the Statutes Service File. Current Law is covered in more detail in chapter 10, para. 10.5.

4.3   MODERN STATUTES FROM THE U.K. PARLIAMENT APPLYING TO SCOTLAND

4.3.1   Bills

A Bill is a draft version of an Act before it is considered by Parliament. It is referred to as a Bill throughout its passage through Parliament and it becomes an Act after it receives the Royal Assent. There are three types of Bills: public, private and hybrid.

4.3.1.1   *Public Bills*

Public Bills affect the general law of the land and every member of the population. A government Bill is a Public Bill which is presented to Parliament by a government Minister. It will have been drafted by parliamentary draftsmen who are civil servants. Private Members Bills are Public Bills (*not* Private Bills) which are introduced by an individual M.P. (or peer in the House of Lords) rather than by the government. Public Bills account for the majority of Bills today. Public Bills become Public General Acts.

4.3.1.2   *Private Bills*

Private Bills tend to be limited in effect to a certain area or organisation or even person. The process is initiated by a promoter instead of an M.P. A promoter is someone who has an interest in the Bill. Historically there were large numbers of Private Bills but they are much less common today. They were used to facilitate major works such as the construction of the railways, harbours and canals. They were also used for some personal matters such as divorce. Private Bills become Local and Personal Acts (also referred to as Private Acts). The procedure relating to Private Bills is different from Public Bills and is dealt with in para. 4.3.3.2 below.

4.3.1.3   *Hybrid Bills*

As its name suggest, this is a Bill which contains elements of both Public and Private Bills. The procedure used is a mixture of Public and Private Bill procedures.

4.3.1.4   *The procedure for a Public Bill in the Westminster Parliament*

This account relates to procedure before the creation of the Scottish Parliament in July 1999. The procedure for U.K. Public Bills will remain the same but the procedure for exclusively Scottish Bills post-July 1, 1999 is unknown at the time of writing.

Most Bills may be introduced in Parliament in either the House of Lords or the House of Commons. A Bill must pass the stages detailed below in both Houses before it can be submitted for Royal Assent.

> *First Reading*. This is the formal presentation of the Bill to Parliament. The name of the Bill is read out and a date set for the second reading. An order is made for the Bill to be printed and to become publicly available.

> *Second Reading*. This is where the House considers the principles contained in the Bill. The debate is recorded in Hansard. Public Bills which have been certified by the Speaker as exclusively Scottish Bills are considered in Scottish Grand Committee. The Committee is made up of the 72 Members of Parliament for Scottish constituencies and an additional number of around 10–15 M.P.s. This is to ensure that the Committee reflects the balance of the parties in the House of Commons. A formal second reading will be moved in the House at a later date.

> *Committee Stage*. This stage involves consideration of the Bill on a clause-by-clause basis. The whole House can consider a Bill at Committee stage but this usually only happens in exceptional circumstances, such as for Bills of constitutional importance. The norm is for a Bill to be considered by a Standing Committee. A Standing Committee consists of around 18 Members of Parliament chosen to reflect the strength of the parties in the House of Commons. Standing Committees are convened as and when they are needed. Bills relating exclusively to Scotland are dealt with by the Scottish Standing Committee.

> *Report Stage*. This consists of the whole House considering the amendments made in Committee. If the Bill was previously dealt with by a Committee of the Whole House and no amendments were made, it by-passes this stage and goes straight to third reading.

> *Third Reading*. This is where the House takes an overview of the amended Bill. When a Bill has completed these stages it then goes to the House of Lords. It has to pass through similar stages in the House of Lords. When both Houses reach agreement about the Bill it goes forward for Royal Assent. Once a Bill receives the Royal Assent it becomes an Act. It does not automatically become law see para. 4.3.4, section [8].

4.3.1.5   *Citation of Bills*

Each Bill is given a number. However, if the Bill is reprinted it will be given a new number. The number of a Bill has no connection with the chapter number that will be allocated when it becomes an Act. If the Bill is amended in a minor way the number is not changed but a lower case letter may be added.

The elements of the citation of a Bill are:

1. The initials of the House, *e.g.* H.C. or H.L.

2. The session of Parliament, *e.g.* 1998–99.

3. The Bill number. If this is in square brackets it means that the Bill is being considered by the House of Commons. In the past round brackets meant that the Bill was being considered by the House of Lords.

The divisions of a Bill are referred to as clauses and not as section as in an Act of Parliament.

Bills may be amended many times as they progress through the various stages outlined above. They may be reprinted in a form that incorporates all the amendments. It is, therefore, very important that you are aware of which version of the Bill you are reading.

4.3.2 Citation of statutes

Acts of Parliament are normally referred to by their short title, *e.g.* Registered Establishments (Scotland) Act 1998. A complete citation would include the chapter number: Registered Establishments (Scotland) Act 1998, c. 25. It could also be cited by referring to the year in which it was passed and the chapter number, *e.g.* 1998, c. 25.

Since 1963 the chapter number has been related to the sequence in which the Acts received the Royal Assent during a calendar year. The above Act was the 25th Act to receive the Royal Assent in 1998. Prior to 1963 the system was not as simple. Each Act was given a chapter number which related to its chronological place within the parliamentary session. Parliamentary sessions do not coincide with calendar years, they run from November to July. They will, therefore, span more than one calendar year. Each parliamentary session was numbered according to the regnal year. This means the years during which the sovereign had reigned. This was calculated from the month of accession to the throne. A table of the regnal years appears at the front of this book. You will notice that no Scottish monarchs are included in the list. This is because Acts of the pre-1707 Scottish Parliaments were referred to as stated above in para. 4.2.2 and not with reference to the regnal year.

The regnal year system means that Acts passed in the same calendar year can be in different regnal years and/or in different parliamentary sessions. This means that care has to be taken when checking the older volumes of statutes.

This cumbersome system was brought to an end by The Acts of Parliament Numbering and Citation Act 1962. Section 1 stated that chapter numbers were to be assigned by reference to the calendar year and not to the parliamentary session.

4.3.3 Local and Personal Acts

Private Bills become Local and Personal Acts. These Acts tend to be limited in effect to a certain area or organisation or even person. There were large numbers of Private Acts in the past but they are much less common today. They were used to facilitate major works such as the construction of the railways, harbours and canals. They were also used for some personal matters such as divorce.

4.3.3.1 *Citation*

Local and Personal Acts are cited in the same way as Public General Acts, except that, in order to differentiate them, the chapter number is printed differently. The chapter numbers of Local Acts appear in small roman numerals, *e.g.* Peterhead Harbours Order Confirmation Act 1992 (1992, c. xii).

The chapter numbers of Personal Acts appear in italicised arabic figures.

4.3.3.2 *Procedure for Private Bills*

The normal procedure involves the presentation of a petition to Parliament by the person or organisation who is promoting the Bill. Information about the contents of the Bill has to be widely circulated and the petitioner has to appear before an examiner. Private Bills then go through the same stages as Public Bills.

A streamlined procedure for Scottish Private Bills is laid down in the Private Legislation Procedure (Scotland) Act 1936. Application has to be made to the Secretary of State for Scotland for a Provisional Order. If an inquiry is deemed appropriate, it is undertaken by Commissioners and sits in Scotland. They make a report to the Secretary of State. If the Order has been approved, the Secretary of State will issue the Order. This does not become law until it has been confirmed by Parliament. The mechanism for this is an Order Confirmation Bill (which is a Public Bill) with the text of the Order appearing as the schedule to the Bill. If the Bill proceeds through a shortened parliamentary procedure, it emerges as a Local and Personal Act.

4.3.4   Anatomy of a statute

This is an example of a Public General Act. It has been chosen because of its brevity — not all Acts are as short as this one — they are usually much longer. While all Acts adopt the same format some, but not necessarily all, features will appear in all Acts. Different features are marked with numbers which correspond to the following list:

[1] The *short title* of the Act. This is the normal way to refer to the Act. The Short Titles Act 1896 and the Statute Law Revision Act 1948 gave short titles to many of the older Acts. Schedule 2 of the Statute Law Revision (Scotland) Act 1962 gave short titles to many of the Acts of the pre-1707 Scottish Parliament.

[2] This is another way of referring to Acts — by their year and *chapter number*. The modern system of assigning chapter numbers dates from 1963. For the position before 1963 see para. 4.3.2 earlier. A chapter number is assigned to each Act in chronological order throughout a calendar year. This means that this was the sixth Act of 1997.

[3] This is the *long title*. It sets out the purpose of the Act in very general terms. It will be more detailed than the short title. However, it is not a detailed guide to the background of the Act. It is no longer the practice for modern Acts to include a preamble but older Acts do contain an explanation of the reasons for the Act. Preambles could be quite detailed — far more so than the brief statement of purpose in modern long titles.

[4] The date which appears at the end of the long title in square brackets is the date of *Royal Assent*. This may or may not be the date that the Act comes into force. See section [8] below regarding commencement generally.

[5] This is the *standard enacting formula*. These words indicate that the Act has the full authority of Parliament.

[6] Acts are divided up into parts called *sections*. Sections are numbered consecutively throughout an Act. Sections can be subdivided into subsections. Subsections can be divided into paragraphs and further divided into sub-paragraphs.

If the Act is long or deals with separate things, it may be divided into parts and chapters, *e.g.* The Environment Act 1995 is divided into five parts:

> Part I The Environment Agency and The Scottish Environment Protection Agency
> Part II Contaminated Land and Abandoned Mines
> Part III National Parks
> Part IV Air Quality
> Part V Miscellaneous, General and Supplemental Provisions

Part I is then subdivided into three chapters:

Local Government (Gaelic Names) (Scotland) Act 1997

1997 Chapter 6

Local Government (Gaelic Names) (Scotland) Act 1997 [1]

1997 Chapter 6 [2]

An Act to enable local authorities in Scotland to take Gaelic names; and for connected purposes. [3]

[27th February 1997] [4]

BE IT ENACTED by the Queen's most Excellent Majesty, by and with the advice and consent of the Lords Spiritual and Temporal, and Commons, in this present Parliament assembled, and by the authority of the same, as follows:- [5]

Power of council to change name into Gaelic and vice-versa. [7]

1. In section 23 of the Local Government (Scotland) Act 1973 (change of name of local government area), there shall be inserted, after subsection (1), the following subsections- [6]

"(1A) Where a council so change the name of their area into Gaelic, they may also, by a resolution passed in accordance with subsection (1) above and notwithstanding sections 2(3) and 3(1)(a) of the Local Government etc. (Scotland) Act 1994, decide that their name shall be "Comhairle" with the addition of the name of their area.

(1B) A council which have so changed their name into Gaelic may, by a resolution passed in accordance with subsection (1) above, change it back into English.".

Short title, commencement and exent.

2. - (1) This Act may be cited as the Local Government (Gaelic Names) (Scotland) Act 1997. [8]

(2) This Act shall come into force on the expiry of the period of two months beginning with the day on which it is passed.

(3) This Act extends to Scotland only.

Chapter I The Environment Agency
Chapter II The Scottish Environment Agency
Chapter III Miscellaneous, General and Supplemental Provisions Relating to the New
Agencies

Chapter II contains sections 20–36:

"S34. general duties with respect to water
(1) It shall be the duty of SEPA —

    (a) to promote the cleanliness of —
        (i) rivers, other inland waters and ground waters in Scotland; and
        (ii) the tidal waters of Scotland; and

    (b) to conserve so far as practicable the water resources of Scotland."

The reference to SEPA's duty to promote the cleanliness of tidal waters is contained in the Environment Act 1995, s. 34(1)(a)(ii). This means sub-paragraph (ii) of paragraph (a) of subsection (1) of section 34 of the Act.

[7] *Marginal notes* are not technically part of the Act. They describe the content of the section in very brief terms.

    N.B. The *interpretation section* is usually, but not always, to be found near the end of the Act. It sets out definitions of certain words which have been used in the Act. Words can be given a particular meaning for the whole of an Act or for a part of it. This Act does not have an interpretation section.

[8] The last section of an Act usually provides for citation of the *short title, commencement and geographic extent*.
Short title. This also appears at the start of the Act. See comments above in section [1].
Commencement. If the Act contains no commencement provision there is a presumption that it comes into force at the beginning of the day on which it receives the Royal Assent. The commencement provisions in an Act can provide for it coming into force in one of three ways:

(a) The Act can specify a particular date;

(b) The Act can specify a period after the passing of the Act when the Act will come into force. This is the case with this Act. It came into force two months after it was passed, *i.e.* April 27, 1997.

(c) The Act can state that it is to come into force on a date to be set by a person, usually the relevant Secretary of State. It would be brought into force by a type of statutory instrument called a Commencement Order.

The whole of an Act can be brought into force at once or sections of it can become law at different times. This means that you need to check the commencement section carefully. There can be considerable time delay between an Act receiving the Royal Assent and becoming law. Some Acts never become law.

    Some terminology can cause confusion. If an Act is referred to as "becoming law" or "coming into force" it has come into operation. If an Act has been "passed" or is referred to as "being on the statute books", it means that it has received the Royal Assent but has not necessarily become law.

Geographic extent. If an Act applies *exclusively* to Scotland the word "(Scotland)" will appear in the short title. However, finding Scottish legislation is not as straightforward as looking for Acts with "(Scotland)" in the short title as it is possible for legislation without "(Scotland)" in the short title to apply in Scotland. There is a presumption that Acts of the Westminster Parliament apply to the whole of the U.K. If the Act is silent then it is taken to apply throughout the U.K.

It is possible for only parts of an Act to apply to Scotland. If an Act applies only to part of the U.K. it has to state this expressly. Acts usually do this in the extent section. This means that you must always check the extent section of an Act.

N.B. Schedules may appear at the end of an Act. A large Act may contain numerous schedules. For instance, the Environment Act 1995 mentioned above contained 24 schedules. Schedules are not divided into sections, instead they are divided into paragraphs and sub-paragraphs. Schedules have equal force in law as the rest of the Act — they do not have a lower status just because they are added on to the end of the Act. Material is usually put into schedules because it is very detailed or technical and it is easier to present in tabular or list form. A common inclusion in schedules is a list of previous legislation which has been amended or repealed by the Act.

4.3.5 **Reading legislation**

Beware of making assumptions.

You cannot presume that because you have found the text of an Act of Parliament that it constitutes the law. Firstly, you cannot assume that an Act is in force. All or part of it may not have been brought into force. See commencement in para. 4.3.4 section [8]. Further, you cannot assume that it has not been amended or repealed. You need to check sources such as Current Legislation Citators to see if any changes have taken place; see para. 5.3.3.

Another assumption that it is dangerous to make is that an Act automatically applies to Scotland. It is safe to make this assumption if the word "Scotland" is included in the short title. If this is not the case, you should check the extent section. This will always be found at the end of the Act. See para. 4.3.4 section [8]. Never assume that Acts without "Scotland" in the title do not apply to Scotland.

You cannot assume that a word used in a statute will have the same meaning as it does in everyday usage. A word can have a special meaning for a section or for the whole Act. Make sure that you check to see if any special meaning has been given to the words of the statute. This involves looking for an interpretation section. This will normally be near the end of an Act. Remember that a definition given in one statute does not necessarily apply in other statutes. Only definitions in statutes which are *in pari materia* (of similar subject matter) can be used.

Do not read an Act from beginning to end. They are not intended to be read in that way. Go straight to the section you are interested in or check the contents of the Act to locate a relevant section.

How do you read a statute? At first sight they bear little resemblance to normal English prose. They are set out in a very formal way and the language used can be difficult to comprehend. The most important piece of advice is to read statutes carefully. The exact wording is very important. Every word has been deliberately chosen. You need to be alert to the smallest of words as they can be crucial to your understanding of a provision. There is a huge difference between the word "may" which suggests that you can do something and the word "shall" which means that you must do something.

Pay particular attention to words at the beginning of a section, *e.g.* "subject to the provisions of s. 10''. This means that the current section is subordinate to the provisions of section 10. If there is any conflict between the two sections, section 10 will prevail.

If you want help in understanding a statutory provision you should consult:

1. Lecture notes, if relevant.

2. A textbook on the subject area. Check the Table of Statutes at the beginning of the book to see if any reference has been made to the Act. The table should give you page references where the Act has been discussed.

3. Annotations to the Act. Some versions of Acts contain annotations, *e.g.* Current Law Statutes. These are written by experts in the relevant area of law. There is usually a long introductory note at the beginning of the Act which explains its significance and places it in context. It will also refer you to the parliamentary debates on the Bill. Throughout the Act there will be shorter annotations which should help to explain the various sections and the effect they have on the existing law. Annotations can be very helpful but you should always remember that they are not authoritative. They are only the view of one person, albeit an expert.

4. Journal commentaries. These can be located by searching:

   (a) The Legal Journals Index since 1986. Check in the Legislation Index. See Chapter 6, para. 6.8.1.1.
   (b) Current Law. Check under the appropriate subject headings in the Year Books and the latest Monthly Digest. See chapter 10, paras 10.2 and 10.3.
   (c) The Scots Law Times and the Journal of the Law Society of Scotland often contain articles on recent legislation.
   (d) Specialist journals may contain commentaries on recent relevant legislation.

5. Cases which have considered the legislation. Current Law Legislation Citator will give you references to any subsequent cases which have considered the legislation. The relevant case reports can then be examined.

4.3.6   Statutory interpretation

When trying to interpret the words of a statute you do not have a free hand. There are rules and conventions governing how to interpret statutory provisions. What should you do if you cannot understand the wording of a statute? Below is a diagram of possible approaches. The detail of statutory interpretation is outwith the scope of this work, but see suggested further reading below for discussion of this topic.

Problem word/phrase: Has it been legally defined?	⇒ definitions section (located within Act itself)
	⇒ Interpretation Act 1978*
Have any cases interpreted this word/phrase as it occurred in this Act?	⇒ Current Law Legislation Citators — see chapter 10
Has it been defined in any statute that is *in pari materia*?	⇒ locate Acts which concern similar subject matter

Have the courts interpreted this word?   ⇒ Judicial Dictionary, chapter 6, para. 6.4,
                                                updated by Words and Phrases Table in
                                                Current Law Year Books and Monthly
                                                Digests

Note that this information may all be contained in an annotation to the Act.

   If this search reveals nothing, try an English dictionary but remember, all that a dictionary
can do is provide evidence of the ordinary meaning of a word. It cannot provide a definitive
answer. Language is a very imprecise medium and a dictionary is likely to give several different
definitions of the word which are equally valid. Dictionaries do not often solve legal problems.

If the word is ambiguous or unclear, use   ⇒ overall approach, *e.g.* purposive, literal
the rules of statutory interpretation   ⇒ grammatical context, *e.g. ejusdem
                                               generis*
                                               ⇒ presumptions, *e.g.* legislation is
                                               presumed not to be retrospective

*Interpretation Act 1978. This is not as helpful as the name would suggest. It contains definitions
of commonly used terms. It deals with matters such as words in the singular should include the
plural and vice versa. It is unlikely to be of much help.

Further reading on statutory interpretation:

V.C.R.A.C. Crabbe, *Understanding Statutes* (Cavendish, 1994).
J.A. Holland and J.S. Webb, *Learning Legal Rules* (4th ed., Blackstone, 1999), chapter 8.
A.A. Paterson and T.St.J.N. Bates, *The Legal System of Scotland* (W. Green, 1993), chapter 13.
W.A. Wilson, *Introductory Essays on Scots Law* (2nd ed., W. Green, 1984), "Interpreting Stat-
     utes".
D.M. Walker, *The Scottish Legal System* (7th ed., W. Green, 1997), pp. 395–413.
R.M. White and I.D. Willock, *The Scottish Legal System* (Butterworths, 1993), chapter 5.

4.4   DELEGATED LEGISLATION

The Westminster Parliament is the supreme law-maker within the U.K. but it is able to delegate its
law-making powers to others. Delegated (sometimes called secondary or subordinate) legislation is
legislation made by individuals or bodies other than Parliament, but with the authority of Parliament. Authority is given by the inclusion of a provision (known as an enabling provision) in an
Act of Parliament. An example is section 245(1) of the Criminal Procedure (Scotland) Act 1995:
"The Secretary of State may make rules for regulating the performance of work under community
service orders or probation orders which include a requirement that the offender shall perform
unpaid work."
   Delegated legislation has been used increasingly throughout the twentieth century and is an
important source of law. Acts of Parliament tend to provide only a broad framework. Delegated
legislation is used to fill out the detail. Delegated legislation is used particularly for areas that
change frequently and for detailed or technical matters. It is also used to implement a lot of
European Community legislation.

There are many different forms of delegated legislation. The most common is the statutory instrument. This is, in fact, not one type of delegated legislation but includes rules, regulations and orders. Before the Statutory Instruments Act 1946 the equivalent to modern statutory instruments were known as "statutory rules and orders". This chapter will concentrate on statutory instruments because they are the type of delegated legislation that you will encounter most frequently. Other types of delegated legislation include by-laws and the peculiarly Scottish Acts of Sederunt and Acts of Adjournal. Acts of Sederunt and Acts of Adjournal are pieces of legislation enacted by the Court of Session and the High Court of Justiciary respectively. Acts of Sederunt are rules which govern procedure in the civil courts while Acts of Adjournal concern procedure in Scotland's criminal courts.

A statutory instrument has the same force of law as a statute. However, there is a key difference between the two. As stated previously an Act of Parliament cannot be challenged in court. A statutory instrument can be so challenged. It is only valid if the person making the legislation has been duly authorised by the "enabling" Act of Parliament and has acted within the limits of the powers laid down in that Act. If this is not the case the statutory instrument could be succesfully challenged on the grounds that it was *ultra vires*.

There are many similaritics with statutes:

Statutory instruments can be general or local. All statutory instruments which have general application are required to be published. Local statutory instruments may not be published.

There is a presumption that statutory instruments, like statutes, apply to the whole of the U.K. However, they may only be applicable to Scotland as in the example below.

Statutory instruments can be amended or revoked (this means the same as repealed in respect of statutes). They remain in force until revoked or until the Act they were made under is repealed.

Greater discussion of delegated legislation will be found in texts such as:

E.C.S. Wade and A.W. Bradley, *Constitutional and Administrative Law* (11th ed., 1993).
A. Carroll, *Constitutional and Administrative Law* (1998).
V. Finch and A. Ashton, *Administrative Law in Scotland* (1997).

4.4.1   Citation of statutory instruments

Statutory instruments are cited either by title and year or, alternatively, by year and running number, *e.g.* Control of Pollution (Silage, Slurry and Agricultural Fuel Oil) Regulations 1991 or S.I. 1991 No. 324. The statutory instruments themselves frequently stipulate the citation by which they should be referred.

The fact that the number is followed by an "S" in brackets and another number shows that this statutory instrument applies only to Scotland, *e.g.* The Restriction of Liberty Order (Scotland) Amendment Regulations 1999 or S.I. 1999 No. 144 (S.6). If you are trying to find a statutory instrument ignore the Scottish number because the indexes for statutory instruments use the main number for the reference.

If the number is followed by a "C" it means that it is a Commencement Order. This is a particular type of statutory instrument which is used to bring an Act or part thereof into operation. They have additional information in their citation, *e.g.* The Environment Act 1995 (Commencement No. 12 and Transitional Provisions) (Scotland) Order 1998 or S.I. 1998 No. 781 (S.40) (C. 16).

If the number is followed by "NI" it applies only to Northern Ireland. If it is followed by "L" it means that it relates to court fees or procedure in England and Wales.

4.4.2 **Anatomy of a Statutory instrument**

STATUTORY INSTRUMENTS

1999 No. 144 (S. 6) [1]

CRIMINAL LAW, SCOTLAND [2]

The Restriction of Liberty Order (Scotland) Amendment Regulations 1999 [3]

Made	*21st January 1999*
Laid before Parliament	*28th January 1999* [4]
Coming into force	*19th February 1999*

The Secretary of State, in exercise of the powers conferred on him by sections 245A(8) and 245C(3) of the Criminal Procedure (Scotland) Act 1995[1] and of all other powers enabling him in that behalf hereby makes the following Regulations: [5]
[6]
Citation and commencement [7]
1. - (1) These Regulations may be cited as the Restriction of Liberty Order (Scotland) Amendment Regulations 1999.
(2) These Regulations shall come into force on 19th February 1999.

Interpretation
2. In these Regulations, unless the context otherwise requires-

"the Principal Regulations" mean the Restriction of Liberty Order (Scotland) Regulations 1998[2].

Amendment of Principal Regulations
3. - (1) The Principal Regulations shall be amended in accordance with the following paragraphs.

(2) In Regulation 2(1), after the definition of "offender" insert the following-

" "Premier Geografix" means Premier Geografix Limited a limited company incorporated under the Companies Acts under number 3522659 having its registered office at Centennial Court, Easthampstead Road, Bracknell, Berkshire RG12 1YQ".

(3) In Schedule 2, after paragraph 3 insert the following-

"4. Devices manufactured by Premier Geografix and sold under the Premier Geografix name:

    (a) GEM Transmitter;
    (b) GEM Site Monitoring Unit;
    (c) GEM Field Management Unit;
    (d) GEM Monitoring Officers Transmitter,
    (e) GEM Central Computer System.".

Henry McLeish [8]
Minister of State, Scottish Office

St Andrew's House, Edinburgh
21st January 1999

EXPLANATORY NOTE [9]

(This note is not part of the Regulations)

These Regulations made under sections 245A(8) and 245C(3) of the Criminal Procedure (Scotland) Act 1995 as inserted by section 5 of the Crime and Punishment (Scotland) Act 1997 amend the Restriction of Liberty Order (Scotland) Regulations 1998 which regulate aspects of the monitoring by electronic and radio devices the compliance of offenders with requirements of restriction of liberty orders.

The amendment to Schedule 2 to the Restriction of Liberty Order (Scotland) Regulations 1998 specifies additional devices which may be used for monitoring.

Notes:
[1] 1995 c.46 sections 245A-245H were inserted by the Crime and Punishment (Scotland) Act 1997 (c.48), section 5.back
[2] S.I. 1998/1802.back

Statutory instruments can vary in length. The example on p. 67 is a particularly short one. Different features are marked with numbers which correspond to the following list:

[1] The citation consists of the year and number. The number refers to the number issued in a calendar year, *e.g.* this is number 144 for 1999. The fact that the number is followed by an "S" in brackets and another number shows that this statutory instrument applies only to Scotland. It is the sixth statutory instrument to apply to Scotland in 1999.

[2] This is not part of the name — it is a subject heading used in official editions of statutory instruments.

[3] This is the short title of the statutory instrument. This is the normal way to refer to a statutory instrument.

[4] This is a list of three dates relating to the parliamentary process involved in creating a statutory instrument. This is a requirement under s. 4(2) of the Statutory Instruments Act 1946, which states that every statutory instrument should include details of when it is to come into force and when it was laid before Parliament. Statutory instruments also usually include details of the date on which they were made.

[5] This paragraph is a recital of the statutory authority and powers that enable the maker of the statutory instrument (here the Secretary of State for Scotland) to issue the statutory instrument. Here he has exercised powers under the provisions of the Criminal Procedure (Scotland) Act 1995, as amended.

[6] Statutory instruments are divided up into parts but these are not referred to as sections as in an Act of Parliament. The name given to the divisions depends on the type of the statutory instrument. In this case the statutory instrument is a regulation and the divisions are called regulations, with further subdivisions called paragraphs and sub-paragraphs. If the statutory instrument is an order the divisions are called articles, but further subdivisions are called paragraphs and sub-paragraphs. If the statutory instrument is a rule, the divisions are called rules but further subdivisions are called paragraphs and sub-paragraphs.

[7] There are several types of regulation (article or rule) which tend to appear in most but not all statutory instruments:
Citation and commencement. This will specify the correct citation to be adopted and give the date on which the statutory instrument will come into force.
Interpretation. This states if particular meanings are to be given to words used in the statutory instrument.

[8] The signature of the person making the statutory instrument, along with their title and the date on which the statutory instrument was made.

It is possible for statutory instruments to have schedules. As with statutes, material in the schedule will tend to be technical and/or very detailed. This statutory instrument does not have any schedules.

[9] In official editions of statutory instruments there is usually an explanatory note at the end of the statutory instrument. It is not technically part of the statutory instrument. They tend to be brief and do not add very much to your understanding of the legislation.

Reading statutory instruments

4.4.3   Reading statutory instruments raises the same issues as reading statutes. See para. 4.3.5. In addition you may find it helpful to read the enabling Act in conjunction with the statutory instrument. The Act (and any annotations to it) may help your understanding of the broader context of which the statutory instrument is part.

4.5   THE SCOTTISH PARLIAMENT (1999–)

4.5.1   Introduction

"The Scottish Parliament, which adjourned on 25 March 1707, is hereby reconvened."*

The first meeting of the new Scottish Parliament was on May 12, 1999 following elections which took place on May 6. The Parliament was formally opened on July 1, 1999. A Parliamentary session is for a fixed period of four years. This is different from the Westminster system where the maximum length of a parliament is five years. The Scottish Parliamentary year covers a 12-month period and the first Parliamentary year started on May 12, 1999.

The Scottish Parliament consists of 129 Members of the Scottish Parliament who are referred to as MSPs. The Scottish Executive is made up of the First Minister, Ministers appointed by the First Minister, the Lord Advocate and the Solicitor General for Scotland. The First Minister is head of the Scottish Executive. He is nominated by the Scottish Parliament and formally appointed by the Queen.

The Presiding Officer (the equivalent of the Speaker in the House of Commons) is one of the important figures of the Parliament. The post is held by one of the MSPs and is elected by the Parliament. This post is currently held by Lord Steel. The Presiding Officer's role is to:

(a) preside over meetings of the Parliament and exercise a casting vote in the event of a tie;

(b) convene and chair meetings of the Parliamentary Bureau and exercise a casting vote in the event of a tie. The Parliamentary Bureau consists of representatives of the various parties who organise the business of the Parliament;

(c) determine any question as to the interpretation or application of the rules governing parliamentary procedure; and

(d) represent the Parliament in discussions and exchanges with any parliamentary, governmental, administrative or other body.

The new post of Advocate General for Scotland has been created. She will provide the U.K. Government with advice on Scots law and is part of the U.K. Government and not the Scottish Parliament.

The Scottish Parliament has only one chamber (unicameral). There is no second chamber. Scottish legislation does not go to the House of Lords. Legislation is scrutinised by the Scottish Parliament as a whole and by its various committees. The proceedings of the Scottish Parliament are regulated by the Scotland Act 1998 (Transitory and Transitional Provisions) (Standing Orders and Parliamentary Publications) Order 1999. This will be referred to as "the Order" throughout this section.

Committees play a key role in the work of the Scottish Parliament. The Parliament may establish committees to deal with specific subject areas in addition to the mandatory committees required by the Order, Chapter 6, Rule 6.1. The mandatory committees are:

Procedures Committee

* Dr Ewing The Official Report 12 May 1999, Col. 5.

Standards Committee

Finance Committee

Audit Committee

European Committee

Equal Opportunities Committee

Public Petitions Committee

Subordinate Legislation Committee

Committees must have at least five but not more than 15 members. The composition of the committees reflects the balance of the parties in the Parliament. The functions of the committees are laid down in the Order, Chapter 6, Rule 6.2. The committees can examine matters within their remit or matters referred to them by the Parliament. They may:

- consider the policy and administration of the Scottish Administration
- consider proposals for legislation in the Scottish Parliament and theWestminster Parliament
- consider E.C. legislation and international Conventions
- consider the need for reform of the law
- initiate Bills
- consider the financial proposals and financial administration of the Scottish Administration

4.5.2   Legislation

A Bill can be introduced by:

- a member of the Scottish Executive, in which case it is referred to as an Executive Bill;
- a Parliamentary Committee, in which case it is referred to as a Committee Bill; or
- a Member of Scottish Parliament, in which case it is referred to as a Member's Bill.

On introduction, a Bill must be accompanied by certain documents (the Order, Chapter 9, Rule 9.3):

- A statement by the Presiding Officer indicating whether the provisions are within the legislative competence of the Parliament. Any provisions which are viewed as outside its competence have to be identified.
- A Financial Memorandum. This sets out a best estimate of the administrative, compliance and other costs arising from the provisions of the Bill. It must distinguish how such costs would fall on the Scottish Administration, local authorities and other bodies, individuals and businesses.
- If a Bill is introduced by a member of the Scottish Executive it must also be accompanied by:

    (a) A statement by the Minister in charge of the Bill that in his view the provisions are within the legislative competence of the Parliament.

    (b) Explanatory notes which summarise objectively each provision of the Bill.

    (c) A Policy Memorandum which sets out:

      (i) Policy objectives of the Bill;

      (ii) Consideration of alternative methods of achieving these objectives and justification of the approach taken in the Bill;

      (iii) Details of any consultation on the objectives;

      (iv) Assessment of the effects, if any, of the Bill on:
          Equal opportunities
          Human rights
          Island communities
          Local government
          Sustainable development
          Any other matter which the Scottish Executive considers relevant.

- If a Bill contains any provision charging expenditure on the Scottish Consolidated Fund, a report from the Auditor General must accompany the Bill. This report sets out whether the Auditor General views the charge as appropriate.

The stages of Bills are governed by Chapter 9 of the Order. There are special rules which apply to Member's Bills (Rule 9.14), Committee Bills (Rule 9.15), Budget Bills (Rule 9.16), Private Bills (Rule 9.17), Consolidation Bills (Rule 9.18), Statute Law Repeals Bills (Rule 9.19), Statute Law Revision Bills (Rule 9.20) and Emergency Bills (Rule 9.21).

The majority of Bills likely to be dealt with by the Parliament are Executive Bills. The procedure outlined below will generally apply to Executive Bills (Rules 9.5–9.8).

Stage 1 — Consideration of the general principles of a Bill.
Once a Bill has been printed it is referred to the committee within whose remit it falls. This committee is known as "the lead committee". This committee considers the general principles and prepares a report for the Parliament. Parliament then considers the general principles of the Bill in the light of this report. It can:

- refer the Bill back to the lead committee for a further report or
- fail to agree the general principles of the Bill (in which case the Bill falls) or
- agree to the Bill.

If the Bill is agreed, it can proceed to stage 2. There must be at least two weeks between the completion of stage 1 and the start of stage 2.

Stage 2 — Consideration of the details of the Bill
This stage is either considered by the lead committee, another committee or a committee of the whole Parliament. Each section, schedule and the long title of the Bill are considered separately. A Bill may be amended at this stage. If the Bill has been amended, it will be reprinted. If it is amended in such a way as to affect powers to make subordinate legislation, the amended Bill must be referred to the Subordinate Legislation Committee for consideration.

If the Bill is amended at stage 2 there must be at least two weeks between completion of stage 2 and the start of stage 3.

Stage 3 — Final consideration
The amended Bill is considered by the Parliament. The Bill can be further amended at this stage.

It is possible for up to half of the sections of the Bill to be referred back to committee for further stage 2 consideration. If this takes place, on resumption of stage 3 proceedings, amendments can only be made to the provisions which were referred back to committee.

If there is a final vote on the Bill, at least a quarter of all MSPs must vote or abstain. If this condition is not met, the Bill will be treated as rejected.

If the Bill is passed, it will be submitted for Royal Assent by the Presiding Officer. Within four weeks of the passing of the Bill the Advocate General, Lord Advocate or Attorney General can refer the question of whether the Bill is within the Parliament's legislative competence to the Judicial Committee of the Privy Council for a decision (Scotland Act 1998, s. 33). The Secretary of State for Scotland has the power to intervene and prohibit the Presiding Officer from submitting the Bill for Royal Assent. He may do this if he has reasonable grounds to believe that the Bill is incompatible with any international obligations or the interests of defence and national security or will have an adverse effect on the law relating to reserved matters (Scotland Act 1998, s. 35).

Once the Bill receives Royal Assent, it becomes an Act of the Scottish Parliament. The full text of all Acts of the Scottish Parliament will be available at the Scottish legislation website (http://www.scotland-legislation.hmso.gov.uk).

4.5.3 Subordinate legislation

The procedures relating to subordinate legislation are governed by Chapter 10 of the Order. Provisions relating to Scottish statutory instruments are contained in the Scotland Act 1998 (Transitory and Transitional Provisions) (Statutory Instruments) Order 1999. All Scottish statutory instruments are to have the heading "SCOTTISH STATUTORY INSTRUMENTS". They are to be numbered consecutively in the order they are received by the Queen's Printer in the series of the calendar year in which they were made. They are to be cited by the letters S.S.I. followed by the calendar year in which they were made and their number, *e.g.* S.S.I. 1999 No. 10.

Details of Scottish statutory instruments will be published by the Queen's Printer in the Scottish Statutory Instruments Issue List. This will contain the following details: number, short title and the date on which the instrument was issued. An annual edition of Scottish statutory instruments will be published at the end of the calendar year. All S.S.I.s will be available at the website mentioned above.

4.5.4 Legislative competence

Any Act of the Scottish Parliament is not law if it is outside the legislative competence of the Parliament (Scotland Act 1998, s. 29). A provision would be outside the Parliament's legislative competence if it related to the reserved matters. The reserved matters are listed in Sched. 5 of the Scotland Act. General reservations include: the constitution, foreign affairs, defence, public service, political parties and treason. There are also a range of specific reservations under the following headings: financial and economic affairs, home affairs, trade and industry, energy, transport, social security, regulation of the professions, employment, health and medicines, media and culture and miscellaneous. The matters which the Scottish Parliament can consider are not listed in the Act. They are to be implied by exception. They include: criminal justice and prosecution, civil and criminal courts, legal aid, judicial appointments, the police and fire services, prisons, health services, education, local government, the environment, agriculture, forestry, fisheries, social work services, liquor licensing, housing, tourism, sport and the arts.

Schedule 6 of the Scotland Act 1998 deals with "devolution issues". These are defined as questions of whether:

(a) The Act (or any of its provisions) is within the Parliament's legislative competence;

(b) Any function being exercised is a function of the Scottish Ministers, First Minister or Lord Advocate;

(c) A function being exercised by a member of the Scottish Executive is within the devolved competence;

(d) The exercise of a function (or failure to act) by a member of the Scottish Executive would be incompatible with the rights under the European Convention of Human Rights or European Communitiy law.

Devolution issues which arise in Scotland may be referred by a court to the Inner House (in respect of civil cases) or to the High Court of Justiciary (in relation to criminal proceedings). The issue may be further referred or appealed to the Judicial Committee of the Privy Council.

4.5.5 The Scottish Parliament Official Report

Chapter 16 of the Order concerns the reporting of proceedings in the Parliament. It states that a substantially verbatim report of proceedings is to be referred to as the Scottish Parliament Official Report. This is the Scottish version of Hansard. It is a record of proceedings in full meetings of the whole Parliament, committee meetings and all written questions and answers. It is published daily throughout the parliamentary session. The Official Report appears on the Scottish Parliament website (see para. 4.5.6 below) by 8.00 a.m. on the following working day. The daily editions are listed in chronological order. Every month the daily editions of the Official Report will be published in a bound volume. This version is to be regarded as the definitive edition.

MSPs are able to read the transcript of their speeches and suggest corrections. They may not change the sense of what has been said or make substantial amendments if what has been reported is correct.

It is intended that a Journal of the Scottish Parliament be published. This will include details of: minutes of proceedings; notice of any instrument or draft instrument or any other document laid before the Parliament and notice of any report of a committee.

4.5.6 Information available from the official website for the Scottish Parliament

The Web address is:
http://www.scottish.parliament.uk/
The website is divided into various sections:

1. What's Happening
   This is the most useful section of the site. It is recommended that you ''bookmark'' this page if you want to keep up to date with developments at the Scottish Parliament. It allows access to the following:

   - News. This lists press releases in chronological order.
   - WHISP (What's Happening in the Scottish Parliament). This is a weekly publication providing information on the work of the Parliament. It also gives details of forthcoming business and publications.
   - Publications. This gives details of Parliamentary publications.
   - The Official Report. See para. 4.5.5 above.
   - Minutes of Proceedings. These are a formal record of the business of the Parliament and any decisions taken.

- Business Bulletin. This is published every day that the Parliament is in session. It details the business of the day. Information in the Bulletin includes:
  ⇒ Daily Business List
  ⇒ Announcements
  ⇒ New written questions
  ⇒ New amendments to legislation
  ⇒ New oral questions
  ⇒ New motions, legislation
  ⇒ Provisional agenda of future business
  ⇒ Progress of Parliamentary business
- Calendar of Events. This lists forthcoming events.

2. The Official Report, see para. 4.5.5 above.

3. Agenda and Decisions
   This section deals with the business of the Parliament and is based on information provided by the Clerking Services Directorate.

4. MSPs
   This section contains the following information:

   - Alphabetical list of MSPs containing biographical information. The information will eventually also include contact details and parliamentary activities.
   - Election results displayed by constituency and by region.
   - Constituencies linked to MSPs. This enables you to find out the identity of your representative in the Scottish Parliament.
   - Register of Interests

5. Welcoming You
   This section provides general information about the Parliament including information about visiting the Parliament. It contains a brief description about how the Parliament works. It also includes a section on the Scottish parliamentary tradition.

6. Young People and Teachers
   This is intended to provide information about the Parliament and is currently under development.

7. The Parliament Buildings
   This section gives information about the temporary home for the Parliament in the Assembly Hall and its future home in the planned building at Holyrood.

Chapter 5

SEARCH STRATEGIES FOR FINDING LEGISLATION

5.1 STATUTES

The searching techniques outlined in this chapter all relate to legislation emanating from the Westminster Parliament. For information services about legislation from the Scottish Parliament, see chapter 4, paras 4.5.2, 4.5.3, 4.5.5 and 4.5.6.

5.1.1 Sources of the text of a recent Bill

Public Bills before Parliament website
http://www.parliament.the-stationery-office.co.uk/pa/pabills.htm
This website is run by the Stationery Office. It contains an alphabetical list of all Public General Bills currently before Parliament. There is a hypertext link to the full text of the Bill. At the top of the entry for each Bill is a reference to which stage the Bill has reached. Some Bills have explanatory notes. Proposed amendments are entered separately under the Bill.

Individual Public Bills are published by The Stationery Office. They form part of a large group of documents known as Parliamentary Papers (see chapter 6, para. 6.11).

Private Bills are more difficult to obtain and you may need to contact the promoter (or his agent) of the Bill.

5.1.2 Finding out which stage a Bill has reached

House of Commons Weekly Information Bulletin (paper and freely available on-line). This is published weekly when the House of Commons is in session. The paper version is published on a Saturday and covers the previous week's events. The full text of the House of Commons Weekly Information Bulletin has been available via the internet since October 1996. The on-line version is published on the following Monday at 12.30 p.m. The web address is:
http://www.parliament.the-stationery-office.co.uk/pa/cm/cmwib.htm

The House of Commons Weekly Information Bulletin includes the following information:

- Reports on the events of the past six days;
- Details of business to be conducted in the forthcoming week (in both Houses);
- Public Legislation — General Notes contains details of abbreviations used in the tables of Bills;
- Cumulative list of Public Bills in the current session;
- Progress of Bills;
- Private Bills in the current session

Public Bills before Parliament website
http://www.parliament.the-stationery-office.co.uk/pa/pabills.htm
See para. 5.1.1 above.

The Daily List is published by The Stationery Office (paper and freely available on-line). The Web address is:
http://www.tso-online.co.uk
Very recent information about a Bill can be found in the *Daily List*, such as the latest developments, the number allocated to a Bill, publication details and whether there have been any amendments moved. The Stationery Office also publishes information about official publications in a Weekly List, Monthly List and Annual Catalogue. See chapter 6, para. 6.11.3.1.

Lawtel (on-line by subscription). This service contains a search facility which allows you to search for Bills by keyword. This takes you to details about the stage the Bill has reached. There is a hypertext link to the full text of the Bill if it is available on the Parliament website. See chapter 13, para. 13.4.2 for more details about Lawtel.

Current Law Monthly Digest. See also chapter 10, para. 10.2. Information about the stages of a Bill is given in the Progress of Bills Table. To find out the stage a bill has reached in the parliamentary process:

⇒ Step 1: Check the most recent Monthly Digest

⇒ Step 2: Turn to the Progress of Bills Table. The bills are arranged in alphabetical order. Opposite the name of the bill will be details of the stage it has reached.

| Example |

Find out which stage the Scottish Enterprise Bill has reached.

⇒ Step 1: Go to the latest Monthly Digest.
⇒ Step 2: Turn to the Progress of Bills Table. Check under ''S'' and locate the entry for the Scottish Enterprise Bill. The name of the Bill is in bold because it is a Government Bill. It is followed by the word ''(Commons)''. This indicates that the Bill originated in the House of Commons. Opposite the entry is the stage the bill has reached. In this case the entry is as follows:

> ''Commons, passed
> Lords, first reading, March 2, 1999 (*Second reading March 22, 1999*)''

The section in italics is provisional.

Journals may contain information about the progress of Bills. In each weekly issue of the *Scots Law Times* there is a News section which contains parliamentary news. This lists new Bills and provides a brief summary of the subject matter. There is also a Progress of Bills section.
Newspapers. The broadsheets contain information about Bills and events in Parliament. This seldom makes the front page unless the Bill is particularly controversial.

5.1.2.1

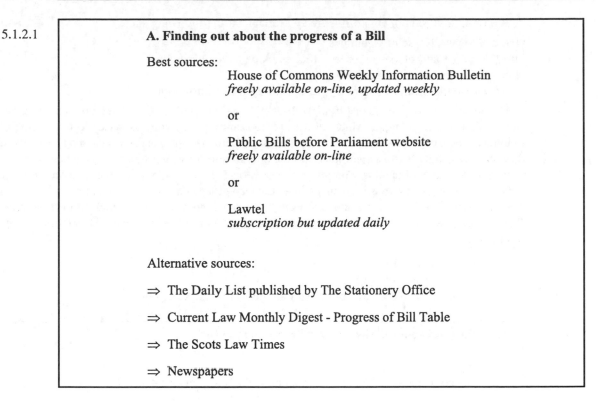

A. Finding out about the progress of a Bill

Best sources:

House of Commons Weekly Information Bulletin
freely available on-line, updated weekly

or

Public Bills before Parliament website
freely available on-line

or

Lawtel
subscription but updated daily

Alternative sources:

⇒ The Daily List published by The Stationery Office

⇒ Current Law Monthly Digest - Progress of Bill Table

⇒ The Scots Law Times

⇒ Newspapers

5.1.3 Finding out about parliamentary debates on a Bill

The House of Commons Weekly Information Bulletin will alert you to the dates of parliamentary debates, see para. 5.1.2.

If the Bill has since become an Act, Current Law Statutes Annotated should contain details of the parliamentary debates relevant to each Act. Look in the first note inserted after the long title.

Parliamentary Debates: Official Report, commonly referred to as Hansard (paper, CD-ROM and on-line), contains a verbatim account of proceedings in Parliament. There are three separate series of Hansard. They cover the House of Commons, the House of Lords and debates of the different Standing Committees when they consider the committee stage of Bills. It is published daily while Parliament is sitting. It is also published weekly and in bound volumes by parliamentary session.

The material appears in columns (like newspapers) and the columns are numbered. Each page contains two columns. References to Hansard are by column number *not* page number. Written answers to parliamentary questions are located in a separate section at the end of the bound volumes. Cumulative indexes are produced throughout the parliamentary session and there is a sessional index in the last bound volume for the session.

The CD-ROM version of Hansard is available from 1988–89. It is updated three times a year. In addition to the information in the bound volumes it contains a database of M.P.s. This gives information about their constituency, party, past and present portfolios and date of entering and, where applicable, leaving Parliament. It is possible to search by keywords, M.P., constituency, portfolio, date, volume, column number.

The on-line version of Hansard is freely available at the following sites:

Hansard for the House of Commons:
http://www.parliament.the-stationery-office.co.uk/pa/cm/cmhansrd.htm
Hansard for the House of Lords:
http://www.parliament.the-stationery-office.co.uk/pa/ld/ldhansrd.htm

The on-line version is available from the 1996–97 session of Parliament. The House of Commons site contains a search engine which allows you to search by keyword (Boolean search), name of individual speaker or question number. The House of Lords website can be searched by a variety of different fields such as Bills, committees off the floor of the House, questions and statements.

Information about Standing Committee Debates on Bills is available on the internet from the 1997–98 session: http://www.parliament.the-stationery-office.co.uk/pa/cm/stand.htm
The information is listed by the title of the Bill being considered. When you click on the title of the Bill you are taken into details of the relevant Standing Committee. You can access the following information:

> Membership of the Committee
> Latest version of the Bill
> Reports of proceedings of the various sittings of the Committee

5.1.3.1

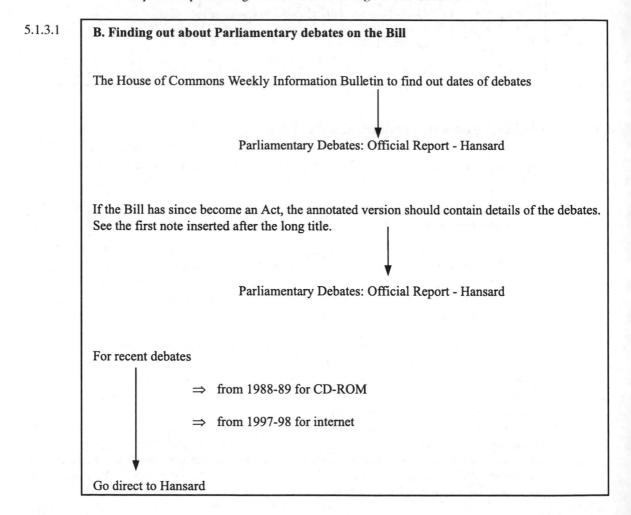

B. Finding out about Parliamentary debates on the Bill

The House of Commons Weekly Information Bulletin to find out dates of debates

Parliamentary Debates: Official Report - Hansard

If the Bill has since become an Act, the annotated version should contain details of the debates. See the first note inserted after the long title.

Parliamentary Debates: Official Report - Hansard

For recent debates

⇒ from 1988-89 for CD-ROM

⇒ from 1997-98 for internet

Go direct to Hansard

5.1.4   Collections of statutes applying to Scotland 1707–1948

For legislation from prior to 1707 see chapter 4, para. 4.2. There are several collections of statutes which applied to Scotland between 1707 and 1948:

Scots Statutes Revised (vols 1–10) covered the period 1707–1900. It includes only Acts applicable to Scotland. Volume 10 includes a subject index to the whole collection. It was continued by *Scots Statutes* which covers the period 1901–1948. This, in turn, was continued from 1949 by Scottish Current Law Statutes, see below.

Public General Statutes affecting Scotland (1848–1947), known as *Blackwood's Acts*, was an annual publication. It included Acts with provisions which related to Scotland. In 1876 legislation from 1707–1847 which was still in force was published in three complementary volumes.

5.1.5   Sources of modern statutes

The official versions of Acts of Parliament are known as the Queen's Printer copies which appear in annual volumes called Public General Acts and Measures, see below. However, these are not the only published editions of an Act. There are many different commercially produced versions of Acts. They may include additional information such as explanatory notes called annotations and/or different search facilities for accessing legislation. Some gather together all legislation relating to a particular subject. Others cover specific periods in time. This means that it is possible for the same piece of legislation to appear in many different publications.

5.1.5.1   *Public General Acts and Measures*

As soon as a Bill receives the Royal Assent it is published as an Act of Parliament by The Stationery Office. Each Act is printed singly and these are known as Queen's Printer copies. The Stationery Office has recently started to publish a separate book of explanatory notes with selected Acts of Parliament. At the end of each year the single Acts are produced together in a publication called *Public General Acts and Measures*. This is the official version of Acts of Parliament. Acts are arranged in chronological order (*i.e.* by chapter number). These do not contain annotations. Alphabetical and chronological lists are contained at the front of each volume. At the end of the final volume for each year are tables of derivations and destinations of the Consolidation Acts for the year. There is also a table called Effects of Legislation. This gives details of Acts (in chronological order) which have been repealed, amended or otherwise affected by legislation passed during the year.

5.1.5.2   *Statutes Revised*

The third edition of *Statutes Revised* covers the period 1235–1948. This is published by HMSO and includes the full text of all Acts in force on December 31, 1948 except pre-1707 Acts of the Parliament of Scotland.

5.1.5.3   *HMSO Website*

Her Majesty's Stationery Office also publishes Acts of Parliament on-line:
http://www.legislation.hmso.gov.uk/acts.htm

This site contains the full text of *all* Public General Acts from the beginning of 1996 and Local Acts from the start of 1997. Acts are available within ten days of their publication in printed form unless they are particularly complex. The material is published in its original form and amendments are not included.

Acts of Parliament do not appear on the web as one document. The reason for this is that, because of their length, it would take an excessive amount of time to load on to your PC. It is usual for a few sections to be grouped together into one document. This means that it takes a lot of time if you want to download a reasonably long Act.

5.1.5.4   *Statutes in Force*

This was published by HMSO but has now practically ceased to exist as an effective information source. Acts were arranged by subject in loose-leaf volumes. The Acts were updated to take account of amendments and repealed Acts were removed. Unfortunately it was never updated frequently enough and now the Acts are no longer amended.

5.1.5.5   *Current Law Statutes Annotated (until 1990 called Scottish Current Law Statutes Annotated)*

Scottish Current Law Statutes Annotated covers 1949–1990; *Current Law Statutes Annotated* covers 1991 to the present.

This part of the Current Law service provides the full text of every Public General Act. (Local and Personal Acts have been included since 1992). The Acts are published in annual volumes and within each volume the Acts are arranged in chronological order. Each Act is annotated by an expert in the relevant field. This means that notes appear throughout the Act explaining its significance. There also tends to be a long introductory note which explains the Act's purpose and puts it into context. It will also refer to the dates of the parliamentary debates on the Bill. There will be notes throughout the Act. The number of notes depends on the complexity of the Act. The notes are intended to clarify the effect of the various sections.

Acts from the current year appear singly in the loose-leaf Statutes Service File. When the more complex statutes first appear they are issued with blue covers. This indicates that only the wording of the statute has been printed and that annotations are still being prepared. See chapter 10, paras 10.6 and 10.7 for more details on Current Law.

How to find details of an Act using Current Law
Check the volume of Statutes Annotated for the appropriate year. The full text with annotations will appear in chronological order.
Alternatively:
A summary of the act will be in the relevant Year Book or Monthly Digest.

| Example |

Find the Local Government (Gaelic Names) Scotland) Act 1997.

⇒ Step 1: Check the Current Law Statutes volumes for 1997. If you know the chapter number, you could check the spines of the volumes to locate the appropriate volume. Otherwise, start by checking the first volume.
⇒ Step 2: Check the alphabetical list of short titles. Opposite the short title is the chapter number.
⇒ Step 3: Turn to the page headed up with the chapter number. The chapter number appears in bold and is followed by a number corresponding to the section number of the Act which appears on that particular page.

5.1.5.6   *Law Reports: Statutes*

These are published by The Incorporated Council of Law Reporting as part of the Law Reports. They include exclusively Scottish legislation. They are not annotated.

5.1.5.7   Justis: *UK Statutes*

This new subscription service contains the full text of all Acts of Parliament from 1880 onwards — there are plans to go back to 1235. The text is as enacted, with visual links between amended and amending legislation. It is currently the only statute law database to contain Scottish legislation. It is available on CD-ROM only and is updated four times a year.

5.1.5.8   *Halsbury's Statutes of England*

This publication provides comprehensive coverage of U.K. legislation but excludes statutes which relate only to Scotland and sections of U.K. statutes which relate to Scotland only. See chapter 7, para. 7.2.

5.1.5.9   *Lexis*

Lexis (on-line by subscription) includes all current Public General Acts for England and Wales. It provides the amended text of the legislation. It does not include exclusively Scottish legislation. Provisions in U.K. Acts which refer to Scotland only are included from 1980. See chapter 13 for more details about Lexis.

5.1.5.10   *Lawtel*

Lawtel (on-line by subscription) indexes statutes and statutory instruments from 1984. Lawtel itself contains only digests of the legislation but it has hypertext links to the full text where it is available on the HMSO site. See chapter 13, para. 13.4.2.

5.1.5.11   *Collections of legislation*

Parliament House Book

The Parliament House Book covers selected areas of private law and court procedure. It includes:

> primary legislation
> delegated legislation
> practice notes
> solicitors practice rules
> notes for guidance issued by public departments

It is published in a loose-leaf format consisting of five volumes. At the front of volumes 1, 3, 4 and 5 are the indices. These consist of alphabetical and chronological indexes of statutes and subordinate legislation covering all five volumes. In addition to this there is also a List of Notes Etc., List of Reports and a Table of Regnal Years.

The Parliament House Book is arranged in different divisions. Within each division the material is arranged chronologically. Statutes are followed by statutory instruments and other regulations, then by tables and notes for guidance. The first page of each division lists its contents. The Parliament House Book is updated four times a year. The date at the foot of each page is the date when the page was last updated. If there is no date there has been no amendment since the Parliament House Book was first published in this form in 1982.

The references given throughout the Parliament House Book are to the division and page number, *e.g.* The Sheriff Courts (Scotland) Act 1971 is referenced as **D** 74. This means that it is contained in Division D at page 74.

N.B.: not all pieces of legislation are printed in full. Statutes may only be printed in part or the statute may be divided up and placed in different divisions of the Parliament House Book.

Volume 1	Indices
	Division A — Fees, Stamps etc.
	Division B — Courts, Upper
	Division D — Courts, Lower
Volume 2	Division C — Greens Annotated Rules of the Court of Session
Volume 3	Indices
	Division E — Licensing
	Division F — Solicitors
	Division G — Legal Aid
	Division H — Bankruptcy and other mercantile statutes
Volume 4	Indices
	Division I — Companies
	Division J — Conveyancing, Land tenure and registration
Volume 5	Indices
	Division K — Family Law
	Division L — Landlord and Tenant
	Division M — Succession, Trusts, Liferents and Judicial Factors
	Division N — Tribunals, Inquiries
	Division O — Valuation for Rating
	* Division P — Practice and Procedure of the Scottish Parliament
	* To be added in December 1999

The criminal procedure section which used to be in the Parliament House Book has now been moved to Renton & Brown's Criminal Procedure Legislation Service.

Specialised collections of legislation

An increasing number of subject-specific collections of legislation are now being produced. They tend to be annotated. Examples include: Renton & Brown's Criminal Procedure Legislation, Scottish Conveyancing Legislation, Scottish Landlord & Tenant Legislation, Scottish Local Government Legislation and Scottish Social Work Legislation.

There are numerous collections of legislation produced for the student market. They tend to contain a selection of subject-specific legislation; some include annotations but many do not. They are usually single-volume paperback works which are updated annually. Texts without annotations are sometimes allowed to be taken into open book exams.

Legislation may also be found in the growing number of loose-leaf encyclopaedias. These tend to reprint the text of selected legislation.

5.2   AIDS TO TRACING STATUTES

There are different types of aids to tracing statutes:

1. Various specialist indexes such as Index to the Statutes (see para. 5.3.1.4 below). There are also indexes contained in collections of legislation, reference works, encyclopaedias and textbooks.

2. Full-text electronic databases such as Lexis and Legislation Direct and Justis — *UK Statutes*. The latter is currently the only statute law database to contain exclusively Scottish legislation.

3. Major collections of statutory material such as *Halsbury's Statutes of England* but this excludes exclusively Scottish legislation.

4. Digests of legislation contained in collections which are indexed in various ways such as Lawtel and the Current Law Year Books.

5. Citators such as Current Law Legislation Citators.

6. There is an increasing amount of recent material freely available via the internet. However, the text of legislation is not updated, which limits the usefulness of this as a source for research.

5.3 SEARCH STRATEGIES FOR FINDING STATUTES

This section deals with the different ways of finding legislation. This will allow you to find legislation from different starting points. There are usually numerous ways of finding legal information. This section contains lists of various alternative sources along with comments as to their strengths and weaknesses. The most comprehensive sources are listed first, followed by the more limited sources. It is not a simple matter of listing the best and worst sources. A lot may depend on the facilities that you have available to you. You may be fortunate enough to have access to a well-resourced law library or you may be faced with finding information with much more limited facilities available to you. Resources are also important. The cost of some of the electronic sources is not inconsiderable and access may be restricted on cost grounds.

The following search strategies are considered:

- Finding statutes by subject. This should allow you to search where you may be interested in a specific subject area. See para. 5.3.1.
- Current status of a statute. It is vital to know whether a statute has been brought into force or whether it has been amended or repealed. See paras 5.3.2 and 5.3.3.
- Finding out about Local and Personal Acts. This is becoming much easier than in the past. However, it is something that you will rarely be expected to do at university. See para. 5.3.4.
- Finding cases on legislation. This covers the situation where you know of a specific legislative provision and you want to find out if any cases have considered it. See chapter 3, para. 3.2.4.

5.3.1 Finding statutes by subject

5.3.1.1 *Major textbooks/reference works*

Look at the Table of Statutes which will be located at the beginning of the book. This will list statutes in chronological order.

The *Stair Memorial Encyclopaedia*. Check the Consolidated Index. This should lead you to the relevant volume. Each subject area has its own Table of Statutes. This information can be updated by checking the Annual Cumulative Supplement and the Service Binder. See chapter 6, para. 6.3.1.1 for more details.

5.3.1.2 *Current Legal Information*

Current Legal Information (on-line by subscription) allows you to search for legislation by keyword. You can search all the databases at once or you could run a search through Badger. It is also possible to browse the Legislation Index. This is arranged alphabetically by short title. Current Legal Information is discussed in chapter 13, para. 13.4.5.

5.3.1.3 *Current Law*

Current Law Year Books and Monthly Digests. Check the subject headings. There are consolidated indexes in the master volumes of the Year Books, see chapter 10, paras 10.2 and 10.3.

5.3.1.4   *Index to the Statutes*

This is published by The Stationery Office. It provides an alphabetical subject index to the statutes in force. Scottish material is included. In areas where the law is markedly different in the two jurisdictions there is a separate section for Scottish legislation at the end of the entry for the subject. It tends to be at least two years out of date.

5.3.1.5   *Halsbury's Statutes*

This is an excellent source of information about legislation — accessed by subject. Unfortunately, it does not include exclusively Scottish legislation, see chapter 7, para. 7.2.1 for details about its use.

5.3.1.6   *Legislation Direct*

This service is available on-line by subscription but does not include exclusively Scottish legislation, see chapter 7, para. 7.2.3.

5.3.1.7   *Lexis*

Lexis (on-line by subscription) includes all current Public General Acts for England and Wales. It does not include exclusively Scottish legislation. Provisions in U.K. Acts which refer to Scotland only are included from 1980. See chapter 13 for more details about Lexis.

5.3.1.8

C. Finding statutes by subject

Best starting point for Scottish material :

      Stair Memorial Encyclopaedia
      comprehensive and updated regularly
      or
      Dedicated textbook
      use the most up to date edition

Alternatives:
⇒   Index to the Statutes
    but it tends to be at least two years out of date
    need to update with another source

⇒   Current Legal Information
    subscription and coverage currently limited

⇒   Current Law Year Books and Monthly Digests
    subject headings can be problematic and consolidating indexes cumbersome

Best source for U.K. material:

      Halsbury's Statutes
      comprehensive with good updating service

Alternatives:
⇒   Legislation Direct
    subscription
⇒   Lexis
    subscription

5.3.2 Current status of a statute—Is It In Force Yet?

5.3.2.1 *The Act itself*

The date the Act comes into force may be the date of Royal Assent or it may be detailed in the commencement section at the end of the Act. See chapter 4, para. 4.3.4, section [8].

5.3.2.2 *Current Law Legislation Citators and Annotated Statutes*

The information in the Citators is updated by the Statutes Service File which contains a Commencement Diary. This notes, alphabetically by statute, the commencement of statutes from January of the current year as initiated by Orders and by statutory provisions. There is also a Commencement Diary covering the year in the annual volumes of Statutes Annotated. From 1992 Commencement Orders have been reprinted in the annual volumes. See chapter 10 for more details.

How to find out if a Commencement Order has been issued in relation to an Act.
Check the Commencement Diary in the relevant Statutes Annotated.
Check the Dates of Commencement Table in the latest Monthly Digest or the Commencement Diary in the Statutes Service File.

Example

Asked in January 1999 — how much of the Scotland Act 1998 had become law?

⇒ Step 1: Check the latest Monthly Digest (December 1998). Look in the Dates of Commencement. The Acts are listed in alphabetical order. The entry for the Scotland Act has the following information:

> "ss. 1–18, 84–116, 125 (part), 126–132, Sched. 1, Sched. 6, Sched. 7, Sched. 8, paras 10, 11, 19, 23(1), 23(6) commenced on Nov 19 1998."

The authority for this is given as s. 130 of the Act.

The legislation citator is available as part of Current Legal Information. However, at present this only covers Acts from 1989 to date.

5.3.2.3 *Is It in Force?*

This is an annual publication which covers the previous 25 years. The current edition is *"Is It in Force 1999?"* and it covers January 1, 1974 to December 31, 1998. This includes Scottish legislation.

The years are presented in chronological order and within each year the statutes are listed alphabetically. Opposite the short title details are given of the relevant commencement provisions. the same Act applies to England/Wales and Scotland but there are differences in, *e.g.* commencement date, this is acknowledged by separating the Scottish information and following it with an "(S)".

Note that this publication does not include full information on amendments and repeals. You should use other publications to check this information, see para. 5.3.3. As it is an annual publication it is always out of date so be sure to use another source to check from the date of publication to the present. There is an on-line version which is available from Butterworths as part of the Legislation Direct database. The on-line version is updated as new Commencement Orders are issued.

Example

Using the paper version of *Is It in Force?*

Has s. 2 of the Crime and Punishment (Scotland) Act 1997 been brought into force?

Check the latest edition of *Is It in Force?* Turn to the entries for 1997. The statutes are listed in alphabetical order, so check under "C". You will find the title of the Act and the sections listed underneath. Opposite s. 2 is the information that it came into force on October 20, 1997. The authority is S.I. 1997 No. 2323.

5.3.2.4 *Lawtel*

This service is available on-line by subscription. It is updated daily and covers all statutes since 1984. This *includes* Acts applying solely to Scotland. Enter the commencement and repeal section. You can search by keyword. It will list the sections of the Act in a table, with entries relating to commencement, amendment and repeal. See chapter 13, para. 13.4.2.

5.3.2.5 *Journals*

Journals such as *Scots Law Times* contain information about legislation which is coming into force.

5.3.2.6 *The Stationery Office Daily, Weekly or Monthly Lists*

These will contain details of Commencement Orders. See chapter 6, para. 6.11.3.1.
The free on-line version of the Daily List:
http://www.tso-online.co.uk

5.3.2.7 *Lexis*

Available on-line by subscription, see chapter 13.

5.3.2.8 See diagram on the facing page

5.3.3   Current status of a statute—Finding Amendments And Repeals

5.3.3.1 *Current Law Legislation Citator*

This is by far the easiest way of locating changes to Scottish legislation — see the worked example below and chapter 10, para. 10.5. The legislation citator is available as part of Current Legal Information. However, at present this only covers Acts from 1989 to date.

5.3.2.8

D. Finding out about whether a statute is in force?

First step : Check the commencement section of the Act.

If no entry ⟶ statute came into force when received royal assent

If entry says specific date or time period ⟶ that is relevant date

If entry says Act (or part of it) to come into force at time set by Minister

You need to check to see if a Commencement Order has been issued AND
find out which part (s) of the Act have been brought into force.

Sources:

⟹ Commencement diaries in Current Law Legislation Citators and Annotated Statutes

⟹ Is It in Force?

⟹ Lawtel

⟹ Journals such as Scots Law Times

⟹ The Stationery Office Daily, Weekly or Monthly Lists.

⟹ Lexis

Using Current Law to find out if an Act has been amended or repealed.
⟹ Step 1: Check the Statute Citators in the volumes of Legislation Citators in chronological order starting from the date of the Act. In order to locate the chapter number, check the alphabetical list of Acts at the beginning of the volume. Once armed with the chapter number you can turn to the Statute Citator itself. Under the entry for the Act, the citator will list any amendments that have been made.
⟹ Step 2: In order to be aware of all amendments (up to the last month) check through all the Statute Citators up to the most recent update for the citator in the Statutes Service File.

Example

Find out if any amendments have been made to the Freshwater and Salmon Fisheries (Scotland) Act 1976?

⇒ Step 1: Check the Statute Citator in the Legislation Citators volume 1972–88. In order to locate the chapter number, check the alphabetical list of Acts at the beginning of the volume. Once armed with the chapter number (22) you can turn to the citator itself. Look under 1976 and within that year at the entry for 22. In this case the entry contains the following information:

> "Royal assent, June 10, 1976
> S. 1 — a list of various orders issued under this section
> s. 6, 7, 9, 10 amended by 1981, c.29, s. 38*
> s. 7, Sched. 3 amended and repealed in pt: 1986, c.62, Sched. 4
> Sched. 3 see *Taddale Properties v. IRC* [1988] S.T.C. 303, C.A."

From this information we can see that several sections of the Act had been amended by the end of 1988.

⇒ Step 2: Check the Statute Citator in the Legislation Citators volume 1989–95. Again check under 1976 number 22. In this case the entry contains the following information:

> "s. 1 — a list of various orders issued under this section
> s. 1 amended: 1995, c.40, Sched. 4 (S)
> Sched. 1, order 95/2683."

This means that we can now add s. 1 to the list of sections which have been amended.

⇒ Step 3: Check the Statute Citator in the Legislation Citators volume 1996–98. The only entry is:

> "s. 1 enabling S.I. 96/57, S.I. 96/58."

This shows that no further amendments have taken place.

⇒ Step 4: Check the latest edition of the statute citator in the Statutes Service File. Again check under 1976, no. 22. This time there is no entry at all for this Act. This means that no developments have taken place.

We can now be certain that (up to the last month) the only sections of the Freshwater and Salmon Fisheries (Scotland) Act 1976 to have been amended are ss. 1, 6, 7, 9, 10 and Sched. 3.

*Note that if you wanted to discover exactly how the Act had been changed you would need to look at the amending legislation. In order to identify the short title from the information provided in the Statute Citator you could (i) look in the same citator under 1981, c. 29 and find the short title or (ii) go to the 1981 volume of Statutes Annotated and check the chronological list of statutes. If you use (ii) you will then have instant access to the text of the Act itself. The short title in this case is the Fisheries Act 1981.

5.3.3.2   *Halsbury's Statutes*

Halsbury's Statutes is a great source for U.K. legislation. It contains the amended text of legislation currently in force and has an effective updating service. Unfortunately, it does not include exclusively Scottish legislation, see chapter 7, para. 7.2.1 for details about its use.

5.3.3.3   *Chronological Table of the Statutes*

This is published annually by The Stationery Office and is in two volumes. It is a chronological table of the statutes for the period 1235 to the year of publication. Statutes are listed chronologically by year and chapter number. When the title of the Act appears in italics it means it has been repealed. If it appears in bold type then the Act is still, at least in part, in force. Details of amendments and repeals are given. Acts of the pre-1707 Parliaments of Scotland are included in a separate table at the end of the second volume. This is an annual publication but tends to be a couple of years out of date. This greatly reduces its usefulness. Another method would have to be employed to bring your search in the Chronological Table of Statutes up to date.

5.3.3.4   *Lawtel*

Lawtel (on-line by subscription)
This service is updated daily and covers all statutes since 1984. This *includes* Acts applying solely to Scotland. Enter the commencement and repeal section. You can search by keyword. It will list the sections of the Act in a table with entries relating to commencement, amendment and repeal. See chapter 13, para. 13.4.2.

5.3.3.5   *Lexis*

Available on-line by subscription, see chapter 13, para. 13.4.3.

5.3.3.6

E. Finding amendments and repeals

Most comprehensive source for Scottish material:

    Current Law Legislation Citator

Alternatives:

⇒   Chronological Table to the Statutes
    tends to be a couple of years out of date

⇒   Lawtel
    The most up-to-date source for statutes from 1984

Most comprehensive source for UK material:

    Halsbury's Statutes

    Lexis

5.3.4   Aids to tracing Local and Personal Acts

5.3.4.1   *Chronological Table of Private and Personal Acts 1539–1997*

Published by The Stationery Office in 1999. This lists the Private and Personal Acts passed by the Westminster Parliaments between 1539 and the end of 1997. They are listed in chronological order along with references to amendments and repeals. Also recently published is the *Statute Law Revision: Report on the Chronological Table of Private and Personal Acts 1539–1997*. The table and the reports have been prepared jointly by the Law Commissions of Scotland and England. This has superseded the *Chronological Table of Local Legislation* which was published by HMSO in 1996. It covered the period 1797 to 1992.

5.3.4.2   *Chronological Table of the Statutes*

Has a table of amendments and repeals to Local and Personal legislation which have taken place since 1974.

5.3.4.3   *Index to Local and Personal Acts 1801–1947/Supplementary Index to Local and Personal Acts 1948–1966*

Published by HMSO. These allow you to locate Local and Personal Acts by subject. This work has been continued by an annual table and index.

5.3.4.4   Local and Personal Acts are listed in alphabetical order in the bound volumes of Public General Acts and Measures.

5.3.4.5   The Daily List and its cumulative versions list Local and Personal Acts.

5.3.5   **Sources of Local and Personal Acts**

From 1992 the full text of Local and Personal Acts is published in the final volume of Current Law Annotated Statutes for the year.

The full text of Local and Personal Acts from the beginning of 1997 is freely available via HMSO's website. They appear in original format and do not take account of amendments. http://www.legislation.hmso.gov.uk/acts.htm

The texts of older Local and Personal Acts can be difficult to locate. Some can be purchased from The Stationery Office. However, you may have to consult one of the collections of Local and Personal Acts held at different libraries (see below) or approach a library local to the area covered by the Act or contact the organisation directly. Collections of Scottish Local and Personal Acts are held by: Aberdeen University library, the Advocates' Library, Edinburgh University library, Glasgow University, Mitchell library, St Andrews University library, Scottish Record Office, Scottish Office Solicitors' library and the Signet library.

5.4   STATUTORY INSTRUMENTS

Statutory instruments are not printed with statutes. They are printed separately and then published in annual volumes. Not all statutory instruments are automatically published — local statutory instruments are not always published by The Stationery Office. However, all statutory instruments which are of general application will be published.

As stated in chapter 4, para. 4.4.1 Scottish statutory instruments have a main number and an additional number. The additional number relates to its sequence in the issue of Scottish statutory instruments during a year. The Scottish number should be ignored when trying to trace an instrument. The indexes all use the main number for the reference.

5.4.1   **Sources of statutory instruments**

1. There is an official consolidation called *Statutory Rules and Orders and Statutory Instruments Revised*. This contains all statutory instruments in force up to the end of 1948 and is arranged under subject headings.

    Statutory instruments (1949–) is an official publication published by The Stationery Office. It contains the full text of general statutory instruments. It is made up of annual volumes arranged in numerical order with a subject index. Before 1961 it was arranged by subject with a numerical index. It contains a list of local statutory instruments (both printed and non-printed).

    General statutory instruments are published individually and can be purchased from The Stationery Office.

2. *SI-CD, Statutory instruments on CD-ROM*
    This database contains the full text of statutory instruments from 1987 to date and a short form of statutory instruments from 1980 onwards. It is updated six times a year. It includes Scottish statutory instruments. A statutory instrument can be traced by keyword, number and title.

3. From the beginning of 1997 all new statutory instruments are published in full text on the internet by HMSO. Access is free:
    http://www.hmso.gov.uk/stat.htm
    They are available within 15 days of their publication in printed form unless they are particularly complex. They are produced in chronological and numerical order. The site can be searched by year and by number. There is also a search engine which allows you to search by keyword(s) and conduct a Boolean search.

    From November 1997 all new draft statutory instruments which are awaiting approval are available at this site. They are available until superseded by an official version or withdrawn. They are arranged by subject.

4. *Halsbury's Statutory Instruments* contains information on every current statutory instrument of general application in England and Wales. It is updated on a monthly basis. It does not reprint *all* statutory instruments, many are only summarised. It does not include exclusively Scottish statutory instruments. This is covered in more detail in chapter 7, para. 7.2.2.

5. Specialist loose-leaf encyclopaedias may contain copies of selected statutory instruments relevant to their subject area.

6. Statutory instruments are digested in the Year Books and Monthly Digests of Current Law. The full text of Commencement Orders is printed in the Year Books (for each successive year since 1992) and in the loose-leaf service file (for the current year).

7. Lexis (on-line by subscription) Statutory instruments applying only to Scotland are not included. Full texts of U.K. statutory instruments are included. The text is amended to take account of any changes.

Note
For sources of Scottish statutory instruments emanating from the Scottish Parliament, see chapter 4, para. 4.5.3.

Statutory instruments made by the National Assembly for Wales are accessible on the internet: http://www.wales-legislation.hmso.gov.uk

5.4.1.1   *Sources of Acts of Sederunt, Acts of Adjournal*

These appear in the Statutory Instrument series published by The Stationery Office, see above. They also appear in the *Scots Law Times* when they are enacted. They were included in Current Law Statutes Annotated but this ceased from 1991 onwards.

An annotated version of Acts of Sederunt which are currently in force is contained in the volume 2 of the *Parliament House Book*. An annotated version of Acts of Adjournal currently in force is contained in *Renton & Brown's Criminal Procedure Legislation*.

5.4.2   Aids to tracing statutory instruments

5.4.2.1   *Table of Government Orders*

This useful publication lists statutory instruments in chronological order and numerically within each year. The title is given in bold if the instrument (or any part of it) is still in force. If the whole instrument has been revoked the title appears in italics. If it is still in force brief details are given of any amendments effected after 1948. If revoked, brief details are given of the revoking provision. Unfortunately the publication is irregular and tends to be out of date by several years.

5.4.2.2   *Index to Government Orders*

Published by The Stationery Office, this lists statutory instruments under subject headings. It is a two-volume work which is published every two years, with a supplement between editions. This will help you find whether a statutory instrument is in force on a given subject. The green paper indexes at the beginning of the volume contain a Table of Statutes, which lists enabling Acts along with the relevant sections, and details of the statutory instruments issued under these powers are listed beneath. A reference is also given to the subject heading. This table allows you to locate statutory instruments made under a particular Act.

5.4.2.3   *List of statutory instruments*

The monthly *List of Statutory instruments* is published by The Stationery Office. It includes details of general and local statutory instruments (printed and non-printed) published during the previous month. They are arranged under subject headings. Each entry includes information about the:

> enabling power,
> date of issue,
> date the instrument was made,
> date the instrument was laid,
> date it comes into force,
> effect on other legislation,
> territorial extent,
> classification.

The same statutory instruments are also listed numerically. There are separate lists of instruments with subsidiary numbers. This section contains a list of Scottish statutory instruments. There are also separate lists for Commencement Orders, Orders in Council relating to Northern Ireland and instruments relating to English court fees and procedure. There is also a cumulative subject index and a list of Northern Ireland statutory rules. The publication is consolidated at the end of a year and appears as an annual *List of Statutory instruments*.

5.4.2.4   *Halsbury's Statutory Instruments*

See chapter 7, para. 7.2.2.

5.4.2.5   *SI-CD Statutory Instruments on CD-ROM*

See para. 5.4.1.

5.4.2.6   *Current Law*

The Current Law Statutory Instrument Citators (1993–) allow you to trace new statutory instruments and amendments and revocations. See chapter 10, para. 10.5.2.

5.4.2.7   *Lawtel (on-line by subscription)*

Lawtel indexes statutory instruments from 1984. See chapter 13, para. 13.4.2.

5.4.2.8   *Lexis (on-line by subscription)*

See chapter 5, para. 5.4.1 and chapter 13, para. 13.4.3.

5.4.2.9   *Daily List*

The *Daily List* published by The Stationery Office (see chapter 6, para. 6.11.3.1) lists statutory instruments published by the Stationery Office.

Information about very recent statutory instruments will also be available in journals such as the *Scots Law Times* and in England the *New Law Journal* and the *Solicitors' Journal*.

5.4.2.10

F. Aids to tracing statutory instruments

Sources for Scottish material:

    Table of Government Orders
    need to update with another source

    Index to Government Orders
    need to update with another source

    List of Statutory Instruments
    annual and monthly

    S.I.-CD Statutory Instruments on CD-ROM
    from 1987

    Current Law
    from 1993

    Daily List

    Lawtel
    from 1984, updated daily

Best sources for UK material:

    Halsbury's Statutory Instruments

    Lexis

5.4.3   Finding statutory instruments by subject

5.4.3.1   *Best sources for Scottish material*

Index to Government Orders (see para. 5.4.2.2) updated by Lawtel.
or
Stair Memorial Encyclopaedia. Check the Consolidated Index. This lists detailed subject headings and will lead you to the relevant volume. You can update this information by checking the Annual Cumulative Supplement and the Service Binder.
Alternatives:
SI-CD Statutory Instruments on CD-ROM; (see para. 5.4.1)
General reference work/text book;
Current Law Yearbooks and Monthly Digests. (see chapter 10)

5.4.3.2   *Best source for U.K. material*

Halsbury's Statutory Instruments (see chapter 7, para. 7.2.2)
Alternative:
Lexis (on-line by subscription).

5.4.4   Current status of statutory instruments — finding amendment and repeals

5.4.4.1   *Best source for Scottish material*

Current Law Statutory Instrument Citator. See worked example below at para. 5.4.4.4 and chapter 10, for more details. Its disadvantage is that it only dates from 1993 onwards.

5.4.4.2   *Best source for checking pre-1993 amendments to statutory instruments*

Table of Government Orders. Entries in bold type are still wholly or partly in force and details of any amendment and repeals are noted. See worked example below at para. 5.4.4.5.
Alternative:
Lawtel (on-line by subscription) has information about amendments and repeals from 1984.

5.4.4.3   *Best source for U.K. material*

Halsbury's Statutory Instruments. This is up to date to within a month and contains the amended versions of statutory instruments. (see chapter 7, para. 7.2.2).
Alternatives:
Lexis (on-line by subscription). This also contains the amended versions of statutory instruments. (see chapter 13, para. 13.4.3).
SI-CD Statutory Instruments on CD-ROM. This contains statutory instruments in full text from 1987 to date. The text is the original and not the amended form. See para. 5.4.1.

5.4.4.4   **Using Current Law to find if a statutory instrument has been amended or revoked.**
⇒ Step 1: Check the Statutory Instrument Citators in the volumes of Legislation Citators in chronological order starting from the date of the statutory instrument. You will need to know the number of the statutory instrument in order to search for it. Under the entry for the statutory instrument, the citator will list any amendments that have been made.
⇒ Step 2: In order to be aware of all amendments (up to the last month) check through all the Statutory Instrument Citators up to the most recent update for the citator in the Statutes Service File.

> Example

Find out if the Control of Pollution (Silage, Slurry & Agricultural Fuel Oil) (Scotland) Regulations 1991 have been amended.

⇒ Step 1: The Statutory Instrument Citators started to appear from the beginning of 1993. How can we check if the regulations changed between 1991 and 1993?

Check the Table of Statutory Instruments Affected 1989–92 which appears as Appendix 2 of the Legislation Citator volume 1989–1995. Check under 1991. The statutory instruments are listed in numerical order. Check under 346. There is no entry, therefore there were no amendments made during this period.

⇒ Step 2: Check the Statutory Instrument Citator 1993–1995 in the Legislation Citator volume 1989–1995. Check under 1991. The material is listed in numerical order. Check for number 346. There is no mention of the regulation, therefore no developments have taken place.

⇒ Step 3: Check the Statutory Instrument Citator in the Legislation Citators volume 1996–98. Check under 1991. The entry shows that the regulations were amended by S.I. 96 No. 973, Reg. 2, Sched. para. 12.

⇒ Step 4: How do you find out the full title of the statutory instrument which amended the regulations? Check earlier in the same volume of the Legislation Citators — under 1996 number 973. You will find the statutory instrument is called the Environment Act 1995 (Consequential & Transitional Provisions) (Scotland) Regulations 1996.

5.4.4.5   **Using the Table of Government Orders to find out about amendments to statutory instruments.**

Find out if the Pensions Appeal Tribunals (Scotland) (Amendment) Rules 1979 No. 94 are still in force.

Go to the latest edition of the Table of Government Orders. It is arranged chronologically so turn to 1979 and look down the numbers for 94. The title of the rules is in italics. This means that they are no longer in force. They were revoked by 1981/500.

5.4.5   **Finding statutory instruments made under the enabling Act**

5.4.5.1   *Best source for Scottish material*

Current Law Statute Citator (see worked example at para. 5.4.5.4 and chapter 10, para. 10.5 below).
Alternative:
The Index to Government Orders (see para. 5.4.2.2 above). It will always be out of date and you will need to update your search by checking Current Law.

5.4.5.2   *Best source for U.K. material*

Halsbury's Statutes of England (see chapter 7, para. 7.2.1).

5.4.5.3   *Most up to date source for material after 1984*

Lawtel (on-line by subscription), (see chapter 13, para. 13.4.2).

5.4.5.4 **Using Current Law to find out if any statutory instruments been made under an Act or section of an Act?**

⇒ Step 1: Check through the Legislation Citators in chronological order. Look under the piece of legislation. If any statutory instruments been made under the Act, their details will appear opposite the statute or section thereof.

⇒ Step 2:You should then check the most recent update for the citator in the Statutes Service File.

Example

Have any statutory instruments been made under s. 175 of the Criminal Procedure (Scotland) Act 1995?

⇒ Step 1: Check the Statute Citator in the Legislation Citators volume 1989–95. In order to locate the chapter number, check the alphabetical list of Acts at the beginning of the volume. You find that it is c. 46. Once armed with the chapter number you can turn to the citator itself. Look under 1995 and within that year at the entry for 46. The entry just mentions when the Act got the Royal Assent.

⇒ Step 2: Check the Statute Citator in the Legislation Citators volume 1996–98. Check under s. 175 and it says "enabling SI 96/2548". This means that S.I. 96 No. 2548 has been made under s. 175.

⇒ Step 3: Check the latest edition of the statute citator in the Statutes Service File. This time there is no mention of any statutory instruments under s. 175.

We can now be certain that (up to the last month) the only statutory instrument to be made under s. 175 of the Criminal Procedure (Scotland) Act 1995 is S.I. 1996 No. 2548.

5.4.5.5 **Using Current Law to find out about a statutory instrument made under an Act of Parliament**

⇒ Step 1: You need to know either the year or full citation of the statutory instrument. If you know the year and its name, check the Alphabetical List of Statutory Instruments for the year in the appropriate Year Book. If you know the full citation and not the name of the statutory instrument, check the Numerical List of Statutory Instruments for the year in the appropriate Year Book. In both cases opposite the entry for the statutory instrument will be a reference to a paragraph number.

⇒ Step 2: Turn to the appropriate paragraph and you will find a digest of the statutory instrument. It will provide details of its full title, a short summary of its content, details of the legislation it is made under and the date it was brought into force.

Example

Find details of S.I. 1996 No. 2548.

⇒ Step 1: Check the Numerical List of Statutory Instruments in the 1996 Year Book. Opposite 2548 is a paragraph reference for a summary of the statutory instrument — paragraph 6791.

⇒ Step 2: Turn to paragraph 6791. It will provide you with the following details about the statutory instrument:

Full title (Prosecutor's Right of Appeal in Summary Proceedings (Scotland) Order 1996 S.I. 1996, 2548 (S197)).

Legislation it is made under: The Criminal Procedure (Scotland) Act 1995 s. 175(4).

Date brought into force: November 1, 1996.

Summary of content: The Criminal Procedure (Scotland) Act 1995, s. 175(4) enables the Secretary of State by order to specify a class of case in summary proceedings in which the prosecutor may appeal to the High Court against the sentence or other disposal passed or made on the grounds that the sentence or disposal is unduly lenient or otherwise inappropriate. This Order specifies the class of case for this purpose as being any case in which, on or after November 1, 1996, the sentence or other disposal is passed or made.

Further reading

A. Bradney *et al.*, *How to Study Law* (3rd ed., Sweet & Maxwell, 1995).

P. Clinch, *Using a Law Library* (Blackstone, 1992).

J. Dane and P.A. Thomas, *How to Use a Law Library* (3rd ed., Sweet & Maxwell, 1996), chapter 8.

D.R. Hart, "Scotland" in J. Winterton and E.M. Moys, *Information Sources in Law* (2nd ed., Bowker Saur, 1997).

G. Holburn, *Butterworths Legal Research Guide* (Butterworths, 1993), chapter 3.

D.D. Mackey, *How to Use a Scottish law library* (W. Green, 1992).

V. Stevenson, *Legal Research in Scotland* (2nd ed., Legal Information Resources Ltd, 1997).

Chapter 6

INSTITUTIONAL WRITERS AND SECONDARY SOURCES OF SCOTS LAW

6.1 ### INTRODUCTION

This chapter contains short sections on a range of information sources of relevance to the Scots lawyer. Some of the sources could be described as exclusively legal but other sources cover many different areas, including law. Many of the information sources are U.K.-wide and, where this is the case, the Scottish element has been stressed.

6.2 ## Institutional Writers

Institutional writings are a closed class of works which have considerable authority. They are the third formal source of Scots law, after legislation and case law. As you will see from the dates of the works given below they were all written a considerable time ago. However, you should not infer that they are unimportant today. They are still taken to represent the law if there is no statute or case law on a point in an area where society's norms have undergone little fundamental change. It is no longer true to say that the Scots lawyer frequently turns to the works of the Institutional Writers in day to day practice. However, the influence of these works is still very much with us. In the past they have had considerable influence on the development of case law and the doctrine of judicial precedent means that this will endure long into the next century.

The list of Institutional Writers is a closed list in that no new works may be added to it. However, there is no unanimity as to the complete list and you will find that it varies. The most widely accepted institutional works are:

> Civil law:
>
> Sir Thomas Craig, *Jus Feudale*, 1603
>
> Andrew McDouall, Lord Bankton, *An Institute of the Laws of Scotland*, 1751
>
> James Dalrymple (Viscount Stair), *The Institutions of the Law of Scotland*, 1681
>
> John Erskine, *An Institute of the Law of Scotland*, 1773
>
> George Joseph Bell, *Commentaries on the Law of Scotland*, 1804 and *Principles of the Law of Scotland*, 1829

Criminal law:

Sir George Mackenzie, *The Laws and Customs of Scotland in Matters Criminal*, 1678

David Hume, *Commentaries on the Law of Scotland Respecting Crimes*, 1797

Archibald Alison, *Principles of the Criminal Law of Scotland*, 1832 and *Practice of the Criminal Law of Scotland*, 1833.

6.3   REFERENCE WORKS

6.3.1   Legal Encyclopaedias

6.3.1.1   *The Laws of Scotland: Stair Memorial Encyclopaedia*

This encyclopaedia gives a commentary on Scots law. It is arranged alphabetically in broad areas of the law and consists of substantial articles on each area. The style of the articles varies as they are written by many different contributors. Each contributor has specialist knowledge of the area of law discussed. Within each area of law, the articles are divided into numbered paragraphs. These are the basis of the referencing system for the encyclopaedia. References are to the paragraph number not the page number.

The encyclopaedia consists of 25 volumes which began to appear from 1986 onwards. The final volume was published in 1996. Each volume consists of the following:

> List of abbreviations
> Table of Statutes
> Table of Orders, Rules and Regulations
> Table of Other Enactments
> Table of Cases
> Articles in alphabetical order of the subject area with each subject area having its own table of contents

At the back of the volume there is an index. There is one index for each subject covered in that volume.

As some of the volumes are becoming increasingly out of date a re-issuing programme has started. Each new issue is to be in a separate booklet to be stored in a binder as opposed to bound volumes. This may cause confusion as the re-issued subject will supersede the subject in the original bound volume but the bound volume will still have to remain on the shelf until all subjects within it are re-issued.

The encyclopaedia is kept up to date by an annual Cumulative Supplement. This brings all the volumes up to date to December 31 of the previous year. The Cumulative Supplement contains:

> Table of Statutes
> Table of Orders, Rules and Regulations
> Table of Cases
> Updates on a volume by volume basis.

Further updating is provided by the loose-leaf Service Binder. Changes are listed by volume number and then by subject within the volume. The Service Binder is updated three times a year. It consists of:

>   Noter-up
>   Glossaries of Scottish and E.C. legal terms
>   Tables of: Statutes
>   Orders, Rules and Regulations
>   Other enactments
>   Cases
>   Competition Decisions and Reports

The current issue of *Is It In Force?* is kept up to date in the Service Binder.

A Consolidated Index was published in 1997. It is organised in alphabetical order of subject. References are to volume and paragraph number. Volume numbers are in bold.

A Consolidated Table of Cases and Consolidated Tables of Statutes, Orders etc. were published in 1996. The Table of Cases is listed by first party's name. This is useful for tracing Scottish cases. The Consolidated Tables of Statutes, Orders etc. consist of consolidated tables of: Statutes, Orders, Rules and Regulations, E.C. legislation, Treaties and Conventions and other enactments.

Using the Stair Memorial Encyclopaedia

To search by subject:

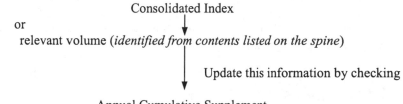

To access information from a case name:

Consolidated Table of Cases
↓
relevant volume

To access information by title of statute:

Consolidated Table of Statutes, Orders, etc.
↓
relevant volume

See also the worked example using the *Stair Memorial Encyclopedia* in chapter 3, para. 3.2.2.11.

6.3.1.2 *Halsbury's Laws of England*

Halsbury's Laws of England is the equivalent of the *Stair Memorial Encyclopaedia* for English law — see chapter 7, para. 7.4.

6.3.2 Reference Books

Reference works tend to run to many editions and it is important to make sure that you use the most up to date edition. Examples are Gloag & Henderson, *An Introduction to the Laws of Scotland* (10th ed., 1995) and D.M. Walker, *Principles of Scottish Private Law* (4th ed., 1989). D.M. Walker's *Oxford Companion to Law* (1980) is a single volume work which is becoming increasingly dated but is still very useful, particularly as a starting point for a literature search.

6.3.3 Loose-leaf Encyclopedias

There are now an increasing number of specialist encyclopedias covering a variety of subjects. They tend to be produced as loose-leaf publications which are updated regularly. Always make sure that you check the date of the most recent update. This is usually indicated at the beginning of the work. Loose-leaf publications are updated by the removal of out-of-date pages and the insertion of new pages. It is not uncommon to find that pages have been misfiled. Great care should be taken when consulting such publications.

Examples of specialist encyclopedias include: *Scottish Planning Encyclopedia*, *Renton & Brown's Criminal Procedure*, *Butterworth's Scottish Family Law Service*, *McEwan & Paton on Damages for Personal Injuries in Scotland*, *Scottish Financial Services Manual*, *Employment Tribunal Practice in Scotland*, *Armour on Valuation for Rating*, *Encyclopaedia of Health & Safety at Work*, *Garner's Environmental Law*, *Harvey on Industrial Relations and Employment Law* and *Encyclopaedia of Information Technology Law*.

6.4 DICTIONARIES

Language is the everyday tool of the lawyer and the precise meaning of words is very important. General English dictionaries are used but there are two types of dictionary which are more important for lawyers. Judicial dictionaries contain definitions given to words by the judiciary. You would consult a judicial dictionary to find out how a judge had defined a certain word. A legal dictionary seeks to explain technical legal terms in a way that can be understood by the student or lay person. Legal dictionaries are not authoritative. Legal dictionaries are often referred to as glossaries.

6.4.1 Judicial Dictionaries

6.4.1.1 *Scottish*

Scottish Contemporary Judicial Dictionary of Words & Phrases by W.J. Stewart (1995). This is a dictionary of words and phrases interpreted by the Scottish courts. It claims to cover every case in which a word has been judicially considered between 1946 and 1993.
Scottish Judicial Dictionary: Dictionary of Words & Phrases by A.W. Dalrymple and A.D. Gibb (1946). This work is a dictionary of words and phrases interpreted by the Scottish supreme courts (not the sheriff court) between 1800–1944.

6.4.1.2 *United Kingdom*

Stroud's Judicial Dictionary of Words and Phrases. The fifth edition of this work consists of six volumes published in 1986. It is updated by cumulative supplements.
Words and Phrases Legally Defined. The third edition of this work was published in four volumes in 1987 and it is also updated by supplements.

Health warning: you should update any search carried out in the above dictionaries by checking their date of publication and using the Words and Phrases Tables in Current Law (or Halsbury's Laws) to bring the search up to the present.

6.4.2 Legal Dictionaries/Glossaries

6.4.2.1 *Scottish*

The classic dictionary of Scots law is *Bell's Dictionary and Digest of the Law of Scotland* (7th ed., 1890). More modern works include:
Green's Glossary of Scottish Legal Terms by A.G.M. Duncan (3rd ed., W. Green, Edinburgh 1992).
Glossary: Scottish Legal Terms, Latin Maxims and EU Legal Terms, R.P. Moore (ed) (Butterworths and The Law Society of Scotland, Edinburgh 1992).
Latin Maxims & Phrases by J. Trayner (4th ed., W. Green, Edinburgh 1993).
Scots Law Terms and Expressions by J.A. Beaton (W. Green, Edinburgh 1982).
A.D. Gibb, *Students' Glossary of Scottish Legal Terms* (2nd ed., W. Green, Edinburgh 1982).
The Laws of Scotland: Stair Memorial Encyclopaedia contains a glossary in the loose-leaf Service Binder. It consists of two parts: Scottish legal terms and Latin maxims and terms used in E.C. law.

6.4.2.2 *English*

Jowitt's Dictionary of English Law. The second edition consisted of two volumes published in 1977. There is a 1985 supplement. Other, shorter dictionaries include: *Concise Dictionary of Law*, P.G. Osborn (8th ed., 1993), *Concise Dictionary of Law* (3rd ed., 1994), *Law Dictionary*, H.N. Mozley and G.C. Whiteley (11th ed., 1993) and *Dictionary of Law*, L.B. Curzon (4th ed., 1993).

6.5 BOOKS AND SEARCH STRATEGIES FOR BOOKS

6.5.1 Legal Books

Legal books contain certain unique features which help the researcher find information. These features include:

1. A statement (usually in the *preface*) of a date up to which the law can be taken as accurate. It is very important that you are aware of this date. It alerts you to the period from which you will have to update your research. The timescale of the publishing process means that most law books are at least six months out of date on the day they are published. You will always need to update information found in a book.

2. *Table of abbreviations.* This will give you the meaning of any abbreviations used in the text.

3. *Table of cases.* This lists all the cases referred to in the text in alphabetical order of the first named party. If you want to find discussion of a case, check this table and it will refer you to the relevant part of the text.

4. *Tables of statutes.* This is a chronological list of all the statutes referred to in the text. This means that if you want to search for discussion of a specific piece of legislation, you can check this table and it will refer you to the relevant page of the text.

One way of finding out about books on a certain subject is to search your library catalogue using a keyword search. It is now easy to search other university libraries via the internet. Another way of finding out about books on legal topics is to search a legal bibliography. They contain lists of books grouped under subject headings.

6.5.2   Legal Bibliographies

D. Raistrick, *Lawyers' Law Books* (3rd ed., Bowker Saur, 1997). This contains bibliographical listings by subject. It includes encyclopaedias, periodicals and texts. It concentrates on U.K. legal literature but does include material relating to other legal jurisdictions. There is a section on Scots law and various Scots terms appear, *e.g.* delict.

Information Sources in Law, J. Winterton and E.M. Moys (eds.) (2nd ed., Bowker Saur, 1997).This is a very useful book. It is designed to provide a starting point for research in an unfamiliar area. It contains chapters written by information specialists in many different areas ranging from the law of the E.U., Albania, Austria to Turkey and the states of the former Yugoslavia.

Scottish Current Law Year Books and Monthly Digests contain details of books and articles. The Monthly Digests are a useful way of finding out about recent publications.

Another useful source of information about legal books is Hammock's Legal Catalogue. It is published annually and contains details of many legal texts arranged under subject headings. Individual publishers' catalogues can also be helpful. They are available both on-line and in paper versions.

For information about older Scottish material: *An Introductory Survey of the Sources and Literature of Scots Law*, Publication of the Stair Society, No. 1, Stair Society, Edinburgh, 1936. Information on older U.K. material: Sweet & Maxwell's *Legal Bibliography of the British Commonwealth of Nations* (2nd ed., Sweet & Maxwell, 1957). Volume 5 covers Scots law up to 1956.

6.5.2.1   *Law Books Published*

This is published every six months with an annual cumulation. Books are indexed by author, title, subject, publisher and series. It covers mainly U.K. and U.S. publications.

6.5.2.2   *Law Books in Print*

This work gives details of books published in English and currently in print. It purports to cover the world.

6.5.2.3   *International Legal Books in Print*

This concentrates on material published in English but excluding the U.S.

There are many specialist legal bibliographies, *e.g.* E. Beyerly, *Public International Law: A Guide to Information Sources* (1991) (see chapter 9 para. 9.4.1).

Information about recent legal books can be gleaned from book reviews which appear in legal journals. These can be located by checking the Legal Journals Index for book reviews.

6.5.3   **General bibliographic sources**

The following works are sources of general bibliographic information including legal materials:

Global Books in Print CD-ROM. This refers to books currently in print.

British National Bibliography. This is a complete listing of all books published in the U.K. since 1950, which have been received and catalogued by the British Library. It references all books regardless of whether or not the work is in print. It is available in paper, CD-ROM and on-line.

Whitaker's Books in Print (formerly British Books in Print). This is available on CD-ROM which is called *Bookbank*. This lists all books published in the U.K. and still in print.

Books in Print. This lists all books published in the U.S. which are still in print.

Bibliography of Scotland. This is a database of material that has been written about Scotland. It excludes material published in Scotland if it has no Scottish content. It includes books, serials and periodical articles. It is possible to search by author, title, subject and keyword. Information from 1976–1987 is available on microfiche. It is available on-line (free access) from 1988 onwards:

http://www.nls.ac.uk/catalogues/bos.htm

Catalogue of the *National Library of Scotland.* It is possible to search the catalogue of printed books on-line. The site currently covers material acquired since 1978. It is possible to search by author, title, subject and keyword.

6.6   **THESES**

You can locate theses by checking the *Index to Theses of Great Britain and Ireland.* This contains details and abstracts (where provided by the institution) of theses accepted for higher degrees in Great Britain and Ireland. The on-line version currently covers the period 1970–1997. It is a subscription website:
http://www.theses.com/
    The paper version goes back to 1950. It is published four times a year by Aslib (London). You can search under subject and author. Not all the law theses are categorised under law. They could be under other headings, *e.g.* political science. Not all Scottish universities are covered by the Index to Theses. In order to read a copy of a thesis you will have to apply to borrow it through the inter-library loan scheme. An alternative is to contact the relevant university directly.
    Legal Research in the United Kingdom 1905–1984 is a classified list of postgraduate legal theses and dissertations accepted by U.K. institutions (published in 1985 by the Institute of Advanced Legal Studies, London).

6.7   CONFERENCE PROCEEDINGS

Index to Conference Proceedings. This is an annual publication which started in 1964. It is produced by the British Library Document Supply Centre. It is available on CD-ROM on a quarterly basis and on-line (subscription) since 1993. It is possible to search alphabetically by subject using key terms such as ''law'' and ''legal''.

6.8   LEGAL JOURNALS

There are many different types of legal journals and they are available in different formats and produced at different times. They range from journals which are aimed at the student, the academic and the practitioner. The practitioner journals tend to be published frequently and aim to provide a current awareness service as well as practical information about the law. Academic journals tend to be published less frequently and contain lengthy articles about more theoretical issues. Student journals contain short articles on recent legal developments.

Some journals are general in that they contain information on all areas of law. Others are restricted to one area. Journals also cater for different legal jurisdictions. There are Scottish legal journals, U.K. legal journals and journals which cover European and International law.

There is no standard format for a legal journal. Journals vary as to length. Some journals are produced as a collection of scholarly articles and are reasonably large publications, while others are slim updating services. Some legal journals are only published electronically but the majority are still paper-based.

In the law library, legal journals will be stored in alphabetical order. Usual practice is to separate the current edition from back issues of the journal. The latest editions will be placed where they are designed to be browsed. Older editions will be shelved elsewhere.

Scottish journals aimed at the profession:

Journal of the Law Society of Scotland (J.L.S.S.) (1956–)	published monthly	*Contents*: professional information, articles, book reviews, news features, letters and interviews.
Scots Law Times (S.L.T.) (1893–)	published weekly	*Contents*: articles, Acts of Adjournal/Sederunt, appointments, obituaries, parliamentary news, book reviews, general information, forthcoming events, information about the courts, business changes and taxation.
Scottish Law Gazette (S.L.G.) (1933–)	published quarterly by the Council of the Scottish Law Agents Society	*Contents*: articles, news, book reviews and book information.

English journals aimed at the profession These include: *New Law Journal, Solicitors' Journal* and the *Law Society Gazette*. These are all published weekly.

Scottish academic journals include:

Juridical Review (J.R.) (1889–)	published six times a year	*Contents*: articles, case and comment.
Edinburgh Law Review (E.L.R.) (1996–)	published three times a year	*Contents*: articles, significant developments in the law and book reviews.
Scottish Law & Practice Quarterly (S.L.P.Q.) (1995–)	published four times a year	*Contents*: articles and updates

English academic journals include:

Law Quarterly Review (L.Q.R.) (1885–)	published every two months
Modern Law Review (M.L.R.) (1937–)	published every two months
Cambridge Law Journal (C.L.J.) (1921–)	published every four months
Oxford Journal of Legal Studies (O.J.L.S.)	published quarterly

Specialist journals published in Scotland include:

Scottish Planning and Environmental Law (SPEL) (1993–) (formerly Scottish Planning Law and Practice) (S.P.T.L.)	published every two months
SCOLAG (Scottish Legal Action Group) (1975–)	published monthly
Green's Criminal Law Bulletin, Green's Civil Practice Bulletin, Green's Employment Law Bulletin, Green's Family Law Bulletin, Green's Reparation Law Bulletin, Green's Property Law Bulletin, Green's Business Law Bulletin	all published every two months

UK-wide specialist journals include: *British Journal of Criminology, Journal of Law and Society, Criminal Law Review, Journal of Planning and Environmental Law*

An example of a journal aimed at students is the *Student Law Review* (S.L.R.) It is published quarterly. An example of an electronic legal journal is the *Journal of Information Law & Technology* (J.I.L.T.) (1996–). This is available free:
http://elj.warwick.ac.uk/jilt/
It covers topics relating to information technology law and IT applications in law.

The Law Librarian is not usually classed as a legal journal but contains much useful material about legal information sources.

6.8.1   Search strategies for finding articles in journals

6.8.1.1   *Legal Journals Index (1986–)*

This index covers all journals published in the U.K. which are devoted to law or frequently contain articles on legal topics. It contains details of all the various publications covered. There is access to the material via five indexes:

> subject
> author
> case
> legislation
> book review — indexed under the author and title of the book reviewed.

The paper version of *Legal Journals Index* is published in monthly issues which are cumulated every quarter. It is also available as part of Current Legal Information. It is available on CD-ROM which is updated monthly and on-line. The electronic versions allow you to search by field (which includes subject, keyword, case, legislation and source) or by free text. They allow you access to the journals database which gives you details of the various publications covered, including the appropriate abbreviation. There is also a "What's new this month" section which arranges recent articles under subject headings.

From 1993 material relating solely to European law and the laws of the countries in Europe is contained in the *European Legal Journals Index*. Material which involves both U.K. and E.C. law is indexed in both the Legal Journals Index and the European Legal Journals Index.

6.8.1.2   *SALSER*

This is a free on-line service which allows you to search for journals in all the university libraries in Scotland, the National Library of Scotland, the Mitchell Library and Edinburgh City Libraries.
http://edina.ed.ac.uk/salser/
You can search by keyword. There is also a useful facility to allow you to limit your search to one or a group of institutions. This means that, for example, if you are local to Edinburgh, you could search all the libraries in the Edinburgh area.

6.8.1.3   *Periodical Contents Index*

This is available on-line by subscription and allows you to search the tables of contents of journals back to the date of their inception up to 1990. It does not just contain legal journals. It is a useful way of searching information contained in back issues of older journals, *e.g.* the *Juridical Review*.

6.8.1.4   *Index to Legal Periodicals*

This index references legal periodicals and books which are published in Great Britain, Ireland, U.S., Canada, Australia and New Zealand. It is an American publication and the majority of material is American. Information can be accessed by subject and author indexes.

6.8.1.5   *British Humanities Index*

This is an extensive abstracting service covering around 250 journals and newspapers. It includes material on the arts, music, philosophy, religion, economics, politics, history and society. Between 1962–1992 the material was arranged by A–Z listing of subject headings but since 1993 the layout has changed. The material is now arranged in a numerical sequence followed by an alphabetical subject index. The index is issued quarterly with an annual bound volume.

   The index starts with an abstracts sequence. This is arranged alphabetically in order of subject headings. Each article has an abstract number which allows it to be traced from any of the three indexes:

   • Alphabetical subject index.

   • Author index which is an alphabetical list of author's names and abstract numbers.

   • Source index which is an alphabetical list of journals covered in the specific volume along with abstract numbers for each article.

To find information on Scots law, go to the subject index and look under law, Scotland.
   British Humanities Index is also available on CD-ROM and on-line (subscription).

6.8.1.6   *Current Law*

Current Law Year Book and Monthly Digests contain details of articles under subject headings. See chapter 10, paras 10.2 and 10.3.

6.8.1.7   *Lexis*

Available on-line by subscription, see chapter 13, para. 13.4.3.

6.8.1.8   *Business Periodicals Index*

This is a U.S. publication. Check under ''law''.

6.8.1.9   *The Reports Index*

This includes official and semi-official reports to do with business. Check under ''law and order'' or ''legal''.

6.8.1.10   *Research Index*

Check under ''law and order'' and ''legal''. It cumulates every quarter into separate indexes. One is for industry and the other for companies. Check the industry index for legal materials.

6.8.1.11   *Union List of Periodicals in Law Report Holdings*, C. Wilcox (Scottish Law Librarian's Group, Edinburgh, 1997). This lists alphabetically by periodicals and law reports by title. It provides references to libraries which hold the material in Scotland and the period covered.

6.9   NEWSPAPER ARTICLES

Most newspapers now have websites that allow you to search back into their archives. However the period is not usually very extensive and tends to be only a couple of years. Access to the websites is free.

Scottish newspapers available on
the internet include:

Scotsman	http://www.scotsman.com/
Herald	http://www.theherald.co.uk/
Dundee Courier & Advertiser	http://www.thecourier.co.uk/febcourierrede/index.htm
Aberdeen Press & Journal	http://www.pressandjournal.co.uk/
Stornoway Gazette	http://www.stornoway-gazette.com/1999/0401.htm
Shetland News	http://www.shetland-news.co.uk/
Shetland Times	http://www.shetland-times.co.uk/

U.K. newspapers with websites include:

The Times	http://www.the-times.co.uk/
The Daily Telegraph	http://www.telegraph.co.uk/
The Independent	http://www.independent.co.uk/
Guardian	http://www.guardian.co.uk/
Financial Times	http://www.ft.com/

There are various indexes which allow you to search newspapers. These include: *The Scotsman Index*, the *Index to the Financial Times* and *The Times Index*. This covers: *The Times*, *The Sunday Times* and *Magazine*, *The Times Literary Supplement*, *The Times Educational Supplement* and *The Times Higher Education Supplement*. The subject headings are arranged by topic and are in alphabetical order for items about Great Britain. Items about other jurisdictions are arranged in alphabetical topic order under the heading of the relevant country. For items relating to Scots law check "Scotland" and "law".

   British Newspaper Index is available on CD-ROM but does not include all British newspapers. It includes the Times group of newspapers, the *Independent*, the *Guardian* and the *Observer*.

   The British Humanities Index indexes articles and features but not news items and editorials. The papers it covers are *The Times*, *Guardian*, *Independent*, *Daily Telegraph* and the *Financial Times*. *The Research Index* includes topics related to commercial and industrial matters. It includes the newspapers above and the *Scotsman*.

   The majority of newspapers now appear in full text on CD-ROM (subscription) and can be searched by keywords. *The Scotsman* now has a full text on-line (subscription) version that allows archival retrieval.

6.10   CURRENT AWARENESS

There are an increasing number of sources of current information available via the internet. Here is a selection:

Current awareness section   http://194.247.69.28/news2/news.asp
of the Scottish Executive
site (free)

Today's Press Releases from Government departments (free)	http://www.coi.gov.uk/ coi/depts/today.html	
Government Information Service What's new (free)	http://www.open.gov.uk/	
CLI Badger Alerter (free)	http:// www.smlawpub.co.uk	A daily current awareness service providing items relating to law, regulation and compliance.
Butterworths News Direct (free)	http://www.butterworths.co.uk/ newsdirect/index.asp	
Butterworths Scots News Direct (free)	http://www.butterworthsscotland. com/scottishnewsdirect/index.htm	
Butterworths Law Direct (subscription)		There is a daily alerting service which provides summaries of Acts, statutory instruments, cases, House of Commons papers, Government press releases and consultation papers.
What's new at HMSO (free)	http://www.hmso.gov.uk/ whatsnew.htm	Details new material added to the site over the previous two weeks.
What's new at the House of Commons (free)	http://www.parliament.uk/ commons/CMNEW.HTM	
No.10 Downing Street (free)	http://www.number-10.gov.uk/ public/news/index.html	This contains a section on the U.K. today.
Foreign Office current news section (free)	http://www.fco.gov.uk/ news/	
BOPCAS (British Official Publications Current Awareness Service) (subscription)		
BBC Scotland (free)	http://www.bbc.co.uk/ scotland/	
BBC news on-line (free)	http://news.bbc.co.uk/	
ITN news on-line (free)	http://www.itn.co.uk/	
CNN (free)	http://www.cnn.com/	
The Press Association	http://www.pa.press.net/	
Scots Law News	http://www.law.ed.ac.uk/ elr/news.htm	This contains news items prepared by H. MacQueen, the editor of the Edinburgh Law Review.

6.11   Government Publications

Bills and parliamentary debates are both classed as parliamentary publications and have already been covered in chapter 5. Other parliamentary publications which you are likely to encounter at university are:

> Command Papers
> House of Commons papers
> House of Lords papers

6.11.1   Command Papers

A Command Paper is technically presented to Parliament "by the Command of Her Majesty" but in practice is presented on the initiative of a person or body other than Parliament. They are usually presented by Government Ministers. They are documents which have been produced for Parliament to consider; they have not been produced by Parliament. There are many different types of Command Papers:

> White Papers (proposal for legislation which is put forward by the Government)
> Green Papers (consultation documents)
> Reports of Royal Commissions
> Reports of Committees of Enquiry
> Annual reports and statistics produced by certain bodies
> State Papers including treaties
> Some Law Commission reports are Command papers.

There are six series of Command Papers. They are all numbered less than 10,000 and (apart from the first series) preceded with a different form of abbreviation for Command:

1833–1866	1 – 4222
1870–1899	C.1 – C.9550
1900–1918	Cd.1 – Cd.9239
1919–1956	Cmd.1 – Cmd.9889
1956–1986	Cmnd.1 – Cmnd.9927
1986–	Cm.1 –

As the same numbers are used in the different series, it is very important to note the precise abbreviation so that you can locate the appropriate Command Paper.

6.11.2   House of Commons and House of Lords Papers

House of Commons papers are not just papers which are produced from the work of the House of Commons, such as Select Committee Papers and Minutes of Proceedings of Standing Committees. They also include some reports and accounts which are required to be presented to Parliament. House of Commons papers are given a reference which consists of H.C., the relevant parliamentary session (*e.g.* 1998/99) and the number of the paper. House of Lords papers are numbered in a similar way but with H.L. as the prefix.

A selection of House of Commons papers are available from the House of Commons Publications website:
http://www.parliament.the-stationery-office.co.uk/pa/cm/cmpubns.htm
The Register of Members' Interests is included.
Select Committee Reports from the beginning of the 1997–98 session are available:
http://www.parliament.the-stationery-office.co.uk/pa/cm/cmselect.htm

6.11.3 Aid to tracing official publications

6.11.3.1 *Bibliographic services provided by the Stationery Office*

You will notice that many older official publications refer to and were published by HMSO. HMSO was privatised in October 1996. The Stationery Office Ltd has taken over its book publishing and sales work. HMSO still exists as a residual Crown body. It is responsible for supervising statutory publishing and the administration of Crown copyright. It is a division of the Cabinet Office and is separate from The Stationery Office Ltd.

The Stationery Office publishes various bibliographic services for its own publications. These include:

1. The Daily List is divided into several sections:

> Parliamentary publications
> Official publications
> Stationery Office publications
> Agency publications
> Statutory Rules of Northern Ireland
> Statutory Instruments
> Forthcoming publications

The Daily List is available in paper format and for free over the internet: http://www.tso-online.co.uk. The Daily Lists for a week are published in paper format together as a Weekly List. The information is also published as monthly catalogues and again as an annual catalogue.

2. The Stationery Office database is available on-line on BLAISE-LINE (subscription). This contains details of its publications from 1976. It is updated monthly.

3. The Stationery Office also publishes an *Index to Chairmen: reports of official committees*. This is published quarterly and appears in an annual cumulative form. It lists chairmen of all committees, commissions and working parties whose reports have been published by The Stationery Office throughout the year. This is a useful aid to finding the reports as they are often known by the name of the chairman.

4. A selection of Command Papers are available on The Stationery Office's website: http://www.official-documents.co.uk/menu/compap.htm
The selection is listed in alphabetical order.

6.11.3.2 *Collections of parliamentary publications*

Some libraries will hold a full set of parliamentary papers. These can be searched by a Sessional Index. The National Library of Scotland holds House of Commons papers since 1715 and House of Lords papers since 1801.

6.11.3.3 *UKOP (Catalogue of United Kingdom Official Publications)*

This is available on-line (subscription) and on CD-ROM. It contains records of *all* British official publications from 1980 onwards. It is compiled from The Stationery Office's database and

Catalogue of Official Publications Not Published by the Stationery Office. The on-line version is updated monthly and the CD-ROM is updated every two months.

6.11.3.4   *BOPCAS (British Official Publications Current Awareness Service)*

This is available on-line by subscription. This database allows access to publications emanating from Government published since July 1995. It includes Acts, Bills, Command Papers, House of Commons papers, House of Lords papers, departmental publications and Standing Committee Reports.

6.11.3.5   *BADGER*

This is available as part of Current Legal Information (subscription only). It stands for Broad All-Purpose Database Geared for Easy Retrieval and is available either on CD-ROM or on-line from 1994. It is an electronic index to:

> Press comment
> Press releases
> Parliamentary publications
> Command Papers
> Bills
> English, Welsh, Scottish and Northern Irish Statutory Instruments and Northern Irish Statutory Rules of general effect and those of local effect made under a Public Act
> White and Green Papers
> European Commission documents (COMdocs); Documents of the Secretariat General of the European Commission (SEC)
> Proceedings of the European Court of Justice
> Practice directions.

This index can be searched by field (this includes subject, keywords, case, legislation, company and entry type) or by free text. Recent developments are arranged under a subject index in the ''What's new'' section. This is a very useful information source. It has brought together many of the types of information which were difficult to find and made them accessible by user-friendly search facility.

6.11.3.6   *Lawtel*

Lawtel has the facility to search for Command Papers including White and Green Papers. It is updated weekly and contains hypertext links to full text when this is available from Government websites. See chapter 13, para. 13.4.2 for more details.

6.11.3.7   *Justis — Parliament (subscription)*

This is based on POLIS (Parliamentary On-line Information Service) which is available to M.P.s and officials at Westminster. It is available on CD-ROM which is updated twice a year or on-line which is updated on a daily basis. It is a bibliographic database which indexes all parliamentary papers from both Houses of Parliament since 1980.

6.11.4   **Non-parliamentary publications**

The main way of tracing the large number of non-parliamentary publications is the *Catalogue of British Official Publications Not Published by The Stationery Office.* This is published by Chadwyck-Healey and is issued bi-monthly and bound into annual volumes. This includes references to a large amount of material emerging from over 500 different organisations. The main body of the publication is made up of two indexes. The first lists entries for the publication under the name of the organisation which published it. The details provided include the author, date of publication, price and source. Some of the material is freely available but most of it is available from the publishers for a fee.

The second listing which appears at the end of the issue is a subject index. The reference given in this section relates to a reference number given to the titles in the order that they are listed in the first section. The references are not page numbers. This can cause some initial confusion when trying to marry together the information in the two indexes.

6.11.5   Government Department Press releases

These can now be traced from a number of different sources, *e.g.*
BADGER (CD-ROM and on-line by subscription) see para. 6.11.3.5 above.
Government Information Service website:
http://www.open.gov.uk/
Check the website for the relevant Government department. These will contain back issues for a limited period. For current information visit the site produced by the Central Office of Information Internet Services. It gathers together the day's press releases for all government departments:
http://www.coi.gov.uk/coi/depts/today.html

6.11.6   Additional information about the workings of Government

6.11.6.1   *The Civil Service Year Book*

This is published annually by The Stationery Office. It is available in paper, on CD-ROM and on-line (subscription).

6.11.6.2   *The Directory of Westminster and Whitehall*, 4th ed., 1998/99.

This directory is split into two sections: House of Commons, which gives information about M.P.s, their staff and constituencies, and Government departments, which lists civil service responsibilities.

6.11.6.3   *Informaton about the Scottish Parliament*

Information abouth MSPs, their constituencies, a Register of Interests along with the details of the working of the Parliament is available free via the Scottish Parliament website. See chapter 4, para. 4.5.6.

6.11.7   Law Commission Papers

The Scottish Law Commission and the Law Commission were both created by the Law Commissions Act 1965.

The Chairman of the Scottish Law Commission is a Senator of the College of Justice. He is assisted by four Commissioners. Its purpose is to promote the reform of the law of Scotland. It proposes reforms in the law, prepares Consolidation and Statute Law Repeals Bills. The Law Commission publishes consultation papers and at a later stage it prepares a report with recommendations. These usually include a draft Bill. The Law Commission does not have the power to alter the law, merely to contribute to debate and to make proposals. The Government makes the final decision whether to adopt the proposals.

6.11.7.1   *How do you find out if the Scottish Law Commission has written about something?*

The Scottish Law Commission publishes Annual Reports. In the appendices to these reports you will find lists of all their reports, consultative memoranda/discussion papers and other published and unpublished documents. They are listed in chronological order and also give the Commission number for the reports and references for other documents. The Annual Reports also contain a section on the progress of current law reform projects.

6.11.7.2   *How do you find out if the Law Commission has written about something?*

The English Law Commission has a website:
http://www.gtnet.gov.uk/lawcomm/homepage.htm
The site contains summaries of the Law Commission's more recent publications with a selection being available in full text. There is a list of all Consultation Papers and Reports.

6.11.8   **Statistical information about Scotland**

The Scottish Executive website (previously the Scottish Office website) allows access to much statistical information about Scotland. Information is available in paper and on-line. The website is:
http://194.247.69.28/stats/default.htm
This contains a section entitled Scotland in Figures. If you enter this page you can access statistics under various subject headings. Crime and Justice is one of the subject headings. The site also contains information about new and forthcoming publications. There is also access to Statbase. This is a newly available on-line database of official government statistics.

The Scottish Office had recently started producing a twice-yearly Criminal Justice Information Bulletin. This is available in paper or on-line:
http://www.scotland.gov.uk/library/documents-w/cj-00.htm
This contains a lot of useful information about prosecution rates, sentencing and other issues. It also contains a section on publications.

The Scottish Office also published a Criminal Justice Series of statistical publications. These are available in paper or on-line via the Scottish Excutive website. They include statistics about liquor licensing, recorded crime, criminal proceedings, prisons, homicide and crimes and offences involving firearms. Most of these statistics are published on an annual basis. There is also an annual publication called The Scottish Abstract of Statistics. The latest addition is available via the Scottish Executive website.

Information about civil matters is published by The Stationery Office on an annual basis under the title Civil Judicial Statistics Scotland.

Other statistical information about Scotland available on-line includes:

1. General Register Office for Scotland
   http://www.open.gov.uk/gros/groshome.htm
   This provides information about Scotland's population, including the 10-yearly census.

2. Department of Health statistics
   http://www.doh.gov.uk/public/stats1.htm

3. U.K. statistics
   U.K. statistical information is available from the Office for National Statistics
   http://www.ons.gov.uk/ons_f.htm
   This provides information about population in England and Wales and U.K. social and economic statistics.

The following are all prepared by the Office for National Statistics:

> *Annual Abstract of Statistics*. This includes information on population, manufacturing, social services, justice, finance, education, transport and defence.
>
> *Regional Trends*. This is published on an annual basis. It includes Scotland and Northern Ireland as well as the regions of England. It contains information on population, environment, regional accounts, industry and agriculture.
>
> *Social Trends*. This is published on an annual basis. It contains information about life and lifestyles in Britain.
>
> *Economic Trends*. This is published on a monthly and annual basis.
>
> *Britain 1999 — The Official Yearbook of the United Kingdom*. This provides information about the current structure and organisation of the U.K.

6.11.9   Central Research Unit (CRU)

The CRU carries out research on behalf of the Scottish Excutive and other Government agencies. The CRU produces research reports, research summaries and is responsible for various research programmes. There are several research branches which produce research findings in different policy areas. These are: criminal justice, legal studies, local government, housing and transport, rural affairs, social work, urban regeneration and planning and education. The research findings which they produce are available free from the CRU. Many can be accessed via the CRU website: http://www.scotland.gov.uk/cru/pub.htm
Information about research which the CRU plans to commission or has recently commissioned is contained in research programmes. Details of these are available on the above website. There are currently seven research programmes. These include civil legal aid 1997–2000, criminal justice research programme 1998–2001 and the Children (Scotland) Act 1995.
The full research reports are published by The Stationery Office. A cumulative list of CRU publications is available on the website. It is arranged in chronological order.

6.11.10   Other sources of official information of interest to the legal researcher

Details of Scottish Excutive publications (and past publications by the Scottish Office) are available on their website:
http://www.scotland.gov.uk
They are also now listed separately in the Stationery Office *Daily List* and other catalogues.

Details of Scottish Parliment publications (including research papers) are available on the Scottish Parliament website, see chapter 4, para. 4.5.6.

Many official bodies produce information either in the form of annual reports or via a website. These include:

1. The Scottish Legal Services Ombudsman (formerly called the Lay Observer). His role is to investigate complaints about how the relevant professional body (Law Society of Scotland, Faculty of Advocates, Scottish Conveyancing and Executry Board) has dealt with a complaint about a member of the legal profession. Annual reports are produced and more information is available on the website:
   http://www.scot-legal-ombud.org.uk/

2. The Scottish Legal Aid Board also produces annual reports and has a website: http://www.slab.org.uk/

3. The Commissioner for Local Administration in Scotland also produces annual reports. He investigates complaints of injustice arising from the maladministration of local authorities and other bodies.

4. The Crown Office and Procurator Fiscal Service produce an annual report.

5. The recently constituted Scottish Criminal Cases Review Commission has a website: http://www.scotland.gov.uk/structure/sscrc.htm

Many agencies have their own websites which provide much useful information, *e.g.* Scottish Environment Protection Agency
http://www.sepa.org.uk/

For more information on official publications in general see:
D. Butcher, *Official Publications in Britain* (2nd ed., Library Association Publishing, London 1991).
D. Jellinek, *Official U.K.: the essential guide to Government web sites* (The Stationery Office, London 1998). On-line updates to this work are available.

6.12   Legal Directories

The Scottish Law Directory (known as the White Book)
This is an annual publication and contains an official list of certificated solicitors. It is divided into five sections: courts and offices, lawyers, solicitors firms listed alphabetically and geographically, services to the legal profession and charities.

The White Book is accompanied by a Fees Supplement which contains details of fee rates. There is also a new publication called the Scottish Law Directory: Individual Solicitors' Specialisms. This contains lists of solicitors and the areas in which they specialise.

The Blue Book: the *Directory of the Law Society of Scotland.*

This is a joint publication by Butterworths and the Law Society of Scotland. It contains an official list of certificated solicitors, bodies employing solicitors, lists of advocates, chartered surveyors, chartered and certificated accountants, messengers-at-arms and sheriff officers. It also contains information about the courts, legal aid fees and court fees.

6.13   Information aimed at practitioners

6.13.1   Relevant websites

The Law Society of Scotland
www.lawscot.org.uk/
The Scottish Law Agents Society
http://www.slas.co.uk/

The Scottish Courts Website
http://www.scotcourts.gov.uk
This contains much useful information about all the Scottish courts. As well as opinions from the Court of Session and High Court of Justiciary (from Sept. 1998) it contains short biographies of judges, the Rules of the Court of Session and from July 5, 1999, the Rolls of Court.

6.13.2   Styles

There are many books which provide styles for various documents commonly encountered by solicitors. Examples include S.A. Bennett, *Style Writs for the Sheriff Court* (2nd ed.), T. & T. Clark, Edinburgh, 1994 and A. Barr *et al.*, *Drafting Wills in Scotland*, Butterworths/Law Society of Scotland, 1994.

There are now an increasing number of packages which allow the practitioner to download styles and adapt them for his own use. Green's Litigation Styles is a collection of styles for use in the Court of Session and the sheriff court. It is a loose-leaf publication in two volumes and includes diskettes containing styles which can be downloaded. The service is updated twice a year.

Green's also publish Practice Styles. This is also a two-volume loose-leaf publication with diskettes. It covers the following areas: agriculture and crofting, commerce, commercial conveyancing, court, domestic conveyancing, executry, family law, intellectual property, moveable property, trusts and wills.

Software packages for the practitioner are now available. Examples include:
L. Martin, S. Giusti and G. Sinclair, *Summary Criminal File* (1997). This contains a series of pre-drafted templates of documents relating to criminal work which can be adapted by the user.
L. Martin, S. Giusti and G. Sinclair, *Conveyancing* (1997).
Pre-assembled templates of documents in a conveyancing transaction.
D. Convery, *Q-CALs* (1996).
This contains software to help the practitioner carry out the various calculations necessary in order to quantify a claim for damages.
I.L.S. Balfour, *Separation Agreements* (1996).
C. Mcleod, *Company Transactions Using Hotdocs* (1998).
D. Brand, *Wills* (1996).

6.13.3   Practical information about Scottish courts

Two publications provide very useful information for court practitioners:
C. McCaffray, *Green's Guide to Sheriff Court Districts* (2nd ed., W. Green, Edinburgh 1992).
This is an invaluable book for the court practitioner as it lists every Scottish city, town and village and the location of the appropriate sheriffdom and sheriff court.
D.T. Crowe, *Scottish Courts Companion* (T & T Clark, Edinburgh 1997). All of the sheriff courts are listed alphabetically and information is provided on the following: contact details of the court, sheriff clerk and procurator fiscal, location of the court including a map, transport, parking and accommodation.

Details of the supreme courts' administration offices, sheriff courts and district courts are available on the Scottish Courts website (see para. 6.13.1).

6.14   LAW LIBRARIES IN SCOTLAND

Information about libraries in Scotland can be gained from:
1. The Scottish Libraries Across the Internet website (SLAINTE):
www.slainte.napier.ac.uk
2. C. Wilcox, *Directory of Legal Libraries in Scotland* (Scottish Law Librarian Group, Edinburgh 1995). This contains an alphabetical list of all law libraries in Scotland. It includes public and private libraries.
3. Co-operative Academic Information Retrieval Network for Scotland (CAIRNS): http://www.cairns.lib.gla.ac.uk The aim of this project is to produce single searching of major academic research collections throughout Scotland. At present the service is not complete.

Chapter 7

UK-WIDE LEGAL INFORMATION SOURCES WHICH EXCLUDE SCOTS LAW

7.1 INTRODUCTION

This chapter looks at some legal information sources which are relevant for UK-wide legal information but which exclude (either wholly or partially) Scots law. The sources covered have been limited to those which are widely available in Scotland. The major works of English law are *Halsbury's Laws of England* (a legal encyclopaedia), *Halsbury's Statutes of England* (annotated full amended text of statutes currently in force) and *Halsbury's Statutory Instruments* (annotated full amended text of statutory instruments currently in force). These are all covered along with explanations of how to search them. The major series of English law reports are discussed. Reference is made to the increasing number of electronic databases which allow easier and more flexible searching. A small selection of English legal websites is also included.

7.2 LEGISLATION

7.2.1 Halsbury's Statutes of England (4th ed.)

This work is a collection of statutes which are arranged in broad subject headings. It consists of 50 volumes along with an updating service which has three parts: Cumulative Supplement, a Noter-up and Current Statutes Service. It contains statutes which relate to England and Wales or to the U.K. as a whole. Sections of U.K. statutes which relate to Scotland only are not included and statutes which relate only to Scotland are not included.

The full text of each statute is given along with annotations which clarify the legislation and refer to relevant case law. The text of the statute incorporates subsequent amendments (it is not, as in Current Law, the original version). From 1993 onwards reference to parliamentary debates is given. The volumes are arranged in alphabetical order, volume 1 starts with Admiralty and volume 50 ends with Wills and E.C. treaties. The volumes are re-issued periodically. At the start of each volume there is a statement that it represents the law up to a certain date. You should ensure that you always check this date and then use the updating service to check for changes since that date. You may also need to check a very up to date source such as Lawtel to ensure that your knowledge is current.

Each bound volume conforms to the same format:

At the start:

> List of headings in all the volumes
> Table of contents for this volume
> Abbreviations
> Table of statutes covering all the statutes printed in the volume in alphabetical and
> chronological order
> Table of statutory instruments
> Table of cases

Within each subject heading there is:

> Table of contents
> Cross references. This indicates where material has been categorised under a different
> heading and is therefore contained in a different volume.
> Alphabetical list of statutes
> Preliminary note. This explains the legislative background to the subject area.
> Annotated and amended version of legislation

At the end of the volume there is a subject index.

The updating service consists of:

1. Cumulative Supplement. This records changes which affect the published volumes. It is arranged by volume, subject and page order in the same way as the bound volumes.

2. Noter-up. This records the effect of recently published legislation and reported cases on material in the volumes and Current Service Binders. It is arranged by subject in the same way as the volumes and Cumulative Supplement. If the letter ''S'' appears after the volume number it means that the legislation is contained in one of the Current Service Binders. The Noter-up also contains an update for the annual publication *Is It in Force?* The Noter-up is updated three times a year.

3. Current Statutes Service. This is contained in six binders. It is issued six times a year. It includes the text of Acts passed since January 1, 1985 other than those included in a published volume. Again, it is arranged in the same way as the other parts of *Halsbury's Statutes*.

Halsbury's Statutes also includes a paperback volume containing Tables of Statutes and a General Index. This is published annually and contains alphabetical and chronological lists of statutes printed in the volumes and the Current Statutes Service up to a given date. It also contains a volume index. This is a detailed subject index to all the bound volumes.

Another part of *Halsbury's Statutes* is a volume of Destination Tables. These cover Consolidation Acts passed between 1983 and 1994 and a selection of important Consolidation Acts back to 1957. These are useful when you want to find the provision which is currently in force where you only know the pre-consolidated legislative provision.

Using *Halsbury's Statutes* to find an Act on a specific subject:

Table of Statutes and General Index

↓

Relevant volume *(could start from here if you know subject area)*

↓

Update by checking Cumulative Supplement

↓

Update by checking Noter-up

How to use *Halsbury's Statutes*

Example

You want to find out about cruelty to badgers.

⇒ Step 1: Either browse the spines of the hardback volumes which list the subject headings contained in each volume or look in the General Index. This will allow access under several different routes, *e.g.*

Index heading: badgers	Entry: cruelty to, offences of, **2** 323–4
Index heading: animals	Entry: cruelty see cruelty to animals
Index heading: cruelty to animals	Entry: badgers **2** 323–4

⇒ Step 2: Use the reference to locate the information.
2 323–4 means volume 2 pages 323–4.
This leads to the text of the Badgers Act 1973 (c.57), s. 2 which is headed "Offences of cruelty".

⇒ Step 3: Check whether this information is still current. Check the beginning of the volume for a reference to a date. On one of the first pages will be a statement: "This volume states the law as at . . . ." You need to update your information to cover the period from this date to the present. Volume 2 states the law as at May 1, 1992.

⇒ Step 4: Go to the Cumulative Supplement. This includes updated information from the bound volume to the date of the Cumulative Supplement. Check what it says about currency, *e.g.* the 1998 version says that it is "up to date to 1st January 1998". Turn to the entry for volume 2 — Animals. In this section any changes appear in the page order of volume 2. The original reference was to p. 323–4. The entry in the Cumulative Supplement is for p. 322–33:

"Badgers Act 1973 (c.57)
    Whole Act repealed by the Protection of Badgers Act 1992, s. 15(2), schedule"

⇒ Step 5: Again you have to ask, is this the most up to date information? No. This will only be up to date to the date of the last Cumulative Supplement. In order to include later developments you need to check the Noter-up. This is updated three times a year. Turn to the entry for volume 2 — Animals. This time check at the end of the section for volume 2. Any changes to the 1992

Act would now be referenced under vol. 2 (S). There is only one minor amendment to the whole Act which does not concern cruelty.

⇒ Step 6: Having established that the current law covering cruelty to badgers is contained in the Protection of Badgers Act 1992, you will want to look at the text of the Act to establish what the current rule is. Turn to the Current Statutes Service. Go to the relevant binder for volume 2 — Binder A. Turn to volume 2 — Animals. The section contains the full text of the Act with annotations. You can now find out about the law regarding cruelty to badgers.

N.B. If you want to bring this search right up to date, you would need to check one of the electronic databases such as Lawtel, which is updated daily.

7.2.2   Halsbury's Statutory Instruments

This service provides information about every statutory instrument of general application in England and Wales. It does not reproduce every statutory instrument in full text. Those which are regarded as of little general importance are summarised. This can be the cause of frustration when you need to look at the full text.

Halsbury's Statutory Instruments consist of 22 volumes. They are arranged by subject in a similar format to *Halsbury's Laws* and *Halsbury's Statutes*. Volume 1 starts with a section about statutory instruments. The rest of the work is alphabetical by subject from agriculture to wills. At the beginning of each volume is the date at which the law is stated in that volume. It is very important to check this date so that you can update your search accordingly.

If you want to find a statutory instrument on a specific subject then you can go to the relevant volume, *e.g.* volume 9 for health and safety. Alternatively, if you are unsure of the relevant subject heading, you can check the detailed subject index in the separate paperback Consolidated Index. This will direct you to the relevant volume. Turn to the health and safety section. It has a table (referred to as an ''arrangement'') showing contents of the section. In this case the section is large and is split into three parts. There is a list of cross-references to allow you to see where material has been categorised under a different subject heading, *e.g.* slaughterhouses are dealt with under animals and food.

A preliminary note explains the legislative background to the subject area. This is followed by cross-references to *Halsbury's Statutes*. The next part of the volume is a chronological list of statutory instruments. This shows instruments in the subject area. It lists: year and number of the instrument, full title, remarks indicating if it is an amending instrument and a reference to a page number where the instrument is either printed in full or summarised. There is also a Table of Instruments No Longer in Operation. This lists instruments which have ceased to have effect since the last re-issue of the volume.

The texts of the statutory instruments are printed in amended form. Where amendments have been printed the added or substituted words appear in square brackets. Omissions are indicated by three dots. Each volume has a subject index at the end.

The service is kept up to date by re-issuing the volumes periodically. Between re-issues it is updated on a monthly basis through the Service. This is a loose-leaf work that consists of two binders. Binder 1 contains the following information:

1. Chronological list of all statutory instruments in the main volumes and in the Service and the subject heading under which they can be found.

2. Table of Statutes which lists all the enabling legislation under which statutory instruments in Halsbury's Statutory Instruments have been made.

3. Annual Cumulative Supplement. This updates the bound volumes and contains changes made since they were published. It contains a chronological list of new instruments, table of instruments no longer in operation, noter-up to pages of the main volumes and summaries of new instruments.

4. Monthly Survey. This contains updates subsequent to the last Annual Cumulative Supplement. It is divided into two sections: summaries of statutory instruments which are arranged numerically and a key which relates the numbers to subject headings.

There is a separate paperback Annual Consolidated Index and Alphabetical List of Statutory Instruments which is published each year. This contains a consolidated version of all the subject indexes to the current volumes. It also covers information in the current Annual Supplement. This means that the Consolidated Index is never more than a year out of date. The Alphabetical List contains references to all statutory instruments which are included in the Service in alphabetical order. This is very useful if you want to find the number for a statutory instrument when you only know the title.

There are different ways of locating statutory instruments, by:

1. Subject matter

Start at either the Annual Consolidated Index or the volume subject index

↓

relevant volume and page reference

↓

update by using Annual Cumulative Supplement and the Monthly Survey.

2. Number

Start by looking at the chronological list in Binder 1 of the Service. This lists all statutory instruments in Halsbury's Statutory Instruments. This will give you the relevant heading.

↓

Turn to the relevant volume. Check the chronological list in this volume. This will lead you to the statutory instrument. If the instrument is very recent, check the Monthly Survey and the additional texts in Binder 2.

3. Title

Use the Alphabetical List of Statutory Instruments. This will indicate the number of the instrument and the relevant subject heading. The bound volume can then be consulted and the statutory instrument located by checking the chronological list at the beginning of the subject area.

4. Enabling power

To find out if any statutory instruments are made under an Act. Check the Table of Statutes in Binder 1. This lists all the enabling powers under which the instruments included in *Halsbury's Statutory Instruments* have been made. It also references the appropriate subject heading. This allows you to access the statutory instruments in the bound volumes.

7.2.3   Legislation Direct

This is an on-line subscription database published by Butterworths. It contains the full text amended versions of all Public General Acts and general statutory instruments currently in force in England and Wales. Scottish material is not included. It is updated daily. Statutes are organised alphabetically and statutory instruments are organised chronologically. You are also able to search by keyword. It also contains a version of *Is it in Force?* and a Progress of Legislation Database.

7.3   Law Reports

South of the border the *Law Reports* are the most authoritative reports. The judge is given the opportunity to check the text before publication. They are also the only reports to include a summary of the argument of counsel. They should be cited in preference to other reports where there is a choice. Publication has traditionally tended to be slow and weekly law reports appeared to fill in the gap. The two most widely used weekly series are the *Weekly Law Reports* and the *All England Law Reports*.

7.3.1   The Law Reports

This series started in 1865 and is published by the Incorporated Council of Law Reporting. It was originally published in several different series but is now published in four series:

> Appeal Cases (A.C.)
>
> Queen's Bench (Q.B.) This becomes Kings Bench if a King is on the throne.
>
> Chancery Division (Ch.)
>
> Family Division (Fam.)

All these different parts usually appear together under "L" for Law Reports in a law library.

7.3.1.1   *Justis — Electronic Law Reports (eLR)*

This subscription service provides the full text of the *Law Reports* from 1865. It consists of two CD-ROMs.

7.3.1.2   *The Law Reports Index*

The *Law Reports Index* provides a continuous indexing system from 1951 to date. This includes *all* cases reported in: *Law Reports*, *Weekly Law Reports* and *Industrial Case Reports*. It also includes references to cases reported in: *All England Law Reports*, *Criminal Appeal Reports*, *Lloyd's Law Reports*, *Local Government Reports*, *Road Traffic Reports*, *Tax Cases* and *Tax Case Leaflets*.

There are currently four volumes. They are referred to as the "Red Indexes". The four volumes are: 1951–60, 1961–70, 1971–80 and 1981–90. There is also a Red Book which consolidates the Index from January 1, 1991 to the end of each year. The current one is 1991–98.

The Red Index is a very useful way of finding cases. It consists of the following tables of information:

Cases reported — references are to the names of both parties

Subject matter — includes ''Words and Phrases'' as a heading

Cases judicially considered

Statutes judicially considered

Statutory Instruments judicially considered

Standard forms of Contract judicially considered

Overseas legislation judicially considered

E.C. legislation judicially considered

International Conventions judicially considered

The Red Index is updated by periodic pink indexes which are published several times a year. Further updates of the Index can be found at the beginning of each issue of the *Weekly Law Reports*.

Red Index

Pink Index

Weekly Law Reports

7.3.2   **The Weekly Law Reports (W.L.R.)**

This series started in 1953. It is published 44 times a year. The *Weekly Law Reports* for each year are in three volumes:

Volume 1 contains cases which do not merit inclusion in The *Law Reports*.
Volume 2 (January–June) and volume 3 (July–December) cover cases which will be subsequently published in the *Law Reports*. Reports in the *Weekly Law Reports* include cases heard in:

House of Lords
Privy Council
Court of Appeal (Civil and Criminal Divisions)
High Court
European Court of Justice

The annual volumes contain the following information:

- List of judges

- Cases — accessible by either party's name

- Subject Matter Index which includes a ''Words and phrases'' heading

- Case reports

The weekly parts additionally contain the update of The Law Reports Index, namely:

Cases judicially considered
Statutes judicially considered
Statutory Instruments judicially considered
E.C. enactments judicially considered.

7.3.2.1   *Justis — Weekly Law*

This subscription service contains full text of the *Weekly Law Reports* since 1953. It is available on CD-ROM which is updated every two months or on-line which is updated every two weeks.

7.3.3   **All England Law Reports**

This series began in 1936. It is published 48 times a year in weekly parts. The annual volumes contain the following information:

- List of judges

- Table of cases — accessible by either party's name

- Digest of cases accessible via subject matter

- House of Lords Petitions

The case reports contain references to *Halsbury's Laws of England*, *Halsbury's Statutes of England and Wales*, *The Digest* and *Halsbury's Statutory Instruments*.

There are indexes to aid searching for cases. These are currently the All E.R. Consolidated Tables and Index 1936–95 and the Cumulative Tables and Index 1996–97. In 1999 these will be replaced by a Consolidated Index 1936–98.

These indexes consist of the following tables:

Cases reported and judicially considered
Practice directions and notes arranged alphabetically according to their subject matter
Statutes judicially considered
Words and phrases judicially considered
Subject index of cases

7.3.3.1   *Butterworths — All England Direct*

This is a new (subscription) on-line service. It allows access to the All E.R. from 1936 to date.

7.3.4   **The Digest (formerly The English & Empire Digest)**

It covers case law of England and Wales and has a selection of cases from Scotland, Ireland, Canada, Australia, New Zealand and other Commonwealth countries. The current edition consists of 90 volumes. It contains annotated summaries of cases. The *Digest* tends to be the most widely available source of information about Scottish cases in England. The current edition is the green band re-issue edition which dates from 1971. Earlier issues are under the original title The *English & Empire Digest*. The first edition was issued between 1919–32 and consisted of 47 volumes. This was replaced by the blue band issue which was issued between 1950–71.

The Digest is a sister publication to *Halsbury's Laws* and the arrangement is similar. Cross-references are given to *Halsbury's Statutes* and *Halsbury's Laws*. It is updated by volumes being re-issued, an Annual Cumulative Supplement and a Quarterly Survey of recent developments. In order to facilitate searching there are Consolidated Tables of Cases and a Consolidated (subject) Index.

7.4   HALSBURY'S LAWS OF ENGLAND

This is a major encyclopaedia covering all areas of English law. It is the English equivalent of the *Stair Memorial Encyclopaedia*. It has been in existence for far longer than its Scottish counterpart and is widely regarded as the best starting point for research on a UK-wide or English problem. It does not include exclusively Scottish material. This is different from *Halsbury's Statutes*, which contains annotated versions of the text of Acts of Parliament. *Halsbury's Laws* does not contain primary material, it is a commentary on the law of England. It can be used with *Halsbury's Statutes* and contains cross-references to it.

The current edition (4th) of *Halsbury's Laws* was completed in 1986. It consists of 56 main volumes. It is kept up to date by the re-issue of individual volumes. There are now few volumes which date from 1986. In addition there is an annual Cumulative Supplement (two volumes) and a monthly Current Service (two binders). References used throughout are to volume and paragraph number.

There are many component parts to *Halsbury's Laws*:

7.4.1   **Individual volumes**

The following information is given at the beginning of each volume:

> The date at which the law is stated
>
> Table of contents
>
> Table of abbreviations
>
> Table of statutes which contains cross-references to *Halsbury's Statutes* for the annotated text of the Act.
>
> Table of statutory instruments which contains cross-references to *Halsbury's Statutory Instruments* for the annotated text of the statutory instrument.
>
> Table of cases which contains references to entries in the *Digest*.

At the end of the volume there is a detailed index for each subject covered by that volume and a words and phrases index. This lists word and phrases which have been explained or defined in the volume.

7.4.2 Annual Cumulative Supplement

The two-volume Annual Cumulative Supplement brings the work up to date to within a year. It provides an account of the changes which have taken place since publication of the bound volumes. Each annual Cumulative Supplement supersedes the previous supplement. Libraries often leave out-of-date editions sitting on the shelves. Make sure that you are using the most recent edition. The Cumulative Supplement is arranged in the same way as the volumes.

7.4.3 The Current Service

This is contained in two binders and is updated monthly. It details developments in the law which have taken place since the date of the last Cumulative Supplement. Binder 1 contains the following information:

1. The *Monthly Review*. This is published in a journal format. Its prime function is to update *Halsbury's Laws* on a monthly basis but it is designed so that it can be read on its own as a digest of recent developments.
2. Tables of cases (includes a quantum of damages table and a table of cases judicially considered), statutes and statutory instruments.
3. A cumulative index to the monthly reviews. This cross-references the reviews to the bound volumes and the Cumulative Supplement.

Binder 2 contains the following information:

1. Commencement of Statutes Table. This lists statutes which were not in force (wholly or partially) when the latest Cumulative Supplement was published. It specifies commencement dates for statutes or states ''no date'' as appropriate.
2. Destination Tables for Consolidation Acts.
3. Personal Injury Section which includes various model letters.
4. Practice Directions relating to the English courts.
5. Table of Articles which relates recent articles to the Halsbury subject headings.
6. Words and Phrases Judicially Interpreted.
7. E.C. materials.
8. Noter-up. This sets out the latest developments in the same format as the Cumulative Supplement.

7.4.4 The Annual Abridgement

This has been published annually since 1974. The *Monthly Review* contains numerous summaries of cases and legislation which (for reasons of space) are not included in the Cumulative Supplement. The Cumulative Supplement only contains details of the effects of these developments on the previous law. The summaries of the cases and legislation are consolidated from the *Monthly Reviews* into an Abridgement volume.

7.4.5   **Volume 53 Consolidated Table of Statutes etc.**

This includes consolidated tables of statutes, statutory instruments and European material. These list the piece of legislation and the relevant reference for it in *Halsbury's Laws*. This allows you to access *Halsbury's Laws* when you know the title of a piece of legislation but are unsure about the subject area.

7.4.6   **Volume 54 Consolidated Table of Cases**

This lists all the cases referred to in *Halsbury's Laws* in alphabetical order of claimant (previously referred to as plaintiff). This allows access to *Halsbury's Laws* when you only know the name of a case.

7.4.7   **Consolidated Index Volume 55 (A–I) and Volume 56 (J–Z)**

This is a very detailed subject index allowing you to key into the system of categorisation used throughout *Halsbury's Laws*. At the end of Volume 56 is a Words and Phrases Table. This includes words which are defined or explained in *Halsbury's Laws*. This is a very useful feature. Say, for example, you want to find out about how the word ''causing'' contained in water pollution legislation has been defined. Check this table under ''C'' and there is an entry:

   ''causing'' (water pollution)   **49(2)**, 628n2''

Turn to volume 49(2), page 628 and note 2 discusses case law on ''causing''.

N.B. The information in volumes 53–56 will become out of date. You need to check the date of publication. A volume of the main work which has been re-issued since these index volumes were last updated will have more up-to-date information for its own subject area.

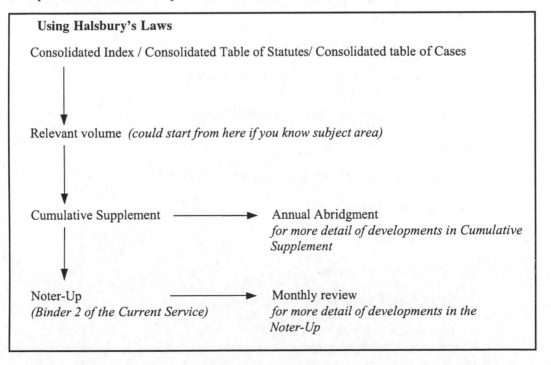

N.B. Halsbury's Laws is always being updated. It is important to make sure that you are looking at the most up-to-date version. There is a check list of materials at the beginning of Binder 1 of the Current Service.

7.4.8   *Halsbury's Law Direct*

Halsbury's Laws of England are also available on-line as part of a service provided by Butter-worths called *Halsbury's Laws Direct*. This allows keyword and natural word searching. It is updated on a monthly basis.

7.5   SELECTION OF ENGLISH LEGAL WEBSITES

7.5.1   The Court Service Web Site

http://www.courtservice.gov.uk/cs_home.htm
This service is free at the moment. It allows access to judgments of the Courts of Appeal (Civil and Criminal Divisions) and Queens Bench Division (Crown Office) since April 1996. Full texts of the judgments are provided. The search facilities allow you to search for judgments from 1998 onwards by keywords. You need to know details of the case in order to search for cases prior to 1998.

7.5.2   The Incorporated Council of Law Reporting for England and Wales website

http://www.lawreports.co.uk
This site gives free access to the details of cases which have been or will be reported in the Law Reports, Weekly Law Reports and Industrial Case Reports. Click on Recent and Forthcoming Law Reports.

7.5.3   Justis — Daily Judgments

This is an on-line subscription service for the English courts.

7.5.4   The Law Society for England and Wales

http://www.lawsociety.org.uk/

7.5.5   The latest edition of the Law Society's Gazette

http://www.lawgazette.co.uk/

7.5.6   The Bar Council

http://www.barcouncil.org.uk/

7.5.7   Judicial Studies Board

http://www.cix.co.uk/~jsb/index.htm
This provides training for judges.

Further information on English legal information sources will be found in:

A. Bradney *et al.*, *How to Study Law* (3rd ed., Sweet & Maxwell 1995).

P. Clinch, *Using a Law Library* (Blackstone 1992).

J. Dane and P.A. Thomas, *How to Use a Law Library* (3rd ed., Sweet & Maxwell 1996).

G. Holburn, *Butterworths Legal Research Guide* (Butterworths 1993).

G. Holburn, ''United Kingdom and dependencies'' in J. Winterton and E.M. Moys, *Information Sources in Law* (2nd ed., Bowker Saur 1997).

J. Jeffries and C. Miskin, *Legal Research in England & Wales* (2nd ed., Legal Information Resources Ltd., Hebden Bridge, 1996).

Chapter 8

E.C. Law

INTRODUCTION

European law makes up an increasingly important part of our body of law. It permeates almost every area of law today and cannot be regarded as a separate subject to be ignored. It is, therefore, essential to be aware of the European dimension to our legal system. This chapter is not intended to provide an overview of the European institutions and the law-making process. Further information on these areas can be found in one of the large number of dedicated European texts (see further reading at the end of the chapter). It is intended to draw your attention to features of the European system which are of relevance to the legal researcher, to introduce you to the key documents of European law and to suggest search strategies for finding information about European law.

There is a vast amount of material published on European law and it is not possible to cover all of it in one chapter. This chapter is designed to introduce you to the principal sources and to make you aware of some of the many alternative ways of locating material. Particular attention will be paid to sources which are official, widely available and those which are free.

There are large numbers of official Community publications. Unfortunately, this does not mean that it is easier to research E.C. law than our own domestic law. Problems can be caused by the sheer volume of material emerging from centralised institutions; significant time delays in publication and a lack of user-friendly indexes to all the information. Many commercial products have appeared which attempt to present the material in a more accessible way. However, you should always remember that the only authoritative version is the official one. Another problem relates to terminology. The indexing systems tend to use Euro-terminology, which can be confusing.

The large amount of information means that electronic sources are coming to the fore. If you want to carry out research on E.C. law you cannot afford to limit yourself to paper sources. There are many official websites and databases which are freely available and updated on a daily basis. A list of European websites is given at the end of this chapter. There are also increasing numbers of commercial databases with different search facilities. Computer-based search skills are essential for studying E.C. law.

One initial point of confusion is the difference between the EEC, E.C. and E.U. The term "Community law" refers to the three communities set up by the Treaty of Paris 1951 and the Treaty of Rome 1957: the European Coal & Steel Community (ECSC), the European Atomic Energy Community (EURATOM) and the European Economic Community (EEC). The Treaty on European Union (the "Maastricht Treaty") came into force in November 1993. It renamed EEC, "EC" (European Community) and established the European Union. The European Union consists of three "pillars": the first pillar is the "Communities pillar" and it is the only pillar to be governed by European Community law. The other pillars (Common Foreign and Security Policy and Co-operation in Justice and Home Affairs) are not subject to the jurisdiction of the Community institutions and the European Court. Those second and third pillars function by way of intergovernmental co-operation.

8.2   LEGISLATION

E.C. laws are made by a completely different process and are different in format to U.K. legislation. See anatomy section, para. 8.2.2.

Some forms of legislation (Regulations) are effective immediately on all Member States, others (Directives) are generally only effective after implementation by Member States into their own national law.

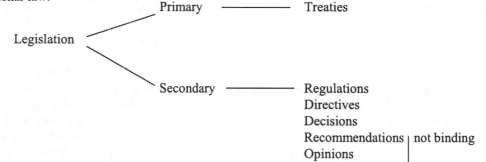

8.2.1   Citation convention

The citation convention for legislation is:

> The institutional origin (Commission/Council)
> The form (Regulation/Directive, etc.)
> The number and year of enactment
>
> > Regulations are cited by number then year
> > *e.g.* Reg. 123/88
> > Directives and Decisions are cited by year and then number
> > *e.g.* Dir. 85/123, Dec. 89/123
>
> The institutional treaty basis (E.C., ECSC, EURATOM)
> Date passed
> Title

Example

Council Directive 96/61/EC of 24 September 1996 concerning integrated pollution prevention and control.

The Treaty of Amsterdam contains amendments to the original treaties which set up the constitution of the European Communities. As a result of article 12 of the Treaty of Amsterdam the articles, titles and sections of the Treaty on European Union and the EC Treaty have been renumbered. This is a recipe for confusion. Many of the recent texts now include tables of equivalences. (see T. Kennedy, *Learning European Law* (Sweet & Maxwell, London 1998, Part 5, V).) The Treaty of Amsterdam came into force on May 1, 1999.

The European Court of Justice has stated that citation of articles of the Treaty where only the number (and not the wording) has changed should be referred to as follows:

Example

Article 81 EC (ex Article 85)

8.2.2   Anatomy of a Directive

31. 12 91   [2]   Official Journal of the European Communities   [1] No L375/1

II

(Acts whose publication is not obligatory)

COUNCIL

COUNCIL DIRECTIVE

of 12 December 1991   [3]

concerning the protection of waters against pollution caused by nitrates from agricultural sources

(91/676/EEC) [4]

COUNCIL OF THE EUROPEAN COMMUNITIES,
[5]

Having regard to the Treaty establishing the European Economic Community, and in particular Article 130s thereof,   [6]

Having regard to the proposal from the Commission ([1])

Having regard to the opinion of the European Parliament ([2]),

Having regard to the opinion of the Economic and Social Committee ([3]),   [7]

Whereas the nitrate content of water in some areas of Member States is increasing and is already high as compared with standards laid down in Council Directive 75/440/EEC of 16 June 1975 concerning, the quality required of surface water intended for the abstraction of drinking water in the Member States ([4]), as amended by Directive 79/869/EEC ([5]), and Council Directive 80/778/EEC of 15 July 1980 relating to the quality of Crater intended for human consumption ([6]), as amended by 1985 Act of Accession;

Whereas the fourth programme of action of the European Economic Communities on the environment ([7]) indicated that the Commission intended to make a proposal for a Directive on the control and reduction of water pollution resulting from the spreading or discharge of livestock effluents and the excessive use of fertilizers;   [8]

Whereas the reform of the common agricultural policy set out in the Commission's green paper 'Perspectives for the common agricultural policy' indicated that, while the use of nitrogen-containing fertilizers and manures is necessary for Community agriculture, excessive use of fertilizers constitutes an environmental risk, that common action is needed to control the problem arising from intensive livestock production and that agricultural policy must take greater account of environmental policy;

Whereas the Council resolution of 28 June 1988 of the protection of the North Sea and of other waters in the Community ([8]) invites the Commission to submit proposals for measures at Community level;

Whereas the main cause of pollution from diffuse sources affecting the Community's waters in nitrates from agricultural sources;

Whereas it is therefore necessary, in order to protect human health and living resources and aquatic ecosystems and to safeguard other legitimate uses of water, to reduce water pollution caused or induced by nitrates from agricultural sources and to prevent further such pollution; whereas for this purpose it is important to take measures concerning the storage and the application on land of all nitrogen compounds and concerning certain land management practices;

Whereas since pollution of water due to nitrates on one Member State can influence waters in other Member States, action at Community level in accordance with Article 130r is therefore necessary;

Whereas, by encouraging good agricultural practices, Member States can provide all waters with a general level of protection against pollution in the future;

([1]) OJ No C 54, 3. 3. 1989, p. 4 and OJ No C 51, 2. 3. 1990, p. 12.
([2]) OJ No C 158, 26. 6. 1989, p. 487.
([3]) OJ No C 159, 26. 6. 1989, p. 1.
([4]) OJ No L 194, 25. 7. 1975, p. 26.

([5]) OJ No L 271, 29. 10. 1979, p. 44.
([6]) No L 229, 30. 8. 1980, p. 11.
([7]) OJ No C 328, 7. 12. 1987, p. 1.
([8]) OJ No C 209, 9. 8. 1988, p. 3.

No L375/2   Official Journal of the European Communities   31. 12 91

Whereas certain zones, draining into waters vulnerable to pollution from nitrogen compounds, require special protection;

Whereas it is necessary for Member States to identify vulnerable zones and to establish and implement action programmes in order to reduce water pollution from nitrogen compounds in vulnerable zones;

Whereas such action programmes should include measures to limit the land-application of all nitrogen-containing fertilizers and in particular to set specific limits for the application of livestock manure;

Whereas it is necessary to monitor waters and to apply reference methods of measurement for nitrogen compounds to ensure that measures are effective;

Whereas it is recognized that the hydrogcology in certain Member States is such that it may he many years before protection measures lead to improvements in water quality;

Whereas a Committee should be established to assist the Commission on matters relating to the implementation of this Directive and to its adaptation to scientific and technical progress;

Whereas Member States should establish and present to the Commission reports on the implementation of this Directive;

Whereas the Commission should report regularly on the implementation of this Directive by the Member States, HAS ADOPTED THIS DIRECTIVE: [9]

Article 1   [10]

This Directive has the objective of:

— reducing water pollution caused or induced by nitrates from agricultural sources and
— preventing further such pollution.

Article 2

For the purpose of this Directive:

(a) 'groundwater': means all water which is below the surface of the ground in the saturation zone an direct contact with the ground or subsoil;

(b) 'freshwater': means naturally occurring water having a low concentration of salts, which is often acceptable as suitable for abstraction and treatment to produce drinking water;

(c) 'nitrogen compound': means any nitrogen-containing substance except for gaseous molecular nitrogen;

(d) 'livestock': means all animals kept for use or profit;

(e) 'fertilizer': means any substance containing a nitrogen compound or nitrogen compounds utilized on land to enhance growth of vegetation; it may include livestock manure, the residues from fish farms and sewage sludge;

(f) 'chemical fertilizer: means any fertilizer which is manufactured by an industrial process;

(g) 'livestock manure': means waste products excreted by livestock or a mixture of litter and waste products excreted by livestock, even in processed form;

(h) 'land application': means the addition of materials to land whether by spreading on the surface of the land, injection into the land, placing below the surface of the land or mixing with the surface layers of the land;

(i) 'eutrophication': means the enrichment of water by nitrogen compounds, causing an accelerated growth of algae and higher forms of plant life to produce an undesirable disturbance to the balance of organisms present in the water and to the quality of the water concerned;

(j) 'pollution': means the discharge, directly or indirectly, of nitrogen compounds from agricultural sources into the aquatic environment, the results of which are such as to cause hazards to human health, harm to living resources and to aquatic ecosystems, damage to amenities or interference with other legitimate uses of water;

(k) 'vulnerable zone': means an area of land designated according to Article 3 (2).

Article 3

1. Waters affected by pollution and waters which could be affected by pollution if action pursuant Article 5 is not taken shall he identified by the Member States in accordance with the criteria set out in Annex I.

2. Member States shall, within a two-year period, following the notification of this Directive, designate as vulnerable zones all known areas of land in their territories which drain into the waters identified according to paragraph 1 and which contribute to pollution. They shall notify the Commission of this initial designation within six months.

3. When any waters identified by a Member State in accordance with paragraph 1 are affected by pollution from waters from another Member State draining directly or indirectly in to them, the Member States whose waters affected may notify the other Member States and the Commission of the relevant facts.

The Member States concerned shall organize, where appropriate with the Commission, the concentration necessary to identify the sources in question and the measures to be taken to protect the waters that are affected in order to ensure conformity with this Directive.

31. 12 91   Official Journal of the European Communities   No L375/3

4. Member States shall review if necessary revise or add to the designation of vulnerable zones as appropriate, and at least every four years, to take into account changes and factors unforeseen at the time of the previous designation. They shall notify the Commission of any revision or addition to the designations within six months.

5. Member States shall be exempt from the obligation to identify specific vulnerable zones, if they establish and apply action programmes referred to in Article 5 in accordance with this Directive throughout their national territory.

Article 4

1. With the aim of providing for all waters a general level protection against pollution, Member States shall, within a two-year period following the notification of this Directive:

(a) establish a code or codes of good agricultural practice, to be implemented by farmers on a voluntary basis, which should contain provisions covering at least the items mentioned in Annex II A;

(b) set up where necessary a programme, including the provision of training and information for farmers, promoting the application of the code(s) of good agricultural practice.

2. Member States shall submit to the Commission details of their codes of good agricultural practice and the Commission shall include information on these codes in the report referred to in Article 11. In. the light of the information received, the Commission may, if it considers it necessary, make appropriate proposals to the Council.

Article 5

1. Within a two-year period following the initial designation referred to in Article 3 (2) or within one year of each additional designation referred to in Article 3 (4), Member States shall, for the purpose of realizing the objectives specified in Article 1, establish action programmes in respect of designated vulnerable zones.

2. An action programme may relate to all vulnerable zones in the territory of a Member State or, where the Member State considers it appropriate, different programmes may be established for different vulnerable zones or parts of zones.

3. Action programmes shall take into account:

(a) available scientific and technical data, mainly with reference to respective nitrogen contributions originating from agricultural and other sources;

(b) environmental conditions in the relevant regions of the Member State concerned.

4. Action programmes shall be implemented within four years of their establishment and shall consist of the following mandatory measures:

(a) the measures in Annex III;

(b) those measures which Member States have prescribed in the code(s) of good agricultural practice established in accordance with Article 4, except those which have been superseded by the measures in Annex III.

5. Member States shall moreover take, in the framework of the action programmes, such additional measures or reinforced actions as they consider necessary if, at the outset or in the light of experience gained in implementing the action programmes, it becomes apparent that the measures referred to in paragraph 4 will not be sufficient for achieving the objectives specified in Article 1. In selecting these measures or actions, Member States shall take into account their effectiveness and their cost relative to other possible preventive measures.

6. Member States shall draw up and implement suitable monitoring programmes to assess the effectiveness of action programmes established pursuant to this Article.

Member States which apply Article 5 throughout their national territory shall monitor the nitrate content of waters (surface waters and groundwater) at selected measuring points which make it possible to establish the extent of nitrate pollution in the waters from agricultural sources.

7. Member States shall review and if necessary revise their action programmes, including any additional measures taken pursuant to paragraph 5, at least every four years. They shall inform the Commission of any changes to the action programmes.

Article 6

1. For the purpose of designating and revising the designation of vulnerable zones, Member States shall:

(a) within two years of notification of the Directive, monitor the nitrate concentration in freshwaters over a period of one year:

(i) at surface water sampling stations, laid down in Article 5 (4) of Directive 751440/EEC and/or at other sampling stations which are representative of surface waters of Member States, at least monthly and more frequently during flood periods;

(ii) at sampling stations which are representative of the groundwater aquifers of Member States, at regular intervals and taking into account the provisions of Directive 801778/EEC;

No L375/4   Official Journal of the European Communities   31. 12 91

(b) repeat the monitoring programme outlined in (a) at least every four years, except for those sampling stations where the nitrate concentration in all previous samples has been below 25 mg/l and no new factor likely to increase the nitrage content has appeared, in which case the monitoring programme need be repeated only every eight years;

(c) review the eutrophic state of their fresh surface waters, estuarial and coastal waters every four years.

2. The reference methods of measurement set out in

Annex IV shall be used.

Article 7

Guidelines for the monitoring referred to in Article 5 and 6 may be drawn up in accordance with the procedure laid down in Article 9.

Article 8

The Annexes to this Directive may be adapted to scientific and technical progress in accordance with the procedure laid down in Article 9.

Article 9

1. The Commission shall be assisted by a Committee composed of the representative of the Member States and chaired by the representative of the Commission.

2. The representative of the Commission shall submit to the Commission a draft of the measures to be taken. The Committee shall deliver its opinion on the draft within a time limit which the chairman may lay down according to the urgency of the matter. The opinion shall be delivered by the majority laid down in Article 148 (2) of the EEC Treaty in the case of decisions which the Council is required to adopt a proposal from the Commission. The votes of the representatives of the Member States within the Committee shall be weighted in the manner set out in that Article. The chairman shall not vote.

3. (a) The Commission shall adopt the measures envisaged if they are in accordance with the opinion of the Committee.

    (b) If the measures envisaged are not with in accordance with the opinion of the Committee, or if no opinion is delivered, the Commission shall, without delay, submit to the Council a proposal relating to the measures to be taken. The Council qualified majority.

    (c) If, on the expiry of a period of three months from the date of referral to the Council, the Council has not acted, the proposed measures shall be adopted by the Commission, save where the Council has decided against the said measures by a simple majority.

Article 10

1. Member States shall, in respect of the four-year period following the notification of this Directive and in respect of each subsequent four-year period, submit a report to the Commission containing the information outlined in Annex V.

2. A report pursuant to this Article shall be submitted to the Commission within six months of the end of the period to which it relates.

Article 11

On the basis of the information received pursuant to Article 10, the Commission shall publish summary reports within six months of receiving the reports from Member States and shall communicate them to the European Parliament and to the Council. In the light of the implementation of the Directive, and in particular the provisions of Annex III, the Commission shall submit to the Council by 1 January 1998 a report accompanied where appropriate by proposals for revision of this Directive.

Article 12   [11]

1. The Member States shall bring into force the laws, regulations and administrative provisions necessary to comply. with this Directive within two years of its notification ([1]). They shall forthwith inform the Commission thereof.

2. When Member States adopt these measures, they shall contain a reference to this Directive or shall be accompanied by such reference on the occasion of their official publication. The methods of making such a reference shall be laid down by the Member States.

3. Member States shall communicate to the Commission the texts of the provisions of national law which they adopt in the field governed by this Directive.

Article 13

This Directive is addressed to the Member States.

Done at Brussels, 12 December 1991.

For the Council

The President

J.G.M. ALDERS

([1]) This Directive was notified to the Member States on 19 December 1991.

31. 12 91   Official Journal of the European Communities   No L375/5

ANNEX 1 [12]

CRITERIA FOR IDENTIFYING WATERS REFERRED TO IN ARTICLE 3 (1)

A. Waters referred to in Article 3 (1) shall be identified making use, *inter alia,* of the following criteria:

  1. whether surface freshwaters, in particular those used or intended for the abstraction of drinking water, contain or could contain, if action pursuant to Article 5 is not taken, more than the concentration of nitrates laid down in accordance with Directive 75/440/EEC;

  2. whether groundwaters contain more than 50 mg/l nitrates or could contain more than 50 mg/l nitrates if action pursuant to Article 5 is not taken;

  3. whether natural freshwater lakes, other freshwater bodies, estuaries, coastal waters and marine waters are found to be eutrophic or in the near future may become euthropic if action pursuant to Article 5 is not taken.

B. In applying these criteria, Member States shall also take account of:

  1. the physical and environmental characteristics of the waters and land;

  2. the current understanding of the behaviour of nitrogen compounds in the environment (water and soil);

  3. the current understanding of the impact of the action taken pursuant to Article 5.

ANNEX II

CODE(S) OF GOOD AGRICULTURAL PRACTICE

A. A code or codes of good agricultural practice with the objective of reducing pollution by nitrates and taking account of conditions in. the different regions of the Community should certain provisions covering the following items, in so far as they are relevant:

  1. periods when the land application of fertilizer is inappropriate;

  2. the land application of fertilizer to steeply sloping ground;

  3. the land application of fertilizer to water-saturated, flooded, frozen or snow-covered ground;

  4. the conditions for land application of fertilizer near water courses;

  5. the capacity and construction of storage vessels for livestock manures, including measures to prevent water pollution by run-off and seepage into the groundwater and surface water of liquids containing livestock manures and effluents from stored plant materials such as silage,

  6. procedures for the land application, including rate and uniformity of spreading, of both chemical fertilizer and livestock manure, that will maintain nutrient losses to water at an acceptable level.

B. Member States may also include in their code(s) of good agricultural practices the following items:

  7. land use management, including the use of crop rotation systems and the proportion of the land area devoted to permanent crops relative to annual tillage crops;

  8. the maintenance of a minimum quantity of vegetation cover during (rainy) periods that will take up the nitrogen from the sod that could otherwise cause nitrate pollution of water;

  9. the establishment of fertilizer plans on a farm-by-farm basis and the keeping of records on fertilizer use;

  10. the prevention of water pollution from run-off and the downward water movement beyond the reach of crop roots in irrigation systems.

Different features of the Directive are marked with numbers which correspond to the following list:

[1] Official Journal series, issue and page

[2] Date of publication

[3] Date of adoption

[4] Number of the Directive

[5] The enacting authority

[6] The legal basis (treaty)

[7] The legislative procedure

[8] The series of paragraphs beginning with the word "whereas" are referred to as recitals. They state the main policy considerations that lie behind the Directive.

[9] This is usually printed in capital letters and represents the end of the first part of the Directive.

[10] The substantive part of the Directive. The parts of European legislation are referred to as articles and not as sections.

[11] Provision concerning when the Directive is to be brought into force.

[12] Additional information at the end of a Directive will be contained in annexes (the equivalent of schedules in U.K. legislation).

A Directive has been used as an example of European legislation. Regulations are similar in format.

8.3   CASES

There are two courts which interpret and enforce E.C. law:
The European Court of Justice (E.C.J.) was established in 1952 and the Court of First Instance (C.F.I.), which gave its first judgment in 1990. Both are situated in Luxembourg.
Points to note:

- Avoid using the term the "European Court". This can cause confusion as there are several courts this title could refer to: European Court of Justice, Court of First Instance, the EFTA (European Free Trade Association) Court and the European Court of Human Rights.

- European cases are reported in a different format, see anatomy of a case, para. 8.3.2.

- There is no equivalent to the role played by the Advocate General in our legal system. At present there are nine Advocates General. The Advocate General's role is independent. He has no connection with either of the parties to a case and yet he is not one of the judges. He delivers an Opinion for the court to consider. In the Opinion he reviews the legal issues and puts forward a proposal as to how the case should be decided. The purpose of the Opinion is to help the court come to their decision. The court is not bound to follow the Opinion, but in practice it does so frequently. The Advocate General's Opinion can be persuasive in later cases. The Opinion will consider the legal issues whereas the judgment of the court will tend to be short and concise. Greater understanding of the legal issues of a case can be gleaned from the Opinion.

- There is no strict doctrine of *stare decisis* in the European Court of Justice.

- Statutory interpretation in the European Court of Justice. The European Court of Justice has tended to adopt a purposive approach to statutory interpretation. It has been criticised for taking this too far and attempting to create law.

- Nicknames for cases. It is common for European cases to be referred to by nicknames. This has arisen because the names tended to be long and difficult to remember. This habit can be useful to distinguish similar cases. However, it can cause problems in locating a case as the nickname is seldom referred to in indexes of cases. Problems can also arise if the same nickname has been given to more than one case. An example of a nickname being used is the Bosman case, Case C-415/93 *Union Royale Belge de Societes de Football Association ASBL v. Jean-Marc Bosman* [1995] E.C.R. I-4921.

8.3.1   Case Citation

The case citation is made up as follows:

      case number/year*
      names of the parties
      [year of judgment]
      citation of the report

Example

Case 6/64 *Costa v. ENEL* [1964] E.C.R. 585.

* The year referred to is the year that application was made to the court. It does not necessarily mean that it will appear in the case reports of that year.

In 1990 the Court of First Instance started to issue judgments. In order to distinguish cases from the two courts, the letter "C" was added to cases from the Court of Justice and the letter "T" added to cases from the Court of First Instance. If the letter "P" appears after the year it denotes that the case has been appealed from the Court of First Instance to the European Court of Justice.

Example

Case C-159/91 *Poucet v. AGF* [1993] E.C.R. I-637
Case T-51/89 *Tetra Pak Rousing S.A. v. Commission* [1990] E.C.R. II-309
Case C-36/92 P *Samenwerkende Elektriciteits-produktiebedrijven NV (SEP) v. Commission of the European Communities* [1994] E.C.R. I-1911.

8.3.2   **Anatomy of a European case report**

The following case appears in the format used by the European Court Reports.

Case C-83/97 [1]

Commission of the European Communities [2]

v

Federal Republic of Germany

(Failure to fulfil obligations — Failure to transpose Directive 92/43/EEC)

Opinion of Advocate General Fennelly delivered on 23 October 1997 . . . . I - 7192
Judgment of the Court (Fifth Chamber) 11 December 1997 . . . . I - 7195

Summary of the Judgment [3]

Acts of the institutions — Directives — Implementation by the Member States — Mere administrative practices not sufficient
(EC Treaty, Art. 189, third para.)

Mere administrative practices, which by their nature are alterable at will by the administration and are not given the appropriate publicity, cannot be regarded as constituting the proper fulfilment of a Member State's obligations under Article 189 of the Treaty.

I - 7191 [4]

OPINION OF ADVOCATE GENERAL   [5]
FENNELLY

delivered on 23 October 1997*

1. Council Directive 92/43/EEC of 21 May 1992 on the conservation of natural habitats and of wild fauna and flora[1] (hereinafter 'the Directive') was notified to the Federal Republic of Germany on 5 June 1992. Article 23(1) required Member States to 'bring into force the laws, regulations and administrative provisions necessary to comply with this Directive within two years of its notification [and] forthwith [to] inform the Commission thereof'. For Germany, this deadline therefore expired on 5 June 1994.

2. In the absence of any indication that the Directive had been transposed into German law, the Commission opened the pre-litigation stage of the procedure provided by Article 169 of the Treaty establishing the European Community ('the Treaty') by sending a letter of formal notice on 9 August 1994. Germany did not contest the complaint in its reply of 6 October 1994. The Commission issued a reasoned opinion on 28 November 1995, to the effect that in failing to adopt the necessary provisions, Germany was in breach of its obligations under the Directive, and setting a two-month deadline for compliance. The present proceedings were initiated pursuant to Article 169 of the Treaty by an application registered at the Court on 24 February 1997.

3. In its application, the Commission observes that, as far as it is aware, not all the provisions necessary to comply with the Directive have been adopted or notified, and that the defendant neither answered nor complied with the reasoned opinion. On this ground, it requests the Court to hold that Germany is in breach of its obligations under the Treaty, and in particular the third paragraph of Article 189 and the first paragraph of Article 5 thereof.

4. In its defence, Germany admits that it has not adopted all the necessary measures to comply with its obligations under the Directive. It adds by way of complementary information that the Directive is directly applied by the competent public authorities, and that the existing national provisions are interpreted in conformity therewith. Furthermore, a bill to amend the Bundesnaturschutzgesetz (Federal law on nature protection) has been submitted to the Bundestag (Federal Assembly, lower house of parliament); the legislative

procedure was scheduled to be completed by Autumn 1997.

5. The Directive is predicated on the statement in the first recital in the preamble that, 'the preservation, protection and improvement of the quality of the environment, including the conservation of natural habitats and of wild fauna and flora, are an essential objective of general interest pursued by the Community'. The fourth recital notes that, as 'the threatened habitats and species form part of the Cominunity's natural heritage and the threats to them are often of a transboundary nature, it is necessary to take measures at Community level in order to conserve them'. This Directive is closely linked to Council Directive 79/409/EEC of 2 April on the conservation of wild birds[2] (hereinafter 'the Birds Directive').[3] The definition of the obligation to transpose the Birds Directive laid down by the Court from its earliest judgments in this area seems to me to be applicable, *mutatis mutandis*, to the obligation to transpose the present Directive. In *Commission v Belgium,* for example, the Court held that transposition 'does not necessarily require the provisions of the directive to he cnactcd in prcciscly the samc words in a specific express legal provision national law; a general legal context may be sufficient if it actually ensures the full application of the directive in a sufficiently clear and precise manners'.[4] It added a proviso to this general statement which is especially relevant in the present proceedings, to the effect that 'a faithful transposition becomes particularly important in a case such as this in which the management of the common heritage is entrusted to the Member States in their respective territories'.[5]

6. Germany has expressly admitted its failure to adopt all of the necessary provisions to comply with the Directive; it has not contended that the action of the public authorities, or the interpretation of the relevant national provisions, ensures such compliance, and, indeed, the Court has consistently held that '[mere] administrative practices, which by their nature are alterable at will by the authorities and are not given the appropriate publicity, cannot he regarded as constituting the proper fulfilment of obligations under the Treaty'.[6] In these circumstances, I am of the opinion that the Commission should bc grantcd thc dcclarations which it has requested both on the merits and as regards costs.

---

* Original language: English

[1] — OJ 1992 L 206, p. 7.

[2] — OJ 1979 L 103, p. 1.

[3] — See paragraph 70 of my Opinion in Case C-44/95 *Royal Society for the Protection of Birds* [1996] ECR I-3802, at pp. I-3832 and I-3833.

[4] — Case 247/85 [1987] ECR 3029, paragraph 9 of the judgment.

[5] — Loc. Cit.

[6] — Case C-334/94 *Commission v France* [1996] ECR I-1307, paragraph 30 of the judgment.

Conclusion

7. In the light of the foregoing, I recommend to the Court that it:

(1) Declare that, by failing to adopt the laws, regulations and administrative provisions necessary to comply with Council Directive 92/43/EEC of 21 May 1992 on the conservation of natural habitats and of wild fauna and flora within the deadline set, the Federal Republic of Germany has failed to comply with its obligations under the EC Treaty;

(2) Order the Federal Republic of Germany to pay the costs.

COMMISSION v GERMANY

JUDGMENT OF THE COURT (Fifth Chamber) [6]

11 December 1997*

In Case C-83/97,

Commission of the European Communities, represented by Götz zur Hausen, Legal Adviser, acting as Agent, with an address for service in Luxembourg at the office of Carlos Gómez de la Cruz, of its Legal Service, Wagner Centre, Kirchberg, [7]

applicant,

v

Federal Republic of Germany, represented by Ernst Rösder, Ministerialrat in the Federal Ministry of Economic Affairs, and Bernd Kloke, Oberregierungsrat in the same ministry, acting as Agents, D-53107 Bonn,

defendant,

APPLICATION for a declaration that, by failing to adopt within the prescribed period the laws, regulations and administrative provisions necessary to comply with Council Directive 92/43/EEC of 21 May 1992 on the conservation of natural habitats and of wild fauna and flora (OJ 1992 L 206, p. 7), the Federal Republic of Germany has failed to fulfil its obligations under the EC Treaty, [8]

* Language of the case: German. [9]

COMMISSION v GERMANY

THE COURT (Fifth Chamber),

composed of. C. Gulmann (Rapporteur), President of the Chamber, M. Wathelet, J. C. Moitinho de Almeida, J.-P. Puissochet and L. Sevón, Judges, [10]

Advocate General: N. Fennelly,
Registrar. R. Grass, [11]

having regard to the report of the Judge-Rapporteur, [12]

after hearing the Opinion of the Advocate General at the sitting on 23 October 1997,

gives the following

Judgment [13]

1. By application lodged at the Registry of the Court of justice on 24 February 1997, the Commission of the European Communities brought an action under Article 169 of the EC Treaty for a declaration that, by failing to adopt within the prescribed period the laws, regulations and administrative provisions necessary to comply with Council Directive 92/43/EEC of 21 May 1992 on the conservation of natural habitats and of wild fauna and flora (OJ 1992 L 206, p. 7, 'the directive'), the Federal Republic of Germany has failed to fulfil its obligations under the EC Treaty.

2. In accordance with Article 23 of the directive, the Member States were to bring into force the laws, regulations and administrative provisions necessary to comply with it within two years of its notification, and forthwith to inform the Commission thereof. Since the directive was notified to the Federal Republic of Germany on 5 June 1992, the period allowed for its implementation expired on 5 June 1994.

3. On 9 August 1994, not having been notified or otherwise informed of any measures to transpose the directive into German law, the Commission give the Federal Government formal notice under Article 169 of the Treaty to submit its observations in that regard within two months.

4. By letter of 25 October 1994 the Federal Government replied that the German authorities were drafting the provisions necessary to comply with the directive and that, pending their adoption, the directive was to be applied under the legal rules in force. However, the Federal Government asserted that the provisions of the directive concerning the conservation of natural habitats were not yet relevant for areas of Community interest, that the provisions relating to protection of species had already been to a large extent transposed by the federal law on the protection of nature then in force and, generally, that in certain places the directive was unclear, which complicated its transposition.

5. On 28 November 1995, not having received any communication of the promised transposition measures, the Commission sent the Federal Government a reasoned opinion requesting it to take the necessary measures to comply therewith within two months from its notification. That reasoned opinion went unanswered.

6. Accordingly, the Commission decided to bring the present action.

7. The Federal Government does not deny that it has not adopted all the measures necessary for implementation of the directive. It states, however, that since the passing of the deadline for transposition, the directive has been directly applied by the competent authorities and existing national provisions have been interpreted in accordance with Community law. It goes on to say that a law designed *inter alia* to implement the directive is in the process of being adopted.

8. Since the directive has not been transposed into national law by the Federal Republic of Germany within the pre-scribed period, the action brought by the Commission must be held to be well founded.

9. It has consistently been held that mere administrative practices, which by their nature are alterable at will by the administration and are not given the appropriate publicity, cannot be regarded as constituting the proper fulfilment of a Member State's obligations under Article 189 of the EC Treaty (see, *inter alia,* Case C-242/94 *Commission* v *Spain* [1995] ECR I-3031, paragraph 6).

10. It must therefore he held that, by failing to adopt within the prescribed period the laws, regulations and admin-istrative provisions necessary to comply with the directive, the Federal Republic of Germany has failed to fulfil its obli-gations under Article 23 of the directive.

Costs

11. Under Article 69(2) of the Rules of Procedure, the unsuccessful party is to be ordered to pay the costs if they have been applied for in the successful party's pleadings. Since the Commission has applied for costs and the defendant has been unsuccessful, the Federal Republic of Germany must be ordered to pay the costs.

COMMISSION v GERMANY

On those grounds,   **[14]**

THE COURT (Fifth Chamber)

hereby:

1. Declares that, by failing to adopt within the prescribed period the laws, regulations and administrative provisions necessary to comply with Council Directive 92/43/EEC of 21 May 1992 on the conservation of natural habitats and of wild fauna and flora, the Federal Republic of Germany has failed to fulfil its obligations under Article 23 of that directive;

2. Orders the Federal Republic of Germany to pay the costs.

Gulmann	Wathelet	Moitinho de Almeida
	Puissochet	Sevón

Delivered in open court in Luxembourg on 11 December 1997.

R. Grass   C. Gulmann

Registrar   President of the Fifth Chamber

Different features of the case report are marked with numbers which correspond to the following list:

[1] Case number

[2] Names of the parties

[3] Summary of Judgment. This is similar to the headnote in U.K. cases. It can be a useful guide to the subject matter of the case but it has no binding force of law.

[4] The page number in the E.C.R. The full citation for this case in Case C-83/97: *Commission of the European Communities v. Federal Republic of Germany* [1997] E.C.R. I-7191.

[5] Opinion of the Advocate General, see para. 8.3.

[6] The current composition of the E.C.J. is 15 judges. The court can sit as a full court which has a quorum of seven. It can also sit with smaller numbers of judges in groups which are referred to as "Chambers".

[7] The parties and their legal advisers.

[8] The section beginning with "APPLICATION" outlines the legal issue(s).

[9] The authentic version of the case is in the language used in the case itself. The E.C.J. identifies the original language in a footnote.

[10] Details of the composition of the court in this case.

[11] The Registrar is a close equivalent to the clerk of court in the U.K. system except that he is considered as more important. He deals with the procedure and administration of the court.

[12] Until 1994 the Report of the Judge-Rapporteur was published with the rest of the case in the E.C.R. It is a report for the hearing which gives the background to the dispute, the legislative framework, details of the procedure adopted and a summary of the written observations submitted to the court.

[13] Judgment. Single judgments are given in all decisions. There is no publication of dis-

senting judgments. Judgments are brief (by U.K. standards) consisting of a series of short paragraphs.

[14] The actual ruling of the court is always at the end of the judgment and usually starts with the words "On those grounds". As in this case, the rulings tend to be short.

8.4   SOURCES OF E.C. LEGISLATION

8.4.1   Official Sources

8.4.1.1   *The Official Journal of the European Communities (O.J.)*

The O.J. is the official gazette of the E.C. There can be several issues on one day due to the amount of material it has to cover. It is published in all the official languages. The Official Journal is available in paper, CD-ROM and on-line on a subscription basis. The Official Journal for the previous 20 days is currently available free via the Eur-lex site. See para. 8.4.1.3 below.

There are separate series within the Official Journal:

The L series contains the full authoritative text of *all* legislation whose publication is obligatory and virtually all adopted legislation. There is no standard citation convention for references in the O.J. A commonly used format is:

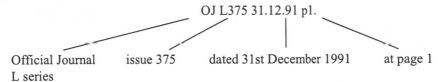

OJ L375 31.12.91 pl.

Official Journal   issue 375   dated 31st December 1991   at page 1
L series

The C series, "Information and Notices", covers a wide range of information including summaries of cases, minutes of plenary sessions and written questions from the European Parliament and details of proposed legislation. Full authoritative case reports from the European Court of Justice and the Court of First Instance are *not* published in the Official Journal. They appear in the Reports of Cases before the Court of Justice and the Court of First Instance (usually known as the European Case Reports see para. 8.6);

The S series contains invitations to tender for public works, services and supply contracts (this information is also available on-line via the Tenders Electronic Daily database (TED) http://www2.echo.lu/ted

The debates of the plenary sessions and oral questions from the European Parliament are published in the *Official Journal: Annex-Debates of the European Parliament.*

8.4.1.2   *Celex*

http://www.europa.eu.int/celex/celex-en.html

Celex is the E.C.'s official legal database. It is available via CD-ROM and on-line. It is a subscription service. It is organised into eight sectors which cover virtually all of the E.C.'s legislative and judicial output. It also includes preparatory acts, parliamentary questions and national implementing measures. It is almost all in full text. It was originally developed for use by officials and not the general public and has been criticised for being user-unfriendly ("many is the information specialist driven to deepest gloom at the prospect of having to interrogate Celex!" I. Mayfield, E.U. Legal Information on the Internet, *The Law Librarian*, vol. 29, no. 4, December 1998, p. 234.). The format of Celex has improved over time but there are now several commercial databases which have developed versions of Celex, see para. 8.4.2.1.

8.4.1.3   *Eur-lex*

http://europa.eu.int/eur-lex
This recent site currently allows free access to a large amount of information. It is part of a European Commission campaign to make Community law more accessible. However, it may become subject to charges in the future. Through this site you can access:

- the full text of the treaties;

- the full consolidated (*i.e.* incorporating amendments) version of legislation. *N.B.* The consolidated texts are not authoritative, only the original legislation is authoritative;

- the Court of Justice website and recent case law

- the Official Journal for the 20 days previously.

Legislation is listed alphabetically by subject index and by areas of Community competence. There is a search facility which allows you to search by keyword(s). This is a very useful free source of information.

8.4.1.4   *European Union: Selected Instruments taken from the treaties*

This official publication contains the text of the treaties but the current edition was published before the Treaty of Amsterdam which has made substantial amendments to the original treaties.

8.4.2   Commercial/unofficial products containing information about E.C. legislation

8.4.2.1   *Commercial databases*

There are several commercial databases which contain versions of Celex. They are all slightly different, with additional features and different search facilities. They are all subscription based and include:

> *Eurolaw* produced by ILI
> *European Law* produced by technical Indexes Ltd
> *Justis Celex* produced by Context Limited
> *OJCD* produced by ELLIS Publications

These databases have recently been evaluated — see E. Davies, "On test — Celex on CD", *European Information*, 1998, vol. 4, p. 23.

8.4.2.2   *European Legislation Service*

This has replaced the old *Encyclopaedia of European Community Law*. It is published by Sweet & Maxwell and is made up of two encyclopaedias. *The Encyclopaedia of European Union Law — Constitutional Texts* contains primary legislation and is published in five loose-leaf volumes. *The Encyclopaedia of European Community Law — Secondary Legislation* is published in 11 loose-leaf volumes. The service is updated four times a year. The service contains the full text of legislation.

8.4.2.3   *Single volume collections of legislation*

These include: N. Foster, *Blackstone's EC Legislation* (9th ed., 1998). This is an annual publication which contains a selection of primary and secondary legislation. There are no annotations. The current edition includes amendments made by the Treaty of Amsterdam.

B. Rudden and D. Wyatt, *Basic Community Laws* (7th ed., 1999). This contains a broad selection of legislation.

Volume 50 of *Halsburys Statutes of England* (see chapter 7, para. 7.2.1) contains amended versions of the Treaties.

8.4.3   Aids to finding E.C. legislation

8.4.3.1   *Official*

The Index to the Official Journal of the European Communities

This index is issued monthly and annually. It is in two parts: an alphabetical subject index and a methodological index which references legislation in numerical order and cases by number.

The Official Journal of the European Communities: Directory of Community Legislation in Force

This is published twice a year. It lists legislation in force (and references any amending legislation) by subject and by reference number. It is available on-line as part of Eur-lex. See para. 8.4.1.3.

EUDOR

This is a document delivery service which operates on a fee basis. However, it is possible to search the site for references at no cost. The site includes secondary legislation and COM documents. http://www.eudor.eu.int/

8.4.3.2   *Commercial/unofficial*

European Communities Legislation: Current Status

This is published by Butterworths. It contains reference to every piece of E.C. legislation both in force and repealed. Annotations beside each entry indicate the status of the legislation and how it has been amended. It consists of two annual volumes, quarterly supplements and a fortnightly updating newsletter. There is also a telephone inquiry service. It lists secondary legislation in chronological/numeric order and also has an alphabetical subject index.

8.4.4   Finding E.C. legislation on a subject

Eur-lex (free), see para. 8.4.1.3.

Celex and its commercial versions: Euro Law, European Law, Justis Celex and OJCD.

European Communities Legislation: Current Status — alphabetical subject index (see para. 8.4.3.2).

The E.U.'s *General Report on the Activities of the European Communities*. This is an annual publication arranged by subject matter. Update by checking the monthly *Bulletin of the European Union*.

Loose-leaf encyclopaedias and texts:

⇒ European Legislation Service (see para. 8.4.2.2).
⇒ D. Vaughan Law of the European Communities Service
⇒ *The Common Market Reporter*

⇒ *E.U. Brief*
⇒ *Butterworths Annual European Review*
⇒ The *Laws of Scotland: Stair Memorial Encyclopaedia* (see chapter 6 para. 6.3.1.1).

N.B. Once you know the year you can use The *Index to the Official Journal of the European Communities*. This is an annual index.

8.4.5   Current status of E.C. legislation

The Official Journal of the European Communities: Directory of Community Legislation in Force. This is available free as part of Eur-lex. See para. 8.4.1.3.

European Communities Legislation: Current Status. See para. 8.4.3.2.

Celex and its commercial versions: Euro Law, European Law, Justis Celex and OJCD.

8.4.6   Tracing if a Directive has been implemented in national law

Butterworths EC Legislation Implementator — This is issued twice a year. It is sold as part of a package with *European Communities Legislation: Current Status* (see para. 8.4.3.2) and is updated by a Current Status fortnightly newsletter. It provides details of the E.C. Directives in numerical order, required dates of implementation and how they have been implemented into U.K. law.

Celex and its commercial versions: Euro Law, European Law, Justis Celex and OJCD.

8.5   OFFICIAL DOCUMENTS

Working documents are published as COM documents. Legislative proposals will first be published as COM documents and will later appear in the C series of the Official Journal.

The E.U. Official documents website contains information on documents such as work programmes, action plans, Green Papers and White Papers.
http://europa.eu.int/comm/off/index__en.htm

Information about legislative proposals and their progress can be found in a site called OEIL. It is called the Legislative Observatory and is produced under the auspices of the European Parliament. It is updated daily.
http://www.europarl.eu.int/dors/oeil/en/inter0.htm

COM documents can also be located by checking:

- *Bulletin of the European Union*, see para. 8.9.3.

- *House of Commons Weekly Information Bulletin*, see chapter 5, para. 5.1.2.

- *European Access* — by subject, see para. 8.8.3.3.

- EUDOR, see para. 8.4.3.1 above
  http://www.eudor.eu.int/

- Celex and its commercial versions: Euro Law, European Law, Justis Celex and OJCD.

- BADGER Index (part of Current Legal Information (subscription)) see chapter 6, para. 6.11.3.5.

A useful source of information about the E.U. is the House of Lords European Communities Committee. This Committee has considered Community proposals and reported on them since 1974. Its reports for parliamentary sessions 1997–98 and 1998–99 are available through the House of Lords website:

http://www.parliament.the-stationery-office.co.uk/pa/ld/ldeucom.htm

8.6   E.C. CASE LAW

8.6.1   Sources of E.C. case law

8.6.1.1   *Law Reports*

There are two main series of law reports:

Title	**European Court Reports** Formal title: Reports of Cases before the Court of Justice and the Court of First Instance
Abbreviation	E.C.R.
Citation	Case C-41/93 *French Republic v. Commission of the European Communities* [1994] E.C.R. I-1829
Period covered	1954 to present
Publisher	Office for Official Publications of the European Communities.
Comments	This is the official series of European law reports. The reports are published in all the official languages of the E.C. The authentic text is that of the language of the case. The production of multiple translations of every case means that the series is slow to appear. The reports include the Advocate General's Opinion beside the decision. This is particularly useful as it is the Advocate General's Opinion which tends to contain the reasoned legal argument in E.C. cases.
Available in	Paper
Coverage	*All* cases from the European Court of Justice and the Court of First Instance are reported, but, since 1989, some may be in summary form.
Format	Indexed by subject matter and in the final volume of the year there is a chronological table of cases. Since 1990 the reports have been divided into two sections: section I for the Court of Justice and section II for the Court of First Instance.

Title	**Common Market Law Reports**
Abbreviation	C.M.L.R.
Citation	T-194/94 *Carvel & Guardian Newspapers Ltd v. Council* [1995] 3 C.M.L.R. 359
Period covered	1962 to present
Publisher	Sweet & Maxwell
Comments	Although they are not official reports, this series has the big advantage of appearing much quicker than the E.C.R. It is published weekly.
Available in	Paper and CD-ROM
Coverage	Decisions from the European Court of Justice and the Court of First Instance, Commission decisions and decisions of national courts, including the U.K., relevant to E.C. law. It does *not* report every case but it does report all cases of significance.
Format	Indexed alphabetically by case name, subject and Community legislative provisions. It also contains tables of Treaties and regulations judicially considered, cases judicially considered, statutes cited and abbreviations.

8.6.1.2   *European Court of Justice website*

European Court of Justice website
europa.eu.int/cj/en/index.htm
There are many sections of this useful site:

- Cases lodged. This contains details of cases lodged in both the European Court of Justice and the Court of First Instance. The cases are listed by case number. A large number of cases are included but some of the older cases have yet to be added to the site. The reports are available in full text but they should not be taken as authoritative. The only authoritative version is the European Court Reports — see para 8.6.1.1.

- *The Proceedings of the Court of Justice and Court of First Instance* weekly bulletin is also available at this site, see para 8.6.1.3 below. The electronic version of this weekly bulletin is always available earlier than its paper counterpart.

- Diary of forthcoming cases before the two courts.

- Press releases. This section gives very brief details about recent judgments and opinions. It is a useful current awareness service. It can alert you to the existence of a new case which you can then read by entering the relevant details into the recent case law section — see below.

- Recent case law. This covers cases from 1997. Judgments are available in full text and on the same day that judgment is delivered. There is a search facility which allows you to search by case number, date, names of parties, subject area or key words.

Other sources of E.C. case law

8.6.1.3 Celex and its commercial versions: Euro Law, European Law, Justis Celex and OJCD.
The Times and *Financial Times* coverage in their law reports.
The Proceedings of the Court of Justice and Court of First Instance. This is a weekly bulletin which summarises judgments and opinions from the previous week. It is available in paper and electronically — see above. It is useful as an easy-to-read guide to recent case law.

8.6.2 Finding E.C. cases

1. *Butterworths E.C. Case Citator and Service*
   This covers most E.C. case law since 1954. This system indexes the information by: case number, first party name, legislation considered, nickname and keywords. It is updated twice a year and in addition subscribers receive a fortnightly updating newsletter.

2. European Court Of Justice website — see para. 8.6.1.2.

3. *European Current Law* (1993–). The Year Books and Monthly Digests contain Tables of Cases. Cases are listed alphabetically and by case number. See chapter 10, para. 10.8.

4. *European Legal Journals Index* (1993–). Case index. See para. 8.8.3.1.

5. D. Vaughan, *Law of the European Communities Service*. Check the Table of Cases.

6. Other European texts. Check tables of cases.

7. Celex and its commercial versions: Euro Law, European Law, Justis Celex and OJCD.

8. Indexes in the European Law Reports and Common Market Law Reports. The indexes are issued annually. If you know the approximate year, it would be feasible to check through the closest annual volumes. If you do not know the date, use another source.

8.6.3   **Finding recent E.C. Cases**

8.6.3.1   *Sources updated daily*

By far the best source: European Court of Justice website (see para. 8.6.1.2), press releases and recent case law sections. Cases appear on the same day as the judgment. See also newspapers and on-line news services.

8.6.3.2   *Sources updated weekly*

The Proceedings of the Court of Justice and Court of First Instance. See para. 8.6.1.3
Butterworths E.C. Law Brief weekly newsletter. See para. 8.7.1.6.

8.6.3.3   *Sources updated monthly*

European Current Law Monthly Digest
European Legal Journals Index

8.7   TRACING RECENT DEVELOPMENTS

8.7.1   **Sources of information about recent developments**

8.7.1.1   What's new on europa? This is a very useful general awareness site covering all kinds of developments. It is updated on a daily basis.
http://europa.eu.int/geninfo/whatsnew.htm

8.7.1.2   European Court of Justice site — press release and recent case law sections, see para. 8.6.1.2.

8.7.1.3   RAPID. This is a daily press release database. It is managed by the Spokeman's Service of the European Commission. It includes press releases from the European Commission, Council of Ministers, Court of Justice, Court of Auditors, Economic and Social Committee and the Committee of the Regions. It is useful for providing a daily view of E.U. activities.
http://europa.eu.int/rapid/start/welcome.htm
The latest documents section is a particularly useful current awareness site.

8.7.1.4   *The Proceedings of the Court of Justice and Court of First Instance.* This is a weekly bulletin which summarises judgments and opinions from the previous week.

8.7.1.5   SCADPLUS
This is available as a weekly bulletin (SCAD Bulletin) or as a website. It is a source of different types of information such as a calendar of events, and summaries of E.U. policies. The website also includes the SCAD database, see para. 8.9.5.
http://europa.eu.int/scadplus/

8.7.1.6   *Butterworths E.C. Law Brief.* This is a four-page weekly newsletter which gives details of the latest developments within the E.C. It is available on-line as part of Butterworth's *Law Direct database.*

8.7.1.7   Newspapers
The E.U. is covered in many newspapers. The most in-depth coverage is to be found in:

The European Voice (a weekly newspaper which covers recent events in the E.U.). It has a website:
http://www.european-voice.com/
The Financial Times
http://www.ft.com/

8.7.1.8   *European Current Law Monthly Digest.* This categorises recent legal developments, books and articles by subject heading

8.7.2   Current awareness strategy

To keep up with the latest legal developments, check the following free services daily:

Europa — what's new
http://europa.eu.int/geninfo/whatsnew.htm

European Court of Justice site, press release section
europa.eu.int/cj/en/index.htm

RAPID — latest documents
http://europa.eu.int/rapid/start/welcome.htm

8.8   SECONDARY SOURCES OF E.C. LAW

8.8.1   Texts

There are numerous texts on European law. The following are some examples:

The entry in volume 10 of *The Laws of Scotland: Stair Memorial Encyclopaedia* "European Community Law and Institutions".

D. Vaughan, *Law of the European Communities Service.* This is a four-volume loose-leaf work which is updated five times a year.

E.U. Brief. This is a four-volume loose-leaf work.

The Common Market Reporter. This is a loose-leaf publication.

Butterworth's Annual European Review. This is an annual publication which indexes legislative and judicial development which have appeared in Butterworths *E.C. Brief* throughout the previous year.

P. Craig and G. De Burca, *E.U. Law: Text, Cases & Materials* (2nd ed., Oxford University Press, 1998).

Shorter, more introductory texts include:

N. Burrows, *Greens Guide to European Law in Scotland* (W. Green, 1995).
W. Cairns, *Introduction to European Union Law* (Cavendish, 1997).
J. Hanlon, *European Community Law* (Sweet & Maxwell, 1998).
T. Kennedy, *Learning European Law* (Sweet & Maxwell, 1998).

8.8.2   **A selection of journals containing legal information about the E.C.**

> *Common Market Law Review* (C.M.L.Rev.) Published bi-monthly.
>
> *European Law Review* (E.L.Rev.) Published bi-monthly.
>
> *Journal of Common Market Studies* (J.C.M.S.) Published four times a year.
>
> *The International and Comparative Law Quarterly* (I.C.L.Q.) Published four times a year.
> *European Law Journal* (E.L.J.) published four times a year.
> *The Yearbook of European Law* (Y.E.L.) This is an annual publication which contains tables of abbreviations, articles, annual surveys, book reviews, tables of cases, decisions and communications, legislation, treaties and rules of procedure, international conventions and agreements, national legislation and an index.

Journals concentrating on specific aspects of E.C. law include:

> *European Business Law Review* (E.B.L.R.) Published 11 times a year.
>
> *European Competition Law Review* (E.C.L.R.) Published eight times a year.
>
> *European Environmental Law Review* (E.E.L.R.) Published 11 times a year.
>
> *European Intellectual Property Review* (E.I.P.R.) Published monthly.
>
> *European Public Law* (E.P.L.) Published four times a year.

8.8.3   **Finding journal articles about E.C. law**

8.8.3.1   *European Legal Journals Index*

Started in 1993 and contains references to journals published in English which frequently contain articles on legal topics relating to the E.C. The material can be accessed via five indexes:

> subject
>
> author
>
> case
>
> legislation
>
> book review

The paper version of *European Legal Journals Index* is published in monthly issues which are cumulated every quarter and again every year. It is also available as part of Current Legal Information as a CD-ROM and on-line.

8.8.3.2   *European Current Law*

Check the subject index at the end of the Year Books. There is also an alphabetical list by title. See chapter 10, para. 10.8.

8.8.3.3   *European Access*

This is a bi-monthly current awareness bulletin covering policies and activities of the E.C. It lists references under subject headings and includes new E.C. proposals, legislation, books, journal and newspaper articles and publications of other bodies. It is a very useful publication for keeping up-to-date with European affairs.

8.8.3.4   *SCAD database*

See para. 8.9.5.

8.9   SOURCES OF INFORMATION ABOUT THE E.U., ITS ACTIVITIES AND POLICIES

8.9.1   Europa

This is the official E.U. website.
http://europa.eu.int/index.htm
This site allows access to a vast amount of information. It can be accessed by four entry points:

1. News. This section covers press releases, a calendar of events, the official Euro rates, statistics and other news services.

2. Institutions. This allows access to the home pages of the E.U. institutions.

3. Abc. This provides basic information about the E.U. It covers the rights of E.U. citizens, information on key issues, access to various sources of information about publications, official documents and legal texts.

4. Policies. This allows access by subject heading to information on the implementation of E.U. policies, legal instruments and current legal developments.

8.9.2   General Report on the Activities of the European Communities

This is an annual publication produced by the Secretariat-General of the Commission. It reviews the previous year's developments. It is available on paper and via the internet:
http://europa.eu.int/abc/doc/off/rg/en/welcome.htm
The reports for 1997 and 1998 and available in full text. Reports for the previous two years are available only in summary.

8.9.3   Bulletin of the European Union

This is a monthly review of the work of the E.U., published by the E.U. publisher. Latest issue and issues back to 1996 are available on-line.
http://europa.eu.int/abc/doc/off/bull/en/welcome.htm

8.9.4   The Week in Europe

This is a two-page newsletter published by the European Commission Representation in the U.K. It is available on paper or on-line.
http://www.cec.org.uk

8.9.5   **SCAD database**

This is the main bibliographic database of the E.C. It allows you to search for references to legislation and preparatory documents, Community publications, a large selection of articles dealing with Community affairs and statements/opinions from both sides of industry.
http://europa.eu.int/scadplus/

8.9.6   **European Access**

See para. 8.8.3.3.

8.9.7   **EUR-OP News**

This is a quarterly periodical which provides an overview of recent developments and lists new publications available from the E.U. publisher. It is available on-line (free).
http://eur-op.eu.int/en/opnews/r.htm

8.10   OTHER SOURCES OF INFORMATION ABOUT EUROPE

8.10.1   **Euristote**

This is a research database. It contains references to thousands of doctoral theses and post-doctoral research on the subject of European integration.

8.10.2   **Euroguide**

This is a website designed to make access to European information easier and contains a subject index with links to relevant sites.
http://www.euroguide.org/

8.10.3   **Websites for European information**

HTTP://www.eia.org.uk/eiaorg/websites.htm

8.10.4   **E.C. Representation offices**

These are located in all E.U. countries. Their purpose is to represent the Commission. In addition, they are a good source of information about the E.U. and E.U. policy. The website for the European Commission Representation in the U.K. is:
http://www.cec.org.uk
The Scottish office is at 9 Alva Street, Edinburgh EH2 4PH. It is a drop-in information centre.

8.10.5   **European Documentation Centres**

Certain libraries have been designated as European Documentation Centres (EDCs). This means
that they will have copies of every publicly available document produced by the E.C. EDCs in
Scotland are the university libraries of Edinburgh, Glasgow, Dundee and Aberdeen.

8.10.6   **European Reference Centres**

Other sites have been designated European Reference Centres (ERCs). They receive a range of
secondary E.C. publications. In Scotland the National Library of Scotland and Stirling University
library are ERCs.

Further reading

N. Burrows, *Greens Guide to European Law in Scotland* (W. Green, 1995, chap. 2).
J. Dane, P.A. Thomas, *How to Use a Law Library* (3rd ed., Sweet & Maxwell, 1996, chap. 11).
V. Deckmyn, *Guide to Information of the European Union* (European Institute of Public Adminis-
    tration, 1996).
T. Kennedy, *Learning European Law* (Sweet & Maxwell, 1998, chap. 7).
I. Mayfield, E.U. Legal Information on the Internet, *The Law Librarian*, vol. 29, no. 4, December
    1998, 234.
F. Shipsey, "European Law" in J. Winterton and E.M. Moys, *Information Sources in Law*
    (Bowker Saur, 1997, pp. 23–46).

8.11 EUROPEAN WEBSITES:

Bulletin of the European Union	http://europa.eu.int/abc/doc/off/bull/en/welcome.htm
Committee of the Regions	http://www.cor.eu.int/
Council of the EU	http://ue.eu.int/en/summ.htm
Court of Auditors	http://www.eca.eu.int/EN.menu.htm
Economic and Social Committee	http://www.esc.eu.int/en/acs/fr_acs_default.htm
EUDOR	http://www.eudor.eu.int/
The Euro	http://europa.eu.int/euro/html/home5.html?lang=5
Eur-lex	http://europa.eu.int/eur-lex
Europa	http://europa.eu.int/index.htm
Europa — what's new	http://europa.eu.int/geninfo/whatsnew.htm
Euroguide	http://www.euroguide.org/
European Agencies and Bodies	http://europa.eu.int/en/agencies.html
European Central Bank	http://www.ecb.int/
European Commission	http://europa.eu.int/index-en.htm
European Commission Representation in the UK	http://www.cec.org.uk
European Court of Justice site	europa.eu.int/cj/en/index.htm
European Investment Bank	http://www.eib.org/
European Ombudsman	http://www.euro-ombudsman.eu.int/home/en/default.htm
European Parliament	http://www.europarl.eu.int/sg/tree/en/default.htm
European Parliament — United Kingdom Office	http://www1.europarl.eu.int/uk/index.html
EUR-OP News	http://eur-op.eu.int/en/opnews/r.htm
The EU Official documents website	http://europa.eu.int/comm/off/index._en.htm
European Voice	http://www.european-voice.com/
The Financial Times	http://www.ft.com/
General Report on the Activities of the European Communities	http://europa.eu.int/abc/doc/off/rg/en/welcome.htm
House of Lords European Communities Committee	http://www.parliament.the-stationery-office.co.uk/pa/ld/ldeucom.htm
IDEA Electronic Directory of the European Institutions	http://europa.eu.int/idea/ideaen.html
RAPID	http://europa.eu.int/rapid/start/welcome.htm
OEIL	http://www.europarl.eu.int/dors/oeil/en/inter0.htm
Office for Official Publications of the EC	http://eur-op.eu.int/indexen.htm
SCAD	http://europa.eu.int/scadplus/
Statistical Office of the European Communities	http://europa.eu.int/en/comm/eurostat/serven/home.htm
Websites for European information	HTTP://www.eia.org.uk/eiaorg/websites.htm

Chapter 9

INTERNATIONAL LAW

9.1 INTRODUCTION

There is a distinction between public international law and private international law. Private international law is also known as "conflict of laws". It is in essence an area of Scots law but with international dimensions. It involves examining the relationship between two or more legal systems. An example of a private international law dispute would be a couple who wished to divorce. They were married in Iceland and the man now lives in France and works in the Netherlands and the wife is Scottish but lives in England.

The sources involved in private international law are principally the same as other areas of Scots law, with the addition of being able to locate international conventions. This subject will not be dealt with separately. Searching for international conventions will be dealt with under public international law.

The purpose of this chapter is to highlight the differences between our domestic legal sources and sources of public international law. It will introduce you to some of the main sources of public international law and ways of locating the different materials. It is intended to be an introduction to researching this increasingly important area of law. More detailed information can be found in the texts listed in para. 9.4.1.

9.2 PUBLIC INTERNATIONAL LAW

Public international law concerns relationships between states. It is a wholly distinct system of law. Public international law is very different from Scots law. It does not have a legislature. The rules of international law do not have the authority of an Act of Parliament. They are unable to bind states in the same way as an Act of the U.K. Parliament binds individuals in the U.K.. To a large extent international law is based on the goodwill of states. If a state chooses not ratify a treaty, it is not bound by that treaty. There is a court, the International Court of Justice, but unlike U.K. courts it does not adopt a system of binding precedent. It does not have jurisdiction over states in the same way as national courts have jurisdiction over individuals within a state.

If there is no legislature, where do the rules of public international law come from? Article 38 (1) of the Statute of the International Court of Justice has come to be regarded as a statement of the sources of international law. It states that the court shall apply:

international conventions

international custom

general principles of law recognised by civilised nations

judicial decisions and the teaching of respected jurists

For a discussion of the sources of international law see I. Brownlie, *Principles of Public International Law* (5th ed., 1998), chap. 1.

One major difference in researching international law is the pre-eminence of electronic material. It is increasingly important in all areas of law but none more so than international law. A list of relevant websites is included at the end of this chapter.

9.3   PRIMARY SOURCES OF INTERNATIONAL LAW

9.3.1   **Treaties**

The Vienna Convention on the Law of Treaties 1969, Article 2(1)(a) defined "treaty" as "an international agreement concluded between States in written form and governed by international law, whether embodied in a single instrument or in two or more related instruments and whatever its particular designation;". Treaties are different from statutes in the U.K. as they do not have universal application. They only apply to states which agree to them. A treaty can be between two states (bilateral) or several states (multilateral). Some international organisations are able to make treaties with states but individuals do not have the capacity to make treaties. Treaties can also be referred to as conventions, covenants, pacts, agreements or charters. A protocol tends to refer to an agreement subsequent to a treaty which has amended the original treaty.

Treaties are divided into articles and paragraphs as opposed to Acts of Parliament which have sections. Treaties do not automatically come into force at the moment the parties come to agreement. The signing of a treaty does not bind a state to ratify it at a later date. Signature only indicates an intention to ratify. There can be a considerable period of time between the signature of a treaty and its coming into force. Individual treaties can specify different periods. It is normal for a treaty to come into force after it has been ratified by a certain number of signatories. As stated earlier, even when a treaty does come into force, it is only binding on states which ratify it.

9.3.1.1 *Citation of treaties*

The normal way of referring to treaties is by their title and the year of signature/adoption, *e.g.* the Vienna Convention on the Law of Treaties 1969. Full citation details will include a reference to the relevant treaty series where the treaty appears. See para. 9.3.1.2 for more information about the different treaty series. The possible citations for this treaty include:

U.K.T.S. 58 (1980), Cmnd. 7964. This relates to the entry in the United Kingdom Treaty Series. This series forms a sub-series to the Command Papers. This means that treaties are referred to by the Treaty Series number, a Command Paper number and the date of issue (treaties are only published in this series *after* ratification).

1155 U.N.T.S. 331. This refers to the United Nations Treaty Series (see para. 9.3.1.2) volume 1155 and page 331.

(1969) 8 I.L.M. 679. This refers to International Legal Materials (see para. 9.3.3.6) 1969 volume 8 and page 679.

9.3.1.2   *Collections of treaties*

1. *The Consolidated Treaty Series* covers the period 1628–1920 and the *League of Nations Treaty Series* covers 1920–1946. The major series of modern treaties is the United Nations Treaty Series (U.N.T.S.) which includes material from 1946 onwards. This is a collection of treaties and international agreements which have been published by the Secretariat of the United Nations. The collection currently has over 30,000 treaties and related material which have been published in over 1,450 volumes. The United Nations Treaty Series is available on-line. It is free but you will be asked to register.

http://www.un.org/Depts/Treaty/enter.htm

This site allows you to search the entire treaty series which has been published in printed form. You can search by: date, party, title, popular name, subject terms, registration number or a combination of these.

The site also allows you access to *Multilateral Treaties Deposited with the Secretary-General*. This publication contains information on the status of major multilateral instruments which have been deposited with the Secretary-General of the United Nations. It is updated on a weekly basis. You will be able to find out about the status of instruments as the process of signature and ratification by states takes place. The printed version is published annually.

2. *The United Kingdom Treaty Series* is the U.K.'s national collection of treaties. It is an official series published by the Foreign & Commonwealth Office. It started in 1892 and forms a sub-series to the Command Papers. Treaties are published in this series only after ratification by the U.K.

3. An excellent and widely available source of information about treaties (and other matters) is *International Legal Materials*. This publishes the texts of treaties along with annotations. See para. 9.3.3.6 below. The text of treaties will tend to appear here much earlier than in the printed series.

4. There are many websites which allow access to a selection of treaties. A good academic treaty collection site is:

http://www.tufts.edu/fletcher/multilaterals.html

This site has been produced as part of a Multilaterals Project. This is an ongoing project to make the texts of multilateral treaties and conventions available. It is run by the Fletcher School of Law and Diplomacy, Tufts University, Massachusetts, USA. It contains the full text of a large selection of important treaties and is easy to use. You can access treaties chronologically (1899–present) or by subject (ranging from atmosphere and space to trade and commercial relations).

The Council of Europe European Treaties website allows free access to treaties and agreements of the Council of Europe.

http://www.coe.fr/eng/legaltxt/treaties.htm

The site is free. It has been constructed for information purposes, the official versions of the treaties are contained in the European Treaty Series (ETS). The Council of Europe was established by the Statute of the Council of Europe in 1949. Its aim as stated in Article 1(b) is to encourage progressive European agreement on economic, social, cultural, scientific, legal and administrative matters and to maintain and work towards the further realisation of human rights and fundamental freedoms. Its principal achievement is the European Convention on Human Rights. See para. 9.5.

5. There are student editions of important treaties such as Blackstone's *International Law Documents*. Student editions tend to have several editions and the latest edition is due out in September 1999. This does not contain any annotations. A widely-used text which includes both primary material and useful commentary is D.J. Harris, *Cases and Materials on International Law* (5th ed., 1998).

6. When a treaty is incorporated into U.K. law it is common practice to include the text of the original treaty in a schedule to the Act or statutory instrument. The ease with which these can be located when you only know the name of the treaty depends on how closely the short title of the U.K. legislation matches the treaty title.

9.3.1.3   *Aids to tracing Treaties*

1. The search facilities available via the websites mentioned in para. 9.3.1.2 above: the U.N.T.S., the Council of Europe European Treaties and the Multilateral project.
2. Each of the paper treaty series mentioned above in para. 9.3.1.2 has extensive indexes.
3. Bowman and D.J. Harris, *Multilateral Treaties: Index & Current Status* (1984) and updated by cumulative supplements. This was a very useful publication but its importance has lessened in recent years with the increasing amount of information becoming accessible via the internet.

9.3.2   Custom

Custom has traditionally been regarded as one of the most important sources of public international law. However, its importance is lessening due to the increase in the number of treaties which are codifying custom. Custom in the international sense does not equate with custom in Scots law. In public international law there are two elements which must be present for a custom to exist: state practice and the belief that a legal obligation binds you to act in a certain way (referred to as *opinio juris et necessitatis*).

How is it possible to find evidence of custom? Brownlie states that:

> "The material sources of custom are very numerous and include the following: diplomatic correspondence, policy statements, press releases, the opinions of official legal advisers, official manuals on legal questions, *e.g.* manuals of military law, executive decisions and practices, orders to naval forces, etc., comments by governments on drafts produced by the International Law Commission, state legislation, international and national judicial decisions, recitals in treaties and other international instruments, a pattern of treaties in the same form, the practice of international organs, and resolutions relating to legal questions in the United Nations General Assembly."

I. Brownlie, *Principles of Public International Law* (5th ed., Clarendon Press, 1998, p. 5).

It is obviously easier to find information about some of the above than others. Sources of information about custom include state papers such as the British & Foreign State Papers produced by the Foreign Office Library between 1812 and 1968. A compilation of British practice is the *British Digest of International Law* edited by C. Parry (this work is incomplete).

The International Law Commission mentioned above exists under the auspices of the United Nations. Its role is to promote the progressive development of international law and its codification. Information about it and its activities can be found at its website: (http://www.un.org/law/ilc/introfra.htm).

Sources of current information about state practice can be gleaned from the "Current Legal Developments" sections in *International and Comparative Law Quarterly* and the *British Yearbook of International Law*. Newspapers and on-line news services are another good source of information.

9.3.3   Cases

The International Court of Justice (ICJ) and sometimes referred to as the "world court" is situated in The Hague in the Netherlands. It was established at the same time as the United Nations in 1946. Its predecessor was called the Permanent Court of International Justice which had been established under the League of Nations.

The International Court of Justice derives its mandate from the Statute of the International Court of Justice which is annexed to the Charter of the United Nations. Article 59 of that Statute states that "the decision of the court has no binding force except between the parties and in respect of that particular case". Although there is no formal doctrine of binding precedent, previous cases are not ignored.

9.3.3.1   *International Court Reports (I.C.J. Reports) (1947 –)*

This is the official series of law reports which has the full title of *Reports of Judgments, Advisory Opinions and Orders of the International Court of Justice*. These reports appear in both English and French. All cases brought before the court since 1946 are available on the web. Some are only in summary form but many of the more recent decisions are in full text.
http://www.icj.cij.org/

9.3.3.2   *Pleadings, Oral Arguments and Documents (I.C.J. Pleadings) (1947–)*

This is also published by the court. The series contains the documentation for each case which is made public after the final decision has been given.

9.3.3.3   *Yearbook of the International Court of Justice (I.C.J. Yearbook)*

This contains information about the work of the court, its members and activities in a year.

9.3.3.4   *Reports of case law of the Permanent Court of International Justice*

The predecessor of the International Court of Justice was the Permanent Court of International Justice (P.C.I.J.). Between 1922 and 1946 P.C.I.J. judgments were published in Series A (Nos. 1–24): Collection of Judgments (up to and including 1930) and Series A/B (Nos. 40–80): Judgments, Orders and Advisory Opinions (beginning in 1931). A selection of its case law can be found in *World Court Reports 1922–1942*. This is a four-volume work edited by Manley O. Hudson.

9.3.3.5   *International Law Reports (I.L.R.)*

This series started in 1919 and was originally called the *Annual Digest of Public International Law Cases*. This is the name for volumes 1–16. From volume 17 (1950) they have been called International Law Reports. The aim of this series is to provide English-language access to judicial matters that have a bearing on international law. It covers the International Court of Justice, European Court of Human Rights, Inter-American Court of Human Rights and other international tribunals as well as national decisions from many countries which have a public international law angle. Cases can be accessed in alphabetical order, by court, by country and by subject headings.

There are three volumes of consolidated indexes:

Volume one contains subject indexes for volumes 1–35 and volumes 36–80.

Volume two contains the following material all relating to volumes 1–80:

List of abbreviations
Consolidated Tables of Cases arranged alphabetically
Consolidated Tables of Cases arranged by jurisdiction
Key Word Index to the Table of Cases
Consolidated Table of Treaties
Index to Treaties by Name in Common Use
Index to Treaties by parties
Index to Treaties by subject

Volume three contains the following material all relating to volumes 81–100:

Abbreviations
Consolidated Table of Cases arranged alphabetically
Consolidated Table of Cases arranged by jurisdiction subdivided into international and national
Consolidated Table of Treaties (in chronological order)
Consolidated Index

9.3.3.6   *International Legal Materials (1962–present)*

This is a bi-monthly publication produced by the American Society of International Law. It provides wide coverage of developments in international law. The main criterion for selection is that the documents are of substantial interest to a large number of legal scholars, practising lawyers and officials dealing with public and private international law. This is a very useful source of information. It is usually the first available source of full text information about key documents. The entries are arranged under the following headings:

Treaties and Agreements

Judicial and similar proceedings

Legislation

Reports and other documents

Notice of documents not reproduced in full

There is a subject index at the end of each annual volume. There are cumulative indexes which cover 1962–69, 1970–79, 1980–89. It is available on-line via Lexis, see chapter 13, para. 13.4.3.

9.4   SECONDARY SOURCES

9.4.1   Books

Key texts include
Oppenheim's International Law edited by R. Jennings (1992).
I. Brownlie, *Principles of Public International Law* (5th ed., 1998)

More introductory texts include:
P. Malanczuk, *Akehurst's Modern Introduction to International Law* (7th ed., 1997)
I.A. Shearer, *Starke's International Law* (11th ed., 1994)
R.M.M. Wallace, *International Law* (3rd ed., 1997).

Bibliographies include:
Contemporary Practice of Public International Law edited by E.G. Schaffer and R.J. Snyder (1997).
Public International Law — A Current Bibliography of Books and Articles (1975–). This is published twice a year.
E. Beyerly, *Public International Law — A Guide to Information Sources* (1991).
Older works could be found in *A Current Bibliography of International Law*, J.G. Merrills (1978).

9.4.2 Journals

The most widely available journals are:

> *International and Comparative Law Quarterly* (I.C.L.Q.)
>
> *American Journal of International Law* (A.J.I.L.)
>
> *European Journal of International Law* (E.J.I.L.)

There are many more international law journals especially in the U.S. There is also an increasing number of journals relating to specialist areas of international law, *e.g. Journal of Air Law & Commerce*.

9.4.3 British Yearbook of International Law (B.Y.I.L.) (1920–present)

This contains the following material for the year under review:

> in-depth articles;
> detailed book reviews;
> decisions of British courts involving questions of international law;
> decisions on the European Convention on Human Rights;
> decisions of the Court of Justice of the European Communities;
> U.K. materials on international law cited from a wide range of sources and arranged by subject within the realm of international law.

9.4.4 Finding journal articles

9.4.4.1 *Public International Law: A Current Bibliography of Books and Articles*

This is published twice a year.

9.4.4.2 *Index to Foreign Legal Periodicals*

This contains a subject index to selected international law and comparative law periodicals and collections of essays.

9.4.4.3   *Index to Legal Periodicals*

This index lists periodicals and books published in the U.S., Canada, Great Britain, Ireland, Australia and New Zealand. The information is indexed under subject and author.

9.4.4.4   *Legal Journals Index*

This index covers all journals published in the U.K. which are devoted to law or frequently contain articles on legal topics. See chapter 6, para. 6.8.1.1 for more details.

Legal Journals Index is published in monthly issues which are cumulated every quarter. From 1993 material relating solely to European law and the laws of the countries in Europe is contained in the *European Legal Journals Index*. Material which involves both U.K. and E.C. law is indexed in both the *Legal Journals Index* and the *European Legal Journals Index*.

9.4.5   Current awareness sources

1. *Bulletin of Legal Developments* published fortnightly by the British Institute of International & Comparative Law.

2. Foreign Office website latest news section:
   http://www.fco.gov.uk/news/
   This site is updated throughout the day with speeches, transcripts and press releases.

3. Focus International section of the Foreign Office website:
   http://www.fco.gov.uk/news/briefs.asp
   This contains a series of papers about international issues. It is free and it is possible to register with the site so that when a new paper is added, you will receive an email telling you of its availability.

4. International Court of Justice — latest press communiqués
   http://www.icj-cij.org/icjwww/ipresscom/iprlast.html

5. BBC news site, world section
   http://news.bbc.co.uk/hi/english/world/default.htm
   This site also allows you access to search all BBC news on-line stories since November 1997.

6. ITN World News
   http://www.itn.co.uk/front/front.htm
   You can also search the ITN archive for the past year.

7. CNN
   http://www.cnn.com/

8. The Press Association
   http://www.pa.press.net/

9. *Keesing's Record of World Events* (originally known as *Keesing's Contemporary Archives*)
   This contains summaries of world events. The entries are short and do not contain much depth.

9.5   HUMAN RIGHTS LAW

Public international law can be divided into discreet areas such as the law of the sea, international environmental law, world trade law and international criminal law. One area of international law which is becoming increasingly important is human rights law. When the Human Rights Act 1998 comes into force, U.K. courts will be under a statutory duty (s. 2) to consider previous jurisprudence relating to the Convention in any case which concerns a Convention right. This means that familiarity with the case law emerging from the European Court of Human Rights will become increasingly important. A short section dealing with human rights law information sources has therefore been included below.

The European Convention on Human Rights (proper title The Convention for the Protection of Human Rights and Fundamental Freedoms) was adopted by the Council of Europe in 1950 and entered into force in 1953. The European Commission on Human Rights was formed in 1953. Its purpose is to deal with violations of the convention. The European Court of Human Rights (E.C.H.R.) was set up in 1959. It is located in Strasbourg. It hears cases which have been referred by the Commission.

9.5.1   Information sources

9.5.1.1   *The Council of Europe*

The Council of Europe European Treaties website allows free access to the full text of the Convention, protocols and status (dates signed and ratified by the various states, date of coming into force and any reservations or declarations).
http://www.coe.fr/eng/legaltxt/treaties.htm

The Council of Europe publishes judgments and decisions in *Publications of the European Court of Human Rights*. Series A contains judgments and Series B pleadings, oral arguments and documents. You can search all the case law of the European Court of Human Rights via its website (free):
http://www.dhcour.coe.fr

Click on Judgments and Decisions or the scales of justice at the foot of the home page. You can search in English and French. Judgments are available on the day of delivery. The Judgments and Decisions section also contains information on the effects of judgments from 1959–1998 and a list of recent judgments.

In addition the site provides the following information:

> General information about the composition of the court
> List of pending cases
> Basic texts. This allows you access to the text of the European Convention on Human Rights and its Protocols and the Rules of Court.
> Press releases. These contain summaries of cases issued by the Registrar of the court.

9.5.1.2   *The European Commission on Human Rights*

The European Commission on Human Rights also has a website (free):
http://www.dhcommhr.coe.fr
This provides information about the organisation and its activities, press releases and full accounts of recent decisions made by the Commission.

An Official Collection of Decisions of the European Commission on Human Rights is also published.

9.5.1.3   *European Human Rights Reports*

The leading paper source for the decisions of the European Court of Human Rights is the commercially produced European Human Rights Reports (E.H.R.R) (1979–present). This covers the case law of the European Court of Human Rights and also includes admissibility decisions of the European Commission on Human Rights.

Information can be accessed via the following tables:

Alphabetical Table of Cases reported in the current volume
Alphabetical Table of Admissibility Decisions reported in the current volume
Numerical Table of Cases reported in the current volume
Chronological Table of European Court Cases reported in volumes 1–current volume
Index of Subject matter in the current volume
Cases Judicially Considered by the European Court in the current volume
Abbreviations

9.5.1.4   *Journal articles*

Journal articles can be found in European legal journals but dedicated sources include:

European Human Rights Law Review (E.H.R.L.R.) is published six times a year

The Yearbook of the European Convention on Human Rights provides an account of the area for a given year. Its publication is usually delayed by several years.

9.6 INTERNATIONAL LAW INTERNET REFERENCES:

American Society of International Law Home Page	http://www.asil.org
Amnesty International	http://www.amnesty.org/
BBC news site, world section	http://news.bbc.co.uk/hi/english/world/default/htm
CNN	http://www.cnn.com/
The Council of Europe European Treaties	http://www.coe.fr/eng/legaltxt/treaties.htm
The Economist	http://www.economist.com/
Europa, the E.U.'s server	http://europa.eu.int/index.htm
European Court of Human Rights	http://www.dhcour.coe.fr
The European Commission on Human Rights	http://www.dhcommhr.coe.fr
European Court of Justice	http://www.curia.eu.int
Foreign Office website latest news section:	http://www.fco.gov.uk/news/
Focus International section of the Foreign Office	http://www.fco.gov.uk/news/briefs.asp
The Foreign Office	http://www.fco.gov.uk/
Indiana University School of Law	http://www.law.indiana.edu
International Criminal Court Home Page	http://www.igc.org/icc/
International Constitutional Law	http://www.uni-wuerzburg.de/law/home.html
International Court of Justice	http://www.icj-cij.org/
International Court of Justice — latest press communiqués	http://www.icj-cij.org/icjwww/ipresscom/iprlast.html
International Federation of Red Cross and Red Crescent Societies	http://www.ifrc.org
International Law Commission	http://www.un.org/law/ilc/introfra.htm
International Law Institute	http://www.ili.org
ITN World News	http://www.itn.co.uk/front/front.htm
Library of Congress	http://www.loc.gov/
Multilaterals Project	http://www.tufts.edu/fletcher/multilaterals.html
One World Home Page	http://www.oneworld.org/index.html
The Press Association	http://www.pa.press.net/
Public International Law Web Resources by Francis Auburn, University of Western Australia	http://www.law.ecel.uwa.edu.au/intlaw/
The Times	http://www.the-times.co.uk
United Nations Headquarters Home Page	http://www.un.org
The United Nations Treaty Series	http://www.un.org/Depts/Treaty/enter.htm
United Nations Documents	http://www.un.org/Docs/
United Nations Scholars' Workstation at Yale University: Research Approaches to U.N. Information	http://www.library.yale.edu/un/un3b4.htm
United Nations High Commissioner for Refugees	http://www.unhcr.ch/
United Nations: Law of the Sea	http://www.un.org/Depts/los/index.html
United Nations: International Criminal Tribunal for the Former Yugoslavia	http://www.un.org/icty/index.html

Chapter 10

CURRENT LAW

　INTRODUCTION TO CURRENT LAW

The reason for an entire chapter being devoted to Current Law is that it has the most comprehensive range of information available in one data-retrieval system. It is also widely available throughout Scotland. It is a very important and useful source of information. The paper version covers legal developments since 1948 and is updated monthly. Recent developments are subsequently incorporated into the Service Files.

Using Current Law can be confusing at first because of all the component parts but it is worth persevering and mastering the system. When you become familiar with it, it becomes the quickest way of checking certain types of legal information.

That is not to say that the system is without its faults. Over the years as the system has expanded and incorporated more information, the format has changed in minor but significant ways. There is very little information about the various changes and this can be confusing. Another criticism is that the classification of material into subject headings can sometimes leave a lot to be desired. You often need to check under several different headings, *e.g.* water pollution material could be classed under water, environmental protection, pollution or utilities. It is also true to say that the subject headings are not used consistently. If there is no relevant material for that month then the heading disappears. However, despite these criticisms Current Law is an invaluable tool to the legal researcher.

A practical exercise (complete with answers) has been included at the end of this book for you to test your ability to use Current Law.

Prior to 1991 the Current Law service was provided in two formats: (a) Scottish Current Law and (b) Current Law. The Scottish Current Law service included the English and Welsh service. The Current Law service excluded all purely Scottish material. From 1991 the service has been called Current Law and now covers the law of England and Wales, Northern Ireland, Scotland and the E.C.

Some components of the Current Law service are available as parts of Current Legal Information. This will be referred to in the sections below as appropriate. The CD-ROM version is updated monthly while the on-line version is updated on a daily basis. Current Legal Information cannot at present be regarded as a replacement for the paper version of Current Law. The limited number of components which are included in Current Legal Information only cover a comparatively short period of time compared to the paper version. There is very poor coverage of Scottish material, *e.g.* currently the case citators do not include Scottish cases.

This chapter concentrates on the *Scottish* version of Current Law and accessing Scottish, U.K. and E.C. material from the system. Reference is made to instances where the English version of Current Law differs significantly from the Scottish version.

Points of note:

- Matters applicable to the U.K. generally are included in the English section of Current Law. Scots lawyers should not just look at the Scottish section.

- Current Law uses a system of references to apply to its various constituent parts. The references appear in the form, *e.g.* 82/4292. The numbers represent the year/paragraph number and not the page number.

Current Law has various component parts:

- Monthly Digests
- Yearbooks
- Case Citators
- Legislation Citators
- Statutes Annotated
- Statutes Service Files
- European Current Law: European Current Law Monthly Digest
  European Current Law Year Book

There is also a publication called Current Law Week. This does not include Scottish material and is designed for the needs of English county court practitioners.

The components of Current Law will now be discussed in turn. The contents will be examined along with directions on using this information service.

10.2   MONTHLY DIGESTS

Monthly Digests provide a *monthly* updating service. Each issue is divided into two parts, Cases and materials and Tables:

10.2.1   Cases and Materials

The subject headings covered in Current Law are listed at the beginning of each Monthly Digest. Not every subject heading will appear in every issue. The subject areas covered in the issue are printed in bold type.

10.2.1.1   *Current Law Notes*

These are brief notes arranged under subject headings. They are designed to provide an overview of recent developments in different fields of law. There is a separate section of Current Law Notes (Scotland).

10.2.1.2   *Digest*

The material is arranged alphabetically by subject. The subject headings are divided into three sections:

U.K., England & Wales and the E.U.

Northern Ireland

Scotland

The material consists of summaries of developments in the law. Developments such as cases, legislation, government department circulars, books and articles.

Excerpt from Monthly Digest Sept 1998 P. 198–199, Legal Aid, with features marked

[1]
LEGAL AID

693. Criminal legal aid — solicitors — employment [2]
SCOTTISH LEGAL AID BOARD (EMPLOYMENT OF SOLICITORS TO PROVIDE CRIMINAL LEGAL ASSISTANCE) REGULATIONS 1998, SI 1998 1938 (S.101); [3]
[4]   [5]
made under the Legal Aid (Scotland) Act 1986 s.28A, s.37. In force: October 1, 1998; £1.10.
      These Regulations provide for solicitors to be employed by the Scottish Legal Aid Board to give criminal legal assistance and to be used in the Sheriff Court district of Edinburgh. [6]

694. Expenses — modification — personal liability of legal aided person —
competency of appeal [7]
[Legal Aid (Scotland) Act 1986 (c.47) s.18(2).] [8]
      In an action between two legally aided parties G was found liable in expenses. The sheriff also refused G's motion under the Legal Aid (Scotland) Act 1986 s.18(2) to modify his personal liability for expenses. G appealed seeking an order that the matter of modification be remitted to the sheriff for reconsideration. [9]
      Held, refusing the appeal, that (1) where a sheriff might have erred in law it was incompetent for a sheriff principal to remit the case to the sheriff, and (2) it was not competent for an appellate court to review a decision on the modification of expenses, *Todd v. Todd* 1966 S.L.T. 50, [1966] C.L.Y. 13387 followed. [10]
      Observed, that *Todd v. Todd* was not consistent with sound policy or the terms of the statute and ought to be reviewed by a larger court. ORTTEWELL v. GILCHRIST 1998 S.C.L.R. 451, CGB Nicholson Q.C., Sheriff Principal, Sh Ct. [11]

695. Articles [12]
[13] No entry! No access! No justice!: J.L.S.S. 1998, 43(7) Supp, 2–3. (Proposed changes to civil legal aid scheme and implications of alternative means of funding litigation). [14]

Key:
  [1] Subject heading
  [2] Subject matter, catchphrases appear in bold
  [3] Title and citation of a statutory instrument
  [4] Enabling legislation
  [5] Date brought into force
  [6] Digest of contents
  [7] Subject matter, catchphrases appear in bold
  [8] Relevant legislation [in square brackets]
  [9] Facts
  [10] Ratio decidendi
  [11] Case name and citation
  [12] Subject matter in bold
  [13] Title of article and reference
  [14] Summary of contents

10.2.2   Tables

A series of tables cover the following:

10.2.2.1   *Quantum of damages*

This provides cumulative information on quantum of damages in personal injuries cases reported in the current year. Information is given in tabular form under five headings: injury, age, case, award and reference. Scottish cases are in a separate table, following the table relating to English cases.

10.2.2.2 *European law*

This details subject areas covering cases heard in the European Court of Justice and the Court of First Instance and European legislation which is digested in that month's digest.

10.2.2.3 *Retail Price Index/Tax and Price Index figures*

10.2.2.4 *Words and phrases judicially considered*

This is a cumulative guide to words and phrases which have been judicially considered throughout the year.

10.2.2.5 *Table of fees*

These relate to the English High Court and the County Court.

10.2.2.6 *Progress of Bills*

This covers Bills in the current parliamentary session and is complete to a date given at the top of the page. Government Bills are given in bold. The word "Commons" or "Lords" appears after the Bill's name to show where the Bill originated.

10.2.2.7 *Dates of commencement*

This gives dates of commencement and details of the instrument that brought the statute into force.

10.2.2.8 *Statutory Instruments*

This is a cumulative alphabetical list of statutory instruments digested in the current year.

10.2.2.9 *European legislation implemented by Statutory Instrument*

European legislation implemented by statutory instruments issued in the current year is listed in chronological order.

10.2.2.10 *Abbreviations*

This is a good place to look for new abbreviations. It covers whatever is included in that issue of the Monthly Digest.

10.2.2.11 *Transcripts subsequently reported*

This is a cumulative list of cases recently digested in Current Law as transcripts and subsequently reported elsewhere.

10.2.2.12 *Table of cases*

This list is cumulative and is in alphabetical order. It covers cases which have been digested or judicially considered in the current year. Cases which have been digested are in CAPITAL LETTERS. Cases which have been judicially considered or commented on are in normal print.

10.2.2.13 *Cumulative index arranged alphabetically within subject headings*

Scottish entries are followed by an "S". The subject headings used here are greater in number and more specific than the broad subject headings in the Cases and Materials section.

10.2.2.14 *List of law books (reference to books can also be found under relevant subject headings)*

This includes books published that month. They are arranged in alphabetical order of author.

10.2.3   Searching the Monthly Digest

Points to note:

1. All indexes are *cumulative* and they refer to the relevant paragraph in the Monthly Digest in which the item is mentioned. This means that you should always check the most recent issue of the Monthly Digest as it will contain information which will allow you to access all the material for the current year.

2. Scottish items are identified by the letter "S" after the Current Law paragraph number.

3. Matters applicable to the U.K. generally are included in the English section of Current Law.

4. Not all digest headings are used in *each* Monthly Digest. They are not used if there is no current information.

5. You will notice that the Monthly Digests use two different referencing systems. This can result in the same reference being given in two different ways in the same volume. The Monthly Digest index refers to previous Monthly Digests as, *e.g.* Mar 442, *i.e.* month and paragraph number, whereas other indexes in the Monthly Digest, *e.g.* alphabetical list of statutory instruments refer to them as 373 3CL, *i.e.* paragraph and volume number for the Monthly Digest.

10.2.3.1 *How to find out about recent developments on a particular subject*

To find out about developments over the last month

Check the relevant subject heading in the latest Monthly Digest. This will tell you if anything has happened over the last month. If the subject heading does not appear it means that there have been no developments in the area for that month.

To find out about developments over the current year

⇒ Step 1: Check the relevant subject heading in the cumulative index at the back of the latest Monthly Digest. This will refer you to the month and paragraph number, *e.g.* Mar 403. If you are looking for Scottish information the references will be followed by the letter "S".
⇒ Step 2: Turn to the March monthly Digest at paragraph 403 and you will find the information.

10.2.3.2 *How to find a recent Scottish article on a subject*

⇒ Step 1: Go to the latest issue of the Monthly Digest.
⇒ Step 2: Check the cumulative index under the subject heading. Various sub-headings will exist and will be listed alphabetically. Check under "articles". You will see various references. If any of the references is followed by an "S", you know that the article is Scottish.
⇒ Step 3: Turn to the entry referred to and you will find details of the article.

| Example |

Find the latest Scottish article on taxation.

⇒ Step 1: Check the latest Monthly Digest (December 1998).

⇒ Step 2 : Check the cumulative index under the subject heading "taxation". Within the heading "taxation" locate the sub-category "articles". Check at the end of the list to find the latest items. You are looking for the latest reference followed by the letter "S". The reference given is Dec 574S.

⇒ Step 3: Check paragraph 574S in the December issue of the Monthly Digest. It gives details of an article by Andrew Hart called "Obtaining Interview records — An Improvement", De Voil I.T.I. 1998, 28, 11–12.

10.3   CURRENT LAW YEAR BOOKS

These are annual volumes which revise and consolidate the Monthly Digests. Items may be regrouped and re-edited. They are not usually available until the middle of the following year. The Year Books are arranged by subject and contain summaries of all legal developments for that year. Over the years the format of the Year Books has changed, the current format (published in two volumes since 1995) is detailed below:

Digest Headings in Use

Table of Cases

Table of Damages for Personal Injuries or Death

Retail Price Index

Tax and Price Index

Alphabetical List of Statutory Instruments for the Year

List of Statutory Instruments arranged alphabetically by subject headings

Numerical Table of Statutory Instruments for the Year

Alphabetical Table of Northern Ireland Statutory Instruments and Orders

Table of Abbreviations

The Law summarised under Subject Headings — U.K., England and Wales and E.U.

The Law summarised under Subject Headings — Northern Ireland

The Law summarised under Subject Headings — Scotland

Words and Phrases Table

Law Books published during the Year

Index

10.3.1 Searching in the Year Books

If you are searching for a particular topic you should check under the appropriate subject heading. Under the subject heading you will find a reference consisting of a year and a paragraph number, *e.g.* 96/6674S. You would locate the material in the 1996 Year Book at paragraph 6674. The "S" denotes that it is Scottish material.

If you know the approximate date you can check the appropriate Year Book. If you do not know the date then you do not have to check every Year Book — in some key volumes the subject index has been consolidated at various times:

1956 Scottish Current Law Year Book Master Volume	contains entries for 1948–56
1961 Scottish Current Law Year Book Master Volume	contains entries for 1957–61
1966 Scottish Current Law Year Book Master Volume	contains entries for 1962–66
1971 Scottish Current Law Year Book Master Volume	contains entries for 1967–71
1986 Scottish Current Law Year Book	contains entries for 1972–86
1990 Scottish Current Law Year Book	contains entries for 1987–90
From 1991 onwards each Year Book should be checked.	contain entries for each year
You should then check the latest Monthly Digest.	contains entries for current year

N.B. The English version has been consolidated at different times

Example

Find out if there have been any developments in the law of succession in Scotland since 1996.

⇒ Step 1: Check the 1997 Year Book in the Scottish section under ''Succession''.
⇒ Step 2: Check the 1998 Year Book in the Scottish section under ''Succession''.
⇒ Step 3: Check the latest issue of the Monthly Digest for the current year in the index under the subject heading ''Succession'' and look for references followed by an ''S''.

Current Legal Information includes a section entitled Current Law Cases. This contains digests of cases from 1986 to date and includes Scottish cases. There is a ''What's new'' section containing recent developments, table of quantum and facilities to search by field (such as case name, court, legislation, subject, keywords) or by free text.

10.4   CASE CITATORS

A case citator is an alphabetical list of cases. If a case has been reported since 1948 it will appear in the list along with its citation(s) and a reference to where you can find a digest of the case in the Current Law service. In addition, every time a case has been commented on or considered by the courts it will appear in the list. This means that pre-1947 cases can also appear in Current Law.

Current Law Case Citators are in three volumes. Scottish Case Citator volumes are currently:
1948–1976,   1977–1997,   1998.

Each volume is divided into three parts:

English, Welsh and Northern Irish cases

Scottish cases

Ship's Names Index (from 1977 onwards)

The English equivalents cover the same periods except that the first citator starts from 1947. The Scottish section of the Case Citator contains the following information:

⇒ Details of cases decided or judicially considered in the Scottish courts for the period covered by the volume of the citator.

⇒ References to English cases judicially considered in Scotland during the period covered by the volume of the citator.

Scottish cases which have been published in English Law Reports are included in both the Scottish and English sections of the citator.

A version of the Case Citator is available in Current Legal Information. It covers the period from 1977 to date but does not include Scottish cases. It does contain cases published in the English law reports.

The Case Citators contain the following information:

⇒ Each volume starts with a list of abbreviations of various series of law reports and journals.

⇒ The full name of any case reported between 1947 and the current year. Cases are listed alphabetically by the first party's name.

⇒ Lists of citations in law reports and journals where the case may have been digested.

⇒ Reference to the Current Law Year Book where the case is digested. Most references have a year before the paragraph number, *e.g.* 85/789. This refers you to the 1985 Year Book, paragraph 789.

⇒ The history of *any* case (irrespective of date) which has been judicially considered from 1947 to date. The reference given is to the digest of the case which considered the case listed.

⇒ The Monthly Digest contains an updated Case Citator (referred to as the Table of Cases) each month.

10.4.1   Searching the Case Citators

The Case Citators up to 1977 are in two parts; since 1977 they are in three parts:

Part I   England, Wales and Northern Ireland

Part II   Scotland

Part III Ship's Names Index

Make sure that you look in the relevant part. It is very easy to make a mistake and look in the English section for a Scottish case.

If you know the approximate year of the case you are looking for, start searching in the appropriate volume and then check all the citators subsequent to the date of the case. This will ensure that you pick up on all subsequent developments.

If you do not know the approximate year of the case, start searching in the first (*i.e.* the earliest) volume and work forward in time. This will make sure that you do not miss any developments.

If the case is not mentioned at all, you may be looking in the wrong section of the citator (England instead of Scotland) or the case may be older than 1947 and have never been considered by the courts since 1947.

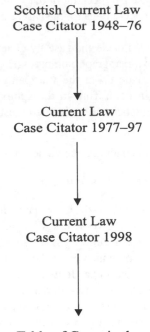

**Scottish Current Law
Case Citator 1948–76**

**Current Law
Case Citator 1977–97**

**Current Law
Case Citator 1998**

**Table of Cases in the
latest Monthly Digest**

Excerpt from Case Citator with features marked.

[2]

[1] Grosvenor Developments (Scotland) v. Argyll Stores, 1987 S.L.T. 738 (Ex. Div.):   [3]
affirming 1987 S.L.T. (Sh.Ct.) 134 ....*Digested*, 87/**4846**: *Followed*, 92/5944, 95/6204:
                                                                                             [4]   *Approved*, 94/5971: *Distinguished*, 94/5970

   Grosvenor Metal Co., *Re* [1950] Ch. 63; (1950) 93 S.J. 774; [1949] 2 All E.R. 948; 65
T.L.R. 755; [67 L.Q.R. 25] .... *Digested*, 50/**1395**: *Approved and followed*, 93/4826
Group 4 Total Security v. Jaymarke Developments, 1995 S.C.L.R. 303. ....*Digested*, 95/**6365**
Group 4 Total Security v. Ferrier, 1985 S.L.T. 287; 1985 S.C. 70 ....*Digested*, 85/**4092**: *Applied*, 86/4023
Grugen v. H.M. Advocate, 1991 S.C.C.R. 526 ....*Digested*, 91/**4644**
Grummer v. H.M. Advocate, 1991 S.C.C.R. 194 ....*Digested*, 91/**4815**: *Commented on*, 92/5570:
                                                                                                                                      Applied, 95/5620

Key:
[1] Name
[2] Citation
[3] References **in bold** indicate where the case has been digested, *e.g.* this case is digested in the 1987 Year Book, paragraph 4846.
[4] References in normal type show where the case has been considered, *e.g.* this case is approved in a case listed in the 1994 Year Book, paragraph 5971.

10.4.1.1   *How to find a citation for a case where you only know the parties' names*

Check through the Case Citators in chronological order. Remember that if it is a Scottish case you should check in the Scottish section. If you are not sure if it is Scottish, you should check *both* the English and Scottish sections of the citators. You should then check the Table of Cases in the most recent Monthly Digest. Cases are listed in alphabetical order of the first named party. If the case appears its full citation(s) will be next to it.

10.4.1.2 *How to find details of a case*

Full text — Locate the case by checking in the Case Citators (see above). Following the name of the case you will find all the citations for the case. For the full text of the case go to the appropriate law report.

A summary of the case — Locate the case by checking in the Case Citators. Opposite the case the first entry will be for a paragraph number where the case is digested in a Current Law Year Book. The reference is made up of the year/paragraph number. The paragraph number of the digest is always shown in bold. Turn to the appropriate Year Book and you will find that the entry for the paragraph number will contain a digest of the case.

Examples using the Case Citators are contained in chapter 3, paras 3.2.1.15 and 3.2.5.7.

10.4.1.3 *Searching the case citations available in Current Legal Information*

Searching the Case Citator (1977–date) available in Current Legal Information enables you to access information either by "Browse cases" which lists cases alphabetically by case name, or by "Search by Field", which allows you to search by various fields. The entry for the case includes the same information which is available in the paper version, with the addition of references to relevant entries in the Legal Journals Index. The key difference between the paper and electronic versions is the ease of cross-referencing. There are hypertext links which allow you to move from one section to another, *e.g.* the reference to the digest of the case, to the digest itself. This is obviously easier than having to go and retrieve another volume from the shelves. Another advantage is the inclusion of the Legal Journals Index in the system. This allows access to details of articles that have considered the case.

10.5 LEGISLATION CITATORS

A Legislation Citator is a chronological list of all Acts passed since 1947 and includes mention of any Acts which have changed or been interpreted by the courts since 1947.

The Current Law Legislation Citators (formerly called Statute Citators) are in four volumes and should be used along with the Current Law Statutes Service File.

The volumes are:

　　　　1948–1971　　　*1972–1988*　　　*1989–1995*　　　*1996–1998.*

The cumulative monthly updates of the Legislation Citator for the current year are to be found in the Current Law Statutes Service File — not in the Monthly Digests.

The English version has a similar format except that the citators start in 1947.

A version of the Legislation Citator is available in Current Legal Information. It covers the period from 1989–date.

The Legislation Citators list *all* amendments, modifications and repeals to primary and secondary legislation made in the years covered by the specific volume.

Since 1993 the Legislation Citators are in fact a combination of two citators — a Statute Citator and a Statutory Instrument Citator.

The Statute Citator is always listed first. It contains:

1. Lists of *all* Public General Acts passed since 1947 along with the date of the Royal Assent. They are listed in chronological order—first by reference to year and then, within year, by reference to chapter number.

2. Details of amendments and repeals since 1947 made to statutes of *any* date, including details of the amending or repealing provisions.

3. In respect of *any* Act, the names and citations of cases in which it has been judicially considered since 1947.

4. In respect of *any* Act, details of statutory instruments issued under its provisions.

5. In respect of *any* Act, where it has been consolidated by an Act passed since 1989.

The Statutory Instrument Citator is arranged in chronological order and contains:

1. Details of amendments and repeals since 1993 made to statutory instruments of *any* date.

2. In respect of *any* statutory instrument, the cases in which it has been judicially considered since 1993.

3. In respect of *any* statutory instrument, details of the statutory instruments issued since 1993 which have been made under its provisions.

4. In respect of *any* statutory instrument, where it has been consolidated by an Act passed since 1993.

Contents of the Legislation Citators are arranged as follows:

- Table of Abbreviations

- Alphabetical Tables of Statutes cited in the Statute Citator and statutory instruments cited in the Statutory Instrument Citator.

- Statute Citator

- Statutory Instrument Citator

- Appendix: Statutory Instruments Affected Table (contained only in the three volumes of citators up to 1995).

- Appendix: European legislation implemented by Statutory Instrument.

10.5.1   Searching the Statute Citators

If you are trying to locate any possible changes, *e.g.* to an Act of Parliament, check the citator covering the period when the Act was passed. After you have found the reference to the Act in that volume, check *all* the subsequent citators right up to the latest citator in the Current Law

Statutes Service File. This will ensure that you locate all subsequent developments relating to the Act in question. If there is no mention of the Act or the section, it means that there has been no alteration made to it within the time period covered by the citator.

Scottish Current Law
Statute Citator 1948–1971

↓

Scottish Current Law
Statute Citator contained in
Legislation Citator volume 1972–1988

↓

Current Law
Statute Citator contained in
Legislation Citator 1989–1995

↓

Current Law
Statute Citator contained in
Legislation Citator 1996–1998

↓

Statute Citator contained in updates for current year in the
Statutes Service File

10.5.1.1   *How to find out if an Act has been amended or repealed*

⇒ Step 1: Check the Statute Citators in the volumes of Legislation Citators in chronological order starting from the date of the Act. In order to locate the chapter number, check the alphabetical list of Acts at the beginning of the volume. Once armed with the chapter number you can turn to the Statute Citator itself. Under the entry for the Act, the citator will list any amendments that have been made.
⇒ Step 2: In order to be aware of all amendments (up to the last month) check through all the Statute Citators up to the most recent update for the citator in the Statutes Service File.

10.5.1.2   *How to find out if any cases have taken place concerning a particular statutory provision*

⇒ Step 1: Check through the Statute Citators in chronological order. Look under the piece of legislation. If a case has taken place, it will appear opposite the statute or section thereof.
⇒ Step 2: You should then check the most recent update for the citator in the Statutes Service File.

10.5.1.3 *How to find out if any statutory instruments have been made under an Act or section of an Act?*

⇒ Step 1: Check through the Statute Citators in chronological order. Look under the piece of legislation. If any statutory instruments been made under the Act, their details will appear opposite the statute or section thereof.
⇒ Step 2:You should then check the most recent update for the citator in the Statutes Service File.

Examples using the Statute Citator are contained in Chapter 5, paras 5.3.3.1 and 5.4.5.4.

10.5.1.4 *Searching the legislation citator available in Current Legal Information*

Searching the Legislation Citator (1989–date) available in Current Legal Information enables you to access information by "Search by Field", which allows you to search by the year; words from the short title of an Act; the number of a statutory instrument or sections of Acts. The entry for a piece of legislation includes the same information which is available in the paper version. The key difference between the paper and electronic versions is the ease of cross-referencing. There are hypertext links which allow you to move from one section to another, *e.g.* the reference to a case which has considered a section of an Act, to the digest of the case. This is obviously easier than having to go and retrieve another volume from the shelves.

The CD-ROM version of Current Legal Information also contains a very useful facility that allows *all* its separate indexes to be searched at once in relation to a piece of legislation.This means that you find information about:

> Statutory Instruments issued under the Act or sections thereof (since 1994)
> Press releases about the Act or sections thereof (since 1994);
> Articles about the Act or sections thereof (since 1986); and
> Cases which considered the Act or sections thereof (since 1986).

10.5.1.5 *Terms used to describe legislative effects*

Current Law uses various terms to describe legislative effects. The following definitions are taken from the latest edition of the Legislation Citators:

> "added" means that new provisions have been inserted by subsequent legislation;
>
> "amended" means that the text of the legislation is modified by subsequent legislation;
>
> "applied" means that it has been brought to bear or exercised by subsequent legislation;
>
> "consolidated" means that previous Acts in the same subject area have been brought together in subsequent legislation, with or without amendments;
>
> "enabling" means giving power for the relevant statutory instrument to be made;
>
> "referred to" means direction from other legislation without specific effect or application;
>
> "restored" means that it has been reinstated by subsequent legislation;
>
> "revoked" means that it has been rescinded by subsequent legislation;
>
> "substituted" means that the text of a provision is completely replaced by a subsequent provision;
>
> "supplemented" means that the scope of previous legislation is enlarged without text being amended.

Excerpt from Statute Citator with features marked

---

[1] 26. Housing (Scotland) Act 1987. [2]
s. 2, amended: 1989, c.42, s.161.
s. 5A, added: 1993, c.28, s.149. [3]
s. 5B, added: *ibid.*, s.151.
s. 17, repealed in pt.: *ibid.*, s.157, sch.22. [4]
ss. 17A–17C, added: *ibid.*, s.153.
s. 19, amended: *ibid.*, s.155. [5]
s. 20, amended: *ibid.*, s.154.
s. 21, see *Pirie* v. *City of Aberdeen District Council* (O.H.), 1993 S.L.T. 1155. [6]
s. 21, amended: 1993, c.28, s.155.
s. 22A, added: *ibid.*, s.152.
s. 24, amended: 1990, c.40, s.65.

Key:
[1] Chapter number
[2] Short title
[3] addition to the Act
[4] part of the Act repealed
[5] changes to the Act
[6] Case concerning a section of the Act

10.5.2   Searching statutory instrument Citators

The 1972–1988 Legislation Citator
contains a Table of Statutory Instruments Affected 1947–1988.
It is arranged chronologically and within each year numerically. It lists amendments
and revocations to Statutory Instruments made from 1947–1988.

↓

1989–1995 Legislation Citator, which includes the
Statutory Instrument Citator 1993–1995 contains a Table of Statutory Instruments
Affected 1989–1992. This lists amendments and revocations to Statutory Instruments
made between 1989–1992.

↓

Current Law Statutory Instrument Citator 1993–1995
contained in the Legislation Citator Volume 1989–1995.

↓

Current Law Statutory Instrument Citator
contained in Legislation Citator volume 1996–98

↓

Statutory Instrument Citator updates for 1999 in the Statutes Service File.

N.B. The material is arranged in chronological order by reference to the year and then within the year, in *numerical order* according to the number of the statutory instrument. In order to locate the number, check the alphabetical list of statutory instruments at the beginning of the volume.

Tables of Statutory Instruments enforcing European Legislation detail statutory instruments issued which give effect to European legislation. The 1989–1995 Legislation Citator has a table covering 1989–1995 and the 1996–1998 Legislation Citator has a table covering 1996–1998.

Excerpt from a Statutory Instrument Citation with features marked

---

[1]   1956. Act of Sederunt (Sheriff Court Ordinary Cause Rules) 1993 [2]
amended: SI 96/2167 r.2, Sch [3]
applied: SI 97/687 Sch.1 Table
Ch.33 Part II, applied: SI 96/125 Art.3
Form G13, see *Stewart v Callaghan* 1996 S.L.T. 12 (Sh Ct) [4]
r.33.22A, applied: SI 96/2444 Reg.18
r.33.29, applied: SI 97/687 Sch.1 Table
r.36.14, applied: SI 96/207 Sch.8 para.43
r.128, applied: SI 96/207 Sch.8 para.43
972. Advice and Assistance (Assistance by Way of Representation) (Scotland) Amendment Regulations 1993
revoked: SI 97/3070 Reg.2 Sch. [5]

Key
[1] S.I. number
[2] Name of S.I.
[3] changes made to the S.I.
[4] case reference
[5] This S.I. has ben revoked

10.5.2.1   *How to find out if a statutory instrument has been amended or revoked*

⇒ Step 1: Check the Statutory Instrument Citators in the volumes of Legislation Citators in chronological order starting from the date of the statutory instrument. In order to locate the number, check the alphabetical list of statutory instruments at the beginning of the volume. You can now turn to the appropriate entry for the statutory instrument, where the citator will list any amendments that have been made.

⇒ Step 2: In order to be aware of all amendments (up to the last month) check through all the Statutory Instrument Citators up to the most recent update for the citator in the Statutes Service File.

10.5.2.2   *How to find out if any cases have taken place concerning a particular statutory instrument*

⇒ Step 1: Check through the Statutory Instrument Citators in chronological order. Look under the entry for the statutory instrument. If a case has taken place, it will appear opposite the entry.

⇒ Step 2: You should then check the most recent update for the citator in the Statutes Service File.

10.5.2.3   *How to find out about a statutory instrument*

⇒ Step 1: If you know the year and name of the statutory instrument check the Alphabetical List of Statutory Instruments for the Year in the appropriate Year book. If you know the full citation and not the name of the statutory instrument, check the Numerical List of Statutory Instruments for the Year in the appropriate Year Book. In both cases opposite the entry for the statutory instrument will be a reference to a paragraph number.

⇒ Step 2: Turn to the appropriate paragraph and you will find a digest of the statutory instrument. It will provide details of its full title, a short summary of its content, details of the legislation it is made under and the date it was brought into force.

10.5.2.4   *Statutory Instrument Citator available in Current Legal Information*

The version of the Legislation Citator included in Current Legal Information gives details of amendments and revocations made to statutory instruments by statutory instruments and statutes from 1994 to date.

Examples using the Statutory Instrument Citator are contained in Chapter 5, paras 5.4.4.4 and 5.4.5.5.

10.6   STATUTES ANNOTATED (1949–)

This part of the Current Law service provides the text of every Public General Act (and Private Acts since 1992). The Acts are published in annual volumes and within each volume the Acts are arranged in chronological order. Each Act is annotated by an expert in the relevant field. This means that notes appear throughout the Act explaining its significance. There tends to be a long introductory note which explains the Act's significance and puts it into context. It will also refer to the dates of the parliamentary debates on the Bill. There will be notes throughout the Act. The number of notes depends on the complexity of the Act. The notes are intended to clarify the effect of the section.

Acts of Sederunt and Acts of Adjournal were included until 1990. For details of current sources, see chapter 5, para. 5.4.1.1.

The English equivalent of Statutes Annotated started in 1948.

Since 1992 Current Law Statutes Annotated have included the following information:

- Chronological Table of Acts in the year

- Alphabetical Index of Short Titles

- Full text of Public General Acts in chronological order with annotations. The annotation after the long title is an introduction and a general note which will include reference to parliamentary debates on the Act. If appropriate, there may also be a more specific note after each or selected sections of the Act.

- Full text of Private Acts.

- Commencement Diary — an alphabetical table of the commencement of statutes in that year.

- Commencement Orders (full text) in chronological order.

- Numerical Table of Statutory Instruments in that year. This lists statutory instruments in numerical order and contains only details of the number and title of the statutory instrument. For details of the statutory instrument see the digest in the Current Law service or the statutory instrument itself.

- Alphabetical list of all Public General Acts passed since 1700.

- Index by subject — Scots law is a heading.

10.6.1   *How to find details of an Act*

Check the volume of Statutes Annotated for the appropriate year. The full text with annotations will appear in chronological order.

Alternatively, a summary of the Act will be in the relevant Year Book or Monthly Digest.

Example

Find the Local Government (Gaelic Names) (Scotland) Act 1997.

⇒ Step 1: Check the Current Law Statutes volumes for 1997. If you know the chapter number, you could check the spines of the volumes to locate the appropriate volume. Otherwise, start by checking the first volume.

⇒ Step 2: Check the alphabetical list of short titles. Opposite the short title is the chapter number.
⇒ Step 3: Turn to the page headed up with the chapter number. The chapter number appears in bold and is followed by a number corresponding to the section number of the Act which appears on that particular page.

10.6.2   *How to find out if a Commencement Order has been issued in relation to an Act*

⇒ Step 1: Check the Commencement Diary in the relevant Statutes Annotated.
⇒ Step 2: Check the Dates of Commencement Table in the latest Monthly Digest or the Commencement Diary in the Statutes Service File.

10.7   STATUTES SERVICE FILES

The Statutes Service Files allow access to a vast amount of information about recent legislative developments. They are structured as follows:

10.7.1   Contents section which includes

Chronological table of Public General Acts which have received Royal Assent in the current year.

Alphabetical list of short titles of Public General Acts which have received Royal Assent in the current year.

Chronological table of Private Acts which have received Royal Assent in the current year.

Alphabetical list of short titles of Private Acts which have received Royal Assent in the current year.

A list of recent White Papers and Green Papers.

Separate cumulative Progress of Bills Tables for Public General Bills and Private Bills.

A cumulative Table of Hansard references for Public Bills currently before Parliament.

Alphabetical and chronological lists of Commencement Orders.

10.7.2   Legislation Not Yet in Force

This table lists alphabetically statutes which have been published in Current Law and remain on the statute book but which, in whole or in part, are not yet in force and for which no coming-into-force date has yet been fixed.

10.7.3   A subject index covering all Acts in the current year

10.7.4   Statute Citator cumulative monthly updates

This is the part you should use to update a search in the Statute Citator part of the Legislation Citator volumes.

10.7.5   Statutory Instrument Citator cumulative monthly updates

This is the part you should use to update a search in the Statutory Instrument Citator part of the Legislation Citator volumes.

10.7.6   Alphabetical Table of Public General Acts 1700–1998

This table is cumulative and is updated each year.

10.7.7   Chronological Table of Statutes (1267–1998)

This contains a list of all Acts printed in the Legislation Citator 1996–1998 and all public general and private Acts passed 1989–1998.

10.7.8   Table of Parliamentary Debates (1950–1998)

This lists Hansard references for substantive debates in both the House of Commons and the House of Lords for Public General Acts 1950–1998.

10.7.9   Commencement Orders

This section includes the Commencement Diary which notes alphabetically by statute the commencement of statutes from January of the current year as initiated by Orders and by statutory provisions. This section also includes a chronological table of European legislation implemented by statutory instrument. Commencement Orders issued appear in chronological order.

10.7.10   Numerical Table of Statutory Instruments

This table is cumulative.

10.7.11   The full text of Public General Acts

When the more complex statutes first appear they will be issued with blue covers. This indicates that only the wording of the statute has been printed and that additional, explanatory annotations are still being prepared.

10.7.12 **The full text of Private Acts**

10.7.13 **Scotland**

This will contain information emerging from the Scottish Parliament.

10.8 EUROPEAN CURRENT LAW

European Current Law started in 1993 and provides a guide to legal developments in Europe. It consists of Monthly Digests which are subsequently consolidated into Year Books. Information can be accessed by subject or by country.

The information contained in European Current Law is divided into four sections:

- Focus. This contains short articles about developments in a specific subject area or jurisdiction.

- The European Union. This section contains details of legislation, cases (from the European Court of Justice and the Court of First Instance), books and articles arranged under subject headings. Each annual volume contains information for that one year.

- National Jurisdictions. Digests of legislation and cases and lists of legislation recently passed are arranged under subject headings and referenced to particular Member States.

- Reference Section. This includes a glossary of courts covering all Member States, a list of abbreviations, Treaty provisions referred to in cases and legislation digested in the volume, cumulative lists of legislation digested and cases reported and a cumulative subject index.

Chapter 11

INTRODUCTION TO INTERNET AND THE WORLD WIDE WEB

11.1 INTRODUCTION TO THE INTERNET

The Internet currently offers a wealth of information for researchers in many areas of study and there is an increasing amount of good legal material available if you know where to look. One of the great advantages of the Internet is that it offers users the ability to access primary and secondary legal source material from all over the world quickly and cheaply without having to leave their computer desk. The Internet has made it possible for students to have free access to articles, legislation, government and case reports that may not be available in their university library.

Research on the Internet can be extremely rewarding and enjoyable but it does have limitations. The Internet, unlike a law library, is not organised in any traditional sense and it is very easy for an inexperienced user to waste a considerable amount of time and energy searching for helpful materials. To learn how to use the Internet for useful legal research takes time, patience and practice. Keeping track of the full range of legal resources available on-line is a difficult task even for Internet enthusiasts. The potential benefits of using the Internet to access legal resources may well have to be set against the time and effort expended in becoming familiar with Internet search methods. Once you have become acquainted with basic search skills it will become clear that there is simply no other method of obtaining such a vast quantity of information virtually automatically. You must therefore take the time to find out for yourself how the Internet works. The purpose of this chapter is not to explain the complexities of Internet technology but to provide a basic reference guide to enable you to quickly acquire the most useful legal information currently available. Further information on the history of the Internet and how it works generally can be found in the following publications.

11.2 DEFINITION OF THE INTERNET

The Internet is the world's largest computer network and an international system for the exchange of information through computers that can contact each other via telecommunication networks. The Internet is not a service run by a commercial organisation but a network of thousands of computers owned by universities, government agencies, companies, non-profit-making organisations and individuals. The Internet is not a physical place but the process of computers interconnecting and communicating with each other.

An Internet user has access to a wide variety of network services including electronic mail (email) and the World Wide Web files. The most important of these services are discussed at paras 11.3.1 to 11.3.7 below.

Further reading:

The World Wide Web Consortium About the Web (1992)

http://www.w3.org/pub/WWW/ http://www.w3.org/WWW/ (Last updated 18/12/97) (Date Accessed 12/4/99)

L. Zeltser, The World-Wide Web: Origins And Beyond (1995)

http://www.seas.upenn.edu/~lzeltser/WWW/ (Date Accessed 10/7/99)

11.3   INTERNET SERVICES/NETWORK TOOLS

There are many different ways to access legal information on the Internet. Before you can access legal resources effectively you need to become familiar with some of the different tools available for finding information. There is a tendency to perceive the Internet as one huge self-contained database rather than as a series of disparate forums and facilities for the exchange of information. For the legal researcher the most important facilities are:

> The World Wide Web
>
> Email
>
> Newsgroups/Usenet
>
> Mailing Lists/Listserv
>
> FTP
>
> Gopher
>
> Telnet

11.3.1   The World Wide Web

The World Wide Web, or the Web, is a system of Internet servers that supports access to the information stored on the computers connected to the Internet. The World Wide Web provides an easy way of accessing files, called Web pages (or home pages) which contain links to resources throughout the Internet. The terms "Internet" and "the Web" are often used synonymously. The Web is actually a subdivision of the Internet that allows users to access, navigate and publish information on the Internet.

The Web consists of thousands of websites containing millions of pages of information on every subject imaginable, including the full text of recent statutes, statutory instruments, international treaties and conventions, case reports and official publications, articles on legal topics and news.

11.3.1.1 *How does the Web work?*

The World Wide Web is a method of retrieving data files, called Web pages, containing links to documents and resources throughout the Internet. The Web is essentially a collection of computer systems (known as "servers") which are accessible through browser applications such as Netscape Navigator. The operation of the Web relies primarily on a system known as "hypertext" for information retrieval.

Hypertext is a way of storing information on a computer as a collection of text documents linked to one another by keywords embedded in the body of the text, known as "hypertext links" or "links". The creators of Web pages set up hypertext links to allow visitors to access documents within their own website or connect to another website. The process of using hypertext links to connect to other documents or websites is known as "surfing".

Hypertext links are represented by words, phrases or graphics normally highlighted in blue and underlined. For example, a typical hypertext sentence may look like this:
In this issue of our on-line magazine we discuss *modems* and list the best new *legal websites*

To use a link

— Position the screen cursor over the highlighted link, and
— Click the mouse button once or press Return on your keyboard.

When you click on a hypertext link you will be taken to other documents, images, animation or sound files stored on the Internet. Some Web pages also use images as links which might have a highlighted border. If the cursor arrow is placed over the image and a small hand icon appears the image will be a link.

11.3.1.2 *Learning how to use the Web — Web Browsers*

To successfully access information on the Web requires familiarity with a software program called a Web browser. A Web browser is an application used to display Web pages using a graphic, user-friendly format. Web browsers translate computer data into a form that can be processed by and displayed on a computer screen.

The aim of this section is to enable you to master basic browsing skills on two major Web browsers — Netscape Navigator and Internet Explorer. If you are accessing the Web at university you will probably be using the Netscape Navigator browser. Currently, Netscape Navigator is offered free for use in educational institutions. If you are connecting to the Internet using a home or office computer you may have Microsoft's Internet Explorer. Each browser navigates the Web using a series of pull-down menus and buttons. For more detailed information about how either browser works, choose **Help** in the menu bar at the top of the screen.
Web browsers include the following common features:

A window that displays the current Web page that is the same as any other window featured on a Macintosh or Windows computer. You can close the window and adjust its size. To view parts of the Web page that are not displayed use the scroll bars at the right-hand side at the bottom of the window. The title of the current page appears in the window's top title bar.

Links that change in colour when they have been used

As stated above hypertext links are represented by words or phrases that are underlined and in colour. Links will usually appear in blue font if you have not used them. Once you have followed a link the colour will change from blue to purple.

The Home button

This button, illustrated by a little picture of a house, is used to relaunch the first page viewed when the browser is opened. The Home page is usually a default page loaded by the browser programmers or by the computer unit at your university and whenever you press this key you will be taken back to this start page.

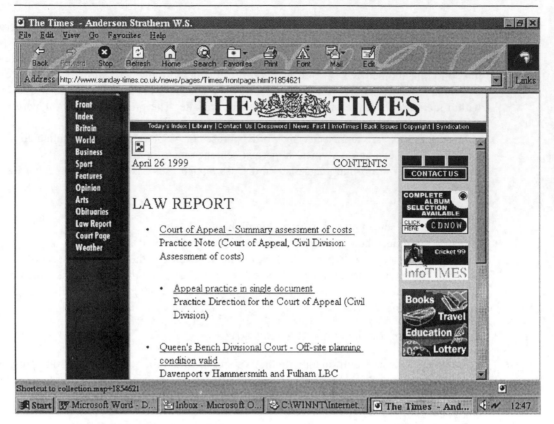

Diagram 11.1

Back and Forward Arrow buttons

The **Back** and **Forward** buttons will display Web pages already viewed during the current Web browsing session. The **Back** button will take you back through all the Web pages that you have visited since starting up the browser program. The **Forward** button performs the reverse role if the **Back** button has been selected previously. You can also use the **Go** menu to trace your way back through any Web pages that you have visited in your current session to prevent you becoming lost while surfing. This prevents you having to click on the **Back** button repeatedly.

Stop button

This button allows you to abort an attempt to retrieve a page from a Web server. If a page is loading very slowly, you may want to change your mind and look at something else. With certain older versions of Web browsers the application can crash if you change your mind and simply click on another hypertext link because the browser can't deal with two conflicting data flows. The **Stop** button cancels any instruction to download Web pages and prevents crashes occurring.

Images

The **Images** button allows images to be turned off while Web pages are being downloaded. It can take a long time to download a page with complex graphics and animation and if the graphics are not needed to understand the informational content of Web pages it is advisable to turn off the graphics using this button. Another way of doing this is to choose the **Options** menu and select the tick next to **Auto Load Images** to prevent graphics being downloaded. When a web page is loaded without graphics small icon boxes will appear in the place that the graphics should have appeared. To view an item simply click on this icon and the browser will then load the image that it represents. To view all graphics after the text has loaded, reverse this process and then select the **Reload** or **Refresh** button.

The Bookmarks or Favourites menu

When you come across a Web page that you would like to visit again in the future use the **Bookmarks** menu (in Netscape Navigator) or **Favourites** menu (in Internet Explorer) to add these pages to an easily accessible list. Bookmarking allows you to save the Web address of an interesting page and store it on the hard drive of your computer to enable you to find it easily at a later date. To bookmark a page using Netscape Navigator simply visit the relevant Web page, select the Bookmarks Menu Option, and choose Add a Bookmark. If you are using Internet Explorer, visit a Web page, click on Favourites in the button bar and than choose **Add** to Favourites.

To access a bookmarked page open the Bookmark or Favourites menu and select the site that you want. This is a very useful feature. Web addresses are difficult to remember and very easy to mistype. This feature allows you to access the site stored quickly and effortlessly.

Netscape Navigator and Internet Explorer have many other useful features not discussed in this section.

11.3.1.3   *Learning to Use the Web — Finding Web Pages*

The first page that you will encounter when you connect to the Web is the Home page. From here there are a number of ways to navigate the Web:

1. Type a Web address (also known as a Uniform Resource Locator or ''URL'') into the browser's location box to access a particular Web page.

2. Follow hypertext links from the Home page to other websites.

3. Use a subject directory or search engine to find useful Web pages. Use of search engines and subject directories is covered in Chapter 13.

Finding Information on the Web using URLs

Every Web page has its own unique address or URL. By using that URL, you can retrieve the Web page it represents from any computer on the Internet. URLs are very similar to e-mail addresses and are simply a user-friendly way of referring to the Internet location of a website which would otherwise appear as a string of computer code numbers. URLs can be found in advertisements, newspaper and journal articles. Some newspapers have special sections dealing with websites such as the Scotsman Interactive section on Tuesdays.

When using URLs it is important to ensure that you take down the details of the ''address'' correctly. URLs are case specific so be careful that you type in lower case letters where these are used and correct punctuation. Many URLs contain unusual character which you may not normally use on your keyboard such as the ~ tilde character and the__underscore character which should not be confused with the - hyphen symbol. URLs must always be typed EXACTLY as they appear including symbols and numbers. It is also important to remember that URLs never contain any spaces. Failure to type the address accurately will mean that you cannot access the website.

You will notice that the URLs in this book are indicated by the use of arrow brackets <> to emphasise that the words and characters shown are part of a Web address rather than text. Do not use the arrow brackets when trying to access websites. The browser will not recognise the brackets as part of the address and you will receive an error message.

To access a Web page using a URL simply type the URL in the location panel which is below the button bar as shown below:

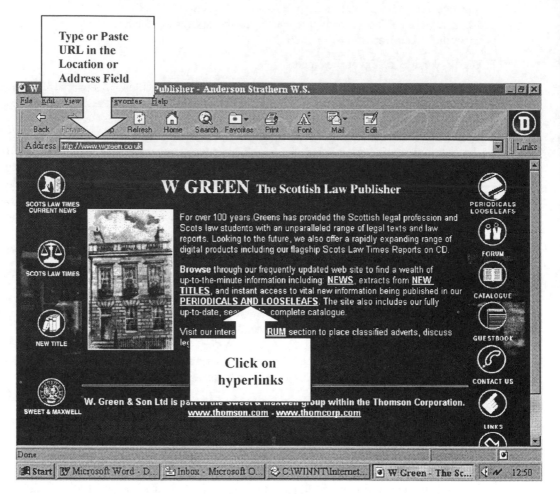

Diagram 11.2

When you have entered the URL, press the Return or Enter key on your keyboard.

Exercise

Try accessing this URL for a Web page on the Microsoft website:
http://www.microsoft.com/magazine/guides/internet

The various parts of the URL tell you where the Web page that you are looking at appears within a website. Each part of the URL is needed to enable you to access the Web page that it represents.

1. Protocol — **http://**

Http stands for HyperText Transfer Protocol, the standard protocol for web servers to exchange information. If someone gives you the address to their web page, they may say, for example, that the Web page is situated at www.napier.ac.uk (the home page for Napier University). Most web browsers need you to include http:// at the beginning of the URL as well so that the browser

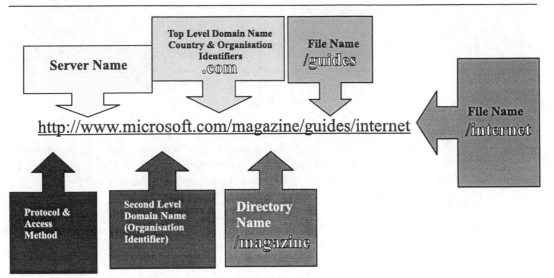

Diagram 11.3: URL Components

knows that you want to visit a web page. More recent versions of Web browsers will allow you to omit the http:// protocol from the URL.

You will also see URLs using other protocols, such as:

gopher:// identifies a file on a gopher server.

news:// identifies an item from a Usenet news group.

ftp:// identifies a file that can be downloaded from an FTP server.

telnet:// identifies a telnet computer.

2. Host computer name — **www**
This section of the URL identifies the type of computer hosting the website. The www suffix is a common name for World Wide Web servers although you will sometimes encounter Web addresses that do not have www as part of the URL.

3. Second Level Domain Name — **microsoft**
This part of the URL is the domain name of the machine on which the file is located. Understanding domain names can help you guess URLs. Interpreting this domain name from right to left, we can decipher some information about the computer.

All computers at Microsoft which are on the Internet are entitled to use an address ending in microsoft.com.

4. Top Level Domain Name — **com**
The Top Level Domain Name (TLD) is **.com** indicating that the website is run by a commercial organisation. Examples of TLDs used in the United Kingdom include:

co.uk   U.K. company or commercial organisation

ac.uk   A school, college or university in the United Kingdom. The U.S. equivalent is edu.

gov.uk   U.K. government departments use this TLD.

| net or net.co.uk | This TLD is allocated to network access provider |
| org | Used mostly by non-profit-making organisations and charities. The URL for the Society of Computers and Law is for example, http://www.scl.org. |

5. Directory and File Names — /magazine/guides/internet

This part of the URL tells you where the directory in which the file containing this Web page is stored on the Web server's computer. In this example, the file for this Web page is /**internet** and it is located in a sub-directory called **guides** within the **magazines** directory.

Using URLs

If you already know the URL for the website that you want to visit, use the **File|Open** location menu option in Netscape Navigator or the **File|Open** menu option in Internet Explorer; type the URL into the dialogue box that appears, then press Return on your keyboard to go to that page. Alternatively, enter the URL that you want into the address window and press **Return**. (See diagram below).

On most computers you can also use the **Cut, Copy** and **Paste** edit options to select a URL from the body of an email message or a Web page. Cut or copy the URL and then paste it into the address window. Alternatively, click on the **Open** button and paste the URL into the dialogue box.

Guessing URLs

It is sometimes possible to guess the URL for a website if you know the country in which the website is likely to be located and the name of the company that hosts the site. Most companies with Web pages use a URL in this format:

www.nameofcompany.com

or

www.nameofcompany.co.uk

For example if you wanted information about a famous science fiction movie series you could try the following URL http://www.starwars.com or http://www.baileys.com for the famous liqueur. While this method is not fool-proof it can be quite useful for tracking down websites when you don't have the address.

Further reading:

The U.S. Domain Registration Services "Overview of the structure of the Top Level .us Domain" (Last modified 2/6/98) http://www.isi.edu:80/in-notes/usdnr (Date Accessed 12/4/99)

Network Wizards Internet Domain Survey http://www.nw.com/zone/WWW/top.html (Date Accessed 28/4/99)

The InterNIC Home pages http://www.networksolutions.com/ (Date accessed 10/4/99) Information about the Internet Domain Name allocation system.

Error Messages

You may occasionally experience difficulties in accessing Web pages. If the URL that you have typed does not open the relevant Web page you should check the original source of the URL to see whether you have typed it correctly. URLs should be typed exactly as they appear with all numbers, symbols and letters in the right place and with no blank spaces between characters. Typographical errors are the most likely reason for URL failure. If the URL that you have typed does not connect to a website this could also be because the resource you are looking for has either been moved to another directory or the name of the resource has been changed or modified. If this is the case the following messages might appear

404 Not Found

or

This server has no DNS

Sometimes a message will be returned that the server requested is busy and in this case you will have to try accessing the site again at another time of day. Servers receiving many simultaneous requests for information will deal with connections on a first-come-first-served basis. The weekend is often the best time to access busy commercial sites.

Other commonly encountered messages include:

Moved 301

This code is usually accompanied by a forwarding message that includes the new URL. Follow any link to the new page, make a note of the new location or update your **Bookmarks/Favourites** list accordingly.

Forbidden 403

This error code simply means that you are not authorised to obtain the requested Web page or document. If you are convinced that the information requested should be available use one of the Search Engines mentioned in Chapter 13 to find the website.

Internal Error 500

This indicates that the server you have contacted may be suffering internal difficulties. In this case you can contact the Web administrator indicated below the error code for clarification or you can retry the location at a later time.

In addition to the error messages mentioned above, sometimes you will find that certain websites will crash your browser or give you an alert message. Generally, this happens when the website includes features that your Web browser cannot access, such as JavaScript or complex animation. If this happens, restart your browser and make a mental note to avoid revisiting a problem site.

Further reading:

Computers Don't Bite http://www.bbc.co.uk/education/cdb (Date Accessed 10/4/99)
A beginner's guide to computers and the Internet compiled by BBC Education.
Webwise http://www.bbc.co.uk/education/webwise (Date Accessed 10/4/99)
Straightforward and easy-to-use guides to the Internet hosted by the BBC to support the television
    series with tutorials and links to other helpful beginner's sites.
Newbie University http://www.newbie-u.com (Date Accessed 26/4/99)
Good basic interactive web tutorials for complete beginners and novices.
Web Monkey http://www.hotwired.com/webmonkey/guides/
Wired magazine's guide to the Internet and the Web for beginners. From Home Page select Web
    Monkey Guides from the pull-down list of menu options
Yahoo How to — A Tutorial for Web Surfers http://howto.yahoo.com/ (Date Accessed 26/4/99)

11.3.2   Electronic mail/email

Electronic mail or email programs allow you to write letters to other people and use the Internet to deliver these letters. Each email user has an electronic mailbox address to which messages are sent. Email messages can theoretically be delivered anywhere in the world in a matter of seconds, but contrary to popular opinion email is neither instantaneous communication nor is it a free service. The time it takes to transmit an email varies depending upon how busy the Internet is at the time you send it. The cost of your email is covered in your service charge to your provider.

In addition to sending messages you can also send whole documents, spreadsheets, computer programs and many other forms of digital data via email, which can then be used by the recipient provided that they have the necessary software to read such enclosures.

11.3.3   Newsgroups/Usenet

''Usenet'' is a shortened form of ''User's Network'', a conferencing system accessed through the Internet. Newsgroups allow users to publicly post email messages via a news server on huge variety of topics that can then be read by anyone visiting that newsgroup. There are thousands of individual newsgroups, each offering a series of articles known as ''postings'' on a set topic. Topics covered by newsgroups range from human rights to the legalisation of cannabis, cat owner-ship, rugby and computer games. The quality of discussion can be either intellectually stimulating or completely inane. Newsgroup postings are the electronic equivalent of a soapbox — anyone with a strong opinion can post an article without taking too much time to consider the content. Occasionally, however, you may well be able to find someone who can help you to find informa-tion that you are looking for, provide technical advice or even offer an informed opinion on your research subject.

Newsgroups are normally set up by an interested individual or organisation who may act as a moderator of the newsgroup. If there is a moderator he or she will read any message submitted to check that it is relevant to that newsgroup and then post the article. Occasionally, the moderator may edit or revise messages that are abusive, inappropriate or simply too long to be included in their entirety. Newsgroup messages are not normally stored on the news server for longer than a week.

Newsgroups are organised into broad subject groups. Some of the main categories are:

alt	Alternative
	Newgroups that do not fit into the other main categories. Alt newsgroups invite discussion on a variety of sometimes quite controversial topics.
bionet	Research Biology
biz	Business and Commercial Subjects
comp	Computer related topics
misc	Miscellaneous topics
news	Information about Usenet itself
rec	Recreational Activities
sci	Sciences
	For natural sciences excluding Research Biology, these newsgroups cover theoretical and technical issues.
soc	Social groups
talk	Debates and discussions, generally political in nature.

Within these categories there are a vast number of sub-categories. Individual newsgroups are named according to their position in the newsgroup hierarchy. For example, rec.arts.movies.reviews is a newsgroup which accepts postings discussing the merits of different films and news.announce.newusers posts articles advising how to use newsgroups. Some newsgroups dealing with legal issues are:

uk.legal

misc.int-property

misc.legal-computing

misc.legal

talk.abortion

Articles posted in one newsgroup may also appear in other groups on a similar topic because Usenet messages travel between host servers which can connect with each other, compare messages and update postings to reflect new articles that have appeared on a specific topic.

To access a list of newsgroups you must first connect to the Internet and then activate the newsreader program through your Web browser. In Netscape choose the **Window** menu and then select **Netscape News** to load the newsreader application. Once loaded (this can take some time if you have never accessed Usenet from your computer before) you will see a list of the newsgroups called **Active Groups** that your ISP or university host enclosed within three separate windows. This list of newsgroups is known as a ''news feed''. News feeds do not allow access to the full list of all newsgroups. There are literally thousands of individual newsgroups and it is not practical for any one news feed to offer access to the sheer volume of data that this represents. Your ISP or university may also decide to prevent access to groups where the content is considered to be offensive or sexually explicit.

Once you have selected a specific newsgroup the contents will be listed in the upper right window. Scroll through the list until you see a discussion thread that looks interesting. Select the thread by clicking on it, and the message selected will appear in the bottom windowpane. Any messages that have still to be read will appear in bold print.

To subscribe to a newsgroup, click in the subscribe box next to the name of the group. A check will then appear in the box. Newsgroups selected in this way will now appear in your list of subscribed groups on your next visit.

If you see any postings that you want to reply to, click on the **Re: News** button on the newsreader Toolbar and a reply window will open. The original message will be quoted in the reply box, together with the address of the newsgroup and all other necessary details. Once you have compiled a suitable reply simply click on **Send** and your reply will be sent to the newsgroup. To send a posting on a new thread click on the **To: News** button.

If you have never posted a message on Usenet before, start by reading any **Help** screens or information included within the newsreader program and if there is a **FAQ (Frequently Asked Questions)** section take time to familiarise yourself with any information that it provides on the purpose of the newsgroup.

One of the best ways to find out whether any useful legal information has been posted to Usenet groups is to search for articles on legal topics on the Deja News database: http://www.dejanews.com.

Exercise

Try searching Deja News http://www.dejanews.com for information on the E.U. Data Protection Directive.

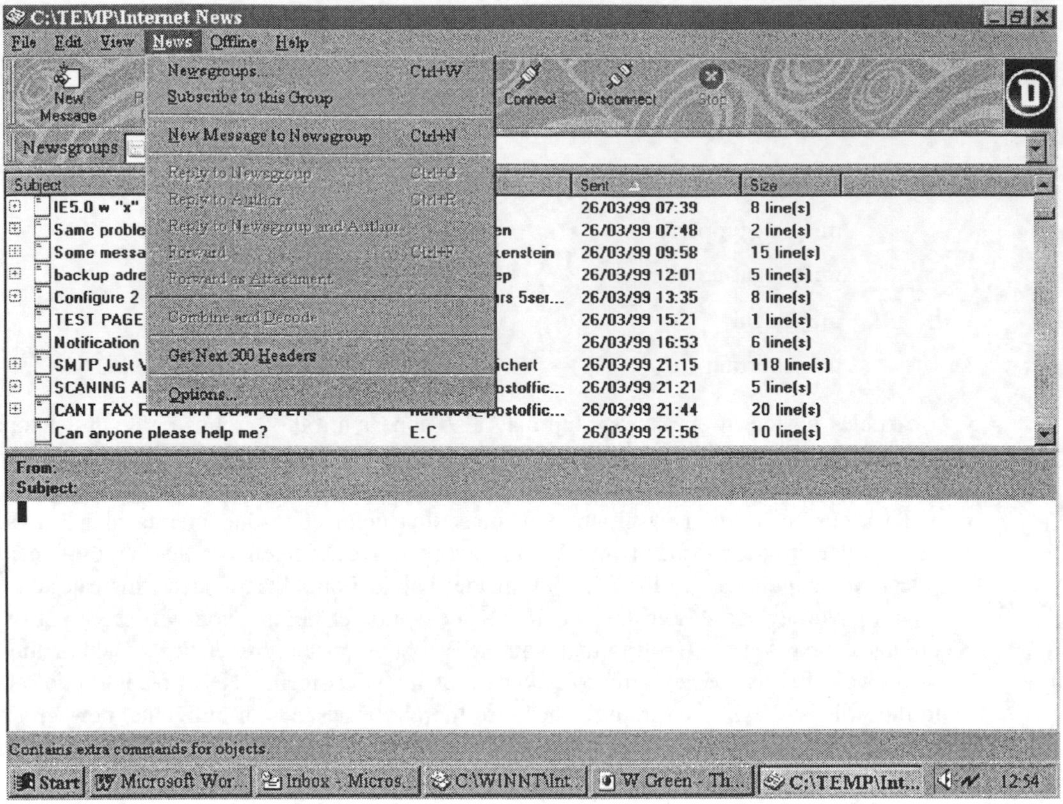

Diagram 11.4: Internet Explorer Newsreader

11.3.4   Mailing Lists and Listserv

A mailing list is a forum for the exchange of email messages between multiple individuals on
selected subjects or themes. You can use mailing lists to share information or news, ask technical
or legal questions and post answers to other users' queries. There are currently in the region of
90,000 mailing lists (April 1999) on the Internet set up to discuss a huge range of topics from
agnosticism to weight loss and Zen. New mailing lists are set up every day as the number of
Internet users grow. Here are examples:

deathlaw   listserv@atbbs.com
A publicly accessible mailing list dedicated to discussion of the legal issues related to death and
dying.

LAWSOURCE
A national daily legal list for law lecturers, librarians, and legal practitioners.

Most mailing lists are open to anybody but sometimes you will find that membership is limited
to specified individuals such as law lecturers or full-time research students. A small percentage
of mailing lists are subscription only. For example, the British Official Publications Current
Awareness Service (BOPCAS) bopcas-scotland mailing list offers weekly updates of the latest
U.K. government publications affecting Scotland and charges a minimum membership fee of

£250. Subscribers receive weekly updates of recent U.K. Official Publications in particular policy areas, including education, health, law, Scotland and defence.

11.3.4.1 *Finding Useful Mailing Lists*

You can use mailing lists to join law-related discussion groups on various issues. To find mailing lists on legal topics requires a fair bit of detective work. You may come across mailing lists by visiting sites that host mailing lists or alternatively you can use an on-line directory of mailing lists or search engine.

Examples of on-line mailing list directories and search engines include:

CataList   http://www.lsoft.com/lists/listref.html
This is an on-line database that provides information on all publicly accessible LISTSERV mailing lists. Lists are categorised by reference to host site, country of origin and number of subscribers. CataList offers a search facility of mailing list topics together with links to list archives.

Liszt   http://www.liszt.com
A very comprehensive catalogue of mailing lists which allegedly stores information on about 71,500 individual lists.

Mailbase   http://www.mailbase.ac.uk
Mailbase archives details of mailing lists that are useful to those in higher education in the U.K.

11.3.4.2 *Subscribing to Mailing Lists*

To receive messages from a mailing list you must first subscribe to it by sending your personal details, including your email address, to the mailing list's administrative address. To join a mailing list you must send an email message containing what is known as a "subscribe" command to the administrative address. To identify a mailing list's administrative address from information contained on a website look for the terms LISTSERV or MAJORDOMO which should appear before the @ symbol in an email address.

| Example |

There is a mailing list called **Lawsource**. This is a publicly accessible legal list designed to encourage distribution of information about new legal resources on the Internet to law librarians, legal scholars, and practising lawyers.

Information about the list and relevant subscription request details and other administrative commands are posted at the following Web address:
http://www.onelist.com

Requests for subscription should be sent to the email address:
lawsource—subscribe@onelist.com

To post information on the **lawsrc-l** list compile a relevant message and then email it to the following address: lawsrc-l@listserv.law.cornell.edu.

If you register on this mailing list you will receive an automatic message confirming your subscription and giving you general information about the aims and objectives of the ist. This message will also tell you how to take your name off the mailing list at a future date. Once you have subscribed, the mailing list address to which messages should be sent is: lawsource@onelist.com

Mailing lists can generate a fair number of email messages and all messages sent to the mailing list are distributed to every subscriber. Receipt of administrative requests will be extremely irritating to other members of the list. Letters should always be sent to the mailing list address. Subscription and other administrative commands should be sent to the mailing list/listserv administrative address.

11.3.4.3 *Sending Messages to Mailing Lists*

Once you have subscribed to a mailing list any email sent to the mailing list address is copied and mass-mailed to the email address of every person subscribed to the list. Recipients can then choose to reply to you or ignore the content of the message.

A person known as a "moderator" supervises some mailing lists. If the mailing list is moderated, the moderator will filter out or edit excessively long messages or those containing immoderate comments or offensive content. An unmoderated list will distribute unexpurgated versions of all email letters sent by individual members to the mailing list subscribers and will allow a free and frank discussion between the mailing list members.

If you decide to contribute to a mailing list consider the following general rules of Internet etiquette or "Netiquette" before sending any message:

- Take the time to familiarise yourself with the topics being discussed in a mailing list.

- Read through the archives without contributing at first to see if the group is appropriate for your needs. If someone asks a question you know the answer to, draft a carefully considered response. You never know whether another mailing list contributor is your tutor, colleague or a potential employer.

- You should include some background information in any messages that you send to help other readers understand the context of your comments. This could include, for example, quoting a section of a previous message that you would like to respond to.

- Avoid posting private email messages sent to you as an individual unless you have permission from the author of the message.

- Remember that someone unfamiliar with your sense of humour can easily misinterpret conversational subtleties as rudeness. In general, therefore, avoid using irony, sarcasm, expletives or off-colour jokes unless you know the other contributors well. If you think that your message is likely to offend someone, don't send it.

- USE CAPITALS VERY SPARINGLY — capitalisation is the email equivalent of shouting. If you want to emphasis a phrase trying use *asterisks instead *.

- You are most likely to receive a reply to a request for information when your query can be answered in either a sentence or two or a short paragraph. Don't write to mailing lists asking for the answers to your coursework or tutorial problems — you will either receive a polite (or not so polite) response from academics who are subscribers or no response at all.

- Ensure that your messages are concise and relevant.

- Check the **FAQ** or **Frequently Asked Questions** file before asking a question of the list group. The FAQ file will tell you a bit more about the group and the topics for discussion.

Exercise

If you are interested in finding out more about how the Internet works try subscribing to the TOURBUS mailing list. This list is essentially an email tutorial designed to introduce new users to the Internet.

1. Subscribe to the listserv by sending an email to "listserv@listserv.aol.com" and typing <u>only</u> the following phrase in the body of the email message:

   SUBSCRIBE TOURBUS

2. Check your email for the confirmation message.
3. Check your email for the welcome message.
4. Unsubscribe from the TOURBUS listserv.
5. Check your email for the confirmation message.

Further reading:

Internet Survival Guide http://aldea.com/bluepages/blue.html (Date Accessed 26/04/99)
Basic information for new users of the Internet that includes a guide to Internet utilities, culture and Netiquette.
A. Rinaldi, The Netiquette Home Page (1998)
http://www.fau.edu/rinaldi/netiquette.html (Data Accessed 26/04/99)

11.3.5   FTP (File Transfer Protocol)

File Transfer Protocol or FTP is both a software program and a method used to transfer computer files rapidly between computers on the Internet. Many computers connected to the Internet are file archives which are publicly accessible containing software, documents, graphic images, song lyrics, video clips and other information. If you connect to another computer using the FTP system you can download data files containing information stored in these file archives. You can use either specially designed software to access FTP sites or simply follow hypertext links from a Web page to an FTP server using your Web browser. You will normally come across FTP sites by following a hypertext link to an archive on a website. You can identify a hypertext link to an FTP site by looking at the URL or Web address. A URL for an FTP site will look something like this:

ftp://domain/path/filename

You can usually access FTP archives in the same way as other Web documents by simply clicking on an appropriate hyperlink. If you have been given the specific location of a file in a public FTP archive, you can use your Web browser's Open Location or Open Page function accessed from the File menu to type in the URL.

Example

North Western University http://www.nwu.edu has an FTP archive that is accessible on the Web by visiting the following address:

ftp://ftp.acns.nwu.edu/

Files on the North Western University archive include information on miscellaneous topics such as law and politics, the music of Crowded House and Hispanic studies.

Very few useful legal resources are available on FTP archives that are not already available on the Web. Accordingly a detailed guide to the use of FTP is outwith the scope of this work. One particularly useful site, however, is the Legal List produced by Tufts University, which attempts to provide a consolidated list of all of the law-related resources available on the Internet and elsewhere. For a full list of instructions that will enable you to get a copy of the Legal List visit the following Web page:

http://www.tufts.edu/departments/fletcher/legallist.txt

If you would like to find out more about how to access FTP archives and download files generally, refer to some of the resources in the Further Reading section below. To search for legal resources stored in FTP archives try the ARCHIE search engine collection available on the Web at http://archie.emnet.co.uk

Further reading:

A. Gaffin, The EFF Guide to the Internet (December 11, 1996)
http://www.eff.org/pub/EFF/netguide.eff (Date Accessed 26/04/99)
alternatively, available by FTP at ftp://ftp.eff.org/pub/EFF/netguide.eff

11.3.6 Gopher

Gopher was once the main system used for retrieving documents and data from the Internet — prior to the introduction of the Web. Gopher presents Internet resources in the form of hierarchical menus, through which you can browse and select and view information. Unlike the Web, it is not possible to provide hypertext links between gopher documents and finding information is more time-consuming. Most of the information previously stored on Gopher is now available on Web pages and while the Gopher system has largely fallen into disuse some useful gopher sites still exist on the Internet. Gopher servers worldwide are registered and listed by the Gopher Consultant Service at the University of Minnesota's Computer and Information Services Department which is available at gopher://gopher.tc.umn.edu/ by selecting the menu items:

Other Gopher and Information Servers

then

All the gopher servers in the world

11.3.7 Telnet

Telnet is a software application that enables you to dial up and connect to a computer at another university and thereafter to use that computer and the databases stored on it as if you were sitting at a computer terminal within that institution. Telnet is used most frequently for accessing library catalogues. When you dial up another computer using a telnet connection you will see what looks like an computer terminal screen with a text-only display. Telnet sites are accessed by following a hyperlink to those sites. A link to a telnet site will look like this:

Example

The following address would be used to access the **Glasgow University Library (GUL)** catalogue:
telnet://eleanor.lib.gla.ac.uk

When you click on a telnet link your computer will launch a telnet program to allow you to dial up the other computer.

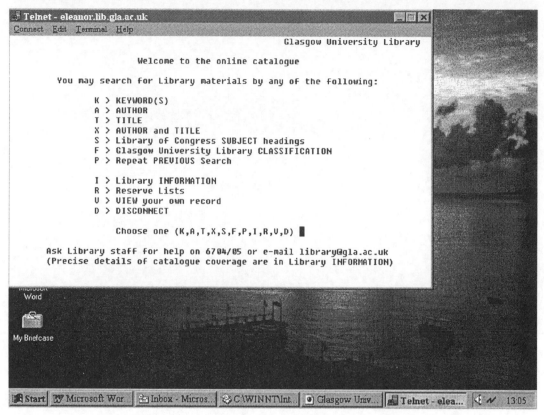

Diagram 11.5: Telnet

Telnet is used primarily for connecting to computerised library catalogues. If you are looking for a textbook or journal that is not stocked by your university library, use telnet to check the library catalogues at another university for that title.

Here are some useful telnet addresses for Scottish university law library catalogues:

University of Aberdeen telnet://library.abdn.ac.uk:23

University of Dundee telnet://library.dundee.ac.uk

Chapter 12

Searching the Web

12.1 Using Search Engines and Subject Directories

Using the Web for legal research can be very time-consuming. Despite the sheer quantity of material available on-line it is not always easy to locate information that is relevant to your research. If you know the URL for a specific site this can be typed into the empty field on the browser's **Location** box on your Web browser toolbar. If you do not have an URL for a relevant site or are looking for more information on a particular topic there are a number of tools available on-line to help you find useful legal information on the Internet. Use a search engine, subject directory or legal information gateway site or law index to help you sift through the millions of Web pages on the Internet. Legal information gateways and law indexes are dealt with in Chapter 13. Subject directories (also known as search directories) are descriptive subject indexes of websites that provide searching options. Search engines will provide a list of websites that correspond to a keyword or phrase such as criminology, copyright or criminal justice. Not all useful law sites are necessarily picked up by either search engines or subject directories and sometimes a good legal information gateway may yield a reference to an unusual or obscure site that might just contain what you are looking for.

12.2 Search Hints and Strategies

12.2.1 Formulate a defined research objective

Before spending an (admittedly) enjoyable afternoon navigating the Web for legal resources, make sure that you have a defined objective. Are you starting out on your research looking for information on a broad subject such as employment law or do you need to find specific articles and materials relating to a particular European Directive? Your search strategy will depend on your individual research objectives.

For general information on a broad subject area start by visiting a search directory or legal information gateway to get a feel for the topic areas covered on the Web. The list of sites featured by search directories and information gateways are rarely complete or totally current but you will probably find links to sites that are more frequently updated. If you are looking for more specific information use a search engine to find current news, materials and articles.

12.2.2 Be clear about the type of resource you are looking for

Try to think about the type of Web resource that is most likely to include the information that you are looking for. Are you looking for articles relating to specific pieces of legislation? If so, visit an on-line journal. Are you looking for current affairs? Then, visit one of the on-line news services or an on-line newspaper.

12.2.3   Think about your search terms and phrases carefully

Make sure your search terms are spelled correctly and use a combination of phrases to narrow down your search.

12.2.4   Give yourself plenty of time to do Web research

The most enticing feature of the Internet is that it theoretically offers you the opportunity to do legal research from your desk. It is quite easy, however, to forget that finding useful websites can take quite a while, perhaps more time than it would take to look up a conventional printed source. Web resources are a supplement rather than a substitute for a conventional literature search. For tips on conducting an effective literature search see chapter 15.

12.3   SUBJECT DIRECTORIES/SEARCH DIRECTORIES

Directories are an excellent source of information for new Web users. Information on the Web is not structured in any traditional way and can therefore be difficult to find. Subject directories are hierarchical subject catalogues, usually compiled by librarians, and which allow keyword searches in addition to the ability to scroll through a list of subject categories. The amount of useful information found by using subject catalogues is limited because links are only provided to websites which the directory administrators have chosen to include and there is no access to sites which they have chosen to omit or are not aware of. The contents of subject directories are not updated as regularly as search engines and, for legal information, are not as comprehensive as law subject indexes such as Hieros Gamos or Findlaw (For more information on Findlaw and Hieros Gamos see chapter 13).

For the best search results use a combination of a good subject catalogues, legal indexes and at least two search engines.

The compilers of subject directories depend to a great extent on the submission of websites by Web authors or users. Once submitted an administrator will physically inspect the site, classify it and then include it in a relevant subject category. Subject directories have been compared to the table of contents in a textbook. Search engines are provided at these sites but it is important to remember that these will only search for keyword matches in the database of websites contained within that directory. Any search results returned may therefore exclude other relevant websites.

Three of the most useful search/subject directories are Yahoo, Magellan and Infoseek.

12.3.1   Yahoo http://www.yahoo.com/
Yahoo (UK) http://www.yahoo.co.uk

Yahoo is extremely easy to use and is therefore one of the most popular subject directories among new Web users. Yahoo is a pure subject directory rather than a search engine but offers access to an extensive catalogue of good research materials by using a careful vetting process. Yahoo administrators will consider including Web pages submitted to them by authors and provide an on-line form for this purpose.

Yahoo employs editors who produce lists of the best sites by category and relies on a team of approximately 50 professional human Web surfers who physically visit websites and prepare catalogue entries of pages viewed. The vetting process is time-consuming and this means that only a small proportion of all current websites has actually been included in the directory. It has been estimated that up to a third of websites seeking a listing in the Yahoo directory are not accepted. (Chris Oakes "Does Yahoo Still Yahoo?" Wired Magazine 11.Feb.98.) In addition, some sites may take months, even years, to get listed at all.

Yahoo is updated daily and offers users an email notification service to receive details of new websites in particular subject areas.

12.3.1.1   *Using Yahoo*

Yahoo is essentially a hierarchical subject index, and allows users to search both general categories as well as specific subjects. The Yahoo internal search engine is a good general-purpose tool which can be used to find legal information stored on Yahoo relatively quickly.

Browse the Yahoo Subject Directory

If you know what you are looking for Yahoo is extremely easy to use for search purposes. To search Yahoo for information, begin by looking at the subject directory. Yahoo provides a compilation of law indices at http://dir.yahoo.com/Government/Law/. If you are looking for information on, for example, Intellectual Property Law you would first select the **Government** directory then choose the **Law** category and the **Intellectual Property** sub-category and follow any links that seem relevant to the topic.

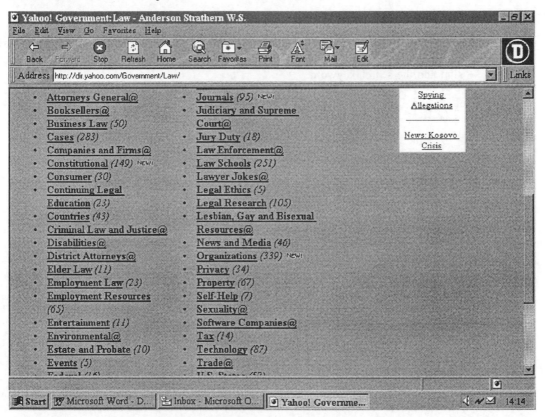

Diagram 12.1: Yahoo categories

Keyword Searches on Yahoo

The subjects indexed by Yahoo are fully searchable. Keyword searching on Yahoo will return results obtained from words in Web page titles, URLs or Web author summaries. Type either a keyword or descriptive phrase which identifies or describes the resources that you are looking for into the query field. Click on the Search button to retrieve a list of resources corresponding with your query. Yahoo is not case-sensitive so there is no need to capitalise proper nouns.

No more than 100 hits will be returned in response to a search request. If a significant number of useful or interesting sites are returned by your request, you can bookmark the Yahoo pages showing the results retrieved by your search and revisit them easily at a later date. If your search request returns no useful results, Yahoo links to Alta Vista to conduct the same query. Alta Vista is a dedicated search engine that will then search the whole of the Web for the same search terms.

You can limit your search area by selecting a search within Yahoo Categories, Today's News, Net Events or websites. Alternatively, choose a time frame during which the listing must have occurred or limit the number of results to be returned.

12.3.1.2   *Refining Your Yahoo Search — Advanced Searches and Search Tools*

If your query returns too many results try refining your search by selecting the Options button in Yahoo. Specify whether you want to include only the most recently posted pages or to use Boolean search terms. (For general tips on Boolean search terms refer to the section on Boolean operators at para. 12.4.2.3.

Including Search Words using the + (Plus Sign)

Inserting a + symbol before a word instructs the search engine to ensure that the word must be found in all of the search results. If you are using this option do not leave any space between the + sign and the search keyword.

| Exercise |

For example try searching for the following keyword

computer

Now try the following query syntax:

computer +crime

Excluding Search Words using the − (Minus Sign)

The use of the minus − symbol in front of a word instructs the search engine to ignore any search results containing that term. Again, do not leave any space between the − sign and the word to be excluded.

| Exercise |

For example try searching for the following word:

tarantino

Now try a search query using the − symbol:

tarantino −quentin

Searching Web page titles only

If you want to restrict a search to words appearing in Web page titles use the following search operator:

t:

| Exercise |

Try searching for the following terms:

anderson strathern

Then try searching using the following key phrase:

t:anderson strathern

Searching URLs

You may want to search for Web pages offered by a specific company or institution. To limit a search to URLs or Web addresses use the following search operator:

u:

| Exercise |

Try searching for the word:

napier

Now try:

u:napier

Phrase Matching

If you are looking for results which only include Web pages featuring a specific phrase, put quotation marks around a set of words to find results that match the words in that particular sequence.

| Exercise |

Try searching for the following:

data protection registrar

Now try using the following search syntax:

"data protection registrar"

Wild cards

Attaching a * to the right-hand side of a word will return left side partial matches.

> Exercise

Try searching for the word:

tax

Now try a search using the * wild card:

tax*

Combining Advanced Search Tools

You can use a combination of any of the query terms as long as the terms are combined in the correct sequence. For Yahoo the correct order for query terms is as follows:
+, −, t:, u:, " and *.

Try a search using the following (correct) combination of query terms:

+t:rugby−Five Nations

Now compare your results with the following (incorrect) combination of query terms:

t:+rugby−Five AND Nations

   The **Options** window also features links to several search engines, including Alta Vista, Open Text Index, and WebCrawler to give you more help in finding what you are looking for.
   If you want to limit your search to Web documents which are more recent than a certain date select the **Time Restrictions** feature from the **Options** page. You cannot use the +, −, t:, u:, " and * search terms if you select a search using the **Time Restrictions** option.

12.3.2   Magellan http://www.mckinley.com

Magellan has a smaller collection of websites in its catalogue than Yahoo but makes up for this by providing a starred rating service, descriptions and reviews of sites. Yahoo is easy to use because it offers the ability both to browse subject categories and to search its indexes. If you want to get the best out of Magellan, however, you will have to take the time to become familiar with the search engine which responds best to specific concept-based searches. Keywords must, therefore, be carefully chosen.

12.3.2.1   *Searching the Magellan Catalogues — Simple Searches*

Magellan has programmed its search engine to look for the words which you have chosen in documents and to look for ideas closely linked to the words in your query.
   Magellan uses a technology known as Intelligent Concept Extraction (ICE) to highlight inherent relationships existing between keywords and concepts. If you conduct a keyword search the search results returned will contain words related to the concepts underlying the words that you are

looking for. To make the most of this facility you should formulate a search based on ideas and concepts rather than keywords. You should, therefore, use a combination of words and phrases to ensure that the search results are relevant to your topic.

Magellan lists 10 search results at a time in decreasing order of relevance, and provides the Web page title, URL and a summary of the contents of the site.

To use the search engine you must select the buttons under the search query box to select either **The Entire Web** or **Green Light Sites Only. The Entire Web** search is a bit of a misnomer as Magellan only claims to have 50 million websites in its database. The **Green Light Sites Only** option offers a focused search of sites reviewed by Magellan's editors which are censored to the extent that sites containing so-called ''adult'' or unregulated content are excluded.

If by using either **The Entire Web** or **Green Light Sites Only** features you find a site that looks interesting you can then use the **Find Similar** request which appears next to the URL for that site. This will return a list of sites that are similar to that selected. The search engine has a limited ability to work out the conceptual relationship between certain words. For example, the term mental illness is related to psychiatry and mental health. If possible you should use as many descriptive words as you can. For example, a search for the term hacking will return a more relevant set of results than the term computer crime.

12.3.2.2 *Searching the Magellan Catalogues — Advanced Searches*

Including and Excluding Search Terms using the + (Plus) and – (Minus) Signs

As for Yahoo make use of the + sign directly before words that the search results must contain. The – sign next to a keyword will specify that that word should be omitted from your search results. Ensure that there are no spaces between the signs and words selected.

Proximity Searches using Quotation Marks

If you are looking for words contained in a certain order within a specific phrase use quotation marks around the phrase for an exact match. For example, ''William Gibson'' +Nuromancer.

Boolean Search Terms

Boolean search terms are particularly helpful in the context of Magellan's concept-based search system. Boolean operators must be typed in capitals and include the AND, AND NOT, OR, and parentheses (brackets) commands. For further information on conducting a search using Boolean operators see para. 12.4.2.3.

12.3.3   Infoseek http://www.infoseek.com/ or http://infoseek.go.com

Infoseek is another popular Web search directory with an extensive index of websites compiled by human editors. It does not claim to produce an exhaustive list of sites in the categories selected but is considered to be more comprehensive than Yahoo and Magellan. Essentially Infoseek is a hybrid search engine and search directory. In response to a keyword search Infoseek sifts through every word in the websites it has catalogued to find results. Words not included in its search results are ''a,'' ''an,'' ''the,'' ''is,'' ''and,'' ''or,'' and ''www.''

12.3.3.1 *Searching Infoseek Categories*

Infoseek lists the search collections it provides both at the top of its home page in a black menu bar and underneath the query box. To conduct a search, simply type your search term into the query box. Be careful to capitalise proper nouns, *e.g.* Edinburgh Festival.

Try, for example, searching Infoseek categories for the following search request:

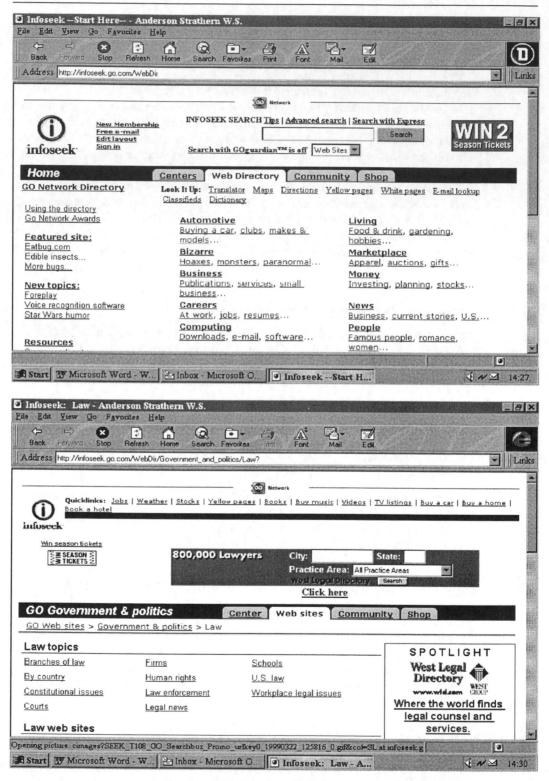

Diagram 12.2: Infoseek Directory categories

alternative health care. To browse legal websites listed by Infoseek choose the **Web Directories** menu tab on the home page, then select **Government and Politics**, then **Law**.

12.3.3.2   *Using the Infoseek Search Engine*

Infoseek uses a unique search language. You must use commas to separate distinct words within phrases and contain those phrases within quotation marks unless they are proper nouns. Capitalised words such as names are treated as a single phrase for search purposes. For example, try searching for **Richard Nixon**. If you are searching for more than one name make sure that you include a comma, otherwise Infoseek will look for both names as a single phrase.

Try Tony Blair Jack Straw

Now try Tony Blair, Jack Straw

Including and Excluding Search Terms using the + (Plus) and − (Minus) Signs

Use the + symbol directly in front of a word to ensure that the search results returned include that particular word. A − (minus) sign typed in front of a word will exclude that word from the search results.

Proximity Searches

Where you are searching for words which should appear in a certain order use the - (hyphen symbol). For example, European-Court-Justice or use brackets () around a pair of words to find sites that feature those two words within 100 words of each other.

Phrase Searches Using Quotation Marks

To find phrases with words in a certain order use quotation marks to highlight the words which must appear next to each other in the text you are searching:

For example, try searching for: reservoir dogs

Now try searching for ''reservoir dogs''

Searching for sub-categories within categories using the | symbol

The | (pipe) symbol will narrow your search results within a broad category to a specific subject.

For example, try searching for:

cycling triathlon

Now try searching for:

cycling|triathlon

   Make sure that the | symbol appears directly adjacent to the sub-category that you are searching for with no spaces.

The ''Search within these results'' Option

The ''search within these results'' command next to the search box field will narrow down your search.

Try searching for: bicycles

To narrow your search to the topic of "Mountain Bikes" type this phrase into the "Search within these results" box to instruct the search engine to retrieve results relating to Mountain Bikes within the general category of "bicycles". You can also use the | symbol to achieve the same result.

Field Searches

To search within newsgroups, Web page titles or URLs use a word or phrase within quotation marks in the Field Search option.

For example to look for legal websites try searching for the following:

ur:legal or

ur:law

Type the colon directly next to the search word or phrase with no space in between the colon and the search word or phrase. Proper nouns, *e.g.* European Union must be capitalised.

To find Web pages with links to the Environmental Protection Agency try using the following search syntax:

link:epa

To find websites dealing with civil liberties try the following search terms:

site:civil-liberties.org.

To search Web page titles for specific search terms use the following format:

title:Parliament

This search format will retrieve Web pages which have the word "Parliament" in the title.

12.4   SEARCH ENGINES

Subject or search directories such as Yahoo require human intervention to select and classify a site for submission. A search engine, however, trawls the Web, FTP servers and Usenet automatically to find specific words or phrases. Search engines are sometimes the only way of accessing information relevant to a research topic and it would be quite impossible to navigate through the enormous volume of information available on the Web without them. While the content of subject directories tends to be better organised, the information obtained from them is less current than search results acquired by using search engines. If you are more interested in broad, general information, the first place to go is to a Web Directory. If you are after narrow, specific information, a Web search engine is probably a better choice of research tool.

12.4.1 How Search Engines Work

Search engines use a variety of software tools to obtain information about websites. The three main software elements are known as (i) the "spider", (ii) the "index" and (iii) the "search engine".

12.4.1.1 *Spider programs*

Spider programs are also known as search "robots" "bots" or "crawlers". A spider program constantly scans the Web and records the URL's for useful pages from a variety of sources such as **"What's New?"** sites and server lists. The spider requests documents from web pages, accesses all links from each page visited and then stores the results of its page search in a database. The results are then used to create an index of Web pages matching pre-selected search criteria. Some spiders keep records to ascertain how often certain Web pages are updated and can also be used to check whether or not Web pages still exist. The results of the spider program's exploration are then incorporated into the index program.

12.4.1.2 *Index program*

The results of the spider's search are compiled using a list of relevant words appearing on Web pages together with a set of locations for the words. The index or catalogue program is a storage facility or database for Web pages recovered by the spider. Some search engines can then produce an index of every word appearing on a website while others tend to store only a condensed copy of certain key words on Web pages.

12.4.1.3 *Search Engine Software*

The search engine software is used to recover information stored in the index database. Generally search engines will respond to search requests for single words or short phrases and produce a list of corresponding Web pages. Some of the search engines currently available, such as Alta Vista and Excite, list search results in decreasing order of relevance depending on the number of references to the search terms in the Web pages found. This is represented by a percentage confidence rating appearing to the left of the search return list. Most search engines will provide a list of websites, a note of the URLs and a brief summary of the contents of each site. The search engine software will generate from a user's request for information a list of links which correspond with that request.

12.4.2 How to Use Search Engines

12.4.2.1 *Keyword Searches*

Search engines filter large amounts of data stored on Web pages. Most users will start a search by selecting a keyword or words to return details of all web pages held on the search engine database containing any or all of the keywords selected.

To conduct a keyword search enter one or more specific words into the relevant form on the search engine Web page, submit the request and the search engine will return a series of Web pages with a list of links (or "hits") to Web pages matching your query. For effective Web research you must be careful to choose very specific search terms. Keyword searches offered by most search engines will simply respond to a keyword search by locating all web pages containing any or all of the terms entered by the user. To conduct a search it is therefore advisable to type words or phrases which are as concise as possible. Try to use words that relate to the information you are looking for rather than general descriptive terms.

```
Example
```

When you are looking for websites with material relating to law and ethics in medicine use keywords such as medical ethics and medical law.

A search for the term "**copyright**" will result in the return of thousands of websites as many Web pages include copyright notices. To make the search more specific select other terms such as "**copyright AND Internet**" or "**copyright AND software NOT piracy**". If you are using a phrase or more than one keyword in your search, read and print off any **Help** information available on the search engine site to ensure that you are entering sufficient information to return relevant results as no two search engines use the same search methods.

A search for keywords will often return a large number of page listings that match the search terms — some relevant, some not. It is therefore important to ensure that the search engine you use is capable of determining the relevance of the results returned to the search terms specified. Each search engine uses a different system to rate how well a particular search result or "hit" matches the search terms used. Hits are normally rated for relevance with the highest scoring results displayed at the top of the list of hits returned by the search engine. Only a few search results will be shown for each page of results and the user must then scroll through as few as 10 or as many as 200 pages of results to find useful information. It is also possible to customise your search to control the maximum number of results returned.

To save time either bookmark any relevant sites or print off the search results page. If you are researching a particular topic you can save time by opening two browser windows. Use one window to display the search results and display the websites retrieved from the results in the other window. To open a second window in Netscape Navigator highlight **File** menu and then choose **New Browser**. In Internet Explorer go to **File** menu and then choose **New Window**.

12.4.2.2 *Advanced Searches*

Most search engines will offer a more refined search option in addition to the keywords search. Advanced Search, also known as Power Search, options are available to narrow down your search where a particular search result does not contain the information you are looking for or where too many irrelevant results have been returned.

Advanced search features commonly include the use of the (+) sign in front of a search word to ensure that all returns contain that word and (−) in front of a search word to ensure that no documents contain that word.

Advanced searches also allow users to search for a segment of a word or phrase. For example, the search term "**tax**" would return **taxation, taxes and taxonomy**; proximity searching to find selected search terms within a defined distance of each other in any text; field searching for searches of page titles, URLs and hyperlinks; and the use of wild cards such as * to fill in any unknown characters.

12.4.2.3 *Boolean Operators*

Many of the search engines, including Excite and Alta Vista additionally claim to recognise the use of the Boolean Search connectors or operators. Boolean operators act as effective filters for finding the information you need on the Web.

The most commonly used Boolean Operators are the words AND, OR, NOT, and NEAR. Always capitalise Boolean search terms when typing your search request.

AND

The AND operator ensures that all the terms specified in your request will appear on the sites selected. If you type environmental AND law your search will return pages about environmental law.

OR

Use OR to return pages which contain either of two terms. For example, Government OR Parliament will find pages that mention either or both terms.

NOT

The NOT connector ensures that certain words will not appear in the search selections retrieved. Intellectual AND property AND patents NOT copyright will restrict your search to sites with information about patents or patent law.

NEAR

Use of the NEAR operators allows you to search for words within a certain distance of each other. Some search engines will allow you to specify the distance in terms of number of characters, while others will fix the distance automatically.

( )

The use of parentheses () allows searches to be further refined. NOT Windows AND Apple-Macintosh will return pages containing the phrase ''Apple Macintosh'' but will not return references to pages including, for example, Windows NT and Apple Macintosh.

''Quotation Marks''

Use quotation marks around any words or names that you want to search as a phrase. If there are terms or phrases that must appear in every document retrieved precede each word by + or combine with the use of the Boolean operator AND. For example, ''rocky +road +ice AND cream''.

12.4.2.4   *Meta Tags*

Search engines retrieve search terms contained in the text of a Web page and can also be used to search the Internet for meta tags. Meta tags are elements of computer code placed in Web documents which are invisible to the human eye but which are capable of being read by Web browsers. Meta tags are designed to provide information about the content of a Web page, in addition to what is actually visible on the page itself. A description meta tag for example, gives the search engine a description of the web page by way of a summary.

Meta tags are used by a number of search engines including Lycos, Alta Vista, HotBot and WebCrawler to ascertain how closely a Web page fulfils the criteria that the search engine administrators have specified for a search.

Meta tags are often employed by commercial website authors to influence the relevance rating of the Web page contents to ensure a higher rating in search engine results. If a search term is uncovered by the spider from a Web page's meta tag, the web page will normally be rated by certain search engines as more relevant and the page will be listed higher in subsequent search results. Some search engine sites will exclude websites which use meta tags for this reason.

12.4.2.5   *Useful Search Engines*

All search engines have the basic components mentioned above but they find information using slightly different criteria. As search engines use different methods to ingather and classify information no two search engines will return the same results for a query. No search engine yet has the ability to index everything on the Internet and it is therefore possible to miss items if you use only one search engine. It is advisable, therefore, to use a combination of at least two search engine sites to locate information corresponding to a specific query. The best-known search engines are listed below, together with a brief evaluation of the effectiveness of each and some useful hints to help you quickly find the information you are looking for.

12.4.3 General Search Engine Hints

1. Focus on the main topic areas within which you want to search. The search engine can't read your mind, exercise judgement on your behalf or ask you questions to refine your search for you.

2. Learn how to formulate search queries. Search engines cannot return hits on keywords which mean the same thing, but which are not actually entered in your query. A query on the subject of **heart disease** would not therefore return a document which used the word **"cardiac"** instead of **"heart"**.

3. Avoid making your searches too general. A search for the topic **"Commercial Law"** is likely to unearth hundreds of law firms' websites. Although there may be useful results returned, there will be so many that you are likely to become quickly discouraged. Make your search as specific as possible.

4. Take the time to try out each of the search engines listed below. Try formulating one advanced search query which you can use for each search engine and then compare results. You will soon get a feel for the search engines which best suit your individual requirements.

12.4.4 The Major Search Engines

The search engines listed below are not the only or necessarily the best but they have proved to be consistently useful to the author. You may find that one or other is easier for you to use or consistently returns the highest number of relevant results.

12.4.4.1 *Alta Vista http://www.altavista.digital.com/*
Alta Vista http://www.altavista.com/

Alta Vista is one of the largest search engines on the web, in terms of pages indexed. Alta Vista allegedly catalogues up to 30 million Web pages and full-text of articles appearing in more than 13,000 newsgroups. Alta Vista uses a robot that searches three million Web pages, including Usenet postings, a day.

Alta Vista will use the specific keywords and phrases which you select to determine the ranking of documents returned by the search engine. Documents will get a high ranking if the keywords are among the first few words in a Web document or if the keywords are found close together in the body of the document or Web page.

Simple Searches on Alta Vista

Alta Vista offers a wide range of advanced search features that are very popular among students and will usually provide the highest number of relevant returns to a particular search request. The Alta Vista robot employs an Exclusion Standard which rates sites according to the Alta Vista Search Onsite Knowledge. Users may conduct a search using a variety of methods such as Advanced Query, Simple Search, Alta Vista Software or Alta Vista help. Alta Vista recognises Boolean search language terms and it is advisable to take some time to become familiar with the Boolean search operators to utilise Alta Vista's capabilities fully. Alta Vista claims to index ALL words, even the articles, "a'," "an'', and "the".

For example, when using Simple or Advanced Search options to search for key phrases, type quotation marks around a selected phrase — **"World Intellectual Property Organisation"** — otherwise the search engine will retrieve every page with any incidence of these words appearing. Type phrases using a sequence of words separated by spaces and enclosed within quotation marks. You can also use the +/– operators to include or exclude certain words in phrases.

Alta Vista is case sensitive — if you use lower case letters in your search request, case insensitive search results will be returned. Capitalising the first letter of a search term will return case sensitive results.

Alta Vista also archives Usenet postings and there may be a useful message thread dealing with a subject that you are researching. To search Usenet select Usenet from the main Alta Vista search page.

Refined Searches on Alta Vista

The **Refine Your Search** button allows you to select complex searches. To make the Boolean logic work for you type AND NOT to exclude certain terms. If you are using the Advanced search option, choose the Results Ranking Criteria box to obtain sorted results. For instance, if you're looking for all pages featuring PLAYSTATION games but have a particular interest in SPYRO THE DRAGON, type Spyro in the Results Ranking Criteria space to bring those listings to the top.

| Exercise |

Try searching for the name of your favourite film actor in Alta Vista

12.4.4.2   *HotBot http://www.hotbot.com/*

Like Alta Vista, HotBot is another favourite among researchers, due to its large index of Web pages (approximately 54 million pages at the time of writing) and many power searching features. HotBot is a fast engine with a catalogue of over 30 million listings, and will return your results ranked by relevance. Hotbot offers optional Boolean and phrase searching capabilities which are recommended for most searches. There is a feature which allows a search for the name of an individuals which is extremely effective.

HotBot is very highly recommended by regular Web users and provides a similar number of accurate results to Alta Vista together with a straightforward **Advanced Search** facility. A list of the most popular sites in a particular subject area can be viewed by clicking on the links provided above the sites listed on the search results page.

12.4.4.3   *Lycos http://www.lycos.com/*

Lycos is one of the more popular search services, despite having a small index that is more out of date than its competitors. While its search engine listings are weak, Lycos does feature an impressive directory of websites called Lycos Community Guides. Lycos also indexes the title, headings, sub-headings and the hyperlinks to other sites, along with the first 20 lines of text and the 100 words which occur most often. Lycos search results can be a bit erratic and you should therefore use it in conjunction with one of the other search engines, preferably Alta Vista.

Lycos is a relatively slow search engine to use, results taking up to two minutes to be returned.

| Exercise |

Try a search on Lycos for the following — The legal profession

12.4.4.4   *Northern Light http://www.northernlight.com/ or http://www.nlsearch.com/*

Northern Light is another favourite search engine among researchers. It features a large index, along with the ability to cluster documents by topic. Northern Light also has a set of "Special Collection" documents which are not readily accessible to search engine spiders. There are documents from thousands of sources, including newswires, magazines and databases. Overall, Northern Light allows over 3,400 full-text published academic and mainstream print journals to be searched. Journals are categorised as "WWW" (Web Pages) or "Special Collection". Searching Special Collection documents is free, but there is a charge of up to $4 (U.S.) to view them. There is no charge to view documents on the Web.

There are four separate search options:

Basic Search from the Northern Light Home Page

The Basic Search feature supports Boolean searches, quotation marks, truncation using wildcards, and the +/– symbols.

Power Search

The Power Search lets you combine all the features mentioned above simultaneously. You can also limit your search results to major languages or countries or specifically selected subjects and types of documents in advance.

Industry Search

This option allows you to limit your search by reference to industry-based subject catalogues — for example, legal or accounting and taxation.

Publication Search

Keyword or phrase searching is possible for journal and periodical titles sorted by relevance of keywords or by the date published. Most recent publications are shown first.

12.4.4.5   *Open Text http://index.opentext.net/*

Open text is a search engine which uses search software robot called Livelink Spider. Open Text offers the following search options:

Simple Search

Simple Search which offers the option of searching for either individual words or a phrase.

Power Search

Power Search allows the user to specify which part of a website to search for a word or phrase and offers the ability to specify a number of search parameters. Information found in Open Text is in the form originally reported to the search robot and therefore is only as accurate as the description originally posted to the Internet. If the information found is accurate, Open Text will report it accurately but, as many users will appreciate, much of the information on the Web is not updated. This may limit the usefulness of Open Text as a research tool. Open Text is recommended as a secondary search tool in addition to, rather than instead of, Yahoo! and Alta Vista.

> Exercise

Try searching Open Text for the name of a specific geographical location in Scotland

12.4.4.6   *Excite http://www.excite.com*

Excite is currently the best-known general-purpose search engine site on the Web which relies on concept-based searching. Excite is one of the most popular search services on the web. It offers an index of over 50 million Web pages and integrates non-web material such as company information and sports scores into its results, when appropriate. It also offers one of the best news search services available: Excite NewsTracker.

Unlike keyword search systems, concept-based search systems try to determine what you mean, not just what you say. In the best circumstances, a concept-based search returns hits on documents that are "about" the subject/theme you are exploring, even if the words in the document do not precisely match the words you enter into the query. This often works better in theory than in practice. Concept-based indexing is a good idea, but it is far from perfect. The results are best when you enter a lot of words, all of which roughly refer to the concept you are seeking information about. Concept-based searches are more effective on Excite if search terms are grouped using parentheses or quotation marks and Boolean syntax.

There are very few refined search features available on Excite and it has a tendency to include sites of low relevance at the start of a search results list. To counteract this, make sure that you scan the following 10 to 30 hits to check whether more relevant hits have been returned.

Exercise

Try the following concept-based search on Excite:

"euthanasia death suicide law ethics"

Now try the same search on Alta Vista

12.4.4.7   *WebCrawler http://www.webcrawler.com/*

WebCrawler has the smallest index of any major search engine on the web and is therefore not the best search engine to use if looking for the place to go when seeking out-of-the-ordinary information. Despite this, WebCrawler does offer a very quick search return rate and has a list of the 25 most popular sites on the Web.

Further reading:

Search IQ Search Engine Tutorials (1998, 1999)
http://www.searchiq.com/directory/index.htm (Date Accessed 24/04/99)

Chapter 13

FINDING LEGAL RESOURCES ON THE WEB

To successfully locate legal resources on the Internet requires effective use of a number of different tools. While search engines attempt to provide the user with an organised route through some of the vast range of documents on the Web, using them for legal research can be frustrating. Very often a search engine request can return vast amounts of irrelevant information. General search engines are not, therefore, necessarily the quickest or most efficient way to find legal resources on the Web. There are a limited number of search engines which aim to return results which specifically relate to legal sources. In addition, there are a number of websites established by individuals and organisations with specialist legal knowledge which are good starting points for legal research on the Web. These sites organise collections of Internet resources on legal topics for the use of students, academics, researchers and practitioners. A well-prepared compilation site can lead you to most, if not all, the Internet resources you need for your research. These resources can be categorised as follows:

> Electronic Libraries
>
> Legal Information Gateway Collections
>
> Legal Subject Directories and Search Engines
>
> Online Legal Databases
>
> The information in this chapter will be updated on-line. For the latest update visit the W. Green website at http://www.wgreen.co.uk

13.1   ELECTRONIC LIBRARIES

Most university libraries now allow access to their catalogues via the Internet either by means of a Web page or Telnet connection. Libraries can be a good place to start your Web research as they will usually provide not only a list of, usually annotated, Web resources but also access to their on-line catalogues to give you some idea of the printed literature available in the area.

13.1.1   The British Library http://www.bl.uk/

The British Library has a huge collection of books, serials and journals and is the home of the national archive of monographs including PhD and Masters theses. The British Library allows visitors to search its catalogues on-line.

13.1.2   **Bulletin Board for Libraries (BUBL)**
           http://bubl.ac.uk

BUBL maintains a Web server with subject tree links to a wide range of information sources.
This site presents an excellent catalogue of selected websites and other Internet resources, including links to law libraries.

13.1.3   **GABRIEL http://www.konbib.nl/gabriel/en/union.html**

This site provides links to websites and telnet servers maintained by major national libraries in
European countries including Austria, the Czech Republic and Slovakia, Denmark, France and
Germany.

13.1.4   **Law Library Links http://law.house.gov/114.htm**

The U.S. House of Representatives has a list of links to Law Schools and Law Libraries. The list
is divided into two parts — Law Schools occupy the top half of the page. Scroll down to find the
library site listings starting with the American Association of Law Libraries.

13.1.5   **LinkMaster http://www.cio.com/central/legal.html**

Legal resources with hyperlinks to libraries and other sites around the world.

13.1.6   **The National Library of Scotland http://www.nls.uk**

A complete list of the National Library catalogues, indexes and databases is accessible on-line.
Catalogues include a general listing of printed books, manuscripts, musical scores, special collections and additions to the Library collections in the previous year. A limited telnet service
accessing some of the same information is available at telnet://library.nls.uk

13.1.7   **LIBIS http://www.libis.kuleuven.ac.be/libis/**

Based in Belgium, the LIBIS Library Network was set up by a number of libraries and information
centres in partnership and catalogues over 2 million bibliographic references to books and journals.
Free access to the LIBIS search facility is offered on the Web.
    Specialised services are offered to registered users, who must be members of a library reco-
gnised as an affiliated organisation — there are no U.K. libraries listed in the membership organisations at present. Registered users can download search results, placing holds on books and documents and may also use the Network's Telnet service.

13.1.8   **National Information Services and Systems (NISS) http://www.niss.ac.uk/**

Aimed primarily at U.K. educational and research communities, NISS allows access to information resources worldwide and includes resources selected by subject experts. The site is free to
all students and academics within higher educational establishments in the U.K. The site has links

to libraries and useful Web resources and is particularly helpful for researchers, as each link is accompanied by an evaluation of the resource which it represents.

13.1.9 OCLC Europe Libraries http://www.oclc.org/oclc/europe/libs.htm

The Online Computer Library Centre is a consortium of over 900 general and specialist libraries worldwide. There are links to member libraries across Europe, including the university libraries of Edinburgh, Glasgow, Dundee and Strathclyde.

13.1.10 Scottish Libraries across the Internet http://www.slainte.napier.ac.uk

A directory of libraries, information about libraries, librarians and the information community in Scotland. You can use this site to find out when public libraries are open and the facilities available at each library are featured.

13.2 LEGAL INFORMATION GATEWAYS

Legal information gateways are collections of Internet resources compiled by individuals and organisations which aim to give you access to law related Internet resources. There are a number of reliable information gateways which are good starting points for legal research. You will find that information gateways provide links to many of the same sites and are often linked to each other. There follows a list of some of the major legal subject directories, together with a short description of their content. Although none of the sites in this section provides a complete list of legal links, they may provide a link to the information that you need to get started. Many of the sites are frequently updated and are well worth bookmarking and revisiting on a regular basis.

13.2.1 Access to Law on the Internet http://www.gointeractive.co.uk/access-to-law/

Offered by GoInteractive, who specialise in Web page design for law firms, this site has a table of links to useful U.K., European, American, Canadian and Australian legal resources. Topics covered include primary and secondary legislation, parliamentary material, case reports and court information, electronic resources and law-related sites by subject. A copy of these links also appears on the Society of Computers and Law website. (see below)

13.2.2 BBC Online Web Guide http://www.bbc.co.uk/webguide/index.shtml

A collection of general resources selected by BBC researchers including a section on legal sites. Sites are vetted for quality and there is a list of the top three sites in each subject category which is updated weekly.

13.2.3 BOPCAS http://www.soton.ac.uk/~bopcas/ukgovw3/ukw3indx.htm

The British Official Publications Current Awareness (BOPCAS) site lists key official publications in major policy areas, with links, and is updated weekly. Brief descriptions of the publications are given rather than full-text documents together with the title, date of publication, publisher and price of each publication featured.

13.2.4   **CCTA Government Information Service http://www.open.gov.uk**

The Government Information Service site has a list of links to all U.K. government departments indexed by organisation and function. There is a search engine facility but this has a tendency to return a large number of irrelevant links so it is advisable to browse through the categories provided initially. Local government sites are not generally included.

13.2.5   **Civil Rights and Civil Liberties
http://www.cyber–rights.org**

The Director of the Civil Rights and Civil Liberties Centre is Yaman Akdeniz a recognised authority on internet law, with a particular interest in censorship and cryptography issues. The site features a series of commentaries on the law affecting cyberspace with a list of links to other useful information sources on the Web.

13.2.6   **The Cyber Law Centre http://www.cyberlawcentre.org.uk**

The Cyber Law Centre, maintained by Hannah Oppenheim, has a list of links to specialist intellectual property resources on the Web.

13.2.7   **Delia Venables Legal Resources Pages http://www.venables.co.uk/legal**

Arguably the best starting point for legal research in the United Kingdom. Delia Venables is an independent IT consultant who advises major law firms on the use of the Internet. The Legal Resources Page offers a list of the most important legal websites in the U.K., links to all firms of U.K. solicitors on the Web and links to the best law directories and gateway sites on the Internet. The What's New section highlights interesting new sites and is updated several times each week. Resources are clearly categorised and content is summarised and evaluated.

13.2.8   **Environmental Law Alliance — Worldwide http://www.elaw.org**

A list of significant environmental law cases presented by topic and country.

13.2.9   **Ethical Updates http://ethics.acusd.edu/applied.html**

If you are looking for resources for medico-legal topics including abortion, euthanasia and assisted reproduction the Ethical Updates pages have an annotated bibliography of recommended books and articles with an emphasis on literature — available on-line.

13.2.10 Europa http://europa.eu.int/index-en.htm

The official gateway to all information held by European Union servers, with links to the European Parliament, European Commission and the European Court of Justice.

13.2.11 Human Rights Internet http://www.hri.ca

The Human Rights Internet site contains descriptions of human rights publications and links to worldwide resources maintained by mostly non-governmental organisations, with a particular emphasis on children's rights.

13.2.12 Human Rights Library http://www1.umn.edu/humanrts/links/ alphalinks.html

An extensive list of unannotated links to human rights resources on the Web.

13.2.13 Human Rights Web http://www.hrweb.org

An introduction to human rights, with links to international treaties, United Nations policy documents and other helpful Web resources categorised by topic.

13.2.14 Information Technology and Legal Issues http://www.brint.com/IntellP.htm

A resource page for articles on Intellectual Property and Cyberspace and links to other sites containing relevant information.

13.2.15 InfoLaw http://www.infolaw.co.uk

This site is maintained by Nick Holmes, an electronic publishing consultant with a particular expertise in legal reference resources. InfoLaw has information on general legal resources with an A to Z of specialist resources listed by topic.

13.2.16 The International Centre for Commercial Law http://www.icclaw.com

This is a Web resource dedicated to the needs of legal practitioners and has a number of articles dealing with commercial law developments in the U.K. and Europe in a wide range of areas such as corporate, employment, tax and media law. The site is hosted by Legalease and has an on-line version of the Legal 500 and links to law firms' websites. This is a useful resource for law students seeking a traineeship with one of the Legal 500 firms.

13.2.17 JURIST http://www.law.cam.ac.uk/jurist/index.htm

JURIST, also known as the Law Professor's Network, has a list of links to valuable teaching and learning resources for law students. Each site linked to is evaluated for quality before inclusion. The subject areas at the time of writing (April, 1999) are commercial law, criminal law, international and comparative law, contracts, legal history, legal research, property equity and trusts and public law.

13.2.18 The Law Commission Law Reform Bulletin
http://www.open.gov.uk/lawcomm/misc/lurhmpge.htm

The Law Commission has provided an alphabetical list of current projects and Law Commission reports awaiting implementation with a brief description of the current position. There are links to a number of Law Commission reports.

13.2.19 Lawlinks http://www.ukc.ac.uk/library/netinfo/intnsubg/lawlinks.htm

This site, compiled by Sarah Carter at the University of Kent at Canterbury, features an extensive list of links to U.K., U.S. and international legal sites.

13.2.20 The Law Society http://www.lawsociety.org.uk

The Law Society has created a large database of links to useful legal resources in the United Kingdom and abroad. The Law Society Gazette is also published on-line.

13.2.21 The Law Society of Scotland http://www.lawscot.org.uk

The Law Society of Scotland site features three easy-to-use database information services. The **"Accredited Specialists"** section allows a search for practitioners by specialism or by firm. The **"All Lawyers"** search facility offers information on over 8,000 solicitors including their email addresses (where relevant), phone and fax numbers. There are links to Scottish universities offering law degrees and legal courses, legal resources on the Web in Scotland and to the home pages of Scottish law firms.

13.2.22 The 'Lectric Law Library http://www.lectlaw.com

The 'Lectric Law Library is a website aimed primarily at consumers to help them find information about U.S. law but there are some good links to U.K. resources. Described as a "virtual law library", this site has a good range of links to legal periodicals. The site is designed to be both informative and entertaining. It is not designed primarily as a tool for researchers as resources are not evaluated but the site is very easy to navigate and can be used to find other gateway sites.

13.2.23 Legal Research on International Law Issues
http://www.lib.uchicago.edu/~llou/forintlaw.html

Compiled by Lyonette Louis Jacques, a law librarian and law lecturer at the Chicago Law School this site contains general advice on Internet research techniques and a list of annotated links to other information gateways and resources.

13.2.24 The Lord Chancellor's Department
http://www.open.gov.uk/lcd/lcdhome.htm

Links to the full text of selected High Court judgments, press releases and policy documentation relating to civil justice reform. There are a considerable number of Patent Court judgments on this site.

13.2.25 PACE Virtual Environmental Law Library
http://www.law.pace.edu/env/vell6.html

A highly-regarded gateway site which allows users to access documents, cases, legislation and a list of links to other sites featuring primary materials.

13.2.26 Society for Computers and Law, Scottish Links
http://www.scl.org/welcome.htm

For a list of links to Scottish legal, political and cultural resources use the left-hand navigational menu on this page. Choose **SCL Groups** then **Scottish** and then **Local Links**.

13.2.27 Social Science Information Gateway (SOSIG) http://www.sosig.ac.uk

SOSIG is an Internet catalogue and gateway site which gives easy access to quality information sources over the Internet for researchers on a variety of topics. There is a particular emphasis on European legal resources. The site features a list of links to approximately 50,000 websites and each link is accompanied by a short summary of the materials on offer. Librarians and academics are responsible for compiling the lists offered by SOSIG and each site is carefully evaluated prior to inclusion on the list. Resources are generally only included if they contain primary information from authoritative sources. Links to other gateway sites are only used where these contain significant added value — bare lists of links are not included.

The SOSIG database is searchable by browsing identified topic areas such as government or law or by conducting a keyword search. The keyword search is enhanced by a Thesaurus option — if your search result does not return any results, use the Thesaurus option to find alternative terms.

13.2.28 UCLA Online Institute for Cyberspace Law and Policy
http://www.gseis.ucla.edu/iclp/hp.html

This site provides reviews and an overview of recent literature in this area, together with a useful and manageable list of links to various U.S. and international resources, U.S. cases, key statutes and topical issues.

13.2.29   **University of Aberdeen, Department of Law, Useful Law Links
           http://www.abdn.ac.uk/~law108/dep/useful.hti**

The University of Aberdeen hosts the Civil Law Centre for the study of Roman law, modern civil
law systems and modern mixed systems of law. If you are researching Roman law and legal
systems there is an extensive list of links prepared by Ernest Metzger at the following URL http://
www.abdn.ac.uk/~law113/rl/rl.htm

13.2.30   **University of Dundee, Legal Web Sites Library
           http://www.dundee.ac.uk/law/legal/index.htm**

Links to general and subject-specific legal information with a particular emphasis on environmental law.

13.2.31   **University of Edinburgh, Faculty of Law Links Index
           http://www.law.ed.ac.uk/links02.htm**

The "Links" section is prepared by Penny Barr and boasts a virtually exhaustive list of links to
Scottish on-line legal resources.

13.2.32   **University of Glasgow, School of Law http://www.law.gla.ac.uk/**

The School of Law website contains original articles and features including the Lockerbie Trial
Briefing, in addition to a list of legal resources.

13.2.33   **University of Strathclyde, Digital Law Library
           http://law-www-server.law.strath.ac.uk/dept/diglib.html**

Links to U.K. and European case reports, government and public information websites, on-line
publications and U.S. cases.

13.2.34   **University of Warwick — National Centre for Legal Information
           http://www.law.warwick.ac.uk/ncle/**

A university site containing links to Internet-based teaching and learning materials. This site
concentrates on providing links to materials which will help academics and researchers to use the
Web more effectively as a learning tool. Choose the link to **the NCLE Resource Bank** which
has links to lecture notes, seminar papers and examination questions.

13.2.35   **WashLaw Web http://www.washlaw.edu**

Hosted by the Washburn University School of Law in the USA this site has a huge collection of
links to primarily U.S. but also European and International legal resources and is fully searchable.

13.2.36 Weekly Information Bulletin
http://www.parliament.the-stationery-office.co.uk/pa/cm/cmwib.htm

Published every Saturday while Parliament is in session the Weekly Information Bulletin lists parliamentary business for the preceding and forthcoming week, including the progress of Bills and European Community documentation received by the House of Commons.

13.3   LEGAL SUBJECT DIRECTORIES AND SEARCH ENGINES

In addition to the search engines discussed in Chapter 12 there are a wide variety of websites dedicated to presenting and cataloguing hyperlinks to law-related information. One of the easiest ways of finding useful topics is to use a hierarchical legal subject directory catalogue, either by means of a keyword search or by scrolling through the list of links provided. Conducting a search using legal subject directories is generally the most efficient way to find information.

13.3.1   Best Environmental Directories http://www.ulb.ac.be/ceese/meta/cds.html

This site lists more than 500 individual topics relating to the environment and environmental law. The Directory is compiled by Bruno Kestemont, a statistician employed by the University of Brussels Library, supported by financing from the Belgian Federal Office for Scientific, Technical and Cultural Affairs. The site is updated twice a month and contains a list of links to authoritative sites dealing with environmental issues. The stated criterion for website inclusion is the number of quality records that it features which are relevant to the specified subject area. No descriptions are given of the sites listed and therefore it can be difficult to ascertain whether or not there is any substantive legal content in the sites linked to.

13.3.2   Findlaw http://www.findlaw.com/index.html
Law Crawler http://www.lawcrawler.com

Findlaw is an important legal subject directory with links to an extensive range of resources. It is situated in the U.S.A but has links to U.K. and other European indexes. Findlaw allows specific searching with its search engine, Law Crawler or users can browse a general index of legal topics. Law Crawler is capable of using Boolean search syntax.

13.3.3   Government Search Engine http://ciir2.cs.umass.edu/Govbot

The Centre for Intelligent Information Retrieval has collected a database of approximately 1 million Web pages relating to U.S. government and military organisations, which is fully searchable.

13.3.4   Hieros Gamos http://www.hg.org/hghm.html

Hieros Gamos is a frequently-updated U.S.-based legal subject directory with links to many resources. You can choose to view text in English, German, French, Spanish or Italian. The site is initially quite difficult to navigate and each page section features a vast amount of information that is visually off-putting. Use the search facility to find information within the site more quickly.

13.3.5   Internet Sleuth's Guide to Law Related Search Engines
http://www.isleuth.com/lega.html

Internet Sleuth is a dedicated search engine and subject directory combined. Search the site by browsing the subject areas provided or conduct a search using keywords or concepts. Each category also provides links to search facilities within the sites linked to. For example, the Berne Convention is listed under the Intellectual Property category and the link featured is to the Legal Information Institute at Cornell University (See the Gateways section above). If you search for a keyword appearing within the text of the Berne Convention, *e.g.* ''author'' and request a search, the results are displayed on a page generated by the Legal Information Institute's server, with links to the relevant sections of the Convention within that site.

13.3.6   The Internet Legal Resource Guide
http://www.ilrg.com/
LawRunner Search Engine http://www.lawrunner.com

The Internet Legal Resource Guide, a legal subject directory offers its own search engine, LawRunner, powered by Alta Vista software in addition to a carefully selected legal database with an index of approximately 30 million Web pages and over 4,000 law-related websites worldwide. The criterion for selection includes the uniqueness of the resource and a consideration of the value of the website content.

   LawRunner allows searches to be limited to a particular jurisdiction, country or to websites with a particular domain name suffix.

13.3.7   Law Server http://www.law.csuohio.edu/lawlibrary/
http://gopher.law.csuohio.edu

Hosted by Cleveland-Marshall College of Law in Ohio, USA. Although this site contains primarily legal discussions and reference material for U.S. law there are also links to foreign and international law sites, human rights resources, legal journals on the Web, library information resources, government agencies, and lists of other legal resources on the Internet.

13.3.8   The Legal Information Institute http://www.law.cornell.edu/

Cornell Law School hosts the Legal Information Institute. There are links from this site to Gopher and Web-based legal resources, including U.S. Supreme Court decisions, the full text of the U.S. Civil Code and state and federal case reports. Sources are listed by topic and all resources are searchable. The links are used to supplement short articles on a variety of topics. For example, an overview of the law of copyright in the U.S. is given, together with links to U.S. Supreme Court and Circuit Courts of Appeals decisions on copyright, international treaties and a list of references to other key resources on the Web.

13.3.9   Yahoo's Government Web Directories
http://dir.yahoo.com/Government/Web_Directories

Yahoo has compiled a list of sites with links to government information gateways. Short descriptions of the sites are provided.

13.4   ON-LINE LEGAL DATABASES

Commercial vendors provide most on-line databases and these can be quite expensive to use. The content tends to be fairly detailed and current. Users must generally pay a subscription fee to use the service and thereafter there may be a charge for specific searches or the time spent connected to the database. In addition to the subscription and search fees, the user will also have to pay their telephone company for the cost of the call used to connect to the database, although this is usually charged at local call rates. The most significant legal databases are:

> Butterworths Law Online
>
> Lawtel
>
> Lexis
>
> New Law Online
>
> Sweet & Maxwell's Current Legal Information Online

13.4.1   Butterworths Law Online http://www.butterworths.co.uk

Butterworths maintain the following databases for Web access by subscribers:

13.4.1.1   *Halsbury's Laws Direct*

Halsbury's Laws are essentially an encyclopaedia of the law and attempts to cover all legislation, cases and European law which applies to England. The closest Scottish equivalent is the *Stair Memorial Encyclopaedia*. The printed version of *Halsbury's Laws* runs to 50 separate volumes encompassing 160 areas of law. The on-line version of *Halsbury's Laws* is updated monthly to take account of legislative and other changes and updates are highlighted in the on-screen text. Halsbury's Laws Direct is fully searchable using two different methods.
— Browsing through subject categories within a set structure of topic menus. Topics are presented in an alphabetical list and clicking the desired item in the list accesses sub-categories within the main topic menus.
— Searching by typing keywords, concepts or natural language requests into the search field box and clicking on the Text Search button. For natural language requests Butterworths have created a search engine called Eureka! which allows search requests to be formulated as questions in plain English. For example, the request "Does my dog need to wear a collar?" would return results from legislation and cases relating to dogs and collars.

All search results are returned ranked by relevance to your query.

There are hypertext links to cases referred to in the Halsbury's Direct database to the All England Reports database and to other relevant sections of Halsbury's Laws Direct.

13.4.1.2   *Daily Update*

Butterworths offer a daily alerting service consisting of summaries of the content of all new cases, statutes, statutory instruments, European legislation, Government press releases and official reports and these summaries are stored in a three-month archive which is fully searchable.

13.4.1.3   *Legislation Direct*

This database allows you to access all Acts of Parliament and statutory instruments passed since 1995 — with hyperlinks to the relevant summary appearing in the Daily Update database where available.

13.4.1.4 *All England Direct*

Full-text All England Law Reports from 1936 are accessible through the All England Direct searchable database, together with case transcripts from the Official Transcripts Archive covering all decisions of the Court of Appeal (Civil and Criminal Division) and a selection of case transcripts from the High Court and Employment Appeal Tribunal (English cases only).

13.4.1.5 *Articles Citator*

Similar to the Legal Journals Index service offered by Sweet & Maxwell (see below) this database allows users to search for legal articles on a range of subjects.

13.4.2   Lawtel http://www.lawtel.co.uk

Lawtel offers subscriptions only access to the following legal databases:

13.4.2.1 *Daily Update*

An email current awareness service that allows you to select and receive email updates of legal developments in a wide range of subject areas.

13.4.2.2 *Case Law Database*

Summaries of all reported and unreported decisions handed down by the House of Lords, Court of Appeal, High Court, Privy Council, Queen's Bench Division, Employment Appeal Tribunal, Lands Tribunal, VAT and Duties Tribunal since 1980 are posted on the Lawtel website within 24 hours of the judgment. There are links to the full-text of cases where these are available on-line and full-text transcripts of decisions can be ordered for delivery by post or fax.

13.4.2.3 *Research Bureau*

Lawtel has a team of legal experts and researchers who will give answers to specific legal queries by fax within six to 24 hours.

13.4.2.4 *Articles*

A database featuring summaries of all articles from the most important legal journals published in the United Kingdom. You can search for articles by subject, periodical and author. It is also possible to search the Articles database for case law or legislation referred to within articles. The full text of some articles can be ordered through Lawtel's **Transcripts Express** service.

13.4.2.5 *PI Interactive*

The PI Interactive service is aimed at legal practitioners and provides access to quantum reports, actuarial tables and summaries of articles from specialist personal injury journals.

13.4.2.6 *Legislation*

Lawtel offers Web access to the following legislative information:

13.4.2.7 *Statutes*

All Acts of Parliament from 1986 are summarised and hyperlinks are available to full-text statutes enacted since 1996. In addition, you can find amendments to statutes, commencement orders and repeals passed since 1986 with hypertext links to the full text from 1996.

13.4.2.8 *Statutory Instruments*

Summaries of all statutory instruments issued from 1984 to the present, with links to the full text of statutory instruments passed since 1997.

13.4.2.9 *Progress of Parliamentary Bills*

You can search for the content of Parliamentary Bills by keywords and the contents of all are summarised. Each entry will tell you the date of each reading of the Bill before Parliament and whether or not the Report stage has been reached.

13.4.2.10 *Green and White Papers*

The Green and White Papers database offers a keyword search facility and links to the full texts.

13.4.2.11 *European Law*

The Lawtel European Law Databases indexes and summarises all case reports from the European Court of Justice, E.U. legislation and proposed legislation, agreements and treaties since 1987.

13.4.3 Lexis http://www.lexis-nexis.com

Lexis is probably the best known full-text legal database. It contains all words which appear in the original printed form of the legal cases, statutes and materials. A limited service is available on the Internet in addition to the tradition legal information retrieval service operated by a computer with specialist Lexis search software connected to a telephone line. Lexis is generally updated every three to four weeks.

Lexis allows you to access U.K. reported and unreported cases and legislation. In addition, you can view full-text Scottish law reports (reported and unreported). The Scottish cases included are those reported in the Scots Law Times from May 1945, Session Cases from November 1944, Scottish Criminal Case Reports from January 1981 and Scottish Civil Law Reports from February 1986. Unreported cases from the Court of Session include Inner House judgments since 1982 and Outer House decisions from January 1985. House of Lords decisions relating to Scotland from July 1986 and selected Scottish cases from the Employment Appeal Tribunal since January 1992 are also accessible through the Lexis database.

Lexis has all Public General Acts and statutory instruments relating to England and Wales but legislation that applies only in Scotland is excluded.

The Lexis CELEX European Communities Library provides access to European Community legislation and cases. The case reports included are decisions of the European Court of Justice since 1954, European Commercial Cases from 1978, judgments from the European Court of Human Rights from 1960 and transcripts of unreported decisions passed down by these courts since October 1980. Legislation includes the basic documents of International Economic Law, European Commission Legislation from January 1980 and European Commission Treaties from November 1979. Other legislative documents include all volumes of the Official Journal of the European Union issued since December 1992, European Commission Parliamentary Questions from 1989, European Commission National Provisions from 1989, preparatory acts, European Commission proposals (from January 1984) and Parliamentary Resolutions (from June 1979). CELEX is offered independently from other databases and is also available on CD-ROM.

Cases and legislation can be searched by keyword and Boolean searching is supported. Any word, excluding connectors such as ''the'' ''and'' and ''or'' can be searched for. Lexis displays search results in a number of ways: the KWIC list highlights the incidences of the search terms whenever they appear in the documents returned, surrounded by 25 words of text and allows you to scan material to decide whether or not it is relevant; the CITE facility simply lists the names of cases, statutes and articles corresponding to the search query; the FULL feature presents the full text of each document retrieved by the search. Each item included in the database can also be searched by segments for the name of the judge, legal counsel, point of law or statutory section. A refined search facility can be used if too many search results are returned and the results of searches can be saved for use at another session at no extra charge. Commonwealth cases and statutes can also be accessed using Lexis provided that the user has subscribed separately to these library services.

13.4.4   New Law Online http://www.newlawonline.com

A database containing English and European Court decisions issued 24 to 48 hours after the original judgment. Each case report is digested, indexed and cross-referenced. There are no Scottish judgments or references to Scottish legislation.

13.4.5   Sweet & Maxwell's Current Legal Information Online
http://www.smlawpub.co.uk

Database services available are similar to the material included in the printed and CD-ROM versions of Current Law publications. The Web version of Current Legal Information from August 1999 will include the Current Law Case Citator from 1947 for English cases but Scottish cases will not be included. The Current Law Cases Digest will incorporate English cases since 1947 and Scottish Cases since 1977. The Current Law Legislation Citator will allow access to all Public General Acts affecting England and Wales from 1989 and statutory instruments passed since 1991. A separate statute service on CD-ROM only will facilitate searches of full-text Public General Acts since 1992 with annotations.

The Web version of Current law will offer the ability to search all databases simultaneously. This facility is at the time of writing available only on the Current Law CD-ROM.

13.4.6   Case Base/Casetrack (Smith Bernal) http://www.smithbernal.com

Smith Bernal's Casetrack service is a Web-based alerting, tracking and full-text transcript service which lists Court of Appeal and High Court judgments. No Scottish case reports are available. Casetrack allows access to all judgments in the Courts of Appeal (Civil and Criminal Divisions), Queen's Bench Division, Chancery Division and the Employment Appeal Tribunal. A selected number of Family Division judgments are also available. Certain cases are excluded where there are reporting restrictions. Casetrack provides access to judgments on-line within 24 hours of the judgment being handed down. Casetrack is a subscription-only service but judgments handed down between July 6, 1998 and December 30, 1998 are searchable free of charge.

You can search the Smith Bernal database by case name, date, case number, Division or Court, judge, court appealed from, barrister or solicitor or by browsing Casetrack subject headings. A menu of subject areas is given — for example, Intellectual Property, Taxation or Employment — with sub-headings which correspond with that subject. To isolate cases on a more specific subject area conduct a search within a sub-heading. Criminal offences are sub-classified by the nature of the offence — for example, assault occasioning actual bodily harm. Boolean search operators AND, OR, NOT, AND NOT are supported, as are the proximity operators NEAR, SENTENCE and PARAGRAPH.

Chapter 14

HOW TO USE YOUR ON-LINE RESEARCH EFFECTIVELY

14.1   EVALUATION OF ON-LINE RESOURCES

The evaluation of documentary sources is dealt with in chapter 16, para. 16.4 and these points apply equally to electronic resources. There are, however, specific issues which relate to on-line sources which merit further consideration.

14.1.1   Criteria for Evaluation of Web Resources

14.1.1.1   *Accuracy of Web Resources*

A major difference between Web resources and paper resources in a law library is that there is no system of quality control for material posted on the Web. In a law library you will encounter official source and material and secondary sources which have been chosen for inclusion in the library stock. They are not selected at random and are of a particular stature, quality and relevance. Web resources are not moderated for either quality or accuracy. You need to be especially wary as a good presentation format can give the illusion of authentic content. In reality there is no guarantee that material on the Web is accurate or well researched. You have to judge this for yourself. Ways of doing this include:

     (a) Checking the source of the website

     (b) Obtaining, if possible, the official source of information

     (c) Using your knowledge to evaluate the source

> Exercise

Visit the website of the Office of Fair Trading http://www.oft.gov.uk. Try to find the OFT's Competition Act guidelines. How accurate would you consider the information contained in these guidelines to be?

14.1.1.2   *Currency of Information*

The importance of ensuring that your research is as up to date as possible has been stressed repeatedly throughout this book. Web pages, unlike printed publications, can be updated or altered by the author at any time, even on a daily basis. In fast-moving areas of law — for example the law affecting the Internet itself — Web resources may be the only way that you can find the most recent cases. However, you should not automatically assume that just because a source is available on-line that it is up to date. Some websites have not been updated for months or years. It is therefore very important to check the date of the last update. The publication date is often located on the first or front page of a website below the name of the author or the publisher. Alternatively, there may be a copyright date or dates displayed on the page you are looking at. If the site has been in existence for at least three years and is regularly updated it is more likely to be a reliable source. A good website will also provide dates for when the website was created and last modified.

Checking the currency of any hypertext links on a Web page will provide another indicator of the currency and therefore the quality of a website. If the author or publisher of a website offers links from within their pages to other websites these should be current. A number of dead or inactive links might suggest that the author of the site is not actively involved in checking these links.

Exercise

Visit the Cyber-Rights and Cyber-Liberties Site http://www.cyber-rights.org hosted by Yaman Akdeniz at the University of Leeds. When was the website first launched? When was the most recent Web item posted on the site? Is there a section listing all the updates mounted on the site?

14.1.1.3   *Content*

It is important to assess the content and coverage of on-line resources.

Jurisdiction

When you first visit a website check whether or not the information at that site relates to Scots law. At the time of writing, there are a small but steadily increasing number of Web resources dedicated to Scots law. There is a significant amount of material relating to the Canadian, North American and Australian jurisdictions. Information relating to other legal systems can however be useful for comparison purposes if the law within that system is similar in any respect to Scots law.

Intended Audience

The treatment of a topic will be influenced by the target audience. Before reading the information contained within Web pages, refer to any notes, prefaces or summaries posted on the site which provide information about the purpose of the website and the range of material covered. A Web author may explain the selection criteria used for inclusion of information on their site. Try to ascertain whether the publications are aimed at a specialist or general audience. If there are no stated selection criteria you will have to browse through the information available to find out whether or not it is relevant to your research. If the author has included bibliographies and references conforming to academic conventions this would suggest that the target audience are academics and researchers.

Relation to Other Works

There is considerable duplication of information resources on the Web. When reading articles you should consider the relationships between the information presented and discard materials which simply duplicate or review pre-existing literature on the subject, unless a new opinion is expressed by the author.

Format and Structure

The Web has no organisational scheme or structure and there are no general guidelines for presentation of material. If the author has taken the time to ensure that the information mounted on a Web page is clearly and logically arranged this is a good sign that the content of the information is likely to have been carefully compiled. However, as stated earlier, good presentation can mask poor content.

Information should appear to you to be supported by valid authority — any theories or arguments on inspection must appear to be reasonable and backed up with appropriate evidence. If the author expresses opinions these should be objective and impartial.

There should be no obvious errors or omissions in the material presented and any text provided should follow basic rules of grammar, spelling and literary composition. Obvious grammatical and spelling errors tend to imply that the text has not been carefully reviewed or edited prior to publication.

14.1.1.4 *Bias*

By determining the intended audience of a particular Web-based resource you will be able to gain an insight into possible bias. Many lobby groups, political parties and individuals have websites whose primary purpose is to persuade others to believe in the same convictions that they do. The objectivity of the resource will therefore help you to determine the accuracy and reliability of the information provided.

A proportion of websites have been created for the purpose of advertising and marketing. Information on law firm sites in particular may have been used for a presentation or may be a brief summary of the law in newsletter form for existing clients. Try to find out the reason for information being published on a website to detect any intrinsic bias which may not be obvious at first glance.

The fact that material contains bias does not automatically render it useless. Postings on newsgroups can, for example, be a useful source of information about public reactions to the effect of legislation.

There should be a link at the foot of the home page of a website to the organisation that sponsors or hosts the site. Investigate the host organisation's Web pages by following any such links. If the Web page is hosted by an academic institution, find out whether the content has been produced by an academic department or researcher. If the host organisation is a commercial or academic publication find out whether the publication is a serial or periodical work or a monograph. A reputable journal or periodical will have an ISSN (International Standard Serial Number). A Web journal which does not have an allocated ISSN is probably not subject to any form of peer review and the articles contained within such a journal will probably have less authority than other publications.

> Exercise

Visit the Journal of Information Law and Technology (JILT) site at http://elj.warwick.ac.uk/jilt/. Is this journal published in printed form? Who is responsible for editing the journal? Are journal articles peer reviewed?

14.1.1.5 *Authority*

There is a prevalence of vanity publishing on the Web. Vanity publishing in the traditional printing environment involves the self-publication by an individual of his or her own work. The nature of the Web allows authors to publish books or articles for public dissemination at low cost and without any intellectual control. There is no need for either peer review or evaluation by a third party, such as a publisher. It can be difficult, therefore, to establish whether or not the author of an on-line article is an expert in their field or simply a person with a passing interest in a subject standing on a virtual soapbox.

Authority of the Author/Creator

When looking at on-line legal articles try to find out if the author is an authority in the field or simply a commentator. The author may be an academic in a known institution or a legal professional with a well-respected organisation. A personal home page or bibliography on a university's Web page may give you useful information about the person responsible for writing or posting the article under consideration. The author's name and email address should be provided at the bottom of every page of the site, or displayed in an obvious place somewhere on the website's home page. If no biographical details are provided by the author take time to examine the URL of a source. If, for example, the source referred to appears at a URL containing the tilde "~" symbol this may indicate that the source is stored within a personal web directory or home page, rather than as a part of the host organisation's official website. Many organisations post disclaimers on websites stating that they do not accept responsibility for the content of material appearing within personal directories.

If there is a link from the site to the author's personal home page, to a biography or other articles they have written, take time to review this information and ask the following questions:

- Has the author published any other articles on the same subject?

- Are there any peer-reviewed print publications among the author's listed works?

- Has the author been quoted in newspapers or other articles?

- If the author has included a list of links to resources on the same area of law, check whether the selection points towards matters of interest; do the selections or annotations suggest that the author may have a bias or special interest?

- Does this author's name appear on any reading lists given to you by your lecturer or tutor?

- Has the author been cited as authority in other articles or bibliographies?

- Try to find out the identity of the publisher or the organisation responsible for posting the information. Articles or newsletters published within a university website are likely to have been carefully compiled for the use of students and researchers. Does the organisation provide any mission statements or other information relating to its aims and objectives or special interest? If so, check to discover whether they have any obvious bias. Evidence of bias is not necessarily a barrier to the provision of high quality legal resources but it should be taken into account in the evaluation process.

| Exercise |

Visit the Electronic Frontier Foundation website at http://www.eff.org. What special interests, if any does EFF seek to promote? What legal resources are available at that site? Now take the time to look at the mission statement posted at the American Civil Liberties Union (ACLU) http://www.aclu.org site. Are the objectives of ACLU identical to those of EFF? Is there any intrinsic bias evident in the resources provided on either site?

Publishers and universities have a vested interest to ensure that any information associated with them is reliable. If the publisher or organisation responsible for maintaining the website on which the source appears does not provide a postal address or contact telephone number, suspicions should be aroused as to the site's credibility and/or accuracy of the information contained on their site.

Title of On-line Journal

Find out whether the journal title is listed in a bibliographic index of legal journals. The Legal Journals Index lists all journals published in the U.K. which carry law-related articles on a regular basis. News items and transient items do not appear in the LJI and this will therefore exclude most of the articles appearing in Web-based periodicals. Other indexes for journals include the European Legal Journals Index (ELJI) and the British Humanities Index. These are considered in more details in chapter 6, paras 6.81.1—6.8.1.10.

14.2   WEB-BASED EVALUATION TOOLS

14.2.1   Evaluative Reviews

It can be useful to locate critical reviews of Web resources. Some legal information gateways offer reviews of websites, discussing the value and currency of content. Gateway sites such as Delia Venables Legal Resources Pages http://www.pavilion.co.uk/legal/welcome.htm, Sarah Carters Law Links http://www.ukc.ac.uk/library/netinfo/intnsubg/lawlinks.htm and the University of Edinburgh Law Links Pages http://www.law.ed.ac.uk/links02.htm also provide links to useful materials. If a site has been included in a comprehensive legal information gateway it will usually contain information which is considered to be useful and reliable.

14.2.2   Search Engine Review Guides

There are a number of search engine sites which attempt to provide evaluations of Web-based resources generally. The criteria for evaluation will depend on the search engine selected. Guides which describe Web resources and allocate starred rating systems can be useful if you find a source which has not yet been included in a gateway site. Lycos Point offers a starred rating guide and links to reviewed sites. Heriot Watt University compiles a database of new websites in subject areas; http://www.hw.ac.uk/libWWW.im. Some search engines offer the ability to find out how many other websites link to a particular resource, signposting sites which other authors in the same field find to be useful.

> Exercise

Visit Lycos Top 5% http://point.lycos.com/categories and Magellan Internet Guide http://magellan.excite.com. What are the selection criteria for recommending websites indicated by these sites? Now try searching for the following website URL:
InfoLaw http://www.infolaw.co.uk
Which Guide produces the best results? Now visit the site yourself. Look at the categories of links and judge for yourself how well the search engines fared. Do you think that the rating would have been higher in each case if Infolaw catalogued primarily North American sites?

Never take evaluation tools at face value. Consider the following for each tool used:

How much descriptive information is given about the Web resources included?

Does the tool take the form of an organisational index with information being catalogued by topic area or other criteria? What level of information is given about the resources included? Does the site give, for example, information about the authors and their professional or other affiliations, details about how the guide was researched and constructed and is the mission of the guide clearly stated?

Summary

When using Web-based resources you must continually attempt to evaluate the quality of source material discovered during your research. Compare any source material found with the content of traditional print-based books and articles on the same subject. If necessary use an intermediary tool such as a legal gateway or resource guide or a search engine. If you suspect that a source may contain incorrect or misleading information, do not include it in your bibliography.

Good legal information should be:

- Accurate

- As up to date as possible

- Complete

- Free from obvious bias

- Obtained from an authoritative source

Further reading:

J. Alexander and M. Tate, *Teaching Critical Evaluation Skills for World Wide Web Resources* (March 28, 1997) http://www.science.widener.edu/~withers/webeval.htm (Date Accessed 20/4/99)

S. Beck, *Evaluation Criteria — The Good, The Bad & The Ugly: or, Why It's a Good Idea to Evaluate Web Sources* (1997). http://lib.nmsu.edu/staff/susabeck/evalcrit.html

Dr N. Everhart, (last revised 10/10/97) *Web Page Evaluation Worksheet* (1996). http://www.slu.edu/departments/english/research/page02.html (Date Accessed 28/8/99)

E. Grassian, *Thinking Critically about World Wide Web Resources* http://www.library.ucla.edu/libraries/college/instruct/web/critical.htm (Date Accessed 28/8/99)

R. Harris, *Evaluating Internet Research Sources* (Sept. 21, 1997) http://www.sccu.edu/faculty/RHarris/evalu8it.htm (Date Accessed 28/8/99)

J. Hendersen, *ICYouSee A to Z: T is for Thinking* http://www.ithaca.edu/library/Training/hott.html (21 Sept 97) (Date Accessed 28/8/99)

J. Ormondroyd, M. Engle, and T. Cosgrave, (Revised October 20, 1996) *How to Critically Analyse Information Sources* http://www.library.cornell.edu/okuref/research/skill 26.htm (Date Accessed 20/4/99)

A.G. Smith, *Criteria for evaluation of Internet Information Resources* (March 2, 1997) http://www.vuw.ac.nz/~agsmith/evaln/index.htm (Date Accessed 28/8/99)

A.G. Smith, *Testing the Surf: Criteria for Evaluating Internet Information Resources*. The Public-Access Computer Systems Review 8, no. 3 (1997) http://info.lib.uh.edu/pr/v8/n3/smit8n3.html (Date Accessed 28/8/99)

L.C. Smith, (1991) Selection and Evaluation of Reference Sources in R.E. Bopp and L.C. Smith, (eds.) *Reference and Information Services: An Introduction* Englewood: Libraries Unlimited

H. Tillman, *Evaluating Quality on the Net* (last revised 2/1/99) http://www.tiac.net/users/hope/findqual.html (Date Accessed 28/8/99)

14.3   REFERENCING WEB-BASED RESOURCES

The World Wide Web, on-line databases and other electronic sources of information are becoming increasingly significant as research tools. It is essential to reference Web-based resources with the same care as printed material.

14.3.1   Purpose of referencing systems/bibliographies

The purpose of providing reference is to attribute material to its original author and to allow subsequent readers to access your research materials. For general information on referencing conventions see chapter 16, para. 16.6. While well-established conventions exist in relation to printed materials there is as yet no uniform system of citing electronic documents, although BILETA http://www.bileta.ac.uk are currently considering the production of appropriate guidelines. A number of different style conventions have been developed by academic institutions in the United States (See Further Reading below) but none of these conventions have yet been adopted by Scottish universities. The aim of this section is not to provide a definitive style for referencing legal and non-legal Web sources but to help you to construct a consistent bibliography for on-line resources where there are no guidelines given by your university in its official course handbook.
Further reading:

X. Li and N.B. Crane, *Electronic Style: A Guide to Citing Electronic Information* (Meckler Publishing, Westport 1993).
J. Gibaldi, *MLA Handbook for Writers of Research Papers* (The Modern Language Association of America, New York 1995).
Publication Manual of the American Psychological Association (4th ed., American Psychological Association, Washington, DC, 1994).
The Bluebook: A Uniform System of Citation (16th ed.,Harvard Law Review Association, Cambridge 1996).
P.W. Martin, *Introduction to Basic Legal Citation* (1998) http://www.law.cornell.edu/citation/citation.table.html (Date Accessed 28/8/99)
Chicago Manual of Style (14th ed., University of Chicago Press, Chicago 1993).
J. Gibaldi, *MLA Style Manual and Guide to Scholarly Publishing* (2nd ed., Modern Language Association of America, New York 1998).
J. Walker, *Style Guide for Citations of Electronic Sources* (The Law Librarian, vol. 27, no. 2, June 1996).

14.3.2   Difficulties in referencing on-line resources

Chapter 16 provides general guidance to help you construct bibliographies and reference lists. On-line resources do not fit easily into the traditional bibliographic format for a number of reasons:

14.3.2.1   *Transient Nature of Web Resources*

The main reason for citing works in bibliographies and footnotes is to provide sufficient information to enable a reader to locate your source material in the future. The temporary nature of much of the material made available on the Internet creates particular problems for researchers. Websites frequently change location or simply disappear without trace. Many commentators have discouraged the use of Web resources for this reason, unless the materials are unavailable or difficult to obtain in printed form. Some on-line versions of newspapers, *The Scotsman* being a notable example, do not post all reports appearing in the printed version. If this is the case make sure that you cite the printed version of the newspaper even if you found an article by means of a Web search.

If you refer to source material found on the Web it is advisable to specify the date you accessed the source, together with a note of the date of any modification of the material. As Internet resources are frequently updated it is essential to provide the reader with a note of the date on which a site was accessed as well as the date on which the page was last modified or updated. Good websites usually have a note at the foot of the home page specifying the date when the site was created and last modified. If this information is not given select the **"View"** menu in your browser's toolbar and choose **"Document Info"** and look for the **"Last Modified"** heading. This will give the date on which a web page was last modified or updated.

14.3.2.2 *Typographical errors*

A typographical error in the bibliographic citation of a printed work will not preclude the reader from finding the original information source. A mistake in citing a URL is a material impediment to accurate retrieval of information. A URL is the sole means to identify and access information on a particular Web page and an incorrect citation will fail completely to provide a link to the referenced material. The fact that URL's contain often strange and unusual symbols makes it much easier to mistype them.

> Example

Try accessing the following URL:

gopher://marvel.loc.gov.70/00/copyright/other/howlong

You will find that the address is incorrect. This URL should link to an article posted on the Library of Congress gopher site entitled "How Long Does Copyright Registration Take?"
The correct URL is:

gopher://marvel.loc.gov:70/00/copyright/other/howlong

Any link to the first URL will fail simply because the substitution of a full stop in place of the colon in this URL makes this reference unusable.

14.3.2.3 *Lack of consistency in presentation of Internet resources:*

Citation styles dictate that you should use references to different types of sources consistently throughout your work. Web authors do not use the same conventions in the presentation of material as traditional publishers; the concept of pagination is unknown in the context of websites. You may find that when you print off an article from the Web that a quotation you would like to refer to appears on page 12 of a document that is 120 pages long. If you use a different printer or print format the same quotation might appear on page 10 of the printed version. If you view the same article while on-line you will notice that it essentially appears on one page. Web browsers generally allow users to search for words and phrases within electronic documents and consequently there is no great need for page references in a traditional sense, provided, of course, that you give the fullest possible reference to enable a reader to find the information to which you are referring.

14.3.3   **Citation formats for on-line resources**

The primary components of a bibliographic reference are the same for most styles of documentation, although the order in which they are presented may vary. These elements include the name
of the author, the title, the place of publication, the publisher's name, the date of publication, and
a designation of the location, or page number, of a reference. Many styles also include a designation of the publication medium. For electronic sources, however, some elements may be missing
or must be translated into elements which make sense in a new era of publishing. For example,
in place of an author's name, on-line authors may only use login names or aliases. Instead of a
title, there may only be a file name. The place of publication and the name of the publisher are
replaced on-line by the protocol and address, and, rather than a date of publication, the date you
access the site may be the only means of designating the specific "edition" of an on-line work.

The basic format for citing electronic resources (As recommended by Janice Walker "Style
Guide for Citations of Electronic Sources" *The Law Librarian*, Vol. 27, no. 2, June 1996) is
shown below:

> Author's Name — Surname, Author's Christian Name Initials
> "Title of Work"
> *The Title of Complete Work in Italics*
> (Date of Work or Document Date and Date Last modified if applicable in parentheses)
> <Complete URL including Protocol (*e.g.* <http://, ftp:// gopher://) within arrow brackets>
> (Date when Resource was Last Accessed in parentheses)
> Navigational Aids (*e.g.* page or section numbers)

N.B. The authors would like to point out that although the recommended convention is to place
URLs within arrow brackets where they appear in a bibliographic reference, this is not the convention used by the publisher. URLs are accordingly only contained within arrow brackets
given in this section of the book only.

| Example |

> Dodd, S.A. Bibliographic References for Computer Files in the Social Sciences: A Discussion
> Paper (Last Revised May 1990)
> <ftp://ftp.msstate.edu/pub/docs/history/netuse/electronic.biblio.cite> (Date Accessed 23/3/99)

14.3.3.1   *Author*

If the author's name is not given and no designation appears for the organisation responsible you
should reference the organisation or department responsible for maintaining the Web page instead.
Alternatively, if no author's name is given but a Web page lists an email address, use the email
address in place of the author's name in the reference.

14.3.3.2   *Title of Work*

Provide the title of the text, file, or website accessed. Web pages are referred to by the page
heading and if no page heading is given, use the title that appears along the top bar of the browser
window.

14.3.3.3   *Publication Date of Work*

Provide the most recent date of publication or a modification date if document undergoes revision.
To find out when a website was last modified or revised use the "View" icon in the directory

menus and select "Document Info". Find the heading which gives the date when the website was "last modified" and cite the last date given under the second heading.

If you are giving a citation for an article appearing in an electronic journal provide the title of the journal together with the actual date of publication.

Example

> Burk, D.L. "Trademarks Along the Infobahn: A First Look at the Emerging Law of Cyberm-
> arks", 1 *Richmond Journal of Law and Technology*, 1 (1995)
> <http://www.urich.edu/~jolt/v1i1/burk.html> (Date Accessed 12/4/99)

If no publication date is given simply note the date of the most recent modification or revision preceded by the term "Last Modified" or "Last Revised". If the publication date and modification dates are unavailable, give the date of access preceded by the term "Last Accessed on" as you would normally after the URL reference.

Example

If there is no publication date given or date of last revision or modification, include the date of access instead, in day-month-year format (*e.g.* 4 April 1999).

URL /Internet Address : For each type of resource specify the relevant protocol first, *e.g.* World Wide Web (http://), Telnet (telnet://), Gopher (gopher://), FTP(ftp://), and then provide the Internet address including the domain name, file name and directory or retrieval pathway.

If you find the same information on a number of different "mirror" websites, reference the URL for the site that you think is likely to be the most permanent. Do not use a full stop or any other punctuation symbols — a period or other punctuation — if it is not part of the Internet address at the end of the URL.

Example

<ftp://ftp.msstate.edu/pub/docs/history/netuse/electronic.biblio.cite.>

If the URL is particularly long and runs over to the next line of text you can break the line at a / symbol provided that the / (forward slash) symbol is the last character on that text line. Never use a - (hyphen) to indicate that the address runs over onto the next line, a reader may take this to be part of the Web address.

Example

<http://dir.yahoo.com/Social—Science/Linguistics__and__Human__Languages/
Languages/Specific__Languages/English/Grammar__Usage__and__Style/
Citation/Internet__Citation/>

14.3.3.4 *Date of Access*

This is the date on which you viewed or downloaded information referred to from the Internet.

14.3.3.5 *Navigational Aids*

List any navigational aids including page, paragraph and section numbers if these are included at the end of the citation, separated by commas. For most electronic sources, however, navigational aids will not be included.

> Riley, M.F. "Using the Internet in your job search" (May 1999)
> : <http://www.dbm.com/jobguide/jobsrch.htmlea> (Date Accessed 28/8/99)

14.3.3.6 *Cases*

All jurisdictions adopt a mandatory universal citation system, citing a decision by stating the year, the unique designator selected by the relevant court, and a sequential number assigned to the decision.

Hoffman-La Roche and Co. AG v. Centrafarm Vertriebsgesellschaft Pharmazeutischer Erzeugnisse mbH (Case 102/77) [1978] E.C.R. 1139

Jurisdictions should use parallel citation for print sources and electronic sources, where one is commonly used in that jurisdiction. While it is always advisable to refer to the printed volume of a case report where this is available this assumes that the electronic version of a case report is derived from a printed volume. Very often the only source will be the electronic version. When a case is unreported and available on a widely-used electronic database, it may be cited to that database. Provide the case name, docket number, database identifier, court name, and full date of the most recent major disposition of the case. The database identifier must contain enough information to enable a reader to identify the database and find the case. If the database has identifying codes or numbers which uniquely identify the case, these must be given. Precede any screen or page numbers, if assigned, with an asterisk. (The Bluebook: A Uniform System of Citation, R. 10.8.1(a) 16th ed., 1996) If a printed copy of an opinion is not available when you are preparing for a moot or debate, you should provide copies of any judgments found on-line to your opposing counsel and the court.

14.3.3.6 *Statutes*

Legislation can be referenced using the same format as statutes in printed form, *e.g.* the Data Protection Act 1998, s. 10.
U.K. statutes are not updated on-line when later legislation or statutory instruments make subsequent amendments. Consequently, unless you are very sure that the legislation has not been updated it is fundamental that you refer to the printed version for accuracy.

14.3.3.7 *Official Reports*

Selected official reports published by the Law Commission and Scottish Law Commission now appear on-line at various locations, including the U.K. Official Documents website http://www.official-documents.co.uk and the Law Commission site http://www.open.gov.uk/lawcomm/homepage.htm/library/library.htm. As these documents are not generally subject to change it is perfectly acceptable to refer to the on-line versions. When citing official reports the following style is recommended:

> Law Commission
>
> "Title"
>
> Report Number
>
> (Date)
>
> <URL>
>
> Paragraph number
>
> (Date Accessed)

14.3.4   **Citations for email, LISTSERV Mailing Lists, and Usenet Newsgroups**

Email and other network communications are essentially unpublished works but can also be very useful, particularly if you have decided to use an on-line questionnaire to obtain research data. You must reference this information if you want to cite its content within your research and it is helpful for readers if you include as much information as possible about the origin of such items.

Messages posted to newsgroups or sent from listserv groups are probably the best sources for research purposes as the authors intend that they be disseminated. Be careful not to include a personal email address where the email has been sent privately to you and avoid using personal email as a reference source unless you have first obtained the author's consent.

The basic form for citing such sources is:

> Author or sender's name (if known)
>
> (Author's email address in parentheses)
>
> ''Subject of Message in Quotation Marks''
>
> Date on which message was posted
>
> Name & Address of the Listserv or newsgroup posted to
>
> Information on how to find the groups archives if available
>
> Date communication was accessed/received
>
> (Recipient's E-mail address in parentheses if relevant)

Most of the information needed to complete the reference will be contained in the subject header of the communication itself.

14.3.4.1 *Sender's Name*

If the author's name is not given, treat the communication as if it were an anonymous source or, alternatively, provide the sender's email address.

14.3.4.2 *Subject of Message or Posting*

Include the subject heading given in the email, listserv message or Usenet posting.

14.3.4.3 *Name of Listserv or Newsgroup*

Provide the name of the listserv or newsgroup from which the message was obtained. Give the email address of the listserv or newsgroup. If the archives of the listserv group or newsgroup are available include information to enable the reader to find the archives.

14.3.4.4 *Date*

Supply the date of the email or listserv message or Usenet posting. News articles should include the unique message ID and the submission date of the article rather than the date it appears in the news spool you have accessed.

14.3.4.5 *Access Date*

Give the date on which the message was accessed.

14.3.4.6 *Email example*

For personal email sent to you use the following form:

> Author's Name,
>
> ''Subject Header of Message''
>
> (Date of Message)
>
> Personal email sent to [Your Name] (Your email address)

14.3.4.7 *Usenet Newsgroup example*

This is an article posted on Usenet with information on how to set up a newsgroup:

> Lawrence, D.C. (newgroups-request@isc.org) How to Create a New Usenet Newsgroup (16/3/99) Guidelines for Usenet Group Creation (newgroups-request@isc.org) Newsgroups: <news.announce.newgroups>, <news.groups>, <news.announce.newusers>, <news.admin.misc, news.answers> (Date Accessed 5/4/99)

14.3.4.8 *Listserv Mailing List example*

This example has been taken from a listserv for NASA's Galileo expedition.

> Orton, G. (1997, February). Back from the original OFJ with some unexpectedsurprises [Online]. Available Email: listmanager@quest.arc.nasa.gov:subscribe updates-jup available (Date Accessed 21/3/97).

14.3.5 Referencing Information Obtained Using Telnet Protocols

If using resources accessed from telnet sites include the following information in your references:

> Author's surname and initials or alias (where available)
>
> ''Title of the work or the name of the Telnet site in quotation marks''
>
> Title of complete work or telnet site
>
> Publication or creation date of work
>
> Address for the Telnet site including telnet protocol
>
> Directions necessary for accessing the publication
>
> (The date when you visited the site enclosed in parentheses)

14.3.5.1 *EXAMPLE: Telnet Reference*

The first example is from the Smithsonian Institute's Telnet site.

> S1 Chronology (Record 28). Rush leaves England with Smithson gold [Online]. Available: telnet://siris.si.edu (Date Accessed March 1997).

14.3.6   **Referencing information obtained using FTP (File Transfer Protocol)**

When referencing documents or files that you have downloaded using FTP, include the following information:

Author's surname and initials (if disclosed)

''The title of the work in quotation marks''

The full title of the document, article, or file in italics if part of a larger work

Date of publication of the document

<The ftp site address including the ftp protocol enclosed within arrow brackets followed by a note of the pathway that you followed to access the information>

(The date on which you visited the ftp site in parentheses)

Ftp Address: To access a document or file stored on an ftp server using a Web browser you must do so using the gopher:// protocol. If you use the ftp:// protocol you will receive an error message in Netscape as the browser will not recognise the DNS server.

14.3.6.1 *EXAMPLE: FTP Reference*

This is an article with information on how to use email to access Internet resources.

''Accessing The Internet By E-Mail: Doctor Bob's Guide to Offline Internet Access''<gopher://ftp.mailbase.ac.uk/pub/lists/lis-iis/files/e-access-inet.txt>

Coverage

Rankin, B. (August, 1994) ''Accessing the Internet by e-mail'' 2nd edition
<gopher://dftnic.gsfc.nasa.gov/general_info/internet.by-email> <ftp dftnic.gsfc.nasa.gov/general_info/internet.by-email>
Information Available Using File Transfer Protocols (FTP) (Date Accessed January 1999).

14.3.7   **Information available using Gopher Protocols**

For referencing information found on the Internet via accessing a gopher site include the following information:

The author's surname and initials or name of organisation

''The full title of the page, article, document or file, enclosed in quotation marks''

The title of the complete work in Italics

The publication date and any previous publication information

<The gopher protocol (gopher://) and address enclosed within arrow brackets>

Details of the search path used or directories that must be followed to access the information, if necessary

(The date the file was accessed in parentheses)

14.3.7.1   *Example*

The following reference relates to an article entitled "How Long Does Copyright Registration Take?" accessed from the Library of Congress gopher server:

> Library of Congress "How Long Does Copyright Registration Take?" (Created 6/4/93) <gopher://marvel.loc.gov:70/00/copyright/other/howlong> gopher/Library of Congress/ Copyright/Other Copyright Topics (Date Accessed 4/4/99)

14.3.8   On-line Databases including Lexis and Lawtel

Much of the information provided by on-line databases will also appear in print form, *e.g.* articles appearing in the Law Society Gazette. If the information is not easily accessible elsewhere — for example unreported cases or articles written especially for that database provider — give the following information:

14.3.8.1   *Unreported Cases*

> Case Name
>
> Date of Report
>
> (Date Last Modified)
>
> <URL or search pathway>
>
> (Date when report was accessed)

14.3.8.2   *Articles*

> Surname of Author and initials /name of editor
>
> The title or edition of the work
>
> [The type of medium in square brackets]
>
> (Publication date)
>
> The name of the Supplier/Database identifier or number
>
> <Available protocol and site reference or search pathway if relevant>
>
> (The date when you accessed the site in parentheses)

Further reading:

X. Li and N.B. Crane, *Electronic Style: A Guide to Citing Electronic Information* (Meckler Publishing, Westport 1993).

J. Gibaldi, *MLA Handbook for Writers of Research Papers* (The Modern Language Association of America, New York 1995).

Publication Manual of the American Psychological Association (4th ed., American Psychological Association, Washington, DC 1994).

The Bluebook: A Uniform System of Citation (16th ed., Harvard Law Review Association, Cambridge 1996).

Chicago Manual of Style (14th ed., University of Chicago Press, Chicago 1993).

J. Walker, *Style Guide for Citations of Electronic Sources*, *The Law Librarian*, vol. 27, no. 2, June 1996.

R. Bohill, *Electronic Citation Guide for Legal Materials.* (No publication date given)
http://law.anu.edu.au/nglrw/lr3.htm (Date Accessed 01/03/99).

A. Greenhill and G.A. Fletcher, *Proposal for Referencing Internet Resources* (1 February 1996)
    http://www.gl.umbc.edu/~khoo/hub_acad.html (Date Accessed 28/8/99)

S.A. Dodd, Bibliographic References for Computer Files in the Social Sciences: A Discussion
    Paper (Rev. May 1990)

ftp://ftp.msstate.edu/pub/docs/history/netuse/electronic.biblio.cite (Date Accessed March 23,
    1999)

MLA Style: Documenting Sources from the World Wide Web by the Modern Language Associ-
    ation of America (1998) http://www.mla.org/main_stl.htm (Date Accessed 28/8/99)

M.E. Page, *A Brief Citation Guide for Internet Sources in History and the Humanities* (Date of
    Article)

http://www.h-net.msu.edu/~africa/citation.html (Date Accessed 28/8/99)

Crouse, M. Citing Electronic Information in History Papers (last revised 26/8/99)

http://www.people.memphis.edu/~mcrouse/elcite.html (Date Accessed 31/8/99)

Excerpts from ISO Draft International Standard 690–2: Information and documentation — Biblio-
    graphic references — Electronic documents or parts thereof (last revised 20/2/99)
    http://www.nlc-bnc.ca/iso/tc46sc9/standard/690-2e.htm (Date Accessed 20/4/89)

C.E. Person, *Citation of Legal and Non-legal Electronic Database Information*

http://www.michbar.org/publications/citations.htm (Reformatted 24/6/97)

Web Extension to American Psychological Association Style (WEAPAS)

http://www.beadsland.com/weapas/ (Date Accessed 20/4/89)

Yahoo Category: Internet Citation

http://dir.yahoo.com/Social_Science/Linguistics_and_Human_Languages/
Languages/Specific_Languages/English/Grammar_Usage_and_Style/Citation/
Internet_Citation/ (Date Accessed 20/4/99)

Chapter 15

AN EXAMINATION OF THE LEGAL INVESTIGATION PROCESS

This chapter examines the legal investigation process. It looks at how to get the most out of lectures and tutorials. It covers various search strategies for the efficient gathering of relevant information. Legal research can involve focusing on the substantive rules such as examining the legal rules for controlling pollution or analysing how the courts have interpreted the wording of the principal pollution offence. However, legal research is not restricted to looking at legal rules in isolation. Socio-legal research examines how law operates in a variety of social spheres, *e.g.* whether the pollution legislation has changed attitudes and behaviour towards polluting activity. In recognition of this fact, this chapter includes a brief discussion of methods of data collection that are common to all the social sciences—questionnaires, interviews and observation studies.

15.1 LECTURES

15.1.1 How to get the most out of a lecture

Make sure that you arrive on time. If you are late you will probably miss the lecturer's outline of the lecture and any handouts. You will then find it an uphill battle to understand what is going on.

Writing down every word like an automaton is a mistake. You may end up with a record of everything that was said — but was everything important? What did the lecturer highlight? You will not know because you were too busy writing to notice. Trying to write down every word will probably also result in completely illegible notes.

It is much better practice to take an active role in the lecturing process. This involves you thinking about what is being said and asking yourself:

Is this important?

Do I understand this? If not, make a note and check the point in the recommended reading or raise it in a tutorial.

Try to identify the structure of the lecture. At the beginning the lecturer may outline the structure of the lecture and/or at the end they may summarise the material. Alternatively, you may be provided with an outline in a handout.

How do you know what is important? There are several clues for you to look out for:

1. The emphasis given by the lecturer. They may say directly that something is important or use terms such as "a leading case";

2. The time spent on a topic. If something is only mentioned briefly it is probably a minor point.

It is very tempting to write down everything, especially at the beginning of your university career. You may feel that you want to do this and gradually build up your confidence in your own note-taking abilities before you move to a more active participation in the lecture.

It is very important that you can easily read your own notes. Several suggestions to aid this:

(a) Develop your own shortened versions of words, *e.g.* do not write out House of Lords each time it is mentioned — put HL.

(b) Mark out cases and statutes in some way, such as underlining.

(c) Do not write in a continuous prose with no breaks. Do not cram everything in together in an attempt to save paper. It will be incredibly difficult to read at a later stage. Try and break up the text with headings. Separate out different points — either by numbering or by leaving a line between them. It will be much easier to use the notes if they are easy to read and you can identify the main points.

Note-taking is covered in more detail in chapter 16, para. 16.3.

Soon after the lecture you should re-read your notes to check that you understand what you have written and that you can read your writing. Do this quickly while the contents of the lecture are still fresh in your mind.

Follow up the lecture by reading any materials recommended by the lecturer. Do not try to read everything — you will not have time. Select the most important materials. Your selection should be based on the emphasis accorded by the lecturer and whether the material is highlighted in your course materials.

15.1.2   Uses to be made of lecture material

1. Your lectures should initially be your principal source of information — they are designed to introduce you to the subject area and to provide a structure and overview for you to flesh out.

2. Do not regard your lecture notes as *all* you will need to pass exams. Lecture notes are just *one* source of material. Your work for a course should include lecture notes but will also include notes from your own reading and interpretation from primary and secondary sources. You are expected to follow up a lecture by reading key materials mentioned by the lecturer. If cases are discussed in a lecture, you should read the case report for yourself. This will not only help your understanding of the topic but it will build up into a bank of notes useful for revision purposes.

3. Your lectures will be more up to date than textbooks. Lectures can include developments which have taken place up to the previous day whereas textbooks are likely to be several months out of date by the time they are published. Do remember that your lecture notes will go out of date quickly. You cannot dig up your old lecture notes years later and assume that they will still apply. The basic underlying principles may still apply but even these can change over time. You must be able to update the information yourself.

4. The information given in one lecture would take you far longer than one hour to find yourself in a library. Those who think that they can complete a course by skipping lectures and just reading a book instead will find that they have chosen the difficult way to study a subject. The most time-efficient way is to attend the lectures and use them as

a basis for your own reading. They will provide a framework and should help identify important areas for you to follow up.

5. Note-taking is a subjective process. Copying out someone else's notes is no substitute for attending the lecture yourself. If you lend notes, make sure that you keep a copy in case the borrower never returns the notes.

6. Lectures are not just useful for the content. You should also pay attention to how the lecturer has structured the material and how they have used legal authority such as cases and statutes. This should help you in structuring your essays and using authority in legal argument.

Further Reading:

H.L. MacQueen, *Studying Scots Law* (Butterworths, 1993), pp. 113–117.
L. Marshall and F. Rowland, *A Guide to Learning Independently* (2nd ed., Open University Press, 1993), chap. 9.
P. Race, *500 Tips for Students* (Blackwell, 1992), pp. 39–41, 54–56.

15.2 TUTORIALS

15.2.1 How to get the most out of a tutorial

Tutorial sessions involve small groups of students having a discussion with the tutor about a topic which has previously been covered in lectures. Tutorials are viewed as a crucial part of the learning process. It is therefore important that you attend all of your scheduled tutorials. If you miss a lecture you can copy someone's notes. Tutorials are much less easy to miss. People will tend to take fewer notes than in a lecture and it will be difficult to find out exactly what was discussed.

The more effort that you put into a tutorial, the more you will get out of it. You will usually be given a tutorial exercise to prepare. Make sure that you have carried out the work expected. If you attend having done no preparation you will not understand the discussion and will probably not be able to take part.

At the tutorial you should be ready to participate in the discussion by asking questions, listening to other people's contributions and responding to issues raised. You should make notes of anything that you consider helpful or if the tutor stresses a particular point. Otherwise you should concentrate on participating and not writing. The best practice is to spend a short time after the tutorial writing up salient points. Do not leave too much of a time-gap between the tutorial and writing up notes as your memory will inevitably let you down.

15.2.2 Uses to be made of tutorials

Use tutorials as an opportunity to raise questions about anything that you have not understood in the lectures. If you are unsure of what is expected from you in a piece of coursework or in the exam, the tutorial is the place to raise it with the tutor.

Tutorial sessions are where you will develop problem-solving skills which will be essential to cope with exam questions and the practice of law generally. Lectures will tend to cover the content of the law in a given area. In tutorials you will apply that law to problem scenarios. The application of the law to factual situations is a fundamental skill for lawyers. Exam questions may be discursive essays or they will consist of problem questions. Working through problem scenarios in tutorials is excellent preparation for the eventual exam at the end of the course.

Tutorials will tend to be the setting for receiving feedback on your assessments. This will give you the chance to see both your strengths and where you are going wrong.

Tutorials also give you the opportunity to improve your oral communication skills. At first it may be nerve-wracking, but the more you speak in the small tutorial setting the more confident you will become speaking generally. This will help you when you come to give presentations.

Tutorials are an important point of contact, not only with the tutor but also with your fellow students. It is always useful to share ideas. It can also be very reassuring to find out that everyone else is finding it as difficult as you are.

Further Reading:

H.L. MacQueen, *Studying Scots Law* (Butterworths, 1993), pp. 117–119.
L. Marshall and F. Rowland, *A Guide to Learning Independently* (2nd ed., Open University Press, 1993), chap. 10.

15.3   LITERATURE SEARCH STRATEGIES

15.3.1   Finding the law on . . .

"All this stuff on cases and legislation is fine, but how do you actually find out what the law is on something?" The diagram on the facing page is intended to provide a guide to finding the law on a given subject.

15.3.2   Updating a legal literature search

Once you have carried out your subject search, your attempt to find out "what the law is on . . ." is not over. You must take steps to update your search. It is vitally important that you are aware of any recent developments that may have changed the law. The appropriate steps may depend on the topic but here are some suggestions of sources you should check:

- Loose-leaf updating services/encyclopaedias. These are useful but make sure that you check the date of the most recent update.
- Current Law Monthly Digest/Statutes Service File, see chapter 10, paras. 10.2 and 10.7. These are updated every month. They tend to be about six weeks behind events.
- Current editions of journals in the appropriate subject area. Weekly journals will have the most up to date information.
- Legal databases on CD-ROM. You need to ensure that you are aware of the date of the most recent update.
- On-line legal databases. Examples include Current Legal Information, Lexis and Lawtel. These will be more up to date than CD-ROM versions but you should still be aware of how often they are updated. They will be at best a day behind events and some are weeks behind.
- Relevant websites. You need to be aware of when the site was last updated. It is dangerous to presume that just because something is on the internet that it is up to date.

Finding the law on a given subject

Library catalogue	Legal Bibliographies chapter 6, para. 6.5.2	Reference works/ Encyclopaedias chapter 6, para. 6.3	On-line legal databases such as Current Legal Information / Lexis / Lawtel / Celex to access	Current Law Year Books & Monthly Digests chapter 10, paras 10.2 and 10.3	Specific sources such as
Books Articles Conference papers	→ Books	Use tables of statutes, cases etc., footnotes, endnotes and references to access			Subject indexes in law reports (cases) chapter 3, para. 3.2.6
		→ legislation cases books articles official publications	→ legislation cases books articles official publications	→ legislation cases books articles	Index to the Statutes (statutes) chapter 5, para. 5.3.1.4
					List of Statutory Instruments (S.I.s) chapter 5, para. 5.4.2.3
					The Stationery Office daily, weekly, monthly & annual catalogues (Government publications) chapter 6, para. 6.11.3.1
					Legal Journals Index (articles) chapter 6, para. 6.8.1.1

For sources of information which make you aware of current developments, see chapter 6, para. 6.10.

15.3.3 Literature search strategy for essays/research projects

This section covers literature strategies appropriate for essays and research projects. Essay writing techniques are covered in chapter 16, para. 17.5.

You should start the investigation process by looking at general information about the topic and moving on to more specific material. Reading general information is not just necessary to become familiar with the topic, it is also important to enable you to put the topic into context.

15.3.3.1 *Starting point*

1. Decide what the essay is about/what your research topic is.

2. Select appropriate search terms. Do not just search using one term. You will inevitably miss lots of material. Think of broad terms, narrow terms and related terms and search under all of them. Do not forget synonyms or alternative terms. If your essay is about the regulation of agricultural pollution you could search using the following terms: environmental protection; pollution; agricultural pollution, water pollution, waste disposal, farm waste, nitrates, silage, slurry, etc.

3. You also need to decide your search parameters. These will affect the range of sources which you consult.

    (a) Jurisdiction — are you just concerned with Scotland? The U.K.? Or is it EC-wide or indeed international?

    (b) Time period to be covered — is it an analysis of the current law or a historical study, and if the latter, which period?

    (c) How up to date does your knowledge have to be? At university you may be told that your work must be current up to a certain date (obviously a solicitor has to ensure that his knowledge is as up to date as possible).

    (d) Is the main thrust of the work to be the substantive law or is it on a more theoretical level such as socio-legal or criminological?

4. Initial search:

    At university ⇒ Lecture notes and/or recommended reading for the course will have identified for you the most relevant and up-to-date textbook.

    For a research project or post university ⇒ The Library catalogue should be consulted. Search under the relevant subject area to identify the most up to date dedicated textbook. Alternatively, try using one of the bibliographies of law books such as D. Raistrick, *Lawyers Law Books* (3rd ed., Bowker Sawer, London 1997). If there are no entries for that subject area try looking in a general reference work such as the *Stair Memorial Encyclopaedia*, Gloag & Henderson, *Introduction to the law of Scotland* (10th ed., W. Green, Edinburgh 1995) or D.M. Walker, *Principles of Scottish Private Law (4th ed., Clarendon, Oxford 1989)*.

    General reference works will not tend to provide much detail but should provide you with an introduction to the subject. They should enable you to identify more specific information sources.

    Remember to make use of one of the best resources in a library — a librarian.

    Also remember that you are not restricted to the materials in the one library. You can use the internet to gain access to the catalogues of other university libraries and order materials through the inter-library loan scheme. There is a charge for this service and you may need a lecturer to authorise your application.

5. Once you have located a relevant textbook, consult the appropriate sections. A textbook is likely to give you some general background information on your topic and to contain references to where more specific/detailed information is located. It should be used as a springboard to the more detailed information sources. Make full use of references listed in footnotes or in any further reading sections. These could identify relevant statutes/ case law/secondary material.

One dedicated text is never going to provide you with the complete answer. At the very least you will want to look at other people's views and interpretations of the issue. This may involve looking for alternative texts and/or journal articles (see chapter 6, para. 6.8.1.). You will probably need to consult primary sources such as cases or statutes to enable you to give *your* view of the law (see chapter 3, para. 3.2.2.1 for searching for cases by subject and chapter 5, para. 5.3.1 for searching for statutes by subject).*Remember that any text will be out of date and you will need to update the information.*

6. Follow up the references you have identified. These may include:

Cases — (see chapters 2 and 3)
Statutes — (see chapters 4 and 5)
Journal articles — (see chapter 6, para. 6.8)
Books — (see chapter 6, para. 6.5)
Newspaper articles — (see chapter 6, para. 6.9)
Scottish Law Commission Reports — (see chapter 6, para. 6.11.7)
Government material — Green Papers, White Papers, Royal Commission Reports, Government Department press releases, Consultation Papers — (see chapter 6, para. 6.11)
Theses — (see chapter 6, para. 6.6)
Conference proceedings — (see chapter 6, para. 6.7)
Relevant websites (see chapter 13)
Specialist legal databases (either electronic or on CD-ROM) (see chapter 13, para. 13.4)

If you are unable to locate any material using the above, try consulting:

The relevant subject heading in the Current Law Year Books and the latest Monthly Digest (see chapter 10, paras 10.2 and 10.3).
On-line databases such as Lexis or Lawtel (see chapter 13, para. 13.4).
The subject indexes contained in the various series of law reports. The following Scottish series contain subject indexes: Session Cases, Scots Law Times, Scottish Criminal Case Reports, Scottish Civil Law Reports and Green's Weekly Digest.

As you search through this material you may wish to alter your search terms or indeed your search parameters. If you cannot find many references, it may be that the original search term used is too narrow. You should try to broaden out your search using a more general term. If you find too many items under the search term, try a more specific term.

7. Even if no journal articles have been identified in the textbook, it will still be worth carrying out a journal search. This is because material could have been written since the

text was published. Journals will be more up to date than a textbook and could help you to update your information. Search strategies for locating journal articles are covered in chapter 6, para. 6.8.1.

8. Ensure that your search is as up to date as possible. You can do this by checking:

   (a) The current editions of relevant journals. They may have been published too recently to have been entered in the indexes;

   (b) Current Law Monthly Digests and Statutes Service File (chapter 16, paras 10.2 and 10.7). This should identify if there have been any legal developments over the last couple of months;

   (c) Updating services available for various sources. Make sure that you check the frequency with which it is updated and the date of the last update. Some updating services are only updated on a six-monthly basis.

   (d) On-line legal databases such as lawtel and lexis should help to locate any very recent developments.

   (e) Newspapers and news organisations for current comment. The search facilities available via their websites are particularly useful (see chapter 6, para. 6.9).

   (f) Relevant websites. This would depend on the topic but might include: House of Commons Weekly Information Bulletin, Hansard, Government departments, The Stationery Office's Daily List, lobby groups, trade organisations.

9. When you do find relevant material you should note down the full bibliographic reference. Bibliographic references are discussed more fully in chapter 16, para 16.6. This will save you a lot of time and frustration later when you come to compile your bibliography. You may wish to compile a database of your own references — a personal bibliography. Personal bibliographies are covered in chapter 16, para 16.8. It is important to be systematic and thorough when checking sources of information and obtaining relevant items. You will stay in control of your research if you keep a check on:

   • Sources which you have already read,
   • Sources which you have photocopied but not read,
   • Sources still to be consulted and
   • Items requested via the library on inter-library loan.

   Failure to do this can result in:

   • Important sources of information being overlooked;
   • The same publication being covered more than once, wasting time and effort by duplicating references;
   • Some vital element in a reference to a publication being missed out, requiring it to be checked;
   • The discovery, when finally writing up the project, that indexes and catalogues should have been checked under a term which you now realise to be important.

The above information is summarised in the diagram on p. 269.

15.3.4   Literature search strategy for problem questions

Techniques for answering problem questions are covered in chapter 17, para. 17.6.

The literature search approach for answering problem questions is very similar to the strategy for essays, see para. 15.3.3. The strategy is different in that you will be limited to looking for

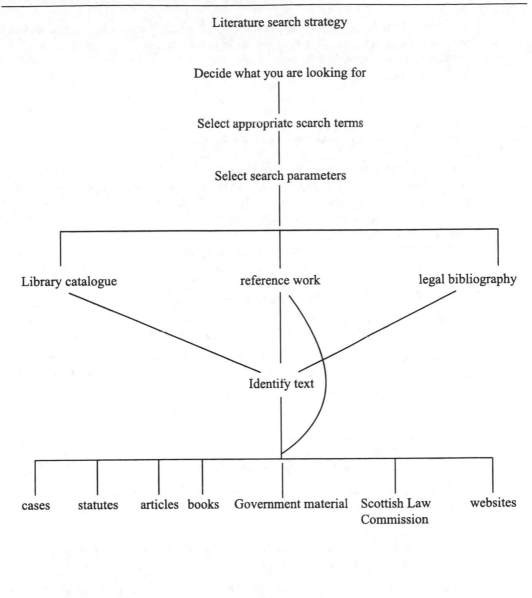

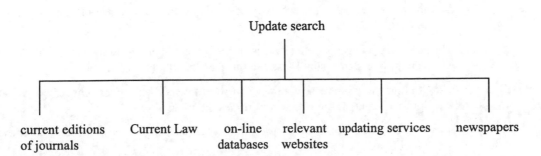

information that is specific to the question. Your reading for an essay question will have to be more general in order to allow the topic to be put in context.

Once you have identified the area of law concerned, you will need to investigate that area and identify the current legal position.

15.4   Time Management

Your success at university depends on YOU. You are in control of your own destiny. One of the most productive things that you can do is to organise yourself and your time at an early stage in your university career. There is no correct way of managing your studies. It is up to you to find ways that suit you and your lifestyle. This section contains some suggestions to help you manage your time effectively.

Time management skills are increasingly important in a world where the majority of students are employed in part-time work. Financial constraints often mean that time that would ideally be spent in the library is instead spent behind a shop counter or bar. It is vital to maintain a balance in your life that does not work to the detriment of your studies.

1. Try to establish a routine and organise yourself into a regular study schedule.

2. Try to be flexible about where you can work. Make use of ''spare'' bits of time such as bus journeys. Make the most of breaks between classes and work in the library.

3. Develop a system for filing your notes. When you start revising for an exam you do not want to be faced with a large file of disorganised notes.

4. Be aware of deadlines. Think ahead and plan your work. Timetables, diaries or planners can be useful aids. Being able to work to deadlines is not only important at university but is a skill which is vital for every kind of job.

5. Set your own target dates for achieving things — choose dates well ahead of any ''external'' deadlines. Make sure that you set realistic deadlines — make an allowance for the unforeseen.

6. Do not leave coursework until just before the deadline for submission. A faulty disk or a broken printer can prove disastrous.

7. Do not put off doing something because you think it is difficult. The sooner you get started, the better your work will be. You will probably find that it is not as difficult as you thought. It will certainly not become any easier by leaving it to the last minute.

8. It can be helpful to make lists of specific goals and cross off each one as you achieve them. Review your list regularly. Prioritise your work depending on its *urgency* and its *importance*.

9. You will find tasks easier to tackle if you break them up into small parts. It is much less daunting to start a small task than to face the whole task at once.

10. It is far more productive to work in short bursts than to work through a whole day and into the night. Taking breaks refreshes the mind.

11. It is also helpful to build variety into your studying — do not spend an entire evening on one task.

12. Finally, do not sit on your own and worry about work. Make use of your lecturers and tutors. Ask for help or additional explanation. You should also make use of your fellow students. Talking and bouncing ideas off each other can be very productive. Even a good moan can be beneficial!

Further reading on time management can be found in:

S. Drew and R. Bingham, *The Student Skills Guide* (Gower, 1997), chaps 3 and 15.
A. Northedge, *The Good Study Guide* (Open University Press, 1990), chap. 1.
P. Race, *500 Tips for Students* (Blackwell, 1992), pp. 12–29.

15.5   EMPIRICAL RESEARCH

This section is going to look briefly at three methods of collecting primary data: questionnaires, interviews and observation studies. Although the methods are dealt with separately, in practice, a researcher may use several methods within one piece of research. The methods will be described, an indication given of the strengths and weaknesses of each approach and details of dedicated texts provided.

There are many different research techniques which can be used to collect data. The choice of which to use will depend on factors such as:

- the purpose of the study;
- the type of information you want to collect;
- accessibility of the subject(s) of the research;
- the nature of the subject(s) of the research;
- time constraints;
- cost;
- the level of skills you possess, *e.g.* if you have an aptitude for figures you may be keen to use questionnaires and statistical analysis;
- personal preference.

15.5.1   Questionnaires

A questionnaire is a data collection technique which involves creating a set of questions which will then be put to each respondent to a survey. The survey may be carried out by post, telephone or on a face-to-face basis. Questionnaires tend to be used for large-scale surveys, particularly those involving a geographically widely distributed population.

15.5.1.1   *Advantages and disadvantages of using questionnaires as a data collection method*

Advantages of using questionnaires

1. Questionnaires are an efficient way of gathering information from respondents who are widely dispersed geographically or who live in inaccessible places.

2. The cost of using questionnaires is relatively low compared with carrying out interviews or observation studies.

3. Questionnaires enable the researcher to gather information from a large number of people in a resource (time and cost) efficient way.

4. The collection of standardised data which can be analysed quantitatively.

Disadvantages of questionnaires

1. The major disadvantage is the low level of response rates currently achievable. This is important because of the bias that can result.

2. There is no opportunity to probe beyond the answers you receive on the questionnaire.

3. There is no opportunity to clarify an ambiguous answer.

4. There is no opportunity to check either the accuracy or truthfulness of the answers.

5. You cannot be sure who, within an organisation, has answered your questionnaire. Has it made its way to the most appropriate person?

6. You have no control over the order in which questions are answered.

7. You have no way of ensuring that all your questions are answered.

8. Questionnaires are unsuitable for certain groups of respondents: people with poor literacy skills or poor sight, the very old, children younger than 10 and people with language difficulties.

Further Reading:

Texts providing an overview of questionnaires:

J. Bell, *Doing Your Research Project* (2nd ed., Open University Press, 1993), chap. 7.
L. Blaxter, C. Hughes and M. Tight, *How to Research* (Open University Press, 1996), chap. 6.
M. Denscombe, *The Good Research Guide for Small-Scale Research Projects* (Open University Press, 1998), chap. 6.
T. May, *Social Research* (Open University Press, 1993), chap. 5.

Texts which contain more practical advice for carrying out a questionnaire exercise:

J.M. Converse and S. Presser, "Survey Questions: Handcrafting the Standardized Questionnaire", *Sage University Paper series on Quantitative Applications in the Social Sciences* (1986).
D.A. de Vaus, *Surveys in Social Research* (4th ed., 1996, UCL), chaps 6 and 7.
G. Hoinville and R. Jowell, *Survey Research Practice* (Gower, 1985).
C.A. Moser and G. Kalton, *Survey Methods in Social Investigation* (2nd ed., 1971, Heinemann Educational), chaps. 11 and 13.
A.N. Oppenheim, *Questionnaire Design, Interviewing and Attitude Measurement* (2nd ed., 1992, Pinter), chaps 7 and 8.

15.5.2   Interviews

There are four different types of interview:

(a) Structured interview: where a questionnaire checklist is completed by the interviewer, not the respondent.

(b) Semi-structured interview: questions are normally specified by the researcher but the interviewer is free to probe beyond the answers.

(c) Informal interview: the respondent is allowed to talk about an issue in any way he chooses.

(d) Group interviews: allow the researcher to focus on group values and group dynamics around the issue under investigation.

15.5.2.1 *Advantages and disadvantages of using interviews as a data collection method*

Advantages of using interviews

1. The response rate will tend to be better than that achievable by mail questionnaires.

2. The interviewer can ensure that the respondent understands what they are being asked by the repetition or rephrasing of questions.

3. An interview ensures that the respondent answers the questions in the sequence intended.

4. There is an opportunity to probe beyond an answer.

5. The respondent has scope to talk about issues in more detail than it would be possible to write down in response to a questionnaire.

6. Respondents who cannot write fluently are able to express their opinions.

7. The interview situation allows data to be collected not only from the answers provided by respondents but also from how they gave their answers. This includes factors such as body language.

Disadvantages of using interviews

1. Interviews can be very time-consuming.

2. Interviews can be costly. Travel costs depend on the location of your interviewees.

3. If too little structure is maintained then it becomes difficult to use the data in a comparative exercise.

4. The possibility of bias being introduced by the interviewer. An interviewee can be influenced by the way a question is asked. This does not just involve the language used but the inflection of the voice and body language.

Texts providing an overview of interviews

J. Bell, *Doing Your Research Project* (2nd ed., Open University Press, 1993), chap. 8.
M. Denscombe, *The Good Research Guide for Small-Scale Research Projects* (Open University Press 1999, chap. 7).
T. May, *Social Research* (Open University Press, 1993), chap. 6.

Texts providing more practical information about carrying out interviews

C.A. Moser and G. Kalton, *Survey Methods in Social Investigation* (2nd ed., 1971, Heinemann Educational), chaps 12 and 13.
A.N. Oppenheim, *Questionnaire Design, Interviewing and Attitude Measurement* (2nd ed., 1992, Pinter), chaps 5 and 6.

15.5.3 **Observation Studies**

Observation not only involves watching, recording and analysing events of interest but also includes talking to people and examining relevant documents such as diaries or records. "The distinguishing feature of observation ... is that the information required is obtained directly,

rather than through the reports of others; in the area of behaviour one finds out what the individual does, rather than what he says he does.''
C.A. Moser and G. Kalton, *Survey Methods in Social Investigation* (2nd ed., 1971, p. 245).

15.5.3.1 *Advantages and disadvantages of using observation studies as a data collection method*

Advantages of using observation studies

1. It allows the spontaneous element of the data to be captured because you are recording behaviour as it takes place.

2. It enables the study of those who are unable to comprehend and provide accurate answers to questions in questionnaires or interviews, *e.g.* young children.

3. It is not dependent on memory. People can distort the past either intentionally or unintentionally. Observation allows the researcher to witness events.

Disadvantages of using observation studies

1. The subjectivity of the researcher. It is the researcher's selection and interpretation of events that will emerge.

2. The bias of the observer. It is not easy to maintain the detachment of an objective observer. The more familiar the observer becomes with the observed, the more likely that data could be omitted or misinterpreted.

3. Observation studies tend to generate a large amount of material which can easily turn into a mass of unstructured notes.

4. Undertaking an observation study can be very time-consuming.

5. You may not end up measuring reality but a false environment because of people's tendency to behave differently as a result of being observed.

6. It is only possible to observe events which have a set duration. Observation is usually not an appropriate way of studying opinions and attitudes. This disadvantage may be mitigated by combining the use of an observation study with one of the other methods of data collection.

7. There are some situations where observation may not be possible, *e.g.* doctor/patient interviews.

8. The research is very dependent on the personality of the researcher. You need to be able to communicate effectively with people and to be adaptable. You will need to be accepted by and build up a relationship with those you are observing.

Further Reading:

J. Bell, *Doing Your Research Project* (2nd ed., Open University Press 1993), chap. 10.
M. Denscombe, *The Good Research Guide for Small-Scale Research Projects* (Open University Press, 1998), chap. 8.
B.R. Dixon, G.D. Bouma and G.B.J. Atkinson, *A Handbook of Social Science* (Oxford University Press, 1987), pp. 69–79.
V. Jupp, *Methods of Criminological Research* (Unwin Hyman, 1989).
T. May, *Social Research* (Open University Press, 1993), chap. 7.
C.A. Moser and G. Kalton, *Survey Methods in Social Investigation* (2nd ed., 1971, chap. 10, 10.3).

Chapter 16

MAKING EFFECTIVE USE OF INFORMATION

16.1 INTRODUCTION

This chapter discusses the effective use of information once it has been located. It includes reading techniques, note-taking, evaluation of documentary material and record-keeping. It also discusses referencing conventions and the construction of a bibliography.

16.2 EFFECTIVE READING TECHNIQUES

The following are suggestions to help you read effectively:

Do not feel compelled to read a book from cover to cover. Use the contents page and the index to identify chapters or shorter sections of the text which are relevant. If this does not help, start by reading the introduction and the concluding chapter.

Critically assess what you are reading. As you read you should be thinking what your opinion is about the text.

Is it easy to understand the author's arguments?

Are the arguments backed up by authority?

Are the arguments consistent?

Do you agree with the arguments?

If yes, why?

If no, why not?

Make notes as you read. This will help you to retain the essential points. It is also one way of keeping your mind active while you read. If you read without taking any notes you will forget a lot of the material. You may even end up having to re-read it. This is duplication of effort and a waste of your time.

One way of making notes is to mark your book by highlighting or underlining sections. This focuses your attention on the text and you will have a permanent reminder of your first thoughts as you read the text. It goes without saying that you should only do this if the material belongs to you. Do not do this to a library book.

Notes made while reading should not be a shorthand copy of the text. As you read you should try to identify relevant information by asking yourself "What exactly is this about?", "What do I need to remember?". Your notes should be clear and concise. It is essential that you can understand your own notes. This is not as simple as it sounds. It is easy to become familiar with a text, grow tired of making full notes and to end up with almost cryptic notes. When you come to read over your notes several months later, they will not make sense.

Make sure you write down sufficient details about the material you read (see para. 16.6 on referencing conventions regarding appropriate details for various sources). In addition, it is advisable to note down the library reference. These precautions enable you to reference the material in a piece of coursework or find it again with a minimum of difficulty. It is very frustrating to find that you have a really good quotation which you want to include in an essay and yet you have no idea where you found it. It is even more frustrating to find that you have finally finished an essay and yet you have not noted down bibliographic details. You then have to spend time rechecking the details.

Before you start reading a book or article make sure you are clear about your reasons for reading it. Reasons for reading a book/article include:

1. The factual content;

2. To gain an insight into the author's interpretation of the law/events;

3. To look at the author's style of writing;

4. To find out which sources the author has used.

Further Reading:

L. Marshall and F. Rowland, *A Guide to Learning Independently* (2nd ed., Open University Press, 1993), chap. 8.
A. Northedge, *The Good Study Guide* (Open University Press, 1990), chap. 2.
K. Williams, *Study Skills* (Macmillan, 1989), chap. 1.

16.3   NOTE-TAKING

When you are taking notes do not merely copy out passages verbatim. Try to think about the material and put it into your own words. If you do use the actual words of the source, make this clear by putting them in quotation marks. This will help avoid unwitting plagiarism (see chapter 17, para. 17.3).

There are various styles that you can use to take notes. There is no "right" way to take notes. Use whichever style suits you:

16.3.1   **Précis**

There are five formal sources of Scots law. The most important of the sources is legislation. The second most important is case law. The institutional writers were very important but their influence has diminished. Custom and equity are the other recognised formal sources of Scots law.

Prose may be appropriate where you want to abstract important details of key ideas. The disadvantage of using continuous prose is that it is rarely easy to scan. Breaking the text up by using paragraphs helps to make it easier to read.

16.3.2 **Headings and sub-headings**

Formal sources of Scots law

- Legislation
- Case law
- Institutional Writers
- Custom
- Equity

16.3.3 **Numbered sections**

1. Formal sources of Scots law

1.1 Legislation

1.2 Case law

1.3 Institutional Writers

1.4 Custom

1.5 Equity

16.3.4 **Annotated diagrams**

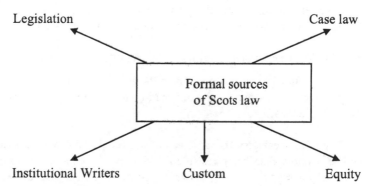

16.3.5 **Colour code**

Using different colours for, *e.g.* case names and details of cases, titles of statutes, etc.

16.3.6 **Annotated photocopied material**

Marking up a photocopy with your own comments. If you use this method be careful not to fall into the trap of photocopying and filing efficiently but failing to actually read the material.

16.3.7   Direct entry into a computer

This can make it easier to manipulate the material using cut and paste functions. However, it does not remove the question of how you should arrange the material.

16.3.8   Card index system

You can put notes of specific items on to a small card index which can then be stored alphabetically. Many people use this method for notes made from cases. It should enable you to find the relevant case note easily. It has the added benefit of forcing you to make your notes concise as they have to fit on to the card.

Further Reading:

K. Williams, *Study Skills* (Macmillan, 1989), chap. 2.

16.4   EVALUATION OF DOCUMENTARY SOURCES ONCE THEY ARE LOCATED

Information sources can be divided into primary and secondary sources. Primary sources include data collected by the researcher and sources which represent the law. Secondary data is material collected and analysed by someone else. Legislation and cases are regarded as primary sources of information. Secondary sources include books, articles, Government statistics, White and Green Papers, etc.

The fact that a document has been compiled by someone else can affect a researcher's use of the document. An example is the crime statistics published by the Government. They can be criticised for failing to reveal the true extent of crime. Reasons for the number of reported crimes being an underestimation of the real extent of crime include:

(a) A large amount of crime is not reported to official authorities for a variety of reasons;

(b) Official statistics also reflect the activities of the authorities, *e.g.* if the authorities decide to concentrate on breath testing the number of reported crimes of drink-driving will increase.

Given this weakness, the official statistics could be used as a piece of evidence about the extent of crime rather than being regarded as definitive. Other pieces of evidence could also be used.

As a general rule, no matter what type of document you are reading, you should not accept it at face value. You should be alert to any possible bias or distortion that it may contain. The distortion need not be deliberate but could be due to the way the information is collected, categorised and interpreted. Even if you do detect bias that does not render the whole document worthless. The important point is that you are aware of the bias and take account of it. The document may still contain some useful information but requires cautious examination.

As you read a document you should consider various questions. The relevancy of the questions will depend on the nature of the document under consideration but here are some suggestions:

1. Who is the author? What are their qualifications for writing on the subject? Are they well respected? What else have they written on the subject? Anything? Are they legally qualified? If they are an academic, which university are they from? What is its reputa-

tion? If the subject matter is practical, has the author qualified as a lawyer or are they "just" an academic who might fail to identify practical issues?

2. What is the date of the publication? You need to ensure that you are reading the most up-to-date information possible. If there is more than one edition, check that you have the latest edition. You will need to be aware of whether the law has changed since the document was produced.

3. Which jurisdiction(s) is the work purporting to cover? Is it referring to Scots law or U.K. law or another jurisdiction? Is it an area that is UK-wide or is that jurisdiction different from Scotland in any key respect?

4. Why was it produced? Has any funding been obtained? If so, from whom? The preface or introduction may contain details of the purpose/objective of the work. Bear in mind that this will be the publicly declared purpose, whereas the real purpose may be very different.

5. Is any bias declared? *e.g.* membership of a particular political party/pressure group?

6. How well has the document been researched? Footnotes/references will provide an indication.

7. How was the research carried out? If the document presents results of research, how much information is given about the research process and the methodologies employed? Can the methodology be justified? Has the methodology been used appropriately? Has it been used according to convention, *i.e.* followed current guidelines. Is it an established methodology? Is it experimental? Further relevant questions would depend on the methodology employed but might include: Is there a copy of the questionnaire, details of sample size or mention of the response rate? Are the results produced in a way which allows the reader to assess their validity, *e.g.* if percentages are used, is there sufficient information to allow the reader to convert them to real numbers?

8. What are its underlying assumptions?

9. How is the argument presented? How well supported and convincing is its argument?

10. Are any conclusions which have been reached based on the evidence presented?

11. What does the document not say? Are there any omissions?

12. How does the document relate to other works? Does it follow on from previous work? Is it part of a trend? Has it disagreed with all previous work? How does it relate to later works? Has anyone taken the research further? Have they confirmed this work or have they contradicted it?

13. What do other sources have to say about it?Has it received critical reviews? If it has, who has been criticising it — experts in the field or competitors?

16.5 RECORD-KEEPING

Make sure that you write down sufficient details to enable you to locate the reference again and to use it in a bibliography. For the specific details required for the different types of sources of information, see para. 16.6.

It is important to be systematic and thorough when checking sources of information and obtaining relevant items. A check on the sources already consulted, those still to be read and a list of items requested via the library on inter-library loan will enable you to remain in control and organised about the progress of your research.

One way of keeping track of things is to create individual records on cards for sources checked and references collected, *e.g.*

Title: Legal Journals Index

Years to be searched			Index term
~~1988~~	~~1993~~	1998	pollution
~~1989~~	1994	1999	
~~1990~~	1995		
~~1991~~	1996		
~~1992~~	1997		

The source cards should be filed alphabetically by title of the publication.

16.6   REFERENCING CONVENTIONS

16.6.1   Bibliographic references

A bibliography is a list of books, journal articles, reports, theses or any other secondary sources of information consulted during the preparation of a piece of research. Primary sources of information (such as cases and statutes) are not included in a bibliography. They should be listed in separate tables of cases/statutes, if appropriate.

A bibliography is used to:

(a) acknowledge the sources which have been consulted and

(b) enable readers of the research to access the material.

References in a bibliography have to convey certain details which give enough information so that others can locate the materials. The information should be accurate, complete and presented in a consistent style. Please note that this book has not adhered to the conventions itemised below. This is because of the need to conform to the publisher's house style.

The following bibliographic details should be included for the type of document listed:

16.6.1.1   *Cases*

case name *in italics*; citation (See chapter 2, para. 2.3.8 for more details about citations).

If you are referring to a particular judgment you should refer to the name of the judge, the page number and corresponding letter in the margin (if included in the series of law reports).

> Example

McNulty v. Marshalls Food Group Ltd 1999 S.C. 195, *per* Lord Macfadyen, p. 206F.

16.6.1.2   *Statutes*

short title; chapter number.

If you are referring to a particular part of the Act, the section number should be given.

> Example

Section 1 of the Protection of Animals (Scotland) Act 1993 (c.15) increased the penalty for certain acts of cruelty to animals.

16.6.1.3 *Books*

author, surname and initials;
title (<u>underline</u>< or *use different script*);
edition (if other than the first edition);
place of publication;
publisher;
date of publication;

> Example

Walker D.M. *The Scottish Legal System*, seventh edition, Edinburgh: W. Green, 1997.
If a book has three or more authors you should include the first named author and then put "*et al*" meaning "and the others".

> Example

Smith C. *et al.*, *Pollution Control in Scotland*. Edinburgh: T & T Clark, 1997.
If you refer to a reference book, *e.g.* dictionaries, encyclopaedias, etc., you should use the title.

> Example

Scottish Law Directory 1991 Edinburgh: T & T Clark, 1991

If a book is produced by a corporate body or institution you should use the name of the institution as the author.

16.6.1.4 *Journal articles*

author;
"title of the article";
title of the journal (<u>underline</u> or *use different script*);
date;
volume number;
part (if appropriate);
page numbers.

> Example

Aubert V., "Some Social Functions of Legislation" <u>Acta Sociologica</u> 1966, vol 10, pp 97–120

16.6.1.5 *Articles or chapters in books*

author;
title of chapter or article;
In: author/editor of main work;
title of main work;

edition (if not the first);
place of publication;
publisher;
date;
volume number (if appropriate);
page numbers.

Example

Carson W.G., ''Symbolic and Instrumental Dimensions of early Factory legislation: A Case Study in the Social Origins of Criminal law'' In: R Hood (ed) *Crime, Criminology and Public Policy.* London: Heinemann 1974 pp.107–38.

16.6.1.6 *Government publications*

name of department/institution/body;
title of report (underline or *use different script*);
(Command number);
place of publication;
publisher;
date.

Example

The Scottish Office, *Scotland's Parliament*, (Cm 3658) London: The Stationery Office, 1997.

16.6.1.7 *Conference proceedings*

author(s);
title (of specific paper);
In: conference title (underline or *use different script*);
place;
publisher;
date;
paper number of specific paper, if given.

Example

Murray A. The nature of law. In: *Proceedings of the Conference on Legal Things.* Dundee, Research Association, 1999, Paper 3.

16.6.1.8 *Theses*

author;
title (underline or *use different script*);
degree or award;
university or other institution;
year.

Example

Smith, A.D. *Some Comparative Aspects of Specific Implement in Scots Law.* PhD Thesis, Edinburgh University, 1989.

16.6.1.9 *Newspaper articles*

author/anon;
"title of article";
name of newspaper;
place of publication;
date;
page number.

Example

Bell I., "Springtime in Quangopolis" *The Scotsman*. Edinburgh, 17th March 1999, p 19

16.6.1.10 *Material on the World Wide Web*

See chapter 14, para. 14.3.3.

16.7 REFERENCING SYSTEMS

There are three referencing systems which you can use to link statements in the text to bibliographic details of documents which support these statements. The choice of which system may be determined by your institution or it may be up to you. The important point is that you use one system *consistently*.

The systems are:

16.7.1 Running notes

With running notes, numerals in the text, [in brackets] or [superscript] refer to notes numbered in the order they occur which contain references and sometimes other information. Multiple citations of the same document receive separate numbers. Details of the documents referred to (*e.g.* page references) should be given in the notes. This system can be used to incorporate explanatory footnotes as well as bibliographic references and is widely used in U.K. legal journals. Running notes can be listed at the foot of the page where reference is made to them (footnotes), or in numerical sequence at the end of the chapter or the work (endnotes).

In the list of references/bibliography the works cited are listed in numerical order.

If more than one reference is made to a document when running notes are used, it is possible to avoid a full re-citing of the document by using the following terms:

> *Ibid* (*Ibidem* — the same) can be used if successive references are made to the same document. Each use of "ibid" should be followed by the page number.
> *Op.Cit.* (*Opere citato* — in the work previously cited) where the document has been cited at an earlier point, but not immediately before this reference. The author's name and page number are required. The original citation should contain full bibliographic information.
> *Loc.Cit.* (*Loco citato* — in the place cited). This is similar to *op.cit.* but is more specific, as it refers to the same part of the work which has already been cited.

Example

Recent research [1] has shown that . . . however a respected author [2] has disagreed. After much debate the findings of the original work [3] have now been accepted.

Excerpt from list of references:

1. Wallace W. *New Law Book* Edinburgh: W. Green, 1998
2. Bruce R. *Even Newer Law Book* Edinburgh: W. Green, 1999
3. Wallace W. *New Law Book* Edinburgh W. Green, 1998.

16.7.2   The numeric system

Documents are numbered in the order in which they are first referred to in the text. At each point in the text at which a reference is required, its number is inserted — [in brackets], or in superscript. Subsequent citations of a particular document receive the same number as the first citation. If details of a particular document, *e.g.* page number are required they should be given after the reference number.

In the list of references/bibliography the works cited are listed in numerical order.

This system produces a list of references which is easy to prepare and easy to look up whilst reading the text, but it is not in any useful order as a bibliography. BS 4821:1990 recommends that this system be coupled with a separate bibliography in alphabetical order of author.

Example

Recent research [1] has shown that . . . however a respected author [2] has disagreed. After much debate the findings of the original work [1] have now been accepted.

[Excerpt from list of references:]

1. Wallace W. *New Law Book* Edinburgh: W. Green, 1998
2. Bruce R. *Even Newer Law Book* Edinburgh: W. Green 1999

16.7.3   The name and date system (also known as the ''Harvard System'')

The author's name and date of publication are inserted in brackets at each point in the text where reference to the particular document is required. If the author's name occurs naturally in the text, the date only should be in brackets. If reference is made to different works by the same author in the same year, distinguish them by small case letters after the year.

The works cited would be listed alphabetically by author in the references/bibliography. The date is given after the name and not repeated at the end of the reference. If there are several works by the same author, they should be listed in chronological order.

Example

Recent research (Wallace 1998) has shown that . . . however a respected author (Bruce 1999) has disagreed. After much debate the findings of the original work (Wallace 1998) have now been accepted.

[Excerpt from list of references:]

Bruce R. (1999) *Even Newer Law Book* Edinburgh: W. Green.
Wallace W. (1998) *New Law Book* Edinburgh: W. Green.

Additional Reading:

David P. Bosworth, *Citing your references: a guide for authors of journal articles and students writing theses or dissertations* (Underhill Press, Thirsk, 1992).

D. French, *How to Cite Legal Authorities* (Blackstone Press, London, 1996).

Further information is also available in the following British Standards:

British Recommendations for References to Published Materials (BS 1629 : 1989).

Recommendations for Citing and Referencing Published Material (BS 5606 : 1990).

British Standard Recommendations for Citation of Unpublished Documents (BS 6371 : 1983).

16.8   CONSTRUCTING YOUR OWN BIBLIOGRAPHY

The purpose of recording all the references that you have found is so that you can find the material in the future and incorporate them into a bibliography, *e.g.* for a piece of coursework. There will tend to be a time gap between collecting the references and making use of the information. In order that you can find the information when you need to use it, you may want to construct your own bibliography as a place of safe-keeping for all these references. This will also enable you to build up your own research base and will help with other work undertaken in the future.

There are different ways of constructing your own bibliography:

1. A manual record card system maintained in alphabetical order of the author's surname.

2. A database in electronic form. This can be achieved by constructing a table in Word (the main word processing package in Britain today) or by using a spreadsheet such as Excel. There are also a number of specialist database software packages such as Access.

In either case you should include full bibliographic details. You may also want to include a keyword system describing the contents of the item. A third section for supplementary information may also be useful. This could include your comments on the work.

Chapter 17

HOW TO USE YOUR RESEARCH TO PRODUCE HIGH QUALITY WORK

This chapter provides practical advice on using your research to produce work of a high standard.

17.1   APPROPRIATE USE OF AUTHORITY

If you are making points or arguments you must back them up with authority. In this case authority means reasons/evidence/justification. If you are talking about legal issues, you must refer to the relevant legal authority. Legal authority means a case, legislation or other authority, such as a statement by one of the Institutional Writers. The best way of developing the technique of using authority is to look at how it has been used by others: judges in their opinions; legal writers in their legal texts; lecturers in their lecture notes.

A statement such as "Distances mentioned in Acts of Parliament should be measured in a straight line" is unsubstantiated assertion. You have produced no evidence to back up your statement. At the other end of the scale, a full reference could consist of the following "Section 8 of The Interpretation Act 1978 states that distances referred to in Acts of Parliament 'shall, unless the contrary intention appears, be measured in a straight line on a horizontal plane'". This version has quoted words from the relevant statute in order to make the position absolutely clear. You may wish to quote from the actual words of the statute if you feel that they would make your point more clearly. However, you should never need to write out the *entire* statutory provision. An acceptable level of reference to authority would be "Unless specifically stated otherwise, references to distance in Acts of Parliament should be measured in a straight line, (Interpretation Act 1978, s. 8)".

When using cases as authority it will rarely be sufficient to refer simply to the correct citation of the authority:

Example

"The offence of causing pollution contained in s. 30F of the Control of Pollution Act 1974, as amended, should be regarded as a strict liability offence — *Alphacell v. Woodward* [1972] A.C. 824."

The narration of excessive factual detail about a case is not appropriate:

Example

"The offence of causing pollution contained in s. 30F of the Control of Pollution Act 1974, as amended, should be regarded as a strict liability offence — *Alphacell v. Woodward* [1972] A.C.

824. This case concerned a company who had premises on the banks of the River Irwell. They treated manilla fibres as part of the process of manufacturing paper. The fibres had to be boiled and the water in which they were boiled became seriously polluted. This water was drained into two settling tanks on the edge of the river. One settling tank was higher than the other and the overflow from the higher tank went into the lower. In a shed nearby there were two pumps which ensured that there was no overflow from the lower tank. If the pumps failed the liquid went straight into the river. This happened one day in November 1969. The court found Alphacell guilty.''

The best practice is to mention what is relevant about the authority to illustrate your point. This will probably be a summary of the *ratio decidendi* of a case either in your own words or as a quotation:

Example

''The offence of causing pollution contained in s. 30F of the Control of Pollution Act 1974, as amended, should be regarded as a strict liability offence, *Alphacell v. Woodward* [1972] A.C. 824. This House of Lords case examined the concept of causation and decided that the word ''cause'' should be given a common sense meaning. Negligence, knowledge and intention were all regarded as irrelevant. The important factor was that an active operation had resulted in polluting matter entering a river.''

17.2   QUOTATIONS

If you want to repeat the exact words used in one of your sources of information you must use quotation marks. Everything between quotation marks, including punctuation, should be exactly as in the original text. If you add something you should put it in square brackets. If you omit something you should mark this by adding a sequence of dots. The quote should be referenced and, in addition, the page from which it was taken should be included in the reference.

> *e.g.* ''In homicide, it is not an offence to kill whether intentionally or recklessly, by omission, unless one is under a duty to act . . . .In the pollution cases the courts have attempted to make a similar distinction.''

N. Padfield, ''Clean Water and Muddy Causation: Is Causation a Question of Law or Fact, or Just a Way of Allocating Blame'', *Crim L.R.* [1995] 683 at p. 690.

17.3   PLAGIARISM

The Oxford English Dictionary defines plagiarism as ''the action or practice of plagiarising: the taking and using as one's own of the thoughts, writing or inventions of another''. Expressing ideas from someone else's work in your own words and acknowledging the source is known as paraphrasing. This is acceptable practice. Expressing someone else's ideas and presenting them as your own is plagiarism. Plagiarism also includes copying out chunks of (or an entire) article, section of a book or another student's essay and submitting it as your own. Plagiarism is not an acceptable academic practice. If you do this your work will be penalised and you may well be awarded no marks at all and/or face disciplinary action.

University study is all about exploring the literature and being influenced by new and different ideas. However, there is a fine dividing line between plagiarism and taking advantage of the many academic influences to which you will be exposed. In order to avoid plagiarism:

(a) make sure that you acknowledge the sources which you have used;

(b) if you want to paraphrase make sure that you refer to it as, *e.g.* X's view of Y is . . . .

(c) alternatively, if you want to use the exact words, use a quotation.

17.4   UNIVERSITY ASSESSMENTS

Different types of assessment are used throughout a law degree. These will include: essays, problem questions, oral presentations, group work and exams. Assessment of a law course is not simply a memory test. You will be required to display more than a knowledge of the law in a particular area. You will have to apply legal rules and principles to particular situations. You will have to display analytical and critical skills and to present argument in a clear and logical manner.

A key part of any assessment is the feedback you receive. Keep a copy of your assessment as it is unlikely that it will be returned to you. You will probably receive a feedback sheet containing comments. If, having read the comments, you do not understand where you went wrong — go and see the person who marked it. It is very important that you find out how to improve your work so that you can ensure that you will perform better in the future.

17.4.1   General points for all types of assessments

Make sure that you understand what is expected of you.

Ensure that you answer the question set.

Do not include unsubstantiated personal opinion.

Always back up your arguments with authority.

It is better practice to reference the person who originated the idea than the people who have written about it subsequently.

Do not include substantive points in footnotes to get round the word limit.

Make sure that your grammar and spelling are accurate. Your work should be intelligible at first reading. If necessary make use of the spell-check facility, a thesaurus or a dictionary. It is important to ensure that your meaning is clearly communicated to the reader.

17.5   ESSAY WRITING TECHNIQUES

Essays are one of the ways in which students are required to express themselves and present information in a written form. Essays are likely to be part of the assessment you encounter at university either as coursework or as part of an exam. This section is designed to help you enhance your essay writing skills.

17.5.1   Compliance with requirements

Make sure that you are aware of any special requirements, such as word limits or format stipulations. Word limits can be useful guides as well as being a requirement. If you are having difficulty finding enough material and are woefully short of the word limit, you may be searching under the wrong terms or you may have misunderstood the question. If you have written far in excess of the word limit, you have included extraneous material. You should re-read it and remove material that does not directly relate to the question.

17.5.2   Understanding the question

Examine the wording of the question and decide what you are being asked to do. This is more easily said than done. One way to help focus your thoughts is to underline key words in the question. You should be aware that essay titles are always carefully chosen. The basic topic will tend to be broad, but one or two key words in the title will narrow the essay's scope.

> Example essay title — *The threat to the environment can only be reduced by strengthening the existing legal controls. Discuss.*

It is a common mistake for students to read a title like this and to conclude that they are being asked to write as much as they know on "the environment" or "strengthening the existing legal controls". These factors are relevant but they are not the major focus of the question. The title is asking you to identify the most probable ways of reducing the threat to the environment and then to assess whether strengthening existing legal controls is more effective than any of the other options.

The title determines what is going to be relevant to the essay. Your answer must address the central question. Everything you write should be relevant to answering the question. You will not gain any marks for irrelevant material — no matter how accurate. The inclusion of irrelevant material will detract from your answer.

17.5.2.1   *Key Words In Questions*

Analyse:	Break up . . . into component parts and examine each part.
Compare:	Look for similarities and differences between . . .
Contrast:	Bring out the differences between . . .
Criticise:	Present and evaluate evidence before reaching a judgement about . . .
Define:	Set out the precise meaning of . . .
Describe:	A detailed account of . . .
Discuss:	Explain the meaning of . . . and examine the reasons for and against . . .
Evaluate:	What is the value/worth of . . .
Explain:	Make . . . plain and understandable and account for it.
Identify:	Establish the nature of . . .
Illustrate:	Make clear by giving examples.
Interpret:	Use your judgement to make clear the meaning of . . .

Justify:	Use arguments to make a case for . . .
Review:	Make a survey of . . . and examine it critically.
State:	Present in brief, clear, concise form.
Summarise:	Give the key points of . . .

This is based on a table by S. Drew and R. Bingham, *The Student Skills Guide* (Gower 1997), p. 57.

17.5.3   Collecting relevant material

Once you have decided what the question is asking, you should start your literature search. See chapter 15, para. 15.3.3.

17.5.4   Planning the essay

Examine all the material you have gathered and select the main points which you want to include in your essay. Do not be tempted to try to use *all* of the material which you have gathered. It may not all be relevant or possible to include due to word limit constraints. You should always keep the essay title uppermost in your mind. You must discard irrelevant material, no matter how interesting it may be.

Construct an essay plan outlining the basic structure of the essay. Essays tend to conform to a basic framework which consists of three parts: introduction, discussion and conclusion.

17.5.4.1   *Introduction*

In your introduction you essentially set out how you are going to tackle the essay. You might include:

- How to interpret the terms in the title (*e.g.* what you understand by "the threat to the environment");

- Any assumptions you are going to make rather than argue in detail;

- The criteria you are going to use to reach your conclusions (*e.g.* "the environment is so important that I shall assume that anything which has an unknown effect must be assumed to have a bad effect");

- How you are going to structure your essay.

17.5.4.2   *Discussion*

This is the main portion of the essay. Each main point should be considered, developed and justified by relevant authority and/or examples. Do not include unsubstantiated opinion. You should not present only one side of an argument. You should show the reader that you have taken account of any apparently conflicting evidence. An outline of a discussion might be Smith's theory of X is well-founded because of (a), (b), (c). However, it can also be said that (d), (e), (f) apply. Consequently . . .

17.5.4.3 *Conclusion*

Your conclusion should bring your whole argument together into a set of points that you want the reader to retain. Do not confuse ''conclusion'' with ''summary''. You do need to summarise all your arguments.

17.5.5   **Writing the essay**

Write a draft of the essay which conforms to your essay plan and includes all your ideas. Do not expect to hand in the first draft. You should use that as a basis and hone your ideas from it. If possible, leave it alone for a couple of days and do something else. Return to the draft with a fresh mind and review what you have written.

Do not just put down everything you know and presume that the marker will extract the relevant/correct sections. YOU should identify the relevant/correct items and should leave out the irrelevant. The inclusion of extraneous material detracts from the appropriate material you have presented.

You should aim to present a clear and concise discussion of the topic. Try to use simple straightforward language. Use short sentences. Do not use any words unless you know what they mean. Each paragraph should deal with a single point.

You should always include a bibliography, which should include references to all books, journals or articles which you have used. Lecture notes and primary sources such as cases and legislation should not be included.

Before submitting your essay you should:

- Re-read the essay to ensure that you have answered the question set.
- Check spelling and punctuation. If in doubt about spelling make use of a dictionary or word processor spell-check facility.
- Check that all your references to authority are accurate and spelt correctly.
- Ensure that your writing is legible.
- See also para. 17.9: ''Evaluation of your own Research''.

The thought of the whole process of writing an essay can be daunting. You may find it easier if you break it down into smaller tasks, *e.g.*:

1. Analyse the title and decide what exactly you are being asked to do

2. Consider possible approaches

3. Collect relevant material

4. Decide on an appropriate structure

5. Write the discussion section

6. Write the conclusion

7. Write the introduction

17.5.6 Receiving feedback

One of the most valuable parts of the essay writing process is receiving feedback from whoever marked it. You should make use of any comments to help you improve your assignments in the future.

Common mistakes made by students include:

- Regurgitation of lecture notes/books;
- Failure to address the question asked;
- The inclusion of material without linking it into the essay question;
- Failure to back up arguments with legal authority;
- The inclusion of too much description and too little analysis;
- Use of colloquial terms;
- Using words inappropriately;
- Inclusion of unsubstantiated personal opinion;
- Failure to communicate ideas clearly;
- Poor use of English language.

Further Reading:

S. Drew and R. Bingham, *The Student Skills Guide* (Gower, 1997), chaps 6 and 17.
G.J. Fairbairn and C. Winch, *Reading, Writing and Reasoning: A Guide for Students* (2nd ed., Open University Press, 1996).
H.L. MacQueen, *Studying Scots Law* (Butterworths, 1993), pp. 154–160.
L. Marshall and F. Rowland, *A Guide to Learning Independently* (2nd ed., Open University Press, 1993), chap. 12.
A. Northedge, *The Good Study Guide* (Open University Press, 1990), chaps 5 and 6.
K. Williams, *Study Skills* (Macmillan, 1989), chaps 7 and 8.

17.6 TECHNIQUES FOR TACKLING PROBLEM QUESTIONS

The problem question format is used frequently in tutorial exercises, coursework and exams. A problem question will provide a set of facts. You will be expected to identify and apply the relevant law to these facts. You will then usually be asked to come to some form of conclusion. This will depend on the question but may involve advising one or more of the parties as to the legal remedies available to them. This section is designed to help you enhance your problem solving skills.

Problem questions are popular forms of assessment at university because problem solving is one of the essential skills for a lawyer. Being presented with a set of facts and asked to advise on their legal implications is an everyday activity of the practising lawyer.

Problem questions are different from essays. Problem questions are far more specific than essay questions. You are not provided with a general topic area for discussion, instead there are particular questions to address. When you construct your answer to a problem question you should not include a long introduction. There is no need to start with a general discussion of the area of law. You should go straight into dealing with the specific issues raised by the question.

Read the question carefully to ensure that you understand it. Problem questions are often quite detailed. Make sure that you have not misread any details. This is particularly easy to do under exam conditions. Do not write out the question. This is a waste of time and if you are required to keep to a word limit it will waste words. Underline key words to help focus your thoughts.

At university, problem questions will tend to be centred around one area of law which is familiar to you. After you leave university you will be faced with problems which do not neatly fit into one subject which you have just studied and which may include elements which are completely new to you.

Even though university questions will tend to concentrate on one area of law that does not mean that they contain just one issue. They may contain several different issues. Do not read the questions through quickly and leap to the conclusion that the problem centres on a single issue. You should also be aware that the answer to a problem question is never "yes" or "no". If you think the answer is very straightforward, re-read the question because you have probably missed something.

Identify the problem by looking at the legal issues which are raised by the facts.

Identify the *relevant* information which you have and the *relevant* information which you do *not* have. In problem questions, as in real life, the complete factual picture is often missing some key details. If facts are missing say so. It may be appropriate to say if X then . . . if Y then . . . (and back up your points with authority).

When you have detected the legal issues you should then begin your literature search to find the current law on the subject. See chapter 15, para. 15.3.4.

Writing your answer

1. Think out a logical structure. The structure will depend on the nature of the problem. In the case of delictual problems the approach might be:

   Is there a duty of care owed?
   Has that duty been breached?
   Did the breach cause loss?
   Is the loss quantifiable?

2. Keep your answer relevant to the question. Do not be tempted to include long descriptive passages. Credit will be give for the appropriate *application* of the relevant law to the factual scenario.

3. Back up your arguments by reference to authority (see para 17.1).

4. You have to apply the law as you find it. If you personally disagree with it or find it unfair, that is irrelevant to answering the question. Personal opinion should not be included.

5. Make sure that you do what has been asked of you. If you are asked to advise X, make sure that you advise X. This does not mean ignoring arguments against X's position. You should take into account any counter-arguments against your adopted position.

6. Do not spent ages agonising over the conclusion to the problem. There is indeed unlikely to be one correct answer. At university level the conclusion that you reach is not *that* important. You will receive credit for the presentation of cogent arguments, backed up by authority. In real life the conclusion is, of course, very important.

```
┌─────────────────────────────────────────────────────────────────────┐
│             Summary of the approach to problem questions              │
│                                                                       │
│                      Examine the available facts                      │
│                                 ⇓                                     │
│               Identify the legal issue(s) raised by the facts         │
│                                 ⇓                                     │
│                        Identify the *material* facts                  │
│                                 ⇓                                     │
│     Be aware of the omission of any material facts. Locate missing facts (if possible). │
│                                 ⇓                                     │
│           Carry out a literature search to find the current legal position │
│                                 ⇓                                     │
│                  Apply the relevant law to the factual scenario       │
│                                 ⇓                                     │
│   Advise client on available options/remedies. In practise this will involve matching the client's │
│        need, desires and resources to possible courses of action (legal and non-legal). │
└─────────────────────────────────────────────────────────────────────┘
```

Further Reading:

H.L. MacQueen, *Studying Scots Law* (Butterworths, 1993), pp 142–147.
V. Tunkel, *Legal Research* (Blackstone Press, 1992), chaps 1 and 8.
G. Williams, *Learning the Law* (Stevens, 1982), chap. 8.

17.7   ORAL PRESENTATIONS

This section concerns oral presentations which are increasingly used as a form of assessment at university. You may be asked to give a presentation either as an individual or as part of a group.

17.7.1   Initial Preparation

Make sure that you know:

> *When* the presentation will take place;
> *How* long the presentation is to last;
> *Where* the presentation is to take place;
> *Who* your audience will be;
> *What* your audience is expecting from you.

17.7.2   Construction of a Presentation

Careful planning is the key to a successful presentation. Once you have identified the information you will need and collected that information, you should:

- establish the main points you want to make;
- ensure that you have material to support these points (support could be in the form of *e.g.* a case, a statutory provision, an example, statistics or a quotation);
- put your main points and supporting material into a clear and logical order.

The structure of the presentation should conform to the essay model: introduction, discussion of the main points and conclusion.

The beginning and end of the presentation require special attention. At the beginning of the talk you want to attract your audience's attention. Ways of making an initial impact include: a controversial statement, a question, a quotation or a joke. You should also always include a clear outline of your presentation.

In a situation that all will find nerve-wracking, do what you feel happy doing. If you are good at telling jokes (and they are appropriate to the subject) then by all means include some. If you shrink in horror at telling a joke in such a setting then the best advice is don't include any.

At the end of the presentation you want to ensure that your audience goes away with a firm understanding of the message of your presentation. You should always provide a brief summary of your main points. Ways of ending your presentation include a recommendation, a challenge or a quotation.

17.7.3   Notes

No matter how good your memory, you will find that you will need some form of notes to guide you through the presentation. Notes help ensure that you do not omit anything from your talk. Some people write out everything they are going to say, others use small cards which contain only the main points of the talk. There is no right or wrong method, it is up to you to choose whichever approach makes you feel comfortable.

If you are inexperienced at giving presentations you may feel happier writing out the full text. If you do this:

> use large writing or typeface;

> use double line spacing;

> use only one side of a piece of paper;

> number the pages (just in case you drop them).

17.7.4   Delivery of the Presentation

Make sure that you are familiar with your talk. Practice speaking it out loud, ideally in the room where you are to give the presentation. This will help you to judge the length of the talk. This should also prevent you becoming too nervous on the day of the presentation.

Organise any visual aids that you are to use. Visual aids help to break up the talk and can help maintain the attention of the audience. Use visual aids that you feel happy operating. If you know that you get nervous and your hands shake do not use a laser pointer. The appearance of a shaky point on a screen will probably gain you the sympathy of your audience but will detract from the message that you are trying to get across. Make sure that you know how to operate any visual aid. When you are nervous it may not be very clear how to switch on or adjust an overhead projector. A few moments familiarising yourself with any equipment will be time well spent.

Examples of visual aids are:

overhead slides

black/white boards

flip charts

physical objects

handouts

videos

If you are going to produce a handout do not include every word of your talk. Your audience will just sit and read it and will not pay any attention to you. A handout should summarise the main points of your talk. Try and make it as attractive as possible. Pay attention to design and layout. The more eye-catching the handout, the more positive an impression will be created.

If you use overhead transparencies make sure that they are not too crowded. Short summaries or bullet points should be used. Do not put large sections of prose on to an overhead. This only results in a loss of visual impact as key sections disappear in the middle of the detail. The writing should be large enough to be read from the back of the room.

Do not read your presentation out word for word. It is important to maintain eye contact with your audience. Try and look at your script, memorise the next few words and then look at members of the audience while you are speaking. They will be very bored if you merely read out material in a monotone! Try and vary the tone of your voice. Put some feeling into your presentation. This will make it much more interesting for your audience.

Be aware of your body language. Good posture shows the audience that you are relaxed and confident. Do not fold your arms or stand with your hands behind your back. Try to avoid waving your arms around — it is very distracting for the audience.

The pace at which you speak is very important. Remember that your audience does not know what you are going to say and will need time to listen and digest your words. At the start of the talk, make a conscious effort to slow down your speech pattern. Do not talk too quickly or you will lose your audience.

Make sure that you speak loud enough so that the people at the back of the room can hear you.

Make sure that you keep to time by putting your watch on the table or somewhere you can see it easily. You should try and work out beforehand which section you could cut if you run out of time. It is also useful to have some extra material if you end up with too much time.

17.7.5   Questions

Waiting for questions can be daunting. The more prepared you are, the easier it will be to answer any questions. If someone asks a question which you do not understand, say so. Ask them to clarify exactly what they mean.

You can give yourself an extra few seconds to think of and structure an answer by repeating the question. You can say that this is so that everyone can hear the question.

If someone asks you something that you do not know it is better to be upfront and admit that you do not know. It may be something outside the ambit of your talk that the questioner knows about. You could always try asking the questioner what they think.

17.7.6   Nerves

Everybody is nervous before making a presentation. There is no way of avoiding nerves altogether but here are some hints to help you control your nerves:

- Be well prepared and practice your talk out loud;
- Remember that you may be only too aware of your nerves but your audience will probably not notice that you are nervous;
- You should be confident that you will know more about the topic than your audience;
- If you drop your notes or lose your place, pause, get yourself organised and take a deep breath. You may feel that the whole process took an hour but the audience will not perceive the delay as anything but minimal;
- If you get short of breath during the presentation, pause and take a deep breath. Then continue . . .

Further Reading:

S. Drew and R. Bingham, *The Student Skills Guide* (Gower, 1997), chaps 8 and 19.

17.8   Research Projects

Presentation of research can take many forms:

1. Abstract
   An abstract is a concise overview of the research highlighting any important findings. Abstracts could be viewed as advertisements for your work. You might send an abstract to a conference organiser or journal editor hoping to get your paper/article accepted. Abstracts also form part of written research, see para. 17.8.1.3 below.

2. Poster
   A poster is a more detailed form of abstract but is shorter than a full paper, usually about six to eight sheets of A4. It is presented as a wall chart, literally a poster. Posters are generally used to present preliminary results and are displayed at conferences. In a conference there will be set sessions in the programme in which delegates can inspect the posters. During this period the researcher has to "man" their poster and answer any questions. This can be a very useful exercise in that it enables you to receive advice as well as to advertise your work.

3. Report/paper/dissertation
   Presentation of research in written form is the principal method of communication and will be dealt with para. 17.8.1.

4. Conference paper/oral presentation
   This is equivalent to giving a short lecture on your research. The normal length would be around 20–30 minutes and you would be expected to deal with questions from the audience. See para. 17.7 on oral presentations.

17.8.1   Structure of written forms of research presentation

The exact structure of the research report/paper/dissertation may vary and indeed may be subject to requirements by various institutions. The following sections represent the conventional form of presenting research:

17.8.1.1   *Title page*

This page should include the title of your work, your name, institution, date and, if the work is being submitted for a particular qualification, you should include the relevant details. The title should be concise and provide an accurate impression of the nature of your work.

17.8.1.2   *Acknowledgements*

It is usual to include any acknowledgements and thanks after the title page. You should bear in mind any assurances of confidentiality which you have given and make sure that these are not breached.

17.8.1.3   *Abstract*

An abstract is usually required in all presentations of academic research. It should be regarded as independent of the research and should not be referred to in the text. The purpose of the abstract is to provide a brief and concise overview of the research and to highlight any important findings.

17.8.1.4   *Contents*

This should include a list of chapter headings and page numbers along with details of any appendices.

17.8.1.5   *Chapter 1 — Introduction*

This should include:

> aims
>
> objectives
>
> research questions/hypotheses which have been investigated
>
> proposed methodology in general terms
>
> indication of why the research topic was chosen
>
> the scope of the work
>
> indication that you are aware of any limitations of the work

17.8.1.6   *Chapter 2 — Literature review*

This should contain a review of previous work on the topic. It should not be a descriptive account of every work published on the topic. You should display skills of critical analysis by commenting on previous works, selecting only relevant material and organising its presentation in an appropriate way.

17.8.1.7   *Chapter 3 — Methodology*

This should include a discussion of the methodology(ies) adopted and a justification of your choice. Another important element of this chapter is to discuss any limitations in the methods employed. The research instruments which were used should be included in an appendix, *e.g.* the questionnaire or interview schedule or descriptions of various statistical tests.

17.8.1.8 *Chapter 4 — Presentation of results/findings*

Presentation of results should be accurate and clear. Detailed comment and interpretation should be left until the following chapter.

17.8.1.9 *Chapter 5 — Discussion*

This is the key section of the work. It should start by mentioning your research questions/hypotheses as outlined in your first chapter. You should then make use of the results/findings from your fourth chapter to back up your lines of argument. You should then tie in these lines of argument with your research questions/hypotheses. You should also refer to how your research relates to the previous works in the area discussed in your chapter two. Any limitations in the research design should be included along with suggestions of alternative approaches.

17.8.1.10 *Chapter 6 — Summary and conclusions*

This should involve bringing all your arguments together and drawing conclusions. You should only include conclusions which can justifiably be drawn from your results/findings. You should not introduce new material in this concluding chapter. It is a good idea to mention whether your work has implications for further research in the area.

17.8.1.11 *Bibliography*

This should include all the sources which you have consulted during your research.

17.8.1.12 *Appendices*

As stated above this should include copies of the research instruments which were used, *e.g.* the questionnaire or interview schedule or descriptions of various statistical tests.

Further Reading:

J. Bell, *Doing Your Research Project* (2nd ed., Open University Press, 1993).
L. Blaxter, C. Hughes, M. Tight, *How to Research* (Open University Press, 1996).
J.A. Sharp and K. Howard, *The Management of a Student Research Project* (2nd ed., Gower, 1996).

17.9   EVALUATION OF YOUR OWN RESEARCH

When you write up your research (be it an essay or research project) be prepared to work through several drafts. One draft will not be sufficient for many reasons: your ideas will evolve; you may need to bring the work more up to date, or you may need to either lengthen or shorten it. In order to facilitate revisions, if you are handwriting you should leave extra room for alterations and only write on one side of a page. If you are word processing, insert a header or footer which includes the number of draft and the date.

Before submission of a piece of work you should put it to one side and forget about it for a period of time. You should then read it again with fresh eyes. This should enable you to pick up any errors which you might have missed previously because you were too close to the work. This requires you to have produced your draft well in advance of any submission deadline. If you find this difficult see chapter 15, para. 15.4 "Time Management".

When revising your work check for the following:

1. Have you answered the question/addressed your research questions?

2. Does it have a logical structure?

3. Is your meaning clear?

4. Are your arguments backed up with authority?

5. Are the most important points sufficiently emphasised?

6. Are there any faults in the logic?

7. Has it taken into account any conflicting arguments?

8. Are the conclusions justified?

9. Does it read well?

10. Are its style, vocabulary, abbreviations, and illustrations appropriate?

11. Is the spelling accurate? Most word processing software will include a spell-check facility. You should, however, ensure that you adopt the British spelling options and do not slip into American-English spelling. A dictionary and a Thesaurus can also be useful.

12. Grammar — is your meaning clear or clouded by clumsy grammatical constructions? Short simple sentences are preferable. It is particularly important to check your use of tenses. It is very easy to slip from one tense to another, especially when you are writing over a period of time. Most software now has a grammar check facility. However, it is generally not as useful as the spell-check facility.

13. Are your references accurately presented?

An additional way of reviewing your work is to persuade a colleague to read your work and to comment on it. Even if they do not belong to the same discipline, they will be able to identify linguistic and stylistic flaws.

Additional Reading:

J. Bell, *Doing Your Research Project* (2nd ed., Open University Press 1993), chap. 12.
L. Blaxter, C. Hughes, and M. Tight, *How to Research* (Open University Press, 1996), chap. 8.
T.R. Black, *Evaluating Social Science Research: An Introduction* (Sage, 1993).

17.10 REVISION STRATEGY FOR EXAMS

There is no one technique that will suit everyone. The following section contains suggestions. You should experiment and pick the way that suits you.

17.10.1 Make sure that you are aware of what is expected of you

Ways of doing this are:

1. Make sure that you know the syllabus of the course and which topics are examinable.

2. Obtain copies of past examination papers. They are useful for guidance but do not be tempted to use them to question spot. This is a very dangerous strategy. If you concentrate only on a few areas and they fail to come up in the exam, you may fail. You cannot presume that the exam set for you will always be in the same format. Courses change over time and you should obtain up-to-date information from your tutor. You should also remember that the law changes and issues relevant in the past may no longer exist. The best way to make use of past papers is to work through them attempting to answer the questions. It can be beneficial to do this with another student. This means that you can pull resources and discuss the answers. If you feel that you are struggling, go and see your tutor and ask the tutor to work through the answer with you.

3. If you have any doubts about what is expected of you, ask your lecturer/tutor.

17.10.2 Make sure that you have all the information you need

Organise your notes. Far in advance of the exam date you should ensure that you have a full set of lecture notes and handouts for the subject. Organising this in advance gives you time to catch up on any notes that you have missed. You will find people more willing to lend notes at some distance from the exam.

Ideally you should have been reading around the lectures and preparing for tutorials throughout the term. When it comes to revising you should have sufficient notes. You should not need to look up textbooks at this stage. It is too late. You should concentrate on the material you already have. The only time you should consult books is to clarify any points that remain unclear.

17.10.3 The process of revising

● Do not sit and look at a thick file of notes. If you do that you will find yourself putting off the evil hour when you have to start revising. All sorts of jobs around the house will suddenly appear far more appealing than sitting and opening this awful file. The way around this is to start by consulting the syllabus for the course. You will find that it can be broken down into several topics or parts. Pick the topic you are most interested in and start with that.

● Try to get a grasp of the major topics. Then move on to the less important points.

● Once you have identified, *e.g.* six topics, gather together all your material on the topics. This may include lecture notes, tutorial preparation and notes, independent reading (could include case notes, notes from statutes, notes from journal articles or texts). Read the material for one topic. Go through it and identify the key points and make revision notes for the topic. These should contain the essential points from all your materials. These notes should not be very long (four to five sides of A4) and should consist of lists with various headings, categories and sub-categories. You should then try to learn these lists.

● Some people like to make notes from notes until they end up with bullet points of vital issues. Others may prefer just to read over and over their original notes. Others prefer to dictate revision notes and to listen to them over and over again.

● Almost all exams aim to test, not just for knowledge of facts, but for understanding and the ability to use them. When revising ask:

(a) What are the key points?

(b) What is the authority/evidence/argument for each proposition?

(c) Is there any counter evidence?

- Test yourself by doing brief outline answers to questions from old examination papers.
- Build periods of free time into any revision schedule. You need to maintain a balance between work and normal life.
- Do not sit up all night the night before an exam. You will end up being exhausted and jaded in the exam. It is far better to organise your revision timetable so that the evening before an exam you can relax. You will then perform much better the next day.
- Do not worry because you do not "know everything". No one ever does. Constantly remind yourself of what you do know rather than worrying about what you do not know.
- Finally, make sure that you know the correct *date*, *time* and *location* of the exam.

17.11   EXAM TECHNIQUE

1. Arrive in good time for the exam.

2. Remember to conform to any university requirements such as bringing your matriculation card for identification purposes.

3. Read any instructions *carefully*. Make sure that you know how many questions you are required to answer and if any questions are compulsory. Always answer the required number of questions even if your last answer(s) are short and scrappy. The few marks you gain may be vital for your final result. Never leave a question blank. Make sure that you answer all parts of a question.

4. Read quickly through the whole paper to get an idea of the content of the questions. Re-read the paper *slowly and carefully* and decide what each question is actually asking. Underline "key words" which indicate the kind of answer you should give. Then select the questions that you intend to answer.

5. Before writing anything, decide on the order you will tackle the questions. Choose the question that seems "easiest" first and work through to the "hardest". By answering the first question well you will be better able to tackle the more difficult ones.

   Do not be phased by people who sit down and immediately start to write. You are better advised to sit and take stock, rather than ploughing straight in and realising later that you have misread/misinterpreted the question.

   Make notes for each question, jotting down ideas. Try to make these brief notes for all questions *before* you start writing. This gets you thinking about other questions even when you are writing your first question. In jotting down some ideas, questions that appeared impossible to answer may become clearer. More ideas about other questions will come to you as you are answering the first one.

6. Allocate your time properly. If each question bears an equal number of marks, spend an equal amount of time on each question. If the marks are different for different questions spend an appropriate proportion of your time on each question. If you use up your time-limit on a question you will already have gained most of the marks that you are going to get. Another five or ten minutes writing is unlikely to get you many more marks. The same time spent concentrating on the key issues in a new question will earn you more marks. Remember that the first few marks in each question are the easiest ones to get.

7. Do not write out the question — this just wastes valuable time.

8. Answer the question set, not the one which you would like to have answered. No credit will be given for irrelevant material, no matter how accurate it may be. For each question, sort out the main points, weeding out irrelevancies. Do not attempt to write down everything you know about the topic; expect to have to go into depth on only part of what you know.

9. The use of authority in an exam. You must back up your arguments with authority. You will not be required to remember the full citation of a case. Ideally you should put down the names of the parties, *e.g. Smith v. Bloggs* but in exam conditions it is easy to forget the precise name of a case. As a minimum you should try to write down sufficient details to show the examiner that you have identified the correct case. If you cannot remember the names of either of the parties, you should put down some detail about the case that identifies it, *e.g.* the case about the XXX. In a hand-written exam you should underline case names. When referring to a case do not include a descriptive account of the facts of the case. The part of the case that you should use is the *ratio decidendi*. Writing down lots of facts will not gain you any extra marks — it will merely waste precious exam time and detracts from the cogency of your answer.

10. If you miscalculate the time badly, finish the question in note-form. This is better than nothing and may pick up a few valuable marks.

11. Re-read everything at the end to check for errors and inaccuracies.

17.11.1 Open Book Exams

It would appear to be a student's dream come true to be allowed to take statutory material into the exam. But the author has certainly found open book exams to be more difficult than unseen exams. It can be reassuring to have a volume of statutes sitting on your desk but if you are not familiar with the material you can waste large chunks of the exam time just trying to find the relevant provisions. Learn to find your way round the statute.

    Never copy out statutory provisions. This just shows the examiner that you are able to copy from one document to another. You should be trying to display understanding and analytical skills.

17.11.2 What NOT to do in an exam

1. Getting the time/date wrong!

2. Failing to answer the question asked.

3. Failing to use authority to back up your arguments.

4. Including lots of description (narration of facts of cases) instead of critical analysis.

5. Failing to stick to a plan about time.

6. Failing to write enough., *e.g.* a question worth 25 marks is not going to be answered sufficiently in six or seven lines.

7. Making jokes and/or frivolous comments. This is not appropriate.

8. Failing to express yourself clearly.

9. Messy handwriting. You will be under pressure in an exam but do try to write legibly.

Further Reading:

S. Drew and R. Bingham, *The Student Skills Guide* (Gower, 1997), chaps 13 and 24.
H.L. MacQueen, *Studying Scots Law* (Butterworths, 1993), pp. 161–168.
H. McVea and P. Cumper, *Learning Exam Skills* (1996).
A. Northedge, *The Good Study Guide* (Open University Press, 1990), chap. 7.

Exercises

LIBRARY EXERCISE

1. What is the name of the original song in:
ZYX Music GmbH v. King and Others [1995] 3 All E.R. 1.

2. What is the name of the property at the centre of:
City of Edinburgh Council v. Secretary of State for Scotland 1998 S.C. (H.L.) 33.

3. With what drinks is the following concerned:
Georg von Deetzen v. Hauptzollamt Oldenburg [1994] 2 C.M.L.R. 487.

4. What kind of pollution is mentioned in:
Commission v. Germany [1991] E.C.R. I-2607.

5. What animal is mentioned in:
Brady v. Barbour 1995 S.C.C.R. 258.

6. What was the activity of the company at the centre of this case:
MacDonald v. HMA 1996 S.L.T. 723.

7. What type of fish are referred to in:
Bishop of the Isles v. James Hamilton (1664) Mor. 15633.

8. What kind of property was being purchased in:
Fortune v. Fraser 1995 S.C.L.R. 121.

9. What industrial action took place in:
Miles v. Wakefield Metropolitan District Council [1987] 2 W.L.R. 795.

10. What did Jones have in the waistband of his trousers in:
R v. Jones (Terence) [1995] Q.B. 235.

11. How many judges heard this case?
Nelson v. HMA 1994 S.C. (J.C.) 94.

12. Which river is mentioned in:
National Rivers Authority v.Welsh Development Agency [1993] Env.L.R. 407.

13.   What is the name of the judge in:
Fry's Metals v. Durastic 1990 G.W.D. 5-272.

14.   Which legislation is mentioned in:
Berrisford v. Woodard Schools (Midland Division Ltd) [1991] I.R.L.R. 247.

15.   What sort of equipment is the subject of this case:
Sabre Leasing Limited v. Copeland 1993 S.C. 345.

16.   Which country other than England is mentioned in:
Eagle Star Insurance Co Ltd v. Provincial Insurance Plc [1994] 1 A.C. 130.

17.   What was the pursuer's job title in:
McCart v. Queen of Scots Knitwear Ltd 1987 S.L.T. (Sh. Ct.) 57.

18.   In which country were the parties married in:
In re A (Minors) (Abducation: Custody Rights) [1992] Fam. 106.

19.   What official activity was the applicant unhappy about in:
Kopp v. Switzerland (1999) 27 E.H.R.R. 91.

20.   Which Act is referred to in:
Education (Student Loans) Act 1990 (c. 6) Sched 2., para. 6.

21.   What animal is mentioned in:
Law Reform (Miscellaneous Provisions) (Scotland) Act 1985 (c. 73) s. 32.

Current Law — Practical exercise

1.   Give details of a case in 1996 which considered the meaning of the term "sex shop".

2.   *Grierson v. HMA*

   (a) What is the citation for this case?
   (b) Give the details of each time this case has an entry in Current Law. You should state what happened to it each time it appeared and state the Year Book and the paragraph number for each of these occasions.

3.   You remember a case called *Stakis v. Boyd* was reported in 1989.

   (a) Give the reference for where you would find the digest of the case in Current Law.
   (b) Which legislation did the case concern?

4.   The Water (Scotland) Act 1967 — the status of this Act altered in 1994. What happened to it?

5. Have any cases been brought concerning s. 12 of the Housing (Scotland) Act 1988?

6. The Land Drainage (Scotland) Act 1935 appears in Current Law. Why?

7. Are the Civil Legal Aid (Scotland) Amendment Regulations 1994 still in force?

8. Is s. 49 of the Sewerage (Scotland) Act 1968 still in force?

9. Find the most recent Scottish article on contract law.

10. *Crawford v. Royal Bank* 1749 Mor. 875 appears in Current Law. Why?

Answers to the library exercise

1. "Please Don't Go".
2. A former riding school described as "Redford Barracks".
3. Milk.
4. Air pollution — lead.
5. Salmon.
6. Maintenance and repair of machinery for Scotrail.
7. Herring.
8. Sandwich bar.
9. Refusal to conduct weddings on a Saturday.
10. Browning 9 mm pistol and 14 bullets.
11. Five.
12. Nant Mychudd Stream.
13. Lord Dervaird.
14. Sex Discrimination Act 1975, s. 1(a), s. 6(2)(b) and EEC Equal Treatment Directive 72/207, Article 2(1).
15. Telephone system.
16. The Bahamas.
17. An unrover.
18. Australia.
19. Telephone tapping.
20. Bankruptcy (Scotland) Act 1985.
21. Sheep.

Answers to Current Law Exercise

1. 1996 Year Book; Words & Phrases table; paragraph 6751; *Rees v. Lees* 1996 S.C.C.R. 601.

2.   (a) 1993 S.C.C.R. 145
     (b) Digested 93/5760; Distinguished 93/5104; Applied 95/6279.

3.   (a) 4389
     (b) Food & Drugs (Scotland) Act 1956 (c. 30) s. 9(3).

4.   Statute citator in Legislation Citator volume 1989–1995. Repealed by Sched. 14 of the Local Government etc. (Scotland) Act 1994.

5.   *Milnbank Housing Association v. Murdoch* 1995 S.L.T. (Sh. Ct.) 12.

6.   It was repealed by the Statute law Revision Act 1950.

7.   No. They were revoked by the Civil Legal Aid (Scotland) Regulations 1996 S.I. 96 No. 2444, Reg 3, Sched. 1.

8.   No. It was repealed by the Environment Act 1995, Sched. 24.

9.   Check the latest edition of the Monthly Digest Cumulative Index under "contract"; look for most recent article followed by an "S".

10.   It was referred to in *M & I Instrument Engineers v. Varsada* 1991 S.L.T. 106 — Current Law reference 90/5467.

INDEX